PERSUASION, SOCIAL INFLUENCE, AND COMPLIANCE GAINING

Robert H. Gass
California State University, Fullerton

John S. Seiter
Utah State University

Allyn and Bacon
Boston • London • Toronto • Sydney • Tokyo • Singapore

Vice President, Editor-in-Chief, Communication and Political Science: Paul A. Smith
Series Editor: Karon Bowers
Series Editorial Assistant: Leila Scott
Production Editor: Christopher H. Rawlings
Editorial-Production Service: Omegatype Typography, Inc.
Composition and Prepress Buyer: Linda Cox
Manufacturing Buyer: Megan Cochran
Cover Administrator: Jenny Hart
Electronic Composition: Omegatype Typography, Inc.

Copyright © 1999 by Allyn & Bacon
A Viacom Company
160 Gould Street
Needham Heights, MA 02494

Internet: www.abacon.com

Library of Congress Cataloging-in-Publication Data
Gass, Robert H.
    Persuasion, social influence, and compliance gaining / Robert H.
Gass, John S. Seiter.
      p. cm.
    Includes bibliographical references and index.
    ISBN 0-205-26352-6
     1. Persuasion (Psychology)   2. Influence (Psychology)
   3. Manipulative behavior.   I. Seiter, John S.   II. Title.
BF637.P4G34   1999
303.3'42—dc21   98-7618
                                               CIP

Printed in the United States of America
10 9 8 7 6 5 4 3   03 02 01 00

CONTENTS

PREFACE

Persuasion research has changed considerably in the past few decades. Investigations of public or "one-to-many" persuasion are less in evidence now; more prominent are investigations of interpersonal or "face-to-face" influence attempts. Whereas students of persuasion once cut their teeth on various attitude change and consistency theories, they are now introduced to studies on a host of new topics including compliance gaining and compliance resisting, deception and deception detection. It is not so much that traditional approaches to the study of persuasion have vanished—fear appeals come to mind as an area of continued interest—but rather, that there has been a divergence in research interests between traditional and nontraditional spheres of persuasion. We've written this text to embrace this divergence. We demonstrate that traditional and nontraditional approaches to the study of persuasion are part of the same whole, and that whether one uses the term *persuasion, social influence,* or *compliance gaining,* all involve essentially the same human activity: trying to convince others to think, feel, or do what we want, or to resist others' influence attempts.

In addition to integrating both traditional and nontraditional approaches to the study of persuasion, we also have carved out a number of meaningful, albeit contingent, generalizations from the literature. A decade or so ago this would have posed a much more difficult challenge. At that time, persuasion research often was characterized by inconsistent or contradictory findings. The student was left to sift among myriad findings in hopes of finding a few kernels of wisdom that could be generalized beyond laboratory settings to the real world. Fortunately, the recent advent of meta-analysis as a technique for integrating research findings, however, has made it possible to reconcile many of the apparent inconsistencies in the literature. There still are plenty of "ifs," "maybes," and "it depends" to go around, but at least some of the long-standing controversies appear to have been resolved satisfactorily. Accordingly, we offer several dozen generalizations based on the recent literature, all accompanied by the appropriate caveats and limitations.

We also have endeavored to provide practical examples of how empirical findings apply to real life situations and contexts. We offer a number of illustrations of how strategies, principles, and processes related to persuasion can be observed in everyday influence attempts in a number of contexts (e.g., car lots, funeral homes, courtrooms, boardrooms, living rooms, doctors' offices, restaurants). We include several esoteric contexts—namely music as persuasion, subliminal persuasion, and fragrances and persuasion—not commonly found in other texts. By building a bridge between empirical findings and real life applications, students will be better able to comprehend and appreciate the value of persuasion research.

The urge to persuade is a fundamental human impulse. Persuasion, as much as baseball, is our nation's favorite pastime. The wealth of television and radio shows devoted to legal, political, and social commentary reveals the public's near insatiable appetite for persuasive discourse. We view persuasion not only as a desirable form of activity, but as an indispensable feature of human interaction. We hope students will catch our enthusiasm for this field of study and come away with a better understanding of how persuasion functions, an improved knowledge of ways to maximize their own persuasive efforts, and a greater ability to resist influence attempts, especially unscrupulous influence attempts by others.

ACKNOWLEDGMENTS

Although it detracted from playing basketball, all in all we had a pretty good time of it. We would like to thank a number of people who were instrumental in helping us finish this project, most notably our wives, Susan Gass and Debora Seiter, who provided ideas, feedback, support, chocolate, encouragement, endless patience and, on occasion, served as our harshest—yet most appreciated—critics. We would also like to thank Darin J. Arsenault for his help in proofreading chapters, obtaining permissions, and co-authoring the instructor's manual. John Seiter wishes to thank Jill Nagel, Richard Seiter, and Harold Kinzer, all of whom supplied material and stories for the book, and Charles Huenemann, a dear friend and excellent philosopher who read and commented on our ethics chapter. Robert Gass wishes to thank California State University, Fullerton, for granting him a research sabbatical during which he and John completed a rough draft of the book, Jeanine Congalton for enduring his many unsolicited stories about "how the book was going," and Tasha Van Horn who provided references and insights on the ethics chapter. Finally, we'd like to thank our students for sharing their stories about their own persuasive encounters and for serving as "guinea pigs" by volunteering to read and comment on some of the early drafts of the chapters. We couldn't have done it without you.

Our thanks also to the following reviewers for their comments on the manuscript: Richard Armstrong, Wichita State University; Barry Brummet, University of Wisconsin, Milwaukee; Dudley Cahn, S.U.N.Y., New Paltz; Risa Dickson, California State University, San Bernardino; Steve Duck, University of Iowa; Thomas E. Harris, University of Alabama; and John Kares Smith, S.U.N.Y., Oswego. Your comments were invaluable to us during our revision of the manuscript.

In addition, we are grateful to the following people from Allyn and Bacon: Carla Daves, who convinced us to translate our concept into a manuscript, and Karon Bowers, our editor, and Leila Scott, editorial assistant, whose efforts contributed greatly. We also owe thanks to our production editor Kathy Olson, at Omegatype Typography, Inc., for her meticulous attention to detail and her ability to be both personable and professional.

1

WHY STUDY PERSUASION?

One of the authors was enjoying a day at the beach with his family. As he sat in a folding chair, lost in a good book, he could hear the cries of seagulls overhead and the pounding of the surf. Nothing was bothering him. He was oblivious to the world around him. Or so he thought. As he reflected more on the situation, however, he became aware that he was being bombarded by persuasive messages on all sides. A boom box was playing a few yards away. During the commercial breaks, various ads tried to convince him to buy a cellular phone, to switch auto insurance companies, and to try a new, grilled chicken sandwich. At the lifeguard tower a red flag was flying, warning the author and others of dangerous riptide conditions. A plane flew overhead trailing a banner that advertised an upcoming music festival. A nearby sign warned that no alcohol, glass objects, or fires were permitted on the beach. The plastic bag in which his kids had brought their beach toys advertised Wal-Mart on its side.

There were oral influence attempts too. One of his kids said, "Come on in Daddy, the water's not that cold." He wasn't convinced. His kids *always* said that, no matter how cold it actually was. "Would you mind keeping an eye on our things?", a family next to the author's asked. I guess our family looks trustworthy, the author thought. His wife asked him, "Do you want to walk down to the pier in a while? They have frozen bananas." She knew he would be unable to resist the temptation.

And those were just the overt persuasive messages. A host of more subtle messages also competed for the author's attention. A few yards away a woman was applying sun block to her neck and shoulders. The author decided to do the same. Had she nonverbally persuaded him to do likewise? Nearby a young couple was soaking up the sun. Both were wearing Ray-Ban sunglasses, the style popularized by the movie *Men in Black*. Were they "advertising" that brand? A man about 10 yards away had a large, conspicuous tattoo of a spider on his back. Was he trying to convince the author and others that he was tough? A young man with a boogie board ran by, headed for the water. He had a shaved head and enough body piercing to make the author wince. Did his appearance advocate a particular set of

1

values or tastes? Was he a billboard for an "alternative" lifestyle? A trio of attractive young women strolled down the beach. Two were wearing bikinis, the third a thong suit. Every male head on the beach turned in unison as they walked by. Were the males "persuaded" to turn their heads or was this simply an involuntary reflex? Two tan, muscular males were tossing a Frisbee back and forth. Their shirts were cut off at the waist, exposing well-defined abdominal muscles. The author made a mental note to do more sit-ups. Some younger teens were smoking. Were they negative role models for his own children? There seemed to be as many persuasive messages, or potentially persuasive messages, as there were shells on the beach.

The preceding examples raise two important issues. First, persuasion is pervasive. Influence attempts, whether explicit or implicit, are everywhere. Second, it is difficult to say with any certainty what is and is not "persuasion." Where should we draw the line between persuasion and other forms of communication? How do we distinguish between influence attempts and ordinary behavior? We address the first of these issues in this chapter. Here we examine the ubiquitous nature of persuasion and offer a rationale for learning more about its workings. In the next chapter, we tackle the issue of what constitutes "persuasion" and related terms such as *social influence* and *compliance-gaining*.

AIMS AND GOALS

This is a book about persuasion. Its aims are academic and practical. On the academic side, we examine how and why persuasion functions the way it does. In so doing, we identify some of the most recent theories and findings by persuasion researchers. On the practical side, we illustrate those theories and findings with plenty of real-life examples of persuasion. We also offer useful advice on how to become a more effective persuader and how to resist influence attempts, especially unethical influence attempts by others.

If learning how to persuade others and avoid being persuaded seems a bit manipulative, remember, we don't live in a society of Smurfs, Care Bears, or cute purple dinosaurs. The real world is brimming with persuaders. Even as you're reading this book, they're practicing their craft. You can avoid learning about persuasion, perhaps, but you can't avoid persuasion itself.

Besides, we can't tell you everything there is to know about persuasion. We don't know it ourselves. Nobody knows all there is to know about persuasion. Indeed, one of the points we stress throughout this book is that people aren't that easy to persuade. Human beings are complex. They aren't that malleable. They can be stubborn, unpredictable, and intractable, despite the best efforts of persuaders.

At present, persuasion is still as much an "art" as it is a "science." Human nature is too complicated, and our understanding of persuasion too limited, to predict in advance whether a given influence attempt will succeed. Think how often you flip the channel when a commercial costing millions of dollars to produce and air appears on television. Think how many candidates for public office have spent a fortune campaigning, only to lose the election. Or think how difficult it is for the federal government to convince people to stop smoking, practice safe sex, or obey the speed limit.

The science of persuasion is still in its infancy. Despite P. T. Barnum's axiom that "there's a sucker born every minute," people are uncannily perceptive at times. The old saying that "you can fool some of the people all of the time, etc." is easier to recite than accomplish. Yet much is known about persuasion. Persuasion has been scientifically studied since the 1940s.[1] Written texts on persuasion date back to ancient Greece.[2] A number of strategies and techniques have been identified and their effectiveness or ineffectiveness documented. Persuaders are a long way from achieving an Orwellian nightmare of thought control, but a good deal is known about how to capture the hearts and minds of individuals. Before proceeding further, we want to address a common negative stereotype about persuasion.

PERSUASION IS NOT A DIRTY WORD

Unfortunately, the study of persuasion has gotten some bad P.R. over the years. The subject itself is a fascinating one, but some communication scholars are reluctant to be associated with a field of study that conjures up images of manipulation, deceit, or brainwashing. There is, after all, a sinister side to persuasion. Adolf Hitler, Charles Manson, Jim Jones, David Koresh and, more recently, Marshall Applewhite (a.k.a. "Do" of Heaven's Gate fame) were all accomplished persuaders—much to the detriment of their followers.[3] It's not surprising then that advocates for the study of persuasion often find themselves cast into the role of apologists. We, however, adopt no such apologetic stance. We don't think of persuasion as the ugly stepsister in the family of human communication. Rather, we find the study of persuasion to be enormously intriguing. Part of our fascination stems from the fact that persuasion is, on occasion, used for unsavory ends. We believe it is essential that researchers learn all they can about persuasion in order to expose the strategies and tactics of unethical persuaders.

PERSUASION IS OUR FRIEND

Persuasion isn't merely a tool used by con artists, chiselers, charlatans, cheats, connivers, and cult leaders. Nobel peace prize recipients and Pulitzer prize-winning journalists also are persuaders. In fact, most "professional" persuaders are engaged in socially acceptable, if not downright respectable, careers. They include advertising executives, writers, celebrity endorsers, clergy, congresspersons, infomercial spokespersons, lawyers, lobbyists, media pundits, motivational speakers, political activists, political cartoonists, political spin doctors, public relations experts, radio talk show hosts, salespersons, senators, syndicated columnists, and telephone solicitors, to name just a few.

Let's focus on the good side of persuasion for a moment. What are some of the good things persuasion does? Persuasion helps forge peace agreements between nations. Persuasion is crucial to the fundraising efforts of charities and philanthropic organizations. Persuasion convinces motorists to buckle up when driving or to refrain from driving when they've had a few too many drinks. Persuasion helps sway at-risk students to remain in school and complete their educations. Persuasion is used to convince an alcoholic or drug-dependent family member to seek professional help. Persuasion is how the coach of an underdog team inspires the players to give it their all. Persuasion offers a means for warning pregnant women about the dangers of drinking or taking drugs during pregnancy. Persuasion helps convince older adults to seek preventive medical care such as annual breast exams or prostate exams. Persuasion is one of the devices used by managers to promote tolerance and respect among employees in the workplace. Persuasion is what a hostage negotiator uses to convince an armed, barricaded suspect not to kill any hostages. Persuasion is a tool used by parents to urge children not to accept rides from strangers or to allow anyone to touch them in a way that feels uncomfortable. In short, persuasion is the cornerstone of a number of positive, prosocial endeavors. *Very little of the good that we see in the world could be accomplished without persuasion.* That statement is not an exaggeration.

Persuasion, then, is a powerful and often positive social force. Having highlighted the positive side of persuasion, we believe an appropriate starting point for a text such as this is to address the question of *why* the study of persuasion is so valuable. The next section therefore offers a justification for the study of social influence.

THE PERVASIVENESS OF PERSUASION: YOU CAN RUN BUT YOU CAN'T HIDE

We've already mentioned one of the primary reasons for learning about this subject—Persuasion is a central feature of every sphere of human communication. Persuasion is found wherever you find people communicating. We can't avoid it. We can't make it go away. Like the smog hanging over Los Angeles, persuasion is all around us. Like Elvis impersonators in Las Vegas, persuasion is here to stay.

It is fairly obvious that persuasion is an indispensable ingredient in a number of professions. In this regard, Simons (1986) has observed, "the so-called people professions—politics, law, social work, counseling, business management, advertising, sales, public relations, the ministry—might as well be called persuasion professions" (p. 4). Persuasion is part and parcel of such occupations. What you may not realize, however, is that persuasion plays an important role in some not-so-obvious contexts as well. We examine two such contexts in the following sections on the sciences and the arts.

Persuasion in Science

You may not think of them this way, but scientists are persuaders. Even in fields such as chemistry, mathematics, or physics—the so-called hard sciences—persuasion plays a major role.[4] Scientists often have to convince others that their research possesses scientific merit and social value, that their experiments have been properly designed and carried out, and that their interpretations of their results are correct. They also have to argue for the superiority of their theories over competing theories (see, for example, Levy, 1994). In this respect, Thomas Kuhn (1970) argues that all scientists employ "techniques of persuasion in their efforts to establish the superiority of their own paradigms over those of their rivals" (p. 151). Similarly, Mitroff (1974) comments that "the notion of the purely objective, uncommitted scientist [is] naive.... The best scientist...not only has points of view but also defends them with gusto" (p. 120).

What do scientists try to persuade each other about? Everything! Paleontologists argue about whether dinosaurs were more reptilian or birdlike, and what caused their extinction. Astronomers disagree about the age of the universe, its makeup, and the probability that life exists elsewhere. Seismologists argue over the location, probability, and severity of the next major earthquake. Theoretical physicists go back and forth about the relationship between Einstein's general theory of relativity and quantum physics, which includes subatomic phenomena like neutrinos and quarks. Anthropologists debate about humankind's earliest ancestors and where they originated. Epidemiologists differ as to the best approaches to preventing newly emerging diseases such as the Ebola virus, Lassa fever, and Bovine Spongiform Encephalopathy (mad cow disease).

There are controversial issues in every scientific field, and those controversies are arbitrated through persuasion. Granted every now and then a new discovery is made, a new finding emerges, or a key breakthrough takes place that resolves a long-standing controversy. Typically, however, new scientific discoveries, findings, and breakthroughs tend to shift controversies in new directions or prompt whole new controversies of their own. Scientists, then, are no strangers to persuasion. They can and do argue fervently for their points of view. They do not simply rely on their findings to speak for themselves. They persuade with gusto.

Persuasion in the Arts

Another not-so-obvious context for persuasion is the arts. Not all art is created "for art's sake." Art serves more than an aesthetic or decorative function. Artists have opinions, strong opinions, and they don't always keep them to themselves. They lend expression to their opinions in and through their work. Consider movies as an art form. Films like Spike Lee's *Do the Right Thing*, or *Schindler's List* by Steven Spielberg demonstrate the power of the camera to alter attitudes, change beliefs, and shape opinions. Other art forms possess the capability to persuade as well. Playwrights, painters, sculptors, photographers, dancers, performance artists, and others give voice to their political and social views through their art (see for example, Hobbs & Woodard, 1986; Lippard, 1984). As just one example, one of the functions performed by exhibits on L.A. riot art was to promote the process of healing in the aftermath of the devastating riots that took place in Los Angeles in 1992 (Berg, 1993; Sullivan, 1993).

If you don't believe that art persuades, how can you explain the current controversy in Congress over proposals to cut funding for the National Endowment for the Arts? Isn't it precisely because some people believe certain works of art send the *wrong* persuasive messages that they want to end federal subsidies for such artwork? Art can be controversial. It can challenge the existing social order. It can make people angry. At the same time it can heighten people's awareness. It can change the way they see things. And in so doing, it can persuade.

Persuasion, then, can be found in obvious and not-so-obvious places. Before concluding this section, however, we want to examine one additional context in which persuasion occurs. This is the context in which most of the influence attempts we encounter on a daily basis occur. And yet, we often tend to overlook the critical role that persuasion plays in this context. We refer to persuasion in the interpersonal arena.

Persuasion in Interpersonal Settings

Interpersonal encounters, no matter where they take place, function as major arteries for influence attempts. Try to think of a conversation you've had lately that *didn't* involve some persuasion. If you can, we suspect you have a narrower view of persuasion than we do, a topic we take up in the next chapter. We wish we could recite one of those nifty statistics like, "On a given day the average American is exposed to 637.4 influence attempts," or "If you lined all the persuasive messages we're exposed to on a daily basis end to end, they would reach the planet Jupiter." Frankly, though, any such number would simply represent an "unknowable statistic."[5] Suffice it to say that on a daily basis we are bombarded with persuasive requests. Your brother wants you to hurry up and get out of the bathroom. A homeless person asks if you can spare some change. Your parents try to talk you out of getting a nose ring. Or worse yet, your significant other uses the "F" word to redefine your relationship: That's right, she or he just wants to be "Friends." Naturally, we persuade back as well, targeting others with our own entreaties, pleadings, and requests for favors.

The extent of influence exerted in the interpersonal arena should not be underestimated. In fact, although we may think of Madison Avenue as manipulative, persuasion is most effective in face-to-face interaction. Why? Because influence attempts tend to operate less conspicuously in interpersonal encounters. Consider the following scenario:

> **The bait:** *Your friend calls up and says "Hey, what are you doing Friday night?"*
>
> **The nibble:** *Anticipating an invitation to go somewhere, you reply, "Nothing much, why?"*
>
> **You're hooked and reeled in:** *"Well, I wonder if you could help me move into my new apartment, then?"*

At least when you watch a television commercial you *know* the sponsor is after something from the outset. In interpersonal encounters the motives of others may be less transparent. As Wenburg and Wilmot (1973) advise, "most scholars agree that if [one has] a choice in determining which communication arena to utilize when he [or she] wants to affect the attitudes and behaviors of others, he [or she] should definitely choose the interpersonal arena" (p. 28). Thus, persuasion tends to operate at maximum effectiveness in interpersonal settings, because we aren't always aware of what is going on. Our advice: Next time you want to turn a paper in late, talk to the professor in person!

From our discussion thus far, it should be apparent that persuasion functions as a pervasive force in virtually every facet of human communication. Ernst Cassirer (1944) has written that humans are, by their very nature, symbol-using animals. One vital aspect of human symbolicity involves the tendency to persuade others. We are symbol users, and one of the principal functions of symbol usage is persuasion.

The recognition that social influence is an essential, pervasive feature of human symbolic action provides the strongest possible justification for the study of persuasion. If "the proper study of man is man," as the saying goes, then the proper study of human nature should include our natural tendency to persuade others. To deny the importance of the study of persuasion is to ignore one of the major underlying impulses for human communication. By way of analogy, one can't understand how an automobile works without taking a look under the hood. Similarly, one can't understand how human communication functions without examining one of its primary motives—persuasion.

THE KNOWLEDGE FUNCTION: ENQUIRING MINDS WANT TO KNOW

Now that we've examined one of the key reasons for learning about persusasion, namely it's pervasiveness, we now turn our attention to a second reason for studying persuasion—The study of persuasion fulfills a knowledge function. Human beings are naturally curious. Recall all the interest in the criminal and civil trials of O. J. Simpson. The public eagerly awaited each new morsel of information as the persuasive strategies of the opposing sides unfolded. Laboratory studies of persuasion have yielded significant insights into human psychological processes and human communication processes. Quite apart from any knowledge of persuasion's instrumental effects is the knowledge gained from the understanding of how persuasive messages function "inside people's heads." Thus, the study of persuasion can tell us a great deal about how people encode messages, decode messages, and respond to messages of a persuasive nature.

Overcoming Habitual Persuasion

Perhaps you're wondering, "Why do I need to learn about persuasion? I've been doing it my whole life." This is a fair question. Persuasion may seem second nature to you by now, like breathing. However, many people rely on habitual forms of persuasion, whether they are effective or not. They get comfortable with a few strategies and tactics that they use over and over again, regardless of how well they work. Just as runners, swimmers, and other athletes need to learn to adjust their breathing in response to different situations, persuaders—to maximize their effectiveness—need to learn to adapt their methods to different audiences and situations. Persuasion isn't a "one-size-fits-all" form of communication.

Understanding Social Forces

Also included within the knowledge function is a better understanding of the social and cultural forces that give rise to influence attempts. Articles appearing in the recent literature have offered insights into the presidential debates, feminist rhetoric, the pro-life versus pro-choice movements, religious cults, and the neo-Nazi movement, among others. By studying persuasion, we can we learn about the social catalysts for such influence attempts. In the process of studying how people are moved by persuasion, we also discover a great deal about why people create, shape, produce, perceive, interpret, and react to messages the way they do.

THE DEFENSIVE FUNCTION: DUCK AND COVER

A third reason for learning about how persuasion operates is vital in our view— The study of persuasion serves a defensive function. This represents one of the chief benefits of taking a class on this subject. By studying how and why influence attempts succeed or fail, you can become a more discerning consumer of persuasive messages, unlike the hapless fellow depicted in Figure 1.1. If you know how persuasion works, you are less likely to be taken in.

Throughout this text we expose a number of persuasive tactics used in retail sales, advertising, and marketing campaigns. Such efforts advance the cause of the average person-on-the-street. For example, we have found in our classes that after students are given a "behind the scenes" look at how car salespeople are taught to sell (see Box 1.1), several students usually acknowledge, "Oh yeah, they did that to me." Admittedly, a huckster could also take advantage of the advice we offer in this book. We think it is far more likely, however, that the typical student reader will use our advice and suggestions as weapons *against* unethical influence attempts. In later chapters of this book we warn you about common ploys used by all manner of persuaders from cult leaders, to panhandlers, to funeral home directors.

THE DEBUNKING FUNCTION: PUH-SHAW

A fourth reason for studying persuasion is that it serves a debunking function. The study of human influence can aid in dispelling various "common sense" assumptions and "homespun" theories about persuasion. Traditional wisdom isn't always right, and it's worth knowing when it's wrong. Unfortunately, some individuals

"That's it, Henry—you've dialled your last mattress!"

FIGURE 1.1   A little persuasive acumen might save you from yourself.

cling tenaciously to stereotypes and folk wisdom about persuasive practices that are known by researchers who study persuasion to be patently false. For example, many people believe that subliminal messages are highly effective and operate in a manner similar to that of post-hypnotic suggestion. This belief is pure poppycock, as we point out in Chapter 15. Another example concerns the use of logical versus emotional appeals. One might expect people to be able to distinguish between messages that are primarily rational from those that are basically emotional. Such is not the case, however. The findings of several researchers (Bettinghaus, 1968; Reuchelle, 1958) reveal that people are consistently *unable* to differentiate logical from emotional appeals. We discuss this topic more in Chapter 14.

Of considerable importance, then, are empirical findings that are *counterintuitive* in nature, that is, that go against the grain of common sense. By learning about research findings on persuasion, the reader can learn to ferret out the true from the false, the fact from the fiction.

We hope you'll agree, based on the foregoing discussion, that there are quite a few good reasons for studying persuasion. We hope we've persuaded you that the

BOX 1.1   Seventeen Tips on Buying a New or Used Car

Car salespersons, especially *used* car salespersons, have a bad reputation. Many consumers have the impression that a car salesperson will do anything it takes—lie, cheat, misrepresent, flatter, beguile, or sweet talk—to make a sale. These bad reputations may be undeserved. However, because buying a car is a major purchase, one would be well advised to err on the side of caution when negotiating with a car salesperson. *Caveat emptor,* as the saying goes: let the buyer beware.

1. Remember, buying a car is a great American ritual in which the car dealer has the upper hand. This is the prototype for high-pressure sales. They are professionals. They sell cars every day. You are an amateur. The average person only buys a car every 4 to 7 years. Who do you think has more experience with persuasion in this setting?

2. Do your homework *before* you go visit a car dealer. Read up on the makes and models in which you're interested (in automobile magazines like *Road & Track, Car & Driver,* etc.). Find out about performance criteria, standard features, and options before setting foot on a car lot. *Consumer Reports* sells an excellent paperback that compares used cars on reliability, safety, and other criteria based on data from actual owners over a 5-year period.

3. Keep a poker face. If the salesperson can tell you are eager or excited about the car purchase, he or she will smell blood. Once the salesperson knows you are emotionally attached to a particular car, you'll wind up paying more.

4. Take a calculator with you. Car salespersons like to pretend that the prices of things are entirely up to the calculator ("Hey, let's see how the numbers shake out.") The implication is that the numbers aren't negotiable or flexible. Everything is negotiable! Do your own figuring to see if the numbers "shake out" the same way. If not, ask why.

5. Once you are on the car lot, the dealer will try to keep you there. They may put you in a little room or cubicle, keeping you "prisoner" during the negotiations. The psychological strategy is to wear you down. After hours of haggling, you'll become mentally drained and therefore more likely to give in. They may ask for the keys to your trade-in, presumably to look it over and determine its value. They may ask for a check for a nominal amount of money, as a demonstration of your good faith. Once they have your keys or your check, though, you can't leave.

6. The car salesperson will want to *avoid* talking about the total price of the car, opting instead to discuss the monthly payment you can afford. You, on the other hand, should focus on four things: (a) the total purchase price, (b) the finance period, (c) the interest rate, and (d) the monthly payment.

> The addition of $16 per month to a $200 per month car payment may not seem like much, but financed over a 5-year period it is close to a $1,000 difference in the price of a car!
>
> Don't discuss the monthly payment unless you are clear on the finance period involved (a 3-year loan, 4-year loan, 5-year loan, etc.). Once you admit you can afford $300 per month, the salesperson may simply switch to a longer finance period—say, 4 years, instead of 3, thereby adding thousands of dollars to the total purchase price.

7. During the negotiations, the salesperson will probably leave the room a number of times to talk with a mysterious, Oz-like figure known as the "sales manager." The salesperson can't agree to anything without checking with this mysterious figure, so the person with whom you are negotiating really can't commit to anything. You, on the other hand, will be asked to commit to a lot of things. You will also be kept

BOX 1.1   *Continued*

waiting for long periods while the salesperson "negotiates" with the mystery figure.

   8. The salespeople will act like they are your best friends even though you never met them before in your life. They will look for ways to identify with you or ingratiate themselves to you to establish comraderie ("Hey, I used to have an AMC Gremlin myself!" "You like fly fishing? That makes two of us." "Whutta-yuh-know, my granddaughter is named 'Fifi' too!"). During the negotiations the salespeople will pretend they are on your side or are willing to go out on a limb for you ("Well, my sales manager may kick my butt all the way to Tehachapie for even showing her this offer, but hey, I like you!"). Remember these two are working as a team, *against you*. Don't be confused for a moment about where the salesperson's loyalties reside: The better the deal you get, the less commission the saleperson makes!

   9. The car salesperson will do all kinds of things to get you to make a commitment to buy ("What would it take to get you to buy this car? Just tell me, whudda-I-godda-do to get you in this car?"). Often the salesperson will ask you to write down any amount you're offering on a slip of paper or an offer sheet, even though it isn't legally binding (it does increase your psychological commitment, however). The car dealer *wants* you to sit in the car, take it for a test spin, smell the upholstery, because then you will become psychologically committed to owning the car.

   10. If you get close to a deal, or alternatively, if a deal seems to be coming apart, don't be surprised if another salesperson comes in to take over the negotiations. Often a "closer" is sent in (sort of like a relief pitcher in baseball) to complete the sale.

   11. Beware of "loss leaders" (advertised specials in the paper or on television at absurdly low prices). These are come-ons designed to get you onto the lot. Once there, however, you'll be subjected to the "Old Switcheroo."

You'll find there is/was only one car at that price (the serial number or license plate number listed in the ad). You will probably be told "Sorry, it's already sold…but I can make you a honey of a deal on…" You will also be stuck with the color and options the loss leader happens to have.

   12. The sale isn't over just because you've agreed on a price! You still have to deal with the dreaded "finance person." You'll be given the impression that you're just seeing the finance person to sign documents and process paperwork. Don't let down your guard. The finance person will try to add on thousands of dollars in the form of the following:

- Extended warranty packages. Most consumer groups advise against these because the fine print on the contract excludes lots of things (the very things that tend to break). In addition, car dealerships can change ownership (new ownership or reorganization following bankruptcy) and fail to honor previous warranties.

- Protective coatings, undercoatings, alarm systems, etc. You can always shop around for prices on these things later. Don't make a snap decision under pressure.

   13. The interest rate is just as important as the price of the car. Shop around for a car loan from a bank or credit union *before* you shop for a car. You can do this by phone without the high pressure of a car dealer. The rates are often much lower and you can find out exactly how much you qualify for in advance of a car purchase. Interest rates at car dealers tend to be higher because their financing schemes must accommodate "flaky" customers with bad credit histories (known as BK's on your TRW form). Interest rates at car dealers are negotiable, to an extent, but the dealer may be reluctant to admit it.

(Continued)

BOX 1.1   *Continued*

14. Shop around for prices on options such as stereos and car phones before you go to a car dealer. People often bargain well on the purchase price, then give up everything they've gained by failing to bargain on the price of extras. The price of everything is negotiable!

15. Don't discuss options in terms of the cost per day or month. Negotiate on the total price of the option. The salesperson may say, "Hon, I can throw in gen-u-wine factory air for only $1 per day." Over a 36-month period, that would cost you around $1,100 dollars, *plus* the finance charges.

16. Don't let the salesperson know you have a trade-in in advance. Any bargaining gains you make on the purchase price of the new car will just be deducted from the trade-in value of your used car. Sell the used car on your own if at all possible. If that's not possible, you can always mention your trade-in after you've negotiated the price of the new car.

17. Some dealers will offer to show you the "invoice" on the car you're considering as proof you're getting a good deal. They won't mention, however, that they get "holdbacks" or rebates from the car manufacturer which are typically on the order of 2 to 3 percent of the invoice amount. Always verify that the vehicle identification number on the invoice is *identical* to the vehicle identification number on the car you are considering purchasing (the Old Switcheroo again).

---

study of persuasion can be a prosocial endeavor. That brings us back to an earlier point, however. Not all persuaders are scrupulous. The practice of persuasion is often seen as manipulative. At this juncture, then, it seems appropriate that we address two common criticisms related to the study of persuasion.

TWO CRITICISMS OF PERSUASION

Does Learning about Persuasion Foster Manipulation?

We've already touched on one of the common criticisms of studying persuasion; the notion that it fosters a manipulative or coercive approach to communication and/or relationships with others. We address ethical concerns surrounding the study and practice of persuasion more specifically in Chapter 16. For the time being, however, a few general arguments can be mustered in response to this concern. First, our principle focus in this text is on the *means* of persuasion (e.g., how persuasion functions). We view the means of persuasion not so much as moral or immoral, but rather as amoral, or ethically neutral. In this respect, persuasion can be likened to a tool, such as a hammer. Like any tool, persuasion can be put to good or bad use. If this sounds like a cop-out, read what Aristotle had to say on this same point in his *Rhetoric*:

> *If it is urged that an abuse of the rhetorical faculty can work great mischief, the same charge can be brought against all good things (save virtue itself), and especially against the most useful things such as strength, health, wealth, and military*

skill. Rightly employed, they work the greatest blessings; and wrongly employed, they work the greatest harm. (1355b)

Related to this idea is the fact that tools can be used in good or bad ways, depending upon their user. We believe that first and foremost it is a *persuader's motives* that determine whether a given influence attempt is good or bad, right or wrong, ethical or unethical. We maintain that the moral quality of a persuasive act is derived primarily from the ends a persuader seeks, and only secondarily from the means the persuader employs. It isn't so much *what* strategies and tactics a persuader uses, as *why* he or she uses them.

To illustrate this position, suppose you asked us whether the use of "fear appeals" is ethically justified. We would have to say, it depends. If a fear appeal was being used to inform a sexually active teen of the risks of HIV infection from unprotected sex, we would tend to say the fear appeal was justified. If a fear appeal was being used by a terrorist who threatened to kill a hostage every hour until his demands were met, we would tend to say the fear appeal was unjustified. In each case the motives of the persuader would "color" the use of the fear appeal. Consistent with our tool analogy, fear appeals, like other persuasive strategies, can be used for good or bad ends.

A second response to this criticism was highlighted earlier. The study of persuasion performs a *defensive function* insofar as it educates people to become more discriminating consumers of persuasive messages. For instance, we feel our "17 Tips on Buying a New or Used Car" (see Box 1.1) might be useful to a car salesperson, but will probably be far more useful to potential car buyers. By increasing your awareness of the ploys of would-be persuaders, this text performs a watchdog function. You can use the information contained herein to arm yourself against the tactics of unscrupulous persuaders.

A third response that bears mentioning is that in denouncing the study of persuasion, anti-manipulation types are also attempting to persuade. The message that persuasion is controlling, manipulative, or exploitative is itself a persuasive appeal that seeks to engender certain attitudes, beliefs, and values about the "proper" study of communication. When one group claims they know best how human communication should be studied, they are standing on the persuasion soapbox themselves. As was stated earlier, efforts aimed at social influence are pervasive. It is one thing to renounce the value of studying persuasion, but quite another to actually abandon its use.

Are Persuasion Findings Too Inconsistent or Confusing?

An additional complaint that has been leveled against the study of persuasion is that it has led to findings which are trivial, overly qualified, or contradictory in nature. Empirical investigations of persuasion, it is argued, have not yielded clear and consistent generalizations, nor have they offered results that are applicable to real-life. There is no "E = MC^2," no "second law of thermodynamics," no universals when it comes to persuasion. This criticism cannot be taken lightly. And to be honest, there is some merit in this complaint. Nevertheless, several defenses can be mounted in support of learning about persuasion.

First, the conclusion that persuasion isn't worth studying because the findings are often inconclusive or contradictory, doesn't make much sense. Quite the opposite. We feel that persuasion warrants study precisely because it *is* so elusive. Underlying this criticism seems to be the expectation that reality is, or should be, simple and uncomplicated. Our response, in the time-honored words of Ann Landers, is "Wake up and smell the coffee!" Like it or not, understanding reality is hard work. As we've already noted, human beings are complex creatures who rarely respond to messages for one and only one reason. And what works on one person may not work on the next. Actually, we find this to be a redeeming feature of humanity. We rejoice in the fact that we aren't an altogether gullible, predictable, or controllable species.

A second response to this criticism is simply that research *has* revealed a number of significant, relevant generalizations about persuasion. You'll find many such generalizations throughout this book. Newer techniques of statistical analysis, such as meta-analysis,[6] have made it possible to reconcile some of the previous inconsistencies in the literature. In this text, we identify a number of noteworthy, albeit qualified, generalizations that are based on the most recent meta-analyses available.

Lastly, studying about persuasion in a classroom setting doesn't preclude one from learning about how persuasion works in other ways. Textbook authors and classroom instructors don't have a corner on the market. You'll notice in this book that we've drawn on the people in the trenches themselves to learn how persuasion works in particular contexts and settings. We've talked to used car salespersons, funeral home operators, retail clothing clerks, advertising firms, former cult members, door-to-door salespersons, and telephone solicitors to find out, from the horse's mouth, so to speak, how persuasion operates.

There are certainly other avenues for learning about persuasion. Keep in mind, however, that there is a lot of nonsense, hokum, and misinformation that gets bandied about on TV talk shows, tabloids, and other popular media that hasn't been carefully scrutinized or subjected to rigorous review. Just because a self-proclaimed expert has appeared on TV or written a book, doesn't necessarily mean he or she knows what he or she is talking about.

ETHICAL CONCERNS ABOUT THE USE OF PERSUASION

We would be remiss if we concluded this chapter without emphasizing the importance of ethics in the persuasion process. We wish to underscore the point that the use of persuasion is fraught with ethical concerns. We raise a number of such concerns in Box 1.2 for you to ponder. Our position is that in learning how to become a more effective persuader, you should strive to be an ethical persuader as well. In the final chapter we address a number of ethical questions that emanate from the various strategies and techniques of persuasion discussed throughout the text. We wait until the final chapter to fully examine ethical concerns for two reasons: First,

BOX 1.2   Ethical or Unethical Persuasion? You Make the Call

Instructions: For each scenario below, indicate how ethical or unethical you perceive the persuader or the persuasive strategy to be *based on a five-point scale* (with 1 being "highly ethical" and 5 being "highly unethical").

1. A student pretends to cry in a professor's office in an attempt to coax the professor into giving her a makeup exam. Is this ethical persuasion?

2. A teenager is paralyzed from the neck down in a car accident. A physician tells the teen that there is a chance she may be able to walk again (even though the physician knows better) so that the teen won't become despondent about the prospect of spending the rest of her life in a wheelchair. Is this ethical persuasion?

3. A persuader advances an argument he doesn't believe in, but which the persuader thinks will be convincing to his listeners. The argument isn't untrue or invalid, it just happens to be one with which the persuader himself does not agree. Is this ethical persuasion?

4. During a political debate, a candidate brings up a past alleged scandal regarding his opponent. The scandal isn't relevant to the issues being debated, but the candidate notes, "It reflects on my opponent's character." Is this ethical persuasion?

5. A car salesperson emphasizes that the brand of car a customer is considering has "more horsepower and better mileage than the competition." The salesperson fails to mention that the car has worse reliability and a worse safety record than the competition. Is this ethical persuasion?

6. A skilled attorney successfully defends a client she knows to be guilty. Is this ethical persuasion?

7. A minister tells his congregation that a vote for a particular candidate is "a vote for the Devil incarnate" and that the scriptures demand that the faithful cast their ballots for another candidate. Is this ethical persuasion?

8. A persuader sincerely believes in the arguments he is presenting, but the facts and information he cites are incorrect and outdated. Is this ethical persuasion?

9. An accused rapist has his wife, mother, and children come to court and sit in the front row throughout the trial. He hopes the jury will see him as a decent, family man. Is this ethical persuasion?

10. A male student asks another male student if he would like to get together to study for an upcoming test. The student doing the asking is gay and his real reason for wanting to get together is more social than task-oriented. Is this ethical persuasion?

11. Parents use a fear appeal to convince their child to clean her room. "Santa doesn't bring presents to children with dirty rooms," they warn. Is this ethical persuasion?

12. A children's cereal states on the box, "High in the vitamins kids need!", but doesn't mention that the cereal is high in sugar too. Is this ethical persuasion?

13. A newlywed husband is upset his wife wants to go to a dance club with some of her single friends for drinks. "If you go," he warns, "I'm going to a strip club with some of my friends." Is this ethical persuasion?

14. A political campaign runs a series of negative attack ads against an opponent, not because the campaign manager prefers to, but because voter surveys show the negative ads will work, whereas ads that take the political "high road" won't. Is this ethical persuasion?

until you've learned more about persuasion, you may not fully appreciate all of the ethical issues that are involved. Second, after you've studied the full scope of persuasion as we present it in this text, you'll be in a much better position to place these ethical questions in perspective.

SUMMARY

We hope that we've convinced you of the ubiquity of persuasion in human interaction. The capacity to persuade is one of the defining features of humankind. This fact provides the strongest possible reason for studying persuasion. Given that learning about persuasion also serves a knowledge function, a defensive function, an instrumental function, and a debunking function, we feel there is ample justification for studying this topic. Finally, rejoinders to two current criticisms of the study of persuasion were offered. Hopefully, a persuasive case has been made for learning about persuasion. Miller and Burgoon (1978) offer a useful footnote to this entire discussion.

> *No matter how fervently some well-meaning individuals try to deny or wish the fact away, questions concerning control and influence will remain an integral aspect of humanity's daily communicative activities. Given the centrality of these questions, it seems both foolhardy and fruitless to assume that our understanding of human communication can go on advancing without continued research attention to the persuasion process. Thus, we conclude that the case for persuasion research is as strong today as it was a decade or a century ago. (p. 45)*

One other thing: Did we mention that learning about persuasion also can be fun?

ENDNOTES

1. The scientific study of persuasion dates back to the 1940s and 1950s when Carl Hovland founded the Yale Attitude Research Program as part of the war effort. The government wanted to know how to counter enemy propaganda that could affect the morale of troops and how susceptible POWs were to brainwashing.

2. Aristotle's work, *The Rhetoric,* is one such text that has survived the test of time. Written in the fourth century, B.C., his work has had a lasting influence on our understanding of persuasion. Many of his insights and observations are considered valid even today.

3. Note that with the exception of Hitler these charismatic leaders enjoyed a limited following. The rest of us weren't taken in by their claims, suggesting that people, in general, aren't that gullible after all.

4. We don't have sufficient space to devote to this topic here, but suffice to say that the tradi-

tional notion of scientific realism is under siege from the anti-realism camp (see Kourany, 1998). The anti-realists argue that science is neither purely objective nor impartial but heavily value-laden (see also Laudan, 1984; Longino, 1990).

5. Such estimates can actually be found. We just don't place much stock in them. For example, Rosseli, Skelly, and Mackie (1995) stated that, "even by conservative estimates, the average person is exposed to 300–400 persuasive messages a day from the mass media alone" (p. 163).

6. Meta-analysis refers to a statistical technique that allows a researcher to combine the results of many separate investigations and examine them as if they were one big super study. A meta-analysis is capable of revealing trends across a number of studies and resolving apparent inconsistencies among studies.

REFERENCES

Aristotle. (1932). *The Rhetoric* (L. Cooper, Trans.). Englewood Cliffs, NJ: Prentice-Hall.

Berg, M. H. (1993, September 10). "Post-riot theme incorporates optimistic vision." *Los Angeles Times*, p. B4.

Bettinghaus, E. P. (1968). *Persuasive communication*. New York: Holt, Rinehart, & Winston.

Cassirer, E. (1944). *An essay on man*. New Haven, CT: Yale University Press.

Hobbs, R. H., & Woodard, F. (Eds.). (1986). *Human rights/human wrongs: Art and social change*. Iowa City, IA: University of Iowa Museum of Art.

Kourany, J. A. (1998). *Scientific knowledge: Basic issues in the philosophy of science*. Belmont, CA: Wadsworth.

Kuhn, T. S. (1970). *The structure of scientific revolutions* (2nd ed.). New York: Springer.

Laudan, L. (1984). *Science and values*. Berkeley, CA: University of California Press.

Levy, S. (1994, May 2). Dr. Edelman's brain. *The New Yorker*, 62–73.

Lippard, L. R. (1984). *Get the message? A decade of art for social change*. New York: E. P. Dutton.

Longino, H. (1990). *Science as social knowledge: Values and objectivity in scientific inquiry*. Princeton, NJ: Princeton University Press.

Miller, G. R., & Burgoon, M. (1978). Persuasion research: Review and commentary. In B. R. Ruben (Ed.), *Communication yearbook 2*, (pp. 29–47). New Brunswick, NJ: International Communication Association.

Mitroff, I. I. (Nov. 2, 1974). Studying the lunar rock scientist. *Saturday Review World*, pp. 64–65.

Rosseli, F., Skelly, J. J., & Mackie, D. M. (1995). Processing rational and emotional messages: The cognitive and affective mediation of persuasion. *Journal of Experimental Social Psychology*, *31*, 163–190.

Reuchelle, R. C. (1958). An experimental study of audience recognition of emotional and intellectual appeals in persuasion. *Speech Monographs*, *25*, 49–58.

Simons, H. W. (1986). *Persuasion: Understanding, practice, analysis*, 2nd ed. New York: McGraw-Hill.

Sullivan, M. (May 7, 1993). "Galleries plan to revisit riots through the eyes of L. A. artists." *Orange County Register*, p. 36.

Wenburg, J. R., & Wilmot, W. W. (1973). *The personal communication process*. New York: John Wiley & Sons.

2

WHAT CONSTITUTES PERSUASION?

What is persuasion? How broad or narrow is the concept? Is persuasion a subset of human communication in general, much like baseball is a subset of sports? Or is persuasion an element found in all human communication in the same way that coordination plays a role in every sport? Not surprisingly, different authors view the concept of persuasion in different ways and have therefore adopted differing definitions of the term. In this chapter we explore some of the ways persuasion has been defined. We offer our own rather broad-based, far-reaching conceptualization of persuasion based on five limiting criteria. We also offer our own model of what persuasion is (Gass & Seiter, 1997) and examine an additional model (Petty & Cacioppo, 1986a, 1986b) of how persuasion functions.

You may have encountered some unusual uses of the term *persuasion*. For example, we have a friend in the construction industry who refers to his sledgehammer as his "persuader." He tends to err on the side of cutting a 2 × 4 board too long, rather than too short, and then "persuading" it into place. As another example, you may recall seeing one of those old gangster movies in which a mob boss orders his henchman to take somebody out back "for a little gentle persuasion," meaning a beating. Although we don't normally associate persuasion with pounding lumber or pummeling people, even in ordinary usage the term does have a wide variety of meanings. Consider each of the hypothetical situations in Box 2.1, entitled "What Constitutes Persuasion?" Which of these scenarios do *you* consider to be persuasion?

Adding to the difficulty of defining persuasion is the fact that persuasion also goes by a variety of other names. Some of its aliases include terms such as influence, compliance gaining, manipulation, education, propaganda, brainwashing, coercion, convincing, and advising. Of course, whether these terms are considered pseudonyms for persuasion, or simply related terms, depends upon one's definition of persuasion.

Defining a concept is analogous to building a fence. A fence is designed to keep some things in and other things out. In the same way, a definition encompasses some elements or aspects of a concept within its domain while excluding

---

BOX 2.1   What Constitutes Persuasion?

1. Muffin notices a grubby-looking weirdo in one of the front seats of the bus she is boarding. He seems to be muttering to himself and has a noticeable facial twitch. She opts for a seat toward the rear of the bus. Did he "persuade" her to sit elsewhere?

2. Benny Bigot is the principal speaker at a park rally to recruit more members to the American Nazi party. Many of the people who hear Benny are so turned off by his speech that they are more anti-Nazi than they were before they attended the rally. Did Benny "persuade" them?

3. During a dramatic pause in his lecture for his 3-hour night class, Professor Hohum hears a student's stomach growling. The professor then decides it would be a good time for the class to take a break. Did the student "persuade" Professor Hohum?

4. Babbs is standing at a street corner watching passersby. The first three people she sees are wearing sweatshirts with political and/or social slogans emblazoned across the front. The fourth person to pass by is wearing a plain white T-shirt. Are the first three people "persuading" Babbs? Is the fourth?

5. Fiffi is contemplating going on a major diet. She realizes she is overweight because she tips the scales at just under 250 lbs, and her obesity affects her self-esteem. On the other hand, she has read that obese people who lose lots of weight typically gain the weight back within a short period of time and that people are genetically predisposed to a certain weight. She convinces herself that there is no point in dieting. Did Fiffi persuade herself?

6. Bubba is at the supermarket pondering which of two brands of beer to purchase, a cold-filtered brew or a fire-brewed brew. After studying both brands attentively, he opts for the cold-filtered variety. Unbeknownst to him, another shopper observed his deliberations. That shopper then walks over to the display and selects the same brand. Did "persuasion" take place?

7. Trudy is an impressionable freshperson who is in a jam. She has just realized a term paper is due in her philosophy class. Desperate, she asks Rex, who is the captain of the debate squad, if he will help her. Rex offers to give her an "A" paper he submitted when he had the same class two years prior *if* Trudy will sleep with him. Is Rex using "persuasion"?

---

others. Which "species" of human communication are to be found inside the "barnyard" of persuasion for a given author, depends upon the size and shape of the fence that particular author builds. Fortunately, the differences in various definitions can be clarified, if not resolved, by focusing on two key considerations. We turn to these next.

PURE VERSUS BORDERLINE CASES OF PERSUASION

The first consideration is whether one is interested in pure persuasion, or borderline cases of persuasion. By *pure persuasion,* we mean clear-cut cases of persuasion, on which most people would agree. Everyone would agree that a presidential debate, a television commercial, or an attorney's closing remarks to a jury are instances of persuasion. Such examples represent "paradigm cases" (O'Keefe, 1990; Simons, 1986) of persuasion because they are at the core of what we think of when we envision influencing others. Other instances of persuasion, though, lie closer to the boundary or periphery of what we normally think of as social influence. These instances we refer to as *borderline cases* of persuasion. Not everyone would agree that a derelict's mere appearance "persuades" passersby to keep their distance. Nor would everyone agree that involuntary reflexes such as burps, blinking, and pupil dilation constitute "persuasive" phenomena. These cases are less clear-cut, more "iffy." Much of the disparity in definitions is rooted in the fact that some authors are concerned with pure persuasion, while other authors are concerned with borderline cases as well. It isn't so much a matter of being right or wrong as it is a matter of how wide a net each author wishes to cast. The preliminary model of the scope of persuasion shown in Figure 2.1 illustrates this distinction in approaches.[1] As the shading in the model suggests, the dividing line between pure and borderline persuasion is fuzzy, rather than distinct.

Although we don't think there is a single, correct definition of persuasion, we do think there are some things that a functional, contemporary definition of persuasion ought to do. A contemporary definition should take into account the rich complex of verbal, nonverbal, and contextual cues found in interpersonal encounters, which, as we noted in Chapter 1, is the arena in which most influence attempts occur. These elements do not function separately, but rather, they operate in an interrelated manner, each affecting the other. A contemporary definition also should acknowledge the many subtle, implicit cues that accompany face-to-face influence attempts. By implicit cues, we mean communication that occurs at a very low level of awareness, or even unconsciously. As an example, cultural factors might influence a person's choice of compliance-gaining strategies, without the

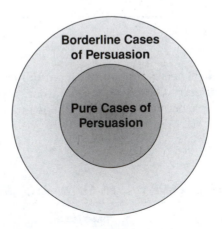

FIGURE 2.1   Preliminary model of persuasion.

person even realizing it (Wiseman et al. 1995). As another example, nonverbal cues are heavily relied upon in deception detection, even though individuals aren't always mindful of how or why they think another person may be lying (Hale & Stiff, 1990; Seiter, 1997). Such implicit communication is, in fact, quite common (Langer, 1989a, 1989b; Roloff, 1980) and an important ingredient in persuasion. The definition and model of persuasion that we offer later in this chapter takes these things into account.

LIMITING CRITERIA FOR DEFINING PERSUASION

A second consideration in defining persuasion involves the limiting criteria that form the basis for a given definition. Five basic criteria can be gleaned from the various definitions offered in the literature. We examine each of these criteria in turn.

Intentionality

Is persuasion necessarily conscious or purposeful? Can social influence occur at a low level of awareness, or even unconsciously? Many who write about persuasion adopt a source-centered view by focusing on the sender's intent as a defining feature of persuasion. Bettinghaus and Cody (1994) adopt this view, stressing that "persuasion involves a conscious effort at influencing the thoughts or actions of a receiver" (p. 5).

Certainly, pure persuasion would seem to be intentional. When we think of obvious cases of persuasion, we tend to think of situations in which one person purposefully tries to influence another. But what about borderline cases of persuasion? We believe that many influence attempts take place absent of any conscious awareness on the part of the persuader. Indeed, an entire branch of psychology is devoted to the subject of implicit perception or the ways in which unconscious stimuli influence experience (Bornstein & Pittman, 1992).

As just one instance, parents quite commonly instill beliefs, impart values, and model behavior for their children (Bandura, 1977). Yet they may not realize how much of what they say and do is absorbed by their young-uns. As any parent will attest, many of the lessons parents "teach" their children are completely unintended. As another example, in children's fairy tales beauty is often equated with "good" (the beautiful princess, the handsome prince) and ugly with "evil" (the ugly witch, the ugly stepsisters). Yet surely the intent in reading children such fairy tales is not to instill false stereotypes in their impressionable young minds.

Another illustration of how persuasion operates at a low level of awareness can be found in "impression management." When we interact with others we spend a good deal of our time trying to project a positive self-image. We want others to think we are intelligent, or charming, or witty. Think of all the time and effort people spend trying to make a favorable impression on a first date or in a job interview. When dating or interviewing, though, many of our attempts to negotiate our identity are unintentional. Without realizing it, a person's table manners, language style, mannerisms, hygiene, attempts at humor, or choice of topics may strongly influence the impressions others form about that person. Much of what we say and do is *reflexive* in nature, as opposed to being *reflective,* even though the messages conveyed carry considerable persuasive potential. In this regard, Cooper and Nothstine (1992) have commented, "those we try to influence through our persuasion may well respond to aspects of our persuasive actions that we are not aware of" (p. 3).

A story involving the father-in-law of one of the authors illustrates how unintentional persuasion can occur. The father-in-law had been backpacking along the John Muir trail in the Sierra Nevada mountains. After 4 days of hiking he emerged from the trail, looking rather grubby. At that time he discovered he had missed the bus he planned to take back to his car, which was parked at the trail head. The bus ran only once per day, so the next bus wouldn't come until the following afternoon. He decided to hitch a ride back to his car and fashioned a sign out of cardboard that read "need ride to Tuolome." No motorists stopped to give him a ride. He thus failed at his intended purpose—hitching a ride. Two motorists, however, stopped to offer a dollar, apparently thinking he was a homeless person based on his unkempt appearance. He thus succeeded at an unintended purpose—panhandling!

As another example of unintentional influence, the author of the syndicated comic, "Rex Morgan, M.D.," came under fire for publishing a comic strip in which the cartoon doctor issued unsound medical advice (see Figure 2.2). In the comic strip, Rex Morgan prescribed baby aspirin for a 13-month-old suffering from a cold. The use of aspirin, however, has been linked to Reye's syndrome, a potentially fatal disease, which can afflict infants and young children following exposure to the flu or chicken pox. Rex Morgan had committed cartoon medical malpractice. He should have prescribed acetaminophen instead.

The cartoon's author, Woody Wilson, was flooded with calls and letters from medical professionals pointing out the potentially dangerous error. He issued an apology and accepted full responsibility for the error. At the same time, however, Wilson warned that the comic strip was intended solely as entertainment and that readers "should never use the medical opinions or treatments illustrated in Rex Morgan, M.D. as a substitute for a visit to a qualified medical professional" (cited

FIGURE 2.2   Rex Morgan, M.D. cartoon.

Reprinted with special permission of North America Syndicate.

in Beyette, 1997). Let's face it, though, millions of readers, with and without medical insurance, intelligent and unintelligent, might have unwittingly followed Rex Morgan's advice. Influence can occur when none is intended.

A second way in which an "intent" criterion is problematic is that people often don't know what they intend or what outcome they are after. Not all persuasion is planned. Face-to-face encounters, in particular, are laden with spontaneity. Sometimes people are mad, or upset, or frustrated, but don't necessarily know what outcome they are seeking. Only *after* talking or arguing with another may they realize what form of influence they wish to exert. Social influence often arises in and through our interaction with others, rather than as a result of planning and forethought.

A third problem with relying on an "intent" criterion involves situations in which there are unintended receivers. Imagine a scenario in which two people are discussing which bets to place on a horse race. One tells the other about an inside tip on a horse that's a "sure thing." A third person overhears the conversation and as a result places a wager on the horse. In such situations persuaders don't intend for third parties to be influenced. Yet they often are. In determining what constitutes persuasion we feel we shouldn't focus exclusively on where a persuader was aiming, but on who the persuader hit.

Two studies (Greenberg & Pyszczynski, 1985; Kirkland, Greenberg, & Pyszczynski, 1987) clearly demonstrate the operation of the "unintended receiver effect." In these studies, the researchers created a situation in which third parties overheard an ethnic slur that was directed against an African American. The results of both studies clearly demonstrated that the overheard ethnic slurs led to lower evaluations by the third parties of the individual at whom the slurs were directed. Notice that a reliance on an intent standard for defining persuasion tends to make senders less accountable for the consequences of their unintended communication. If a message has harmful effects, the source can disavow any responsibility by claiming "that's not what I intended."

A fourth limitation lies in the difficulty of ascertaining another's intent. What if persons disagree as to what someone's persuasive motives or goals happen to be? Complicating the picture, there can be differences between a persuader's *stated* intent versus his or her *actual* intent. Who makes the determination in such cases? The sender? The receiver? A third party? Moreover, in the case of organizations and social movements, which are larger than any one individual, intent may be even more difficult to establish. Large groups often have multiple purposes, some of which are at odds with one another. The intent of the pro-life movement, for example, doesn't reside in any one spokesperson for the cause.

Resolving the issue of intent is particularly difficult in interpersonal contexts, in which both parties may be simultaneously engaged in attempts at influence. When there are two interactants, whose intent counts? Is it one party's actual intent that matters, or the other party's *perception* that there is an intent to persuade? Intent-based definitions, we believe, are ill-suited to modern conceptualizations of human interaction as a two-way venture. The rather linear view of persuasion that such definitions imply, from sender to receiver, ignores the complexities inherent in mutual influence.

Effects

You are probably familiar with the old conundrum, "If a tree falls in the forest and no one is around to hear it, is there any sound?" A similar question can be posed about an "effects" criterion: "Has persuasion taken place if no one is actually persuaded?" Some authors adopt a receiver-oriented definition of persuasion by restricting its use to situations in which receivers are somehow changed, altered, or affected. Daniel O'Keefe (1990) underscores this perspective when he writes:

> *the notion of* success *is embedded in the concept of persuasion. Notice for instance, that it doesn't make sense to say, "I persuaded him, but failed." One can say, "I tried to persuade him, but failed," but to say simply, "I persuaded him" is to imply a successful attempt to influence. (p. 15)*

The strong version of this perspective would view persuasion as being successful if it achieved the specific outcome sought by a persuader. The "weak" version of this perspective would settle for outcomes falling short of what the persuader ideally had in mind. While we recognize the attraction of this point of view, we believe problems arise when the definition of persuasion is limited in this way. We take the position that if a person is communicating badly, he or she is *still* communicating. Similarly, we feel that a person can be engaged in persuasion even if it is *ineffective* persuasion. The same can be said for most activities. A salesperson might fail to close a deal, but would still be engaged in selling. A dancer might dance badly, stepping on his or her partner's toes, but would still be engaged in dancing. In short, a person can be engaged in an activity whether they are doing it well or not.

A second reason we disagree with an effects criterion is that it is less consistent with current conceptions of human communication. Our concern here is twofold. First, an effects orientation emphasizes persuasion as a *product,* rather than as a *process.* If we think of persuasion only as an outcome or a thing, then an effects orientation makes perfectly good sense. We maintain, however, that persuasion is better understood as an activity in which people engage. Such an approach bears greater fidelity to current thinking about human communication as an ongoing, dynamic, process. This is more than semantic quibbling. By approaching persuasion as a process, scholars and researchers are more likely to gain insights into how it functions or what makes it tick, because they are focusing on *what's going on,* not simply how things turn out.

A second weakness is the same as that already associated with an intent criterion: an effects criterion embodies a rather linear view of persuasion, from source to receiver. In face-to-face encounters, however, there isn't simply *a* source and *a* receiver. Both parties may be simultaneously engaged in persuasion, with no clear demarcation between who is the persuader and who is the persuadee. Influence peddling in the interpersonal arena is a two-way street. Who has to succeed for persuasion to occur, one party or both parties? What if each party wins and loses a little, as is often the case?

A third problem with relying on an effects criterion to define persuasion is that it is often difficult, if not impossible, to measure persuasive outcomes. What effects count as indicators of success? Changes in beliefs, attitudes, intentions, motivations, and behaviors can be extremely subtle and therefore difficult to detect. In fact, the ability to measure such changes may hinge entirely on the sensitivity of one's measuring instruments (scales, surveys, etc.). Furthermore, what constitutes the threshold for a successful versus an unsuccessful attempt at persuasion? What if a PBS channel's fund-raising telethon fails to motivate a viewer to donate money, but induces feelings of guilt in the viewer for not donating? What if the American Lung Association's annual "Smokeout" campaign convinces a smoker to quit, but only for a few days? How much attitude or behavior change must take place in order for persuasion to succeed? What if a persuader succeeds in some respects, but fails in others? What if there is a delay or latency period before any effects take place? Or, conversely, what if the persuasive effects wear off quickly? And what about the occasional odd circumstance in which persuasion "boomerangs," for example, a persuader achieves an effect that is *contrary* to his or her intended purpose? Such questions, we believe, point out the many vagaries inherent in relying on an effects criterion.

A fourth problem with an effects criterion is that whether a given attempt to persuade is deemed successful or not often depends on whom one asks. Whether a labor strike is labeled a success or a failure, might well depend on whether one was gathering opinions from management or union representatives. It is often the case that, following a Supreme Court ruling, both sides proclaim victory.

We do agree that, as with an intent criterion, pure cases of persuasion can usually be evaluated by their overall effectiveness. Even then, persuasion is rarely an all or nothing venture. If one also wishes to focus on borderline cases of persuasion, one must accept the fact that partial persuasion is more the rule than the exception. Notice, too, that there is some tension between relying upon intent and effects as limiting criteria: What is achieved isn't always what is intended, and what is intended isn't always what is achieved. We happen to think some of the most interesting persuasive campaigns are those that are unsuccessful, or only partially successful, or which in fact achieve the opposite of the effect being sought.

Degree of Free Choice or Free Will

Many authors endorse the view that there is a distinction between persuasion and coercion. This view also is receiver-based, but focuses on the recipient's choice-making as a limiting criterion. Persuasion, these authors suggest, is noncoercive. As Herbert Simons (1986) puts it, "persuasion is a form of influence that predisposes, but does not impose" (p. 22). Richard Perloff (1993) also makes this point when he states a "defining characteristic of persuasion is free choice. At some level the individual must be capable of accepting or rejecting the position that has been urged of him or her" (p. 16).

On this score, we largely agree. The difficulty is in attempting to draw a bright line between persuasion and coercion. At what point does voluntary action leave off and involuntary action begin? In the last two decades, the courts have been called upon to draw such bright lines, for instance, in distinguishing harmless flirting from sexual harassment or in differentiating between consensual sex and rape ("States Struggle," 1994; Theissen & Young, 1994).

Coercive strategies aren't necessarily limited to negative sanctions. Coercion also can take place in the form of rewards, incentives, inducements, flattery, ingratiation, or bribery. Sting operations by law enforcement agencies, for example, rely on positive inducements to lure criminals in. If the inducements are too strong, however, the cases may be dismissed as entrapment. Thus, positive inducements also can exert coercive pressure.

Persuasion and coercion aren't so much polar opposites as they are close relatives. A message or message strategy can easily cross the line from one to the other. Moreover, many communication encounters contain both voluntary *and* involuntary elements. A simple request by a superior to a subordinate, "Boswell, can you give me a lift to pick up my car?", may carry with it an implicit threat for noncompliance. A parent may give a child three good reasons to eat his or her broccoli, but also may issue a negative sanction as well, "or no dessert for you, young lady."

In fact, we would argue that most influence attempts we encounter in our day-to-day affairs include both persuasive and coercive elements. Rarely in life is one free to make a completely unfettered choice. There are almost always strings attached. This is particularly true in face-to-face encounters. If a friend asks to borrow 20 bucks, we can say "no," but there may be relational consequences for declining.

Rarely, too, are influence attempts completely coercive. For example, holding a gun to another person's head would seem to be an obvious example of coercion. We readily admit this situation is *primarily* coercive. But what if the other person doesn't believe the gun is loaded? Or what if the other person thinks the threatener is bluffing? To be successful, a threat—even a threat of violence—must be perceived as credible. Thus, even in what might seem like a clear-cut case of coercion there are persuasive elements at work. And conversely, even in what appear to be cut and dried cases of persuasion, there may be coercive features operating.

People also have different dispositions and different personalities that may lead them to perceive messages differently. What one person regards as an innocent request another may view as highly coercive. As Trenholm (1989) notes, "Freedom of choice is subjective. Some people seem immune to even the most extreme threats; others feel coerced by the mildest influence attempts" (p. 6). Communication theorists are fond of saying "meanings are in people, not in words." Whether a given message is interpreted as primarily persuasive or primarily coercive is largely in the eyes of the beholder.

Because influence attempts frequently contain both voluntary and involuntary elements, and because the issue of free choice or free will is largely a perceptual phenomenon, we believe it is most useful to distinguish persuasion from coercion based on the degree of choice available. It isn't so much *whether* a situation is persuasive or coercive, but *how* persuasive or coercive the situation is.

"I insist."

"Persuasion" and "coercion" often coexist side by side.

Symbolic Action

A number of authors maintain that persuasion begins and ends with symbolic expression, which includes language as well other meaning-laden acts such as civil disobedience and protest marches. This approach focuses on the means or channel of persuasion as a limiting criterion. Cooper and Nothstine (1992) espouse this view, writing that:

> *Persuasion uses language and symbolic action. Symbolic action includes all the behaviors we engage in that are meaningful—that is, that come to represent to others our attitudes, beliefs or intentions. Language is one kind of symbolic action, and the most essentially human—but there are other kinds of symbolic action as well. These symbolic actions may be shaped and influenced by language, of course, but they need not be language, strictly speaking. Symbolic action includes such group phenomena as rallies, demonstrations, moratoriums, boycotts, and lawsuits; it also includes individual acts of nonverbal (literally "without language") communication. (pp. 2–3)*

Gerald Miller (1980) echoes their sentiments, writing that "persuasion relies upon symbolic transactions…the scholarly endeavors of persuasion researchers—and for that matter, the ordinary language usages of the term 'persuasion'—have consistently centered on the manipulation of symbols" (pp. 14–15).

Authors who limit the scope of persuasion to symbolic action fear that without such a limitation all human behavior could be considered persuasion. Their point is well taken. Yet we remain unconvinced that restricting the medium for persuasion is the best limiting criterion to employ. Again, we see good reasons for restricting our understanding of pure persuasion to symbolic action. Nevertheless, we believe that some of the most intriguing aspects of persuasion can be found in nonverbal behavior, which lies on the periphery of symbolic action. For example, research on the physiological correlates of deception demonstrates that a variety of involuntary nonverbal cues (such as blinking, smiling, and pupil dilation) are positive indicators of lying (DePaulo, Stone, & Lassiter, 1985). We focus on deception as a form of persuasion in Chapter 13. Research on source credibility reveals that physical attributes such as height or attractiveness influence judgments of source credibility (Chaiken, 1979). We examine such factors in Chapter 5. Studies have even demonstrated that aromas significantly influence individuals' moods and behaviors (Steiner, 1986; Walton, 1994). We explore this topic in Chapter 15. We see little justification for excluding such forms of influence from beneath the umbrella of persuasion. Why exclude them when there is credible, revealing research on these topics? Why exclude them when, in fact, real-world persuaders use them?

We can also think of situations in which pure behavior, for example, nonsymbolic actions, are nevertheless persuasive. When a basketball player makes a head fake to fool a defender, we would maintain that the player is *persuading* the defender to go the wrong way. The fake is all behavior, but the player has to *sell* the fake to get the defender to "bite" on it. As another example, some victims of shooting rampages have managed to survive by playing dead. Playing dead is an act of pure nonverbal persuasion. There are numerous other situations in which individuals use nonsymbolic means to influence others.

We believe that restricting the study of persuasion exclusively to symbolic expression leads to a fragmented understanding of the subject. Persuasion involves more than language usage or symbol usage. There are a whole host of factors at work. Physical features about a person, such as height, weight, sex, age, or ethnicity may have persuasive potential. The same may be said for a person's demeanor, mannerisms, involuntary utterances (such as burping or belching), and reflexive actions (such as being startled or laughing). Knowledge of a person's past or other relational cues may carry persuasive weight, as may situational or contextual cues. Unless the notion of symbolic action is expanded to include all of these features, we feel such a restriction offers only a partial picture of the whole of persuasion. Interestingly, many authors who profess an adherence to symbolic action nevertheless treat a variety of nonsymbolic aspects of behavior, such as those just mentioned, in their texts.

Interpersonal Versus Intrapersonal

How many actors are required for persuasion to take place? A last limiting criterion that deserves mention is whether persuasion can involve just one person or whether persuasion requires the participation of two or more distinct persons.

Some scholars adopt the view that engaging in persuasion is like dancing the tango; it takes two (Bettinghaus & Cody, 1994; Johnston, 1994; Perloff, 1993). We agree in the case of the tango, but not in the case of persuasion. In fact, we maintain that attempts at self-persuasion are quite common. A person who is on a diet might tape a picture of a lean, "chiseled" model on the refrigerator door to reinforce his or her motivation to refrain from eating. A person might search for a rationalization to do something he or she wants, such as blowing the rent money on front row concert tickets. In such cases, people engage in self-persuasion by "talking themselves into" whatever it is they wish to do. New Year's resolutions are good examples of self-persuasion. They involve making a commitment to do something or to stop doing something. The act of making the commitment serves to increase one's resolve.

We are sympathetic to the two or more perspective but suggest that, once again, the issue comes down to whether one wishes to focus exclusively on pure cases of persuasion or borderline cases as well. We heartily agree that when we think of pure cases of persuasion, we conjure up an image of one person persuading another. When we also include borderline cases, we imagine instances in which individuals sometimes try to convince themselves.

A MODEL OF THE SCOPE OF PERSUASION

In light of the five limiting criteria just discussed, we can now offer an enhanced model (see Figure 2.3) that encompasses both pure and borderline cases of persuasion (Gass & Seiter, 1997). Note that, as with the preliminary model, the inner circle represents pure persuasion; that is, what we think of as the core or heart of social influence. The outer circle represents borderline persuasion. Superimposed on top of these two circles are five wedges or "pie slices," each representing one of the five limiting criteria previously discussed. The inner portion of each slice represents the pure case for that criterion. The outer portion represents the borderline case. Once again, the shading between the inner and outer circles reflects the fuzzy dividing line that exists between pure and borderline persuasion.

Based on this enhanced model, you can appreciate the fact that different definitions feature different wedges of the inner and outer circles. Source-oriented definitions restrict persuasion to the inner circle of the "intentional-unintentional" wedge. Receiver-based definitions limit persuasion to the inner circle of the "effects–no effects" wedge. Other receiver-based definitions favor the inner circle with respect to the free choice–coercion criterion, and so on.

As you can also see from the enhanced model, some definitions concern themselves with several wedges at the same time, while other definitions are based on a single limiting criterion. It's worth noting that all definitions of persuasion— including our own, which we present shortly—are linguistic constructs. They exist in the "world of words." Whether a given situation involves persuasion is not a matter of fact, but of judgment.

Our own preference is for an expanded view of persuasion, one that includes borderline cases as well as pure persuasion. We tend to side with the view that

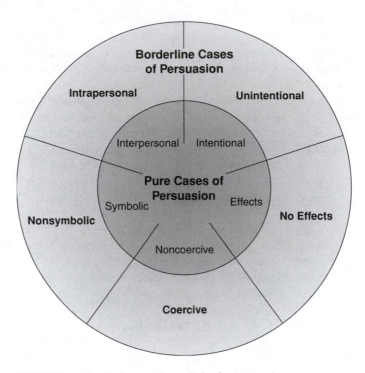

FIGURE 2.3   Enhanced model of persuasion.

persuasion is sometimes unintentional, that it sometimes has no discernable effects, that it often includes at least some coercive features, that it needn't be conveyed exclusively via symbols, and that humans do, on occasion, engage in self-persuasion. Many of the topics discussed in later chapters reside in the outer ring of our model. As we've already indicated, we believe that some of the most interesting aspects of persuasion can be found there. We firmly believe that we must look at both the inner and outer rings to fully understand the phenomenon called persuasion.

THE CONTEXT FOR PERSUASION

Consistent with current conceptualizations of persuasion, we view social influence as a process. Thus far, however, our model has remained relatively static. A final feature must be incorporated into our model to reflect the nature of persuasion as a process. That feature is the context for persuasion. The context in which persuasion occurs, for example, within a small group, via mass media, in an organizational setting, and so forth is crucial because it is the context that determines the nature of the communication process. In a face-to-face setting, for example, influence is a mutual, two-way process. In an advertising setting, influence tends to be more linear, from the advertiser to the consumer (there may be feedback from consumers, but it is delayed). Each context imposes its own unique set of constraints on the options available to persuaders.

By context, we don't simply mean the number of communicators present, although that is certainly one of the factors. The context for communication also includes how synchronous or asynchronous communication is. Synchronous communication refers to the simultaneous sending and receiving of messages. Such is the case in face-to-face interaction. Asynchronous communication refers to a back and forth process that involves some delay. Persuasion via e-mail involves asynchronous communication.

Another contextual factor is the ratio of verbal to nonverbal cues that are present. A print ad consisting entirely of text would rely exclusively on verbal cues (words) to persuade. A charity poster featuring only the picture of a starving child would rely exclusively on nonverbal cues to persuade. Most persuasive messages involve both verbal and nonverbal cues. The ratio of verbal to nonverbal cues available in any persuasive situation imposes particular constraints on the persuasion process.

An additional contextual factor is the nature and type of media used in the persuasion process. Television commercials, radio ads, magazine ads, and telephone solicitations are all mediated forms of persuasion. Face-to-face encounters, such as door-to-door sales and panhandling, are unmediated. As with the other contextual factors, each medium imposes its own requirements and constraints on the persuasion process.

Yet another contextual factor involves the goals of the participants. The prevailing view is that most, if not all, interpersonal communication, is goal-directed (Dillard, 1989, 1990, 1993; Dillard, Segrin & Harden, 1989; Tracy, 1991). That is, participants typically enter into communication encounters with specific objectives in mind. Canary and Cody (1994) break down these goals into three types—*self-presentational goals, relational goals,* and *instrumental goals.* Self-presentational goals have to do with identity management, which we mentioned earlier. People want to project a favorable image of themselves to others. Relational goals have to do with what people want out of their relationships; how to develop them, improve them, change them, terminate them, and so forth. Instrumental goals involve attempts at compliance gaining. The first two types of goals are more closely related to what we call borderline persuasion. The third type of goal is more closely connected to what we call pure persuasion. People's goals may be thwarted or may change during a persuasive encounter. Even so, the nature of the goals they are seeking imposes certain constraints on the persuasion process.

A final contextual variable involves socio-cultural factors that affect the persuasion process. People from different cultures or subcultures may persuade in different ways. They may respond to persuasive messages differently as well. For example, research suggests that some cultures prefer more "indirect" approaches to compliance gaining (hinting, guilt, reliance on group norms), while other cultures prefer more "direct" approaches to compliance gaining (direct requests, demanding) (Wiseman et al., 1995). Different cultural traditions can dramatically affect what is expected or accepted in the way of influence attempts.

Note that all of these contextual factors are operating at once in a given persuasive situation. Each of the contextual factors constrains the process of persuasion in one way or another. The context involves the totality of the relationships among all these factors. The final version of our model, depicted in Figure 2.4, illustrates how persuasion is shaped by context (Gass & Seiter, 1997). Context, then, is what determines the nature of the process involved in a given persuasive situation.

A WORKING DEFINITION OF PERSUASION

At last we arrive at our own definition of persuasion. Our view is that *persuasion involves one or more persons who are engaged in the activity of creating, reinforcing, modifying, or extinguishing beliefs, attitudes, intentions, motivations, and/or behaviors within the constraints of a given communication context.* The advantage of our definition is that it encompasses the full scope of persuasion; both pure *and* borderline cases. Our definition also emphasizes persuasion as an activity or a process; it is something people do. We are uncomfortable with treating persuasion as a product or an outcome, which explains our bias against an effects standard. Our definition encompasses the notion that in face-to face encounters persuasion is a two-way street. Each party has an opportunity to influence the other. This explains our reluctance to label only one party the "sender," as an intent criterion seems to suggest, or only one party as the "receiver," as an effects criterion tends to imply.

With respect to our definition, we also wish to stress that persuasion doesn't involve simply *changing* one's own or another's mind, although that is the most typical connotation. Gerald Miller (1980) calls this common connotation a *response-changing process*. Miller also noted that persuasion can involve creating new beliefs or attitudes, where none existed before, which he termed a *response-shaping process*. And, he observed, persuasion can involve reinforcing, strengthening or solidifying attitudes already held by receivers, which he labeled a *response-reinforcing process*. We believe persuasion also can involve attempts to extinguish or eliminate beliefs and attitudes. Thus, we would add to Miller's (1980) typology a fourth category, a *response-extinguishing process*. The Center for Disease Control's efforts to convince the public that HIV is not casually transmitted fall into this category; HIV isn't casually transmitted, meaning that one doesn't contract HIV by kissing someone, touching a doorknob, speaking on a pay phone, or having lunch with an HIV positive person. This approach is also exemplified in the strategy employed by Alcoholics Anonymous to convince alcoholics to abandon the notion that somehow other people are responsible, or circumstances are to blame, for their dependency.

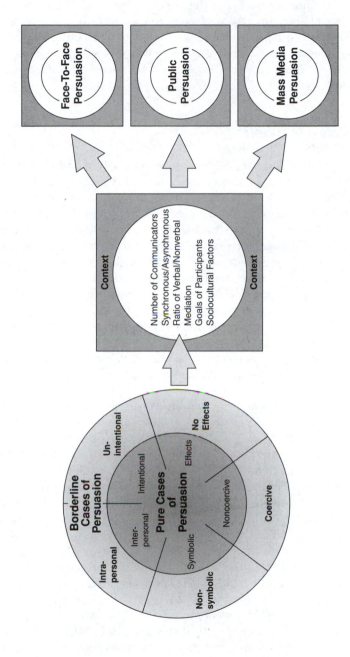

FIGURE 2.4   Completed model of persuasion. (This figure illustrates three of many possible persuasive situations.)

If our definition seems expansive it is because we feel the topic of persuasion itself is rather far-ranging. We wish to examine not only the core of persuasion in this text, but its periphery as well. The majority of our examples will focus on pure cases of persuasion. However, from time to time we will dabble on the fuzzy outer edges. We find some of the borderline cases of persuasion quite interesting, and we believe you will too.

SO WHAT ISN'T PERSUASION?

Given the breadth of our definition, you're probably wondering, "What *isn't* persuasion then?" We address this concern now. Our position is that the ingredients for persuasion can be found in most, if not all, communication transactions. The degree to which these persuasive ingredients are present, not their mere presence or absence, is what matters. We think most human communication involves at least the *potential* to influence, for example, to create, modify, reinforce, or extinguish beliefs, attitudes, intentions, motivations, and behaviors. Of course, one may choose not to focus on the persuasive, or potentially persuasive, elements in a communication situation. One can concentrate on some other aspect of communication instead. The potential for persuasion remains nonetheless. What matters, then, is how persuasive a given communication situation is, not whether a communication situation is persuasive or not.

Our position is not that most, or all, human communication is just persuasion. Many other features of communication can command one's attention. For example, one can examine the role of self-disclosure and relationship satisfaction without discussing persuasion. One can study nonverbal cues and liking without focusing on persuasion. One can look at how people try to save face during conflicts without involving persuasion. Persuasive elements needn't comprise the focus of attention even if they are present. One can focus on other relevant features of human communication to the exclusion of persuasive processes.

Although we believe that nearly all human communication is potentially persuasive, we don't believe the same about all human behavior. The mere act of breathing, in and of itself, doesn't seem like persuasion to us—although given some additional conditions it could be. Tripping over a rock and hitting one's head, by itself, doesn't seem like a persuasive act to us although, again, under the right circumstances it could be (like pretending to be clumsy). A good deal of human behavior, then, we don't consider to be persuasion, unless and until some additional conditions are met. We don't think everything humans do is persuasive.

There are also some forms of communication that we've excluded from consideration in this text, for purely practical reasons. For example, we don't address the possibility of human-to-animal persuasion, or vice versa, though such a case probably could be made. We don't examine the power of hypnotic suggestion as a form of influence. We don't examine attempts to persuade via paranormal or psychic activity either. We've heard that some people with cancerous tumors try to "talk to" their cancer and "persuade" it go away. We don't deal with that topic here, except insofar as it may constitute a form of self-persuasion. We also don't address a host of other intriguing topics, such as prayer or meditation as forms of persuasion. We simply don't have the space to devote to those topics. Thus, as big as the fence that we've built is, there is a lot of human communication we've left out.

THE ELABORATION LIKELIHOOD MODEL OF PERSUASION

Now that we've clarified what we think persuasion is, we want to take a look at how it functions. To accomplish this, we present a brief explanation of Richard Petty and John Cacioppo's (1986a, 1986b) *Elaboration Likelihood Model of Persuasion,* or *ELM,* as it is commonly known.[2] Their model postulates two basic routes to persuasion, that operate in tandem. The first of these they call the *central route.* The central route, or "central processing," as they sometimes refer to it, involves "issue-relevant thinking." That means thinking about the content of a message, reflecting upon the ideas and information contained in it, and scrutinizing the evidence and reasoning presented. The second route to persuasion is known as the *peripheral route.* The peripheral route, or "peripheral processing" as it is sometimes called, involves focusing on cues that aren't directly related to the substance of the message. For example, focusing on a source's physical attractiveness, or the quantity as opposed to the quality of arguments presented, or a catchy jingle as a basis for decision making, would entail peripheral processing.

To illustrate the two basic routes, imagine that Rex and Trudy are out on a date at a restaurant. Trudy is very health conscious, so she studies the menu carefully. She looks to see whether certain dishes are fatty or high in calories. When the food server arrives to take their order, she asks, "What kind of oil is used to prepare the pasta?" She might sound picky, but Trudy is engaging in central processing. She is actively thinking about what the menu says. Rex, on the other hand, is smitten with Trudy's good looks. He hardly looks at the menu, and when the food server asks for his order he says, "I'll have what she's having." Rex is engaging in peripheral processing. He's basing his decision on cues that are unrelated to the items on the menu.

Petty and Cacioppo suggest that when a person is presented with a persuasive message, he or she processes it via both routes simultaneously. They call this *parallel processing* (Petty, Kasmer, Haugtvedt, & Cacioppo, 1987). However, they suggest that a person will tend to favor one route over the other. Whether a person emphasizes the central route over the peripheral route hinges on two basic factors. The first of these is the individual's motivation to engage in central processing. For a person to engage in central processing there must be some motivation for doing so. Typically, this means the person has high involvement with the topic or issue in question. That is, the topic or issue matters to him or her or affects him or her personally. If a person has low involvement with a topic or issue, he or she is less likely to engage in central processing and more likely to resort to peripheral processing.

A personality trait called *need for cognition* also affects a person's motivation to engage in central or peripheral processing. We discuss this trait in Chapter 6.

The second factor that determines whether a person will rely on central or peripheral processing is his or her ability to process information. Let's face it, some people have more going on "upstairs" than others. They are more adept at grasping ideas, understanding concepts, and thinking things through. Some people also have more knowledge or expertise on certain topics or issues than others. In addition to cognitive ability and knowledge, situational factors also can affect a person's ability to engage in central processing. Distractions, for example, such as background noise or poor lighting, can inhibit an individual's ability to concentrate on a message.

In sum, then, receivers are more likely to process a persuasive message via the central route if they are motivated and able to do so. If they lack the motivation, personality, or ability to engage in central processing, they will tend to rely instead on peripheral processing. The ELM model is useful both for explaining and predicting people's reactions to persuasive messages. Literally dozens of studies devoted to testing the explanatory and predictive power of the ELM model have been carried out. They have generally upheld its utility as a comprehensive, integrative model of how persuasion functions.[3]

Among other things, researchers have found that persuasion via the central route tends to be more long-lasting, whereas persuasion via the peripheral route tends to be more short-lived. This seems reasonable: When we think about ideas, they are more likely to sink in. Similarly, persuasion that takes place via central processing also tends to be more resistant to counter-influence attempts than persuasion via peripheral processing. This also makes sense: If you've thought through your position, you're less likely to "waffle." Researchers have also found that if receivers disagree with the content of a message, using central processing will cause them to generate more counterarguments, while they mentally rehearse their objections to the message. If receivers disagree with a message, however, and they rely on peripheral processing, they will be less prone to generate counterarguments or other unfavorable thoughts about the message. We'll develop and amplify these and other principles related to the ELM throughout this text. Because we'll be referring back to the ELM repeatedly, it would be worth your while to familiarize yourself with the basic concepts of the model now for later reference.

SUMMARY

We began this chapter by presenting a preliminary model of persuasion that distinguished pure from borderline cases of persuasion. We argued for an expanded view of persuasion, emphasizing the importance of borderline cases to an overall appreciation of what persuasion is. We then identified five limiting criteria for defining persuasion that were reflected in an enhanced model of persuasion. We discussed what we believed to be the limitations of basing a definition of persuasion on any one criterion. We then introduced our own completed model of persuasion (Gass & Seiter, 1997), which emphasized the role of context in the persuasion process. We followed our model with our own broad-based, far-reaching definition of persuasion. Last, we provided a brief explanation of Petty and Cacioppo's (1986b) Elaboration Likelihood Model of persuasion.

ENDNOTES

1. More than a decade ago, Simons (1986, p. 116) introduced a model of persuasion having concentric circles, representing pure persuasion, peripheral persuasion, and nonpersuasion. Our preliminary model (Figure 2.1) draws upon his work.

2. A rival model, Chaiken and Eagly's Heuristic Systematic Model of persuasion, or ESM, has similar explanatory and predictive power (see Chaiken, 1980, 1987; Chaiken, Liberman, & Eagly, 1989; Eagly & Chaiken, 1993). For our purposes, both models possess enough similarities to be considered somewhat interchangeable. Heuristic processing in Chaiken and Eagly's ESM is roughly analogous to peripheral processing in Petty and Cacioppo's ELM. Similarly, systematic processing in Chaiken and Eagly's ESM is roughly analogous to central processing in Petty and Cacioppo's ELM.

3. Not all scholars are enamored with Petty and Cacioppo's model. Among others, Mongeau and Stiff (1993) and Stiff and Boster (1987) have criticized the ELM for its theoretical and empirical limitations. Petty, Wegener, Fabrigar, Priester, and Cacioppo (1993) and Petty, Kasmer, Haugtvedt, and Cacioppo (1987) have responded to many of the criticisms directed against their model.

REFERENCES

Bandura, A. (1977). *Social learning theory.* Englewood Cliffs, NJ: Prentice-Hall.

Bettinghaus, E. P., & Cody, M. J. (1994). *Persuasive communication,* (6th ed.). Forth Worth, TX: Harcourt Brace.

Beyette, B. (1997, August 1). "Comic strip's error gives creator a dose of reality." *Los Angeles Times,* E-2.

Bornstein, R. F., & Pittman, T. S. (1992). *Perception without awareness: Cognitive, clinical and social perspectives.* New York: Guilford Press.

Canary, D. J., & Cody, M. J. (1994). *Interpersonal communication: A goals-based approach.* New York: St. Martin's Press.

Chaiken, S. (1979). Communicator physical attractiveness and persuasion. *Journal of Personality and Social Psychology, 37,* 1387–1397.

Chaiken, S. (1980). Heuristic versus systematic information processing and the use of source versus message cues in persuasion. *Journal of Personality and Social Psychology, 39,* 752–766.

Chaiken, S. (1987). The heuristic model of persuasion. In M. P. Zanna, J. M. Olson, & C. P. Herman (Eds.), *Social influence: The Ontario Symposium* (Vol. 5, pp. 3–39). Hillsdale, NJ: Erlbaum.

Chaiken, S., Liberman, A., & Eagly, A. H. (1989). Heuristic and systematic information processing within and beyond the persuasion context. In J. S. Uleman & J. A. Bargh (Eds.), *Unintended thought* (pp. 212–252). New York: Guilford Press.

Cooper, M., & Nothstine, W. L. (1992). *Power persuasion: Moving an ancient art into the media age.* Greenwood, IN: Educational Video Group.

DePaulo, B. M., Stone, J. I., & Lassiter, G. D. (1985). Deceiving and detecting deceit. In B. R. Schlenker (Ed.), *The self and social life* (pp. 323–370). New York: McGraw-Hill.

Dillard, J. P. (1989). Types of influence goals in close relationships. *Journal of Social and Personal Relationships, 6,* 293–308.

Dillard, J. P. (1990). Primary and secondary goals in interpersonal influence. In M. J. Cody & M. L. McLauglin (Eds.), *Psychology of tactical communication* (pp. 70–90). Clavendon, England: Multilingual Matters.

Dillard, J. P. (1993). A goal-driven model of interpersonal influence. In J. P. Dillard (Ed.), *Seeking compliance: The production of interpersonal influence messages* (pp. 41–56). Scottsdale, AZ: Gorsuch, Scarisbrick.

Dillard, J. P., Segrin, C., & Harden, J. M. (1989). Primary and secondary goals in the interpersonal influence process. *Communication Monographs, 56*, 19–39.

Eagly, A. H., & Chaiken, S. (1993). *The psychology of attitudes.* New York: Harcourt, Brace, Jovanovich.

Gass, R. H., & Seiter, J. S. (1997, November). On defining persuasion: Toward a contemporary perspective. Paper presented at the annual convention of the Western Communication Association, Monterey, California.

Greenberg, J., & Pyszczynski, T. (1985). The effect of an overheard ethnic slur on evaluations of the target: How to spread a social disease. *Journal of Experimental Social Psychology, 21*, 61–72.

Hale, J. S., & Stiff, J. B. (1990). Nonverbal primacy in veracity judgments. *Communication Reports, 3*, 75–83.

Johnston, D. D. (1994). *The art and science of persuasion.* Madison, WI: William C. Brown.

Kirkland, S. L., Greenberg, J., & Pyszczynski, T. (1987). Further evidence of the deleterious effects of overheard derogatory ethnic labels: Derogation beyond the target. *Personality and Social Psychology Bulletin, 13*(2), 216–227.

Langer, E. J. (1989a). *Mindfulness.* Reading, MA: Addison-Wesley.

Langer, E. J. (1989b). Minding matters. In L. Berkowitz (Ed.), *Advances in experimental social psychology* (Vol. 22, pp. 137–173). New York: Addison-Wesley.

Miller, G. R. (1980). On being persuaded: Some basic distinctions. In M. E. Roloff & G. R. Miller (Eds.), *Persuasion: New directions in theory and research* (pp. 11–28). Beverly Hills, CA: Sage.

Mongeau, P. A., & Stiff, J. B. (1993). Specifying causal relationships in the Elaboration Likelihood Model. *Communication Theory, 3*, 65–72.

O'Keefe, D. (1990). *Persuasion: Theory and research.* Newbury Park, CA: Sage.

Perloff, R. M. (1993). *The dynamics of persuasion.* Hillsdale, NJ: Erlbaum.

Petty, R. E., & Cacioppo, J. T. (1986a). The Elaboration Likelihood Model of persuasion. In L. Berkowitz (Ed.), *Advances in experimental social psychology* (Vol. 19, pp. 123–205). New York: Academic Press.

Petty, R. E., & Cacioppo, J. T. (1986b). *Communication and persuasion: Central and peripheral routes to attitude change.* New York: Springer-Verlag.

Petty, J. T., Kasmer, J. E., Haugtvedt, C. P., & Cacioppo, J. T. (1987). Source and message factors in persuasion: A reply to Stiff's critique of the Elaboration Likelihood Model. *Communication Monographs, 54*, 233–249.

Petty, R. E., Wegener, D. T., Fabrigar, L. R., Priester, J. R., & Cacioppo, J. T. (1993). Conceptual and methodological issues in the Elaboration Likelihood Model of persuasion: A reply to the Michigan State critics. *Communication Theory, 3*(4), 336–362.

Roloff, M. E. (1980). Self-awareness and the persuasion process: Do we really *know* what we're doing? In M. E. Roloff & G. R. Miller (Eds.), *Persuasion: New directions in theory and research*, pp. 29–66. Beverly Hills, CA: Sage.

Seiter, J. S. (1997). Honest or deceitful? A study of persons' mental models for judging veracity. *Human Communication Research, 24*(2), 216–259.

Simons, H. W. (1986). *Persuasion: Understanding, practice, and analysis* (2nd ed.). New York: McGraw-Hill.

"States struggle to define rape: Is force needed? Is 'no' enough? Rulings vary." (1994, June 3). *Star Tribune.* p. 1+.

Steiner, W. (1986). The effect of nose fragrances on human experience and behavior. drom Report, "The Nose, Part 3", 16–21.

Stiff, J. B., & Boster, F. J. (1987). Cognitive processing: Additional thoughts and a reply to Petty, Kasmer, Haugtveldt, and Cacioppo. *Communication Monographs, 54*, 250–256.

Thiessen, D., & Young, R. K. (1994, March). Investigating sexual coercion: Critique of scientific studies on rape and sexual harassment. *Society, 31*(3), 60–63.

Tracy, K. (Ed.). (1991). *Understanding face-to-face interaction: Issues linking goals and discourse.* Hillsdale, NJ: Erlbaum.

Trenholm, S. (1989). *Persuasion and social influence.* Englewood Cliffs, NJ: Prentice-Hall.

Walton, A. S. (1994, October 2). A chemical attraction discovery of pheromonal proportions. *The Atlanta Journal and Constitution,* L-6+.

Wiseman, R. L., Sanders, J. A., Congalton, K. J., Gass, R. H., Sueda, K., & Ruiqing, D. (1995). A cross-cultural analysis of compliance-gaining: China, Japan, and the United States. *Intercultural Communication Studies,* 5(1), 1–17.

3

ATTITUDES AND ATTITUDE MEASURES

The word "attitude" doesn't mean the same thing to social scientists that it does to rappers. When social scientists say someone "has an attitude" they don't mean the person is being defensive or petulant. Social scientists have long been fascinated with the study of attitudes. More than half a century ago Gordon Allport proclaimed that attitudes were "probably the most distinctive and indispensable concept in contemporary American social psychology" (1935, p. 798). They continue to occupy the center stage of persuasion research even today. The recent emphasis on compliance gaining, with its focus on behavioral conformity, has meant that attitudes have had to share the limelight with behavioral measures of persuasion's effectiveness. Nevertheless, attitudes remain a pivotal element in understanding how social influence functions.

Just why are attitudes so important to understanding persuasion? The reason is that attitudes serve as guides for human behavior. This happens in three basic ways. First, an understanding of how attitudes are formed, shaped, or altered helps *predict behavior.* If a persuader knows enough about a target audience's attitudes on a particular topic or issue, he or she can predict with reasonable accuracy how the audience will respond to a persuasive message on that topic or issue. Second, an understanding of attitudes helps *explain behavior.* If a persuader knows enough about receivers' attitudes, he or she can explain how and why they respond to particular persuasive messages the way they do. Third, a knowledge of how attitudes work helps *modify behavior.* By changing receivers' attitudes toward a particular topic or issue, a persuader can modify their actions accordingly. Just as a baker uses yeast as a catalyst in baking bread, persuaders rely on attitude change as a means of inducing behavioral changes in receivers. An understanding of attitudes is therefore an important ingredient in any recipe for persuasion. For this reason, this chapter is devoted to a discussion of attitudes; what they are, how they're formed, and how they function. We also examine the ways they are measured or inferred via standardized scales, roundabout methods, and physiological measures. We discuss the limitations of each of these approaches to measuring attitudes. Last, we examine the all-important relationship between attitudes and behavior.

IN FIFTEEN WORDS OR LESS, WHAT IS AN "ATTITUDE"?

Although once hotly debated, there is now general agreement among social scientists that an attitude is a learned predisposition to respond favorably or unfavorably toward some attitude object (Fishbein & Ajzen, 1975). Let's examine some of the assumptions contained in this definition more closely. First, attitudes are *learned,* not innate. A person isn't born with attitudes already in place. They're acquired. We develop attitudes by interacting with others, through our personal experiences, from the media, and so forth.

Second, attitudes are *predispositions to respond,* which means they precede and, to some extent, direct people's actions. Researchers call attitudes "precursors of behavior" for this reason. We don't have time to reflect on each and every action we take in life, so attitudes provide us with mental short-cuts that guide our behavior.

This is not to say that there is a one-to-one correspondence between attitudes and behaviors. A person may have a favorable attitude toward losing weight, but may not stay on a diet. Just think about how many new year's resolutions are forgotten by the second day of January! To a large extent, though, our attitudes do correspond with our behaviors. Dog lovers tend to own dogs, while cat lovers tend to own cats. People who favor gun control laws are less likely to own guns than people who oppose such laws. After all, there wouldn't be much point in studying attitudes if they weren't, by and large, predictive of behavior. We'll return to the issue of attitude–behavior consistency again in this chapter (see Box 3.1).

A third feature of attitudes is that they represent favorable or unfavorable evaluations of things.[1] In other words, they reflect likes or dislikes, agreement or disagreement, positive or negative feelings. This *evaluative dimension* is, perhaps, the most central feature of attitudes (Dillard, 1993). If a person says, "I can't stand Howard Stern," or "I adore Rush Limbaugh," the person is expressing his or her attitudes toward the two radio talk-show hosts. Evaluative words and phrases, such as "can't stand" and "adore" signal both the direction (positive or negative valence) of the person's attitudes and the degree or intensity of the attitudes.

A fourth and final aspect of attitudes is that they are always directed toward an attitude object. People hold attitudes *about* things or *toward* things. The attitude object can be another person, an idea, a policy, an event, or a situation. In 1995, Timothy McVeigh's hatred of the federal government, for example, was manifested in his choice of a federal building in Oklahoma City as the target for his bombing.

SO HOW DO YOU MEASURE THE DURN' THINGS?

If you want to know how much you weigh, you can stand on a scale. If you want to know how tall you are, you can use a tape measure. But what if you want to measure your own, or someone else's, attitudes? Attitudes can't be directly observed. Attitudes are "in people's heads." They are abstract phenomena. They must therefore be measured indirectly.[2]

You are undoubtedly familiar with the method used by the movie critics, Gene Siskel and Roger Ebert, for evaluating movies. Their well-known "two thumbs up"

BOX 3.1 When Do Attitudes Coincide with Behavior?

Just because a movie goer tends to prefer action–adventure movies over comedies doesn't mean he or she will *always* elect to see movies of the former genre at the expense of movies from the latter genre. So when can we expect attitudes to coincide with behavior? There tends to be greater attitude-behavior consistency when:

1. **Multiple attitudes aren't confused with single attitudes.** A person doesn't have just *one* attitude toward "immigrants," for example. A person's attitudes toward legal versus illegal immigrants, first-generation versus second-generation immigrants, or immigrants from one country versus another, may vary. Attitude–behavior consistency is greater when a single attitude is measured within a specific situation, place, and time.

2. **"Multiple act criteria" are employed.** Giving people different opportunities to manifest their attitudes through their behavior improves the "fit" between attitudes and behavior. If you want to assess a person's attitudes toward homeless people, for example, you should examine her or his behavior toward more than one homeless person. If you want to assess a person's attitudes toward "honesty" you should provide him or her with multiple opportunities to perform honest acts (e.g., returning a lost wallet, declining to cheat on a test, admitting he or she broke something).

3. **The attitudes are based on personal experience.** Attitudes that have been formed as a result of direct personal experience tend to correspond more closely with actual behavior (Fazio, 1986; Fazio & Zanna, 1981). Second-hand attitudes, which are based on what others have told us, or which have been shaped by the media, do not predict behavior as well. For example, a person's attitudes toward alcoholics will more closely coincide with her or his behavior toward alcoholics if she or he has had first-hand experiences with alcoholics, as opposed to simply reading about them.

4. **Attitudes central to the belief system are involved.** Attitudes that are central to an individual's core beliefs and values tend to be more reliable predictors of behavior than attitudes that are tangential to an individual's belief system. A person's attitudes about "marital fidelity" would reveal more about his or her behavior in relationships than his or her preferences regarding pineapple on pizza.

5. **Social desirability bias is removed.** When people know their actions are on public display, they may exhibit what is called *social desirability bias.* That is, they tend to abide by what they perceive to be socially acceptable norms for conduct (Fisher, 1993). During a job interview, for example, a person might express politically correct attitudes toward workplace concerns such as sexual harassment or affirmative action in order to appear to be a good job prospect. Such prosocial behavior may or may not reflect a person's true attitudes. For this reason, the attitude–behavior relationship is stronger when persons feel unconstrained by social norms and are free to engage in "out of role" behavior.

6. **Self-monitoring behavior is taken into account.** Self-monitoring is a trait-like quality found in people. High self-monitors (HSMs) are more likely to adapt their behavior to fit the situation. They rely on other people, circumstances, and the setting for cues on how to behave (e.g., waiting until noon to eat lunch). Low self-monitors (LSMs) tend to respond based on their own internal states. LSMs' actions are the product of what they want or how they feel (e.g., eating when one is hungry). Research suggests that greater attitude–behavior consistency is found among LSMs than HSMs, because the former are less inclined to tailor their behavior to fit perceived situational expectations. We discuss self-monitoring in more detail in Chapter 6.

7. **Actual attitudes as opposed to "non-attitudes" are at issue.** People don't want to appear uninformed or unintelligent. So quite often, when individuals are asked for their attitude on a particular issue, they simply make one up—on the spot! They fear that saying "I don't know" or "I don't care" will make them look foolish. Thus, some attitudes are artificial by-products of people's attempts to appear knowledgeable and informed in front of researchers and/or pollsters. Such non-attitudes, as they are called, are not reliable predictors of behavior.

or "two thumbs down" rating system is a simple, yet effective means of conveying their attitudes toward the movies they review. You are probably also acquainted with the ever popular "10 point scale" used by males and females alike to rate the physical attractiveness of members of the opposite sex. In a not too dissimilar vein, social scientists have developed a variety of means for assessing people's attitudes toward just about everything. Such attitude measures are extremely important to social science research. Without them, it would be nearly impossible to study whether persuasion works.

Standardized Self-Report Scales

One means of measuring attitudes is via standardized scales based on self-reports. These are informally referred to as "paper-pencil" measures of attitude. The earliest standardized scales for measuring attitudes were developed by L. L. Thurstone (1928; Thurstone & Chave, 1929) and Louis Guttman (1944, 1950). The Thurstone and Guttman scales are seldom used nowadays because they are difficult to create and cumbersome to use. More efficient scales for measuring attitudes, such as the Likert scales (Likert, 1932) mentioned below, have supplanted them. Nevertheless, you may still hear or read about Thurstone or Guttman scales from time to time.

Likert Scales

A problem with Siskel and Ebert's rating system is that it is an all-or-nothing approach. What if they "sort of liked" a movie? Likert's (1932) approach overcomes this problem, allowing for gradations in attitudes. His "equal appearing interval" scales remain among the most popular in use today. They are easy to construct and administer to subjects. You've probably already completed a number of them yourself while in college (see Figure 3.1). A Likert scale consists of a series of declarative statements, pertaining to some attitude object, followed by a continuum of choices ranging from "strongly agree" to "strongly disagree" (see Figure 3.1). A respondent's attitude is represented by the average of his or her responses to all the declarative statements asked about.

The reason they are called "equal appearing interval" scales is because each space on the continuum represents the same increment or degree of attitude change as the other spaces. This is an important feature of Likert scales because it allows mathematical comparisons among attitudes to be made. An attitude of "+2" on a 7-point Likert scale would be considered twice as strong as an attitude of "+1" on the same scale.

Likert scales enjoy widespread acceptance in academia, government, and industry. Specialized versions of these scales have been developed to measure teaching effectiveness, job satisfaction, marital satisfaction, ethnocentrism, verbal aggressiveness, homophobia, dogmatism, and communication anxiety, to mention only a few of the uses to which these scales have been adapted.

Semantic Differential Scales

In 1957 Charles Osgood, Percy Tannenbaum, and George Sucie developed the semantic differential scale as a means for measuring attitudes. Although the name

(A)

> 1 = almost never true
> 2 = rarely true
> 3 = occasionally true
> 4 = often true
> 5 = almost always true

_____ I am extremely careful to avoid attacking individuals' intelligence when I attack their ideas.

_____ When individuals are very stubborn, I use insults to soften the stubbornness.

_____ I try to make people feel good about themselves even if their ideas are stupid.

_____ When individuals insult me, I get a lot of pleasure out of really telling them off.

(B)

Newt Gingrich

expert	:_____:_____:_____:_____:_____:_____:_____:	inexpert
untrained	:_____:_____:_____:_____:_____:_____:_____:	trained
unselfish	:_____:_____:_____:_____:_____:_____:_____:	selfish
relaxed	:_____:_____:_____:_____:_____:_____:_____:	tense
timid	:_____:_____:_____:_____:_____:_____:_____:	bold
meek	:_____:_____:_____:_____:_____:_____:_____:	aggressive

FIGURE 3.1   **(A) Sample of Likert-type scale items taken from Infante and Wigley's (1986) Verbal Aggressiveness Scale.   (B) Sample of a semantic differential scale, featuring some of the adjective pairs used by McCroskey (1966) to measure source credibility or ethos.**

Source: Infante, D. A., & Wigley, C. J. (1986). Verbal aggressiveness: An interpersonal model and measure. *Communication Monographs, 53,* 61–69 and McCroskey, J. C. (1966). Scales for the measurement of ethos. *Speech Monographs, 33,* 65–72. Used by permission of the National Communication Association.

of the scale may seem unfamiliar, you are probably already acquainted with this approach to measuring attitudes as well (see Figure 3.1). A semantic differential scale is based upon the *connotative* meanings words have for people. The scale consists of a series of bipolar adjective pairs or, stated more simply, opposites, such as light-dark, fast-slow, happy-sad, and so on. The adjective pairs are separated by a number of spaces, typically seven. In completing the scale a respondent checks the "semantic" space between each adjective pair that best reflects his or her overall attitude toward the concept in question. The subject's overall attitude is represented by the average of the spaces checked on all of the items. As with Likert scales, semantic differential scales presume the spaces on the scale are "equidistant" from one another, making mathematical comparisons of attitudes possible. An example of one of the better known semantic differential scales is McCroskey's "ethos scale," which is used to measure source credibility (McCroskey, 1966; McCroskey & Young, 1981). A few of the bipolar adjectives used in this scale are displayed in Figure 3.1.

Visually Oriented Self-Report Scales

Other more visually oriented methods of measuring attitudes via self-reports have been developed. Ostrum, Bond, Krosnick, and Sedikides (1994) discuss several of these, including an "opinion thermometer" in which the respondent visualizes his or her attitude in terms of degrees on a thermometer. The thermometer shows gradations, in increments of 10, ranging from 0° to 100°. The respondent checks the appropriate degree of his or her attitude with "0°" meaning the respondent is cold toward the attitude object, and "100°" meaning the respondent is warm toward the attitude object.

But let's say you want to measure the attitude of someone who doesn't understand temperatures or complex words. What would you do? These authors also refer to an innovative approach for measuring attitudes utilizing simple drawings of facial expressions. The expressions represent differing degrees of favorability or unfavorability toward the attitude object, ranging from smiling to frowning (see Figure 3.2).

Visually oriented approaches make it easier for respondents to conceptualize their attitudes because they can "see" where their attitudes fit on a scale or continuum. Visually oriented approaches to measuring attitudes are especially useful when dealing with respondents who are less literate, less well-educated, or less conversant with the language in which the survey is being conducted.

Negative Attitudes toward Attitude Scales

Although our discussion thus far might suggest that measuring attitudes is simple and effective, a cadre of researchers and laypersons alike remain suspicious of findings based on attitude scales. They charge that such measures are artificial in nature and don't reflect the real world. In addition to pitfalls such as *social desirability bias* and the problem of "non-attitudes" which are discussed in Box 3.1, there is also the problem of *acquiescence bias* (Ostrum et al., 1994). Some respondents exhibit a tendency to agree with any statement contained in a survey or questionnaire. This tendency is especially pronounced in oral, in-person interviews. Just why some people are so agreeable is unclear. They may feel inclined to express agreement because they believe the researcher favors the issue featured in the survey. This obviously poses a problem for researchers and pollsters who want to know what the respondents actually think or feel, not what the respondents believe the researchers or pollsters want to hear.

1. _____   2. _____   3. _____   4. _____

5. _____   6. _____   7. _____

FIGURE 3.2   Example of a visually oriented attitude scale.

From Ostrum, T. M., Bond, C. F., Krosnick, J. A., & Sedikides, C. (1994). Attitude scales: How we measure the unmeasurable. In S. Shavitt & T. C. Brock (Eds.), *Persuasion: Psychological insights and perspectives* (pp. 15–42). Boston: Allyn and Bacon. Copyright © 1994 by Allyn and Bacon. Reprinted by permission.

Another complaint relates to the issue of mindfulness. For a person to mark the space on any self-report measure the person must first *know* what his or her attitude is. Unfortunately, respondents often, quite literally, don't know their own minds. They have strong attitudes, mind you, they just aren't aware they have them. For example, a person could harbor racist, sexist, or homophobic attitudes, without consciously realizing it. To the extent that persons aren't mindful of their own attitudes, the use of such scales is problematic (Hample, 1984; Nisbett & Wilson, 1977).

Can You Trust What You Can't See?

The various criticisms of attitude scales are well-taken. On the other hand, because attitudes exist "inside" people, the most basic way to measure them is by asking. Until someone "invents a better mousetrap" for measuring attitudes, these standardized scales will continue to enjoy widespread use. Keep in mind, too, that the fact that attitudes must be measured via indirect means doesn't make them any less real. A myriad of mental phenomena, such as beliefs, opinions, emotions, and intentions, cannot be directly observed. The study of attitudes is a bit like astronomy in this respect. Astronomers can't *see* quarks, or black holes, or dark matter in the universe, but they can infer their existence. Social scientists can't see attitudes "in the flesh," as it were, but can infer their existence through their influence on behavior, communication, decision making, and relationships.

Roundabout Methods of Measuring Attitudes

In addition to relying on self-reports gathered from the respondents themselves, a variety of other means are used, by researchers and ordinary folks, to assess people's attitudes. These include inferring attitudes from appearances, from associations, and from behavior.

Judging a Book by Its Cover—Appearances

In addition to, or perhaps instead of, measuring attitudes using self-reports and standardized scales, attitudes also may be inferred from appearances. This process is less scientific than using standardized scales, but we all do this from time to time. A person wearing a sweatshirt with Shaqueel O'Neal's name and likeness on it, for instance, might very likely have a favorable attitude toward the NBA superstar. A person with a swastika tattooed on his arm may well hold anti-Semitic attitudes. In support of this assumption, an experiment conducted by Mathes and Kemper (1976) revealed that observers were able to make reliable determinations about another person's sexual behavior, based on the other's clothing.

The danger of relying on such appearance-based cues, however, is that the person may be engaging in "faulty sign" reasoning. For example, not everyone sporting a bandana or an Oakland Raiders jacket with baggy pants is a member of a gang. A study conducted by Goldberg, Gottesdeiner, and Abramson (1975) illustrates the fallibility of relying on appearances to infer attitudes. In the study, male college students were asked to evaluate 30 photographs of women they had never met and rank them based on physical attractiveness. Another group of male college students were asked to evaluate the same 30 photographs and rank them according to the extent to which they perceived the women in the photographs to be supportive of feminism. The researchers found that the rank orderings from the two groups were *negatively correlated*. That is, the women who were perceived as being the most attractive were perceived as being the least likely to be feminists and vice versa. When the researchers measured the women's own attitudes toward feminism, however, they found *no correlation* existed between attitudes toward feminism and the males' attractiveness rankings. The males in the study thus subscribed to the erroneous stereotype that "feminists tend to be ugly."

Birds of a Feather—Associations

"You can tell a person," so the saying goes, "by the company he or she keeps." If this is true, then memberships and affiliations also can signify attitudes. At least former president George Bush seemed to think so. In June of 1995 he angrily renounced his lifetime membership in the National Rifle Association (NRA). He did so in response to an NRA newsletter that labeled federal agents as "jack-booted thugs...wearing Nazi bucket helmets and black storm-trooper uniforms" (Sidey, 1995). Bush's resignation was designed to indicate that his views were different from those of the NRA, with whom he no longer wished to be affiliated. Can you infer other people's attitudes from the company they keep? Arnold Schwarzenegger and Garth Brooks campaigned for Bob Dole in the 1996 presidential election. Can you guess where they stood on issues such as a balanced budget amendment or a reduction in the capital gains tax? (Hint: Republicans favored these measures.) Steven Spielberg and Barbra Streisand campaigned on behalf of Bill Clinton. Can you guess where they stood on issues like tobacco regulation and environmental protection? (Hint: Democrats supported these measures.)

If you can tell a person by the company he or she keeps, can you also tell a person by the company for whom she or he works? A study by Hartman, Karlson, and Hibbard (1994) demonstrates that attitudes are linked to occupations. The researchers sent questionnaires to 329 prosecutors and defense attorneys. The questionnaires asked about their attitudes toward a variety of hypothetical situations involving potential acts of child sexual abuse (e.g., a child showering with an adult, or a child sleeping in the same bed with an adult). Would it surprise you to learn that the prosecutors were far more likely than the defense attorneys to view the hypothetical situations as immoral or inappropriate? The two groups of attorneys' attitudes are consistent with the adversarial roles they play in the courtroom.

It makes sense that people would enter into careers, join organizations, and establish affiliations with groups of like-minded people. Such associations serve to reinforce the individual's self-image and belief system. Politicians rely on the fact that people who share similar attitudes tend to form memberships. This enables politicians to curry favor with "voting blocks." Members of the American Association of Retired Persons tend to oppose cuts in Social Security funding. Catholics tend to have more negative attitudes toward abortion than Protestants or Jews. Members of the American Civil Liberties Union tend to oppose capital punishment.

How does all of this relate to persuasion? Obviously, by knowing that members of unions, professional associations, churches, and other organizations tend to share similar attitudes, politicians are able to tailor their messages to each group's frame of reference. Studies on the death penalty (cited in Byrne, 1986) indicate that jurors' political party affiliations have a lot to do with their attitudes toward capital punishment. Republicans are more likely to favor the death penalty and to vote for conviction in capital cases than are Democrats. Furthermore, Republicans are more likely to vote for conviction, as opposed to acquittal, in a variety of other, noncapital cases than their Democratic counterparts. Thus, political party affiliation appears to be closely related to attitudes about crime and punishment.

Before concluding this section, we should note that the approach of inferring attitudes based on associations is not without its limitations. If you rely on this approach, exercise caution. People may join organizations for all kinds of reasons, reasons that may have little or nothing to do with the group's avowed purpose. For example, a person might join an organization simply to meet prospective dates! And even within groups that exhibit considerable uniformity, there are differences of opinion. Suffice to say that attitudes among group members vary, as do their personalities, their lifestyles, and their individual tastes.

You Are What You Do—Behavior

A person's overt actions, mannerisms, habits, and nonverbal cues can also be used to infer attitudes. If a person marches in a pro-choice rally, it's a pretty good indication that he or she holds pro-choice attitudes. If a person buys season tickets to the philharmonic orchestra, it's a fairly safe bet that he or she likes classical music. Indeed, concealing one's attitudes can be difficult, precisely because one's actions tend to give one away. By way of example, Kraut (1982) exposed students to pleasant or disgusting odors and filmed their nonverbal reactions. The students were instructed to try to conceal their true emotions and to feign the opposite emotion (e.g., to pretend a foul odor smelled pleasant). Despite their best efforts to control their expressions, observers who viewed the videotapes could detect their true reactions to the smells.

Inferring attitudes from behavior, however, also can be fraught with difficulties. To some extent, the degree of attitude–behavior consistency hinges on subtle nuances in the way that questions asking about attitudes are worded. For instance, Kendzierski and Lamastro (1988) found that asking subjects about their attitudes toward *not* lifting weights better reflected the amount of time they spent weight-lifting than asking about attitudes toward lifting weights.

A recent meta-analysis (Kim & Hunter, 1993) of more than 100 attitude–behavior studies sheds some light on the extent to which attitudes reflect behavior and vice versa. Kim and Hunter found that in many cases, researchers made poor choices as to which attitudes to examine, or how to examine them, in relation to the particular behaviors in question. They found that when the attitude measures employed were truly relevant to the behaviors in question, attitude–behavior consistency was quite high. When attitudes and attitude measures with low relevance to the specific behaviors in question were used, attitude–behavior consistency was low. Past studies that found low or no attitude–behavior consistency may thus have been looking at the wrong attitudes or may have gone about conceptualizing and measuring attitudes in the wrong way. The bottom line is that behavior can be extremely revealing of attitudes, but care must be exercised in determining which attitudes are germane to which behaviors.

Physiological Measures of Attitude

Are you familiar with the expression "It's not too loud, you're too old"? It seems as if the older generation is always telling the younger generation to "turn it down!" Indeed, the volume level at which a person perceives music to be "too loud" is, to a large extent, dependent on that person's musical preferences. If you like rap music you'll tend to "pump up the volume." If you hate country music you'll tend to think it's too loud or regard it as "noise." This tendency illustrates the point that attitudes are often accompanied by physiological reactions. Gruesome photographs of a murder scene, like those shown to jurors in the O. J. Simpson trial, for example, can be so gory that they may induce nausea or dizziness.

An entire field of study, known as *psychophysiology,* is devoted to identifying the physiological bases underlying mental processes. To date, efforts to identify biological indicators of attitude change have produced mixed results (Petty & Cacioppo, 1983). Although a thorough treatment of this field of study is beyond the scope of this text, we take a look at three physiological measures that appear to be connected to attitudes; galvonic skin response (or GSR), pupillary response, and electromyogram (EMG) activity.

Galvonic Skin Response

Galvonic skin response is a measure of the electrical conductivity of the skin. When a person becomes nervous or anxious, his or her GSR increases. The person's skin becomes more sweaty or clammy. We know that strong attitudes *sometimes* produce changes in GSR, but not always (Porier & Lott, 1967; Rankin & Campbell, 1955; Vidulich & Krevanick, 1966). For example, when students were asked to evaluate different ethnic/cultural groups and were then exposed to either complimentary or derogatory statements about those groups, significant changes in GSR were detected (Cooper & Singer, 1956). GSR increased when an admired group was derogated *and* when a disliked group was complimented.

Complicating the picture, though, is the fact that GSR is a *bidirectional indicator,* for example, increases in GSR can signal either strong positive or strong negative reactions toward something. In fact, exposure to almost any novel stimulus can produce increases in GSR, making it a rather ambiguous indicator of attitudes and attitude change. These limitations prompted Eagly and Chaiken (1993) to conclude that "there is general agreement that galvonic skin response is inadequate as a physiological measure of attitudes" (p. 61).

Pupillary Response

Police officers routinely shine their flashlights in suspects' eyes to determine if they are under the influence of a controlled substance. Because pupil dilation (or constriction) is an involuntary reflex, a person has no control over this reaction. Pupillary response has been employed by researchers as a means of measuring arousal or attention level (Beatty, 1986; Hess, Seltzer, & Shlien, 1965). One such intriguing study (Atwood & Howell, 1971) in this area examined the responses of convicted male pedophiles to pictures of nude adult women versus those of nude young girls. The pedophiles exhibited significantly greater pupil dilation when viewing pictures of nude young girls. In contrast, other "control" prisoners (felons convicted of non-sex-related crimes) exhibited greater pupil dilation when viewing pictures of nude adult women. Why would anyone carry out such a "creepy" study in the first place, you ask? Because the results might shed light on the most effective means for rehabilitating such prisoners. If pedophiles' reactions to pictures of naked girls represent an involuntary reflex, as this study suggests, then different methods of rehabilitation may be required for pedophiles than for other categories of felons. For example, if the sexual arousal is involuntary, then psychological approaches, like counseling, might prove ineffective, whereas physiological approaches, such as chemical castration (medication to make pedophiles impotent), might prove more effective.

Although research on pupillary response holds promise, the exact nature of the relationship between pupil dilation (or constriction) and attitudes is still unclear. As with GSR, pupillary response is a bidirectional measure. And of course, pupillary changes can be brought about by a variety of other factors (bright lights, opthamological exams, etc.). At present, researchers (Cacioppo & Petty, 1986; Woodmansee, 1970) tend to believe that pupil dilation is a better indicator of interest or attention level than it is an indicator of attitudes or attitude change.

Facial Expressions and Electromyogram Activity

In the 1960s, Haggard and Isaacs (1966) examined what they termed *micro-momentary facial expressions* as they related to affective responses. Micro-momentary facial expressions are so fleeting that they can't be seen with the naked eye in ordinary conversation, but are visible if a person is videotaped while interacting and the videotape is then slowed down. Knapp and Hall (1992) suggested these movements, which may last only one-fifth of a second, are revealing of emotional reactions, but are of short duration because they are immediately repressed. Ekman, Friesen, and Ellsworth (1982) questioned just how common or rare such expressions are, which suggests the need for further corroborative studies.

In a related vein, other researchers have focused on electromyogram activity, which involves measuring electrical impulses brought about by small changes in facial muscles. Such changes are often below the threshold of human visibility, but can nonetheless be detected as changes in EMG.

Studies have revealed that slight movements in the zygomatic and corrugator muscles around the mouth, which control smiling and frowning, are revealing of emotions. For instance, Cacioppo and Petty (1979) demonstrated that messages that people favored elicited more zygomatic muscle activity, whereas messages people opposed involved more corrugator muscle activity. The study of EMG changes appears to offer promise as a means for discovering physiological correlates of attitudes. For this measure to work, however, a number of conditions must be met. Cacioppo and Petty (1986) note:

> In sum, preliminary evidence suggests that subtle facial muscle changes may reflect the general nature of subjects' affective reactions to attitudinal stimuli as long as the subject is generally relaxed, inactive, involved in the task, and unobtrusively observed so that display rules or deceptive expressions are not invoked and the small muscular signals of interest are not masked by background somatic activity. (p. 668)

Limitations of Physiological Measures

Polygraphs have been around for a long time, but are still inadmissable in criminal trials, due to continued concerns about their validity. The same concerns apply when using other physiological measures as indicators of what people are thinking or feeling. One limitation of research in the area of psychophysiology is that individual researchers have typically relied on single physiological measures to assess attitudes, for example, GSR *or* pupillary response *or* EMG. More studies are needed that incorporate multiple physiological measures to assess attitudes and attitude change. Also bear in mind that the more complex the attitudes are, the more difficult the task of reducing them to purely physiological terms. Another important point to keep in mind is that even physiological responses constitute indirect measures of attitude. One can never "see" an attitude. One can only observe manifestations of attitudes through physiological or biological reactions. Because attitudes are mental constructs or internal phenomena, they can't be observed, or measured, directly.

THE PERSISTENCE OF ATTITUDES

A final feature of attitudes we wish to address is their persistence. Attitudes change over time. They aren't as fleeting as moods or emotions, but neither are they etched in stone. Sometimes a person's attitude will change in response to a single, brief exposure to a persuasive message. Sometimes a person's attitudes will endure for years. What makes some attitudes more durable and others more transitory?

Petty and Cacioppo's Elaboration Likelihood Model (ELM), discussed in the previous chapter, provides a useful answer to this question. You'll recall from Chapter 2 that the ELM maintains that there are two basic routes to persuasion—a "central route," which is based on thought and reflection, and a "peripheral route," which is based on cues such as source attractiveness, quantity of arguments, and so forth. Petty and Cacioppo argue that attitudes formed via the central route are more persistent than attitudes formed via the peripheral route. The reason is that when a person actively thinks about a message, analyzes it, and scrutinizes it, the person tends to internalize the content of the message more. Such active mental effort tends to make any attitudes formed more lasting. Peripheral processing, however, requires little mental effort. As a result, there is less internalization of message content. Attitudes formed as a result of peripheral processing thus tend to be more short-lived.[3]

A study by Elms (1966) illustrates the persistence of attitudes formed via central processing over those formed via peripheral processing. Elms exposed two groups of students to an anti-smoking message. One group actively participated in the design of the message by helping to generate the arguments to be used. Another group passively listened to the message the first group had helped to design. A test of the two groups' attitudes conducted immediately after exposure to the persuasive message revealed that both groups' attitudes had shifted the same amount against smoking. A follow-up test of the two groups' attitudes was administered 3 weeks later. This time the results showed that the group that actively participated in the design of the message retained more negative attitudes toward smoking than the passive group. Thus, the active mental effort exerted by the first group made their attitudes more persistent, compared to the passive processing employed by the second group.

What does this mean for you as a persuader? *If you want a message to have a lasting effect on receivers' attitudes you should design it and deliver it in such a way as to actively promote central processing, that is, thought, analysis, and reflection.* Of course, this assumes that the content of your message is of sufficient quality to survive such scrutiny. How can you encourage central processing? In the previous chapter we noted that increasing receivers' involvement was one way of promoting central processing. Explaining why a topic or issue is relevant to receivers and how it affects them personally will increase their motivation to employ central processing. Adapting your message to the receivers' level of understanding or experience and eliminating potential distractions will increase their ability to engage in central processing. In short, if you can get your listeners to actively think about your message, you are more likely to change their attitudes for the long-term and not just the short-term.

SUMMARY

The concept of "attitude" is central to the study of persuasion. As concepts, attitudes can't be directly observed, yet they can be inferred and measured though a variety of indirect means. One means is to employ self-reports based on standardized scales. Likert scales and semantic differential scales are the most common ones now in use. Another means is to infer attitudes from appearances, associations, and behavior. Physiological measures, such as galvonic skin response, pupillary response, facial expressions, and electromyogram activity, also have been employed as means of inferring attitudes. All of these approaches have inherent benefits and weaknesses. People's attitudes do tend to coincide with their behavior, but only if and when a number of important conditions are satisfied. Finally, attitudes formed via central processing are more persistent than attitudes formed via peripheral processing.

ENDNOTES

1. At one time, attitudes were conceptualized as having three dimensions: cognitive (or thought), affective (or feeling), and conative (or behavior). This tripartite characterization of attitudes no longer enjoys widespread support. Rather, these three elements now tend to be viewed not as dimensions of attitudes themselves, but as ways in which attitudes are manifested (Tesser & Shaffer, 1990).

2. Standardized scales, such as Likert scales, are sometimes referred to as "direct" measures of attitude, meaning that they are taken directly from an individual, or from "the horse's mouth," so to speak. Such measures are still, strictly speaking, indirect, because the researcher cannot observe, measure, or quantify the attitude as an entity in itself, apart from the respondent's self-report about his or her attitude.

3. This explanation is highly consistent with findings based on "inoculation theory," which we discuss in Chapter 10. Inoculating receivers against opposing arguments (e.g., giving them a

54 *Chapter 3*

small dose of the arguments they are likely to hear along with answers to those arguments) requires that they actively think about message content. This increased mental effort makes them more resilient to opposing arguments presented at a later date.

REFERENCES

Allport, G. W. (1935). Attitudes. In C. Murchison (Ed.), *A handbook of social psychology,* (Vol. 2, pp. 798–844). Worcester, MA: Clark University Press.

Atwood, R. W., & Howell, R. J. (1971). Pupilometric and personality test score differences of female aggressing pedophiliacs and normals. *Psychonomic Science, 22,* 115–116.

Beatty, J. (1986). The pupillary system. In M. G. H. Coles, E. Duchin, & S. W. Porges (Eds.), *Psychophysiology: Systems, processes, and applications* (pp. 43–50). New York: Guilford Press.

Byrne, J. (1986). Lockhart vs. McCree: Conviction proneness and the constitutionality of death-qualified juries. *Catholic University Law Review, 36,* 287–317.

Cacioppo, J. T., & Petty, R. E. (1979). Attitudes and cognitive response: An electrophysiological approach. *Journal of Personality and Social Psychology, 37,* 2181–2199.

Cacioppo, J. T., & Petty, R. E. (1986). In M. G. H. Cole, E. Donchin, & S. W. Porgess (Eds.), *Social processes in psychophysiology: Systems, processes, and applications* (pp. 646–679). New York: Guilford Press.

Cooper, J. B., & Singer, D. N. (1956). The role of emotion and prejudice. *Journal of Social Psychology, 44,* 241–247.

Dillard, P. (1993). Persuasion past and present: Attitudes aren't what they used to be. *Communication Monographs, 60*(1), 90–97.

Eagly, A. H., & Chaiken, S. (1993). *The psychology of attitudes.* New York: Harcourt, Brace, Janovich.

Ekman, P., Friesen, W. V., & Ellsworth, P. (1982). Does the face provide accurate information? In P. Ekman (Ed.), *Emotion in the human face,* (2nd ed., pp. 86–97). Cambridge, MA: Cambridge University Press.

Elms, A. C. (1966). Influence of fantasy ability on attitude change through role-playing. *Journal of Personality and Social Psychology, 4,* 36–43.

Fazio, R. H. (1986). How do attitudes guide behavior? In R. M. Sorrentino & E. T. Higgins (Eds.), *The handbook of motivation and cognition: Foundations of social behavior* (pp. 204–243). New York: Guilford Press.

Fazio, R. H., & Zanna, M. P. (1981). Direct experience and attitude-behavior consistency. In L. Berkowitz (Ed.), *Advances in experimental social psychology,* (Vol. 14, pp. 161–202). New York: Academic Press.

Fishbein, M., & Ajzen, I. (1975). *Belief, attitude, intention, and behavior: An introduction to theory and research.* Reading, MA: Addison-Wesley.

Fisher, R. J. (1993). Social desirability bias and the validity of indirect questioning. *Journal of Consumer Research, 20,* 303–315.

Goldberg, P. A., Gottesdeiner, M., & Abramson, P. R. (1975). Another put-down of women? Perceived attractiveness as a function of support for the feminist movement. *Journal of Personality and Social Psychology, 32,* 113–115.

Guttman, L. (1944). A basis for scaling qualitative data. *American Sociological Review, 9,* 139–150.

Guttman, L. (1950). The basis for scalogram analysis. In S. A. Stouffer, L. Guttman, E. A. Suchman, P. F. Lazarsfeld, S. A. Star, & J. A. Gardner (Eds.), *Measurement and prediction* (pp. 45–69). Princeton, NJ: Princeton University Press.

Haggard, E. A., & Isaacs, K. S. (1966). Micromomentary facial expressions as indicators of ego mechanisms in psychotherapy. In L. A. Gottschalk & A. H. Auerback (Eds.), *Methods of research in psychotherapy* (pp. 154–165). New York: Appleton-Century-Crofts.

Hample, D. (1984). On the use of self-reports. *Argumentation and Advocacy, 20,* 140–153.

Hartman, G. L., Karlson, H., & Hibbard, R. A. (1994). Attorney attitudes regarding behaviors associated with child sexual abuse. *Child Abuse and Neglect, 18*(8), 657–662.

Hess, R. D., Seltzer, A. L., & Schlien, J. M. (1965). Pupil response of hetero and homosexual males to pictures of men and women: A pilot study. *Journal of Abnormal Psychology, 70,* 165–168.

Infante, D. A, & Wigley, C. J. (1986). Verbal aggressiveness: An interpersonal model and measure. *Communication Monographs, 53,* 61–69.

Kendzierski, D., & Lamastro, V. D. (1988) Reconsidering the role of attitudes in exercise behavior: A decision theoretic approach. *Journal of Applied Social Psychology, 8,* 737–759.

Kim, M., & Hunter, J. E. (1993). Attitude-behavior relations: A meta-analysis of attitude relevance and topic. *Journal of Communication, 43*(1), 101–142.

Knapp, M. L., & Hall, J. A. (1992). *Nonverbal communication in human interaction* (3rd. ed.). Ft. Worth, TX: Harcourt, Brace, Jovanovich.

Kraut, R. E. (1982) Social presence, facial feedback, and emotion. *Journal of Personality and Social Psychology, 42,* 853–863.

Likert, R. (1932). A technique for the measurement of attitudes (special issue). *Archives of Psychology, 22,* 1–55.

Mathes, E. W., & Kemper, S. B. (1976). Clothing as a nonverbal communicator of sexual attitudes and behavior. *Perceptual and Motor Skills, 43,* 495–498.

McCroskey, J. C. (1966). Scales for the measurement of ethos. *Speech Monographs, 33,* 65–72.

McCroskey, J. C., & Young, T. J. (1981). Ethos and credibility: The construct and its measurement after three decades. *Central States Speech Journal, 32,* 24–34.

Nisbett, R. E., & Wilson, T. D. (1977). Telling more than we know: Verbal reports on mental processes. *Psychological Review, 84,* 231–259.

Osgood, C. E., Tannenbaum, P. H., & Suci, G. J. (1957). *The measurement of meaning.* Urbana, IL: University of Illinois Press.

Ostrum, T. M., Bond, C. F., Krosnick, J. A., & Sedikides, C. (1994). Attitude scales: How we measure the unmeasurable. In S. Shavitt & T. C. Brock (Eds.), *Persuasion: Psychological insights and perspectives,* (pp. 15–42). Boston: Allyn and Bacon.

Petty, R. E., & Cacioppo, J. T. (1983). The role of bodily responses in attitude measurement and change. In J. T. Cacioppo & R. E. Petty (Eds.), *Social psychophysiology: A sourcebook* (pp. 51–101). New York: Guilford Press.

Porier, G. W., & Lott, A. J. (1967). Galvonic skin responses and prejudice. *Journal of Personality and Social Psychology, 5,* 253–259.

Rankin, R. E., & Campbell, D. T. (1955). Galvonic skin response to Negro and white experimenters. *Journal of Abnormal and Social Psychology, 51,* 30–33.

Sidey, H., (1995, May 22). "For pride of service." *Time,* p. 44.

Tesser, A., & Shaffer, D. R. (1990). Attitudes and attitude change. In M. W. Rosenzweig & L. W. Porter (Eds.), *Annual review of psychology* (pp. 479–573). Palo Alto, CA: Annual Reviews.

Thurstone, L. L. (1928). Attitudes can be measured. *American Journal of Sociology, 33,* 529–544.

Thurstone, L. L., & Chave, E. J. (1929). *The measurement of attitude.* Chicago: University of Chicago Press.

Vidulich, R. N., & Krevanick, F. W. (1966). Racial attitudes and emotional responses to visual representations of the Negro. *Journal of Social Psychology, 68,* 85–93.

Woodmansee, J. J. (1970). The pupil response as a measure of social attitudes. In G. F. Summers (Ed.), *Attitude measurement* (pp. 514–533). Chicago: Rand-McNally.

4

CONSISTENCY AND COMMITMENT

Imagine the smell of a brand new box of Crayola crayons, one of those big boxes with the built-in sharpener. If you never had Crayola crayons, try imagining the smell of Play-Doh instead. Does it make you feel nostalgic? Does it bring back childhood memories of home or school? What associations do you have with the smell of crayons? How about other childhood smells, like Johnson's baby powder, Bazooka Joe bubble gum, or Vick's VapoRub? Do those smells evoke any positive or negative memories or trigger any favorable or unfavorable associations? If you're like most people, remembering one thing, such as a favorite childhood smell, will trigger memories of other related things and events. One memory can lead to another memory, and so on.

Attitudes are related to one another in much the same way as our memories. Our attitude toward one thing is connected to our attitudes toward other related things. From the previous chapter you now understand what attitudes are, how they are formed, and how they are measured. In this chapter we extend that discussion by taking a look at how attitudes are related to persuasion. We'll talk about how our attitudes are interconnected and how persuaders try to link their messages to favorable images and associations in our minds. We'll also talk about persuasion as it relates to consistency theories, which relate to people's efforts to maintain psychological harmony among their attitudes, beliefs, and behavior. Finally we'll examine the role of psychological commitment and persuasion.

ATTITUDES AS ASSOCIATIVE NETWORKS: YOUR MIND IS A WEB

In some ways our attitudes, beliefs, and values can be likened to a spider's web. Like the fine silky threads of a spider's web, they are interrelated to one another in a delicate balance. Attitudes exist in elaborate *associative networks* (Tesser & Shaffer, 1990). An individual may or may not be consciously aware of all these connections. To a large extent, these associative networks operate implicitly, that is, without the individual's conscious awareness. A change in one attitude affects other attitudes, beliefs, opinions, and values. Like jiggling a spider's web, a vibration in one attitude can trigger reverberations in other cognitive structures. These mental reverberations may be quite minor or of major consequence to the individual.

MANUFACTURING FAVORABLE IMAGES AND ASSOCIATIONS: JIGGLING THE WEB

Why would anyone buy a brand of beer because three frogs like that brand? Or, for that matter, why would anyone buy a brand of beer because giant people playing frisbee in the Rockies drink that brand? The associative networks in which attitudes exist are critical to such influence attempts. In a nutshell here is why— *Persuaders try to create, reinforce, modify or extinguish the connections that exist among these networks. They want to link their messages with favorable attitudes and avoid associations with unfavorable attitudes.*

A clear case in point can be found in image-oriented advertising. Companies want to associate their goods and services with positive images. Oil companies, for example, don't want you to think about tar-covered birds gasping for air on an oil-stained beach when you envision petroleum products. They want you to associate oil companies with pro-environmental attitudes, hence, Mobil Oil's "People do" advertising campaign. As another example, cigarette manufacturers don't want you to envision patients dying in cancer wards who've undergone laryngectomies for esophagal cancer yet continue to smoke through holes in their windpipes. They want you to think of vibrant, young, healthy, vivacious people playing volleyball on the beach. Or they want you to imagine strong, rugged, "outdoorsy" types like the Marlboro man, when you think of cigarettes. The whole point of image-oriented advertising is to link products with favorable attitudes, values, and life-styles. As Schudson (1984) emphasizes, advertising "does not claim to picture reality as it is but reality as it should be—life and lives worth imitating" (p. 215).

To illustrate, let's examine advertisements and commercials for beer. The ads almost always depict people in pairs or groups, socializing and having a good time. The people in the ads are vibrant, sexy, alive. What is the image or association the ads are projecting? *Beer = fun.* It's a simple formula. Drinking beer is equated with good times and camaraderie. The three frogs we mentioned dance to a reggae tune once they get their beer. The giant people frolicking in the Rockies are depicted as having a wonderful time.[1]

Even nonalcoholic beers designed with alcohol awareness in mind play on this theme. It matters not if one is the designated driver. You can still be popular if you throw back a tall, cool, nonalcoholic brew like O'Doul's, Cutter, or Near beer. But wait a minute. Why does the designated driver need to drink a beer facsimile *at all*? Why can't the designated driver have any of a number of alternatives to beer, like fruit juice, tea, espresso, a soft drink, or an upscale brand of water? Because the

image being portrayed is that if you aren't drinking beer, you aren't having fun.
That is the attitudinal association that is being made.

Sloganeering

One means of fostering favorable associations is through sloganeering. Consider the
products below and their corresponding advertising slogans. Notice the positive
associations that the slogans are designed to instill with respect to each product.

"Like a rock" (Chevy trucks)
"Breakfast of champions" (Wheaties)
"It does a body good" (milk)
"The few, the proud" (U.S. Marine Corps)

The slogans imbue the products with positive qualities which, over time, become embedded in receivers' minds.

Sponsorship

Another way of linking products and services with favorable attitudes is through sponsorship. Watch any automobile race and you'll see corporate logos and insignia plastered all over the cars. In fact, most major sporting events now have corporate sponsors who provide funding in return for the right to associate their products with the event. When the Olympics rolls around every 4 years, advertisers pay handsome fees to become "The official (insert product here—camera, lip balm, snack food, etc.) of the Olympics." Look at the photographs in an issue of *Runner's World* magazine and you'll notice that the tape the winner runs through at the finish line often carries an endorsement. Sponsorship can, on occasion, become problematic, as noted in Box 4.1.

The use of celebrity endorsements follows this same strategy. The star status of famous athletes and movie stars (Candice Bergen for Sprint, Michael Jordan for Nike, etc.) establishes positive associations between the endorser and the product or service. We address the topic of celebrity spokespersons in greater detail in Chapter 5.

Naturally, advertisers aren't the only ones who try to tie themselves to favorable associations. When candidates for political office kiss babies, eat home cooking, and stand next to the American flag, they are trying to link themselves with positive, patriotic values. Negative political campaigning, a.k.a. "mudslinging,"

BOX 4.1   Strange Bedfellows

A few years ago, an interesting controversy involving attitudes and corporate sponsorship surfaced with respect to the Women's Tennis Association. Virginia Slims, a long-time sponsor of the WTA, decided to terminate its sponsorship. When the WTA announced it was seeking a new sponsor, Tambrands, the company that makes Tampax, offered to pay $10 million per year to become the new sponsor. The WTA, however, declined the offer. The organization felt uncomfortable about associating women's tennis with a feminine hygiene product. It seems the idea of playing tennis against the backdrop of a banner or billboard for Tampons was too "yucky" or "gross" for the WTA. As Martina Navratilova, then president of the WTA stated, "It's not our role to crusade to change public opinion and get people over their embarrassment" (Salter, 1995, p. 10A).

The irony is that tampons are a useful, beneficial product. Cigarette smoking, on the other hand, is a scientifically recognized health hazard. A woman can't avoid having periods, but she can certainly avoid smoking. Why was the WTA willing to embrace Virginia Slims as a sponsor for more than a decade, but not Tampax? Is the topic of menstruation really so taboo? The organization's moral conscience seems to be taking a backseat to vanity. Maybe the Women's Tennis Association *hasn't* come a long way, baby.

serves the same purpose in reverse: A candidate seeks to link his or her opponent to negative attitudes and negative values. When philanthropic organizations make appeals for donations, they attempt to link their causes to favorable attitudes, like charity, altruism, and giving. The ability of advertisers, politicians, fund-raisers, and others to establish bonds between receivers' attitudes and their respective products, campaigns, or causes is part and parcel of what persuasion is all about.

A major tenet of persuasion thus involves establishing favorable connections between attitudes and attitude objects. Persuaders try to establish these connections by selling an image or a lifestyle. When you buy a product, you are buying into the image as well. O. K., so maybe you aren't wealthy, don't own a Rolls Royce, and don't have a chauffeur. But you can still use the same brand of mustard as the rich: Grey Poupon.

PSYCHOLOGICAL CONSISTENCY

We now turn our attention to another important aspect of attitudes and persuasion, that of psychological consistency. People like to be consistent. They like to avoid the appearance of being inconsistent. These simple principles form the basis for a whole host of theories, variously known as "attitude change" or "cognitive consistency" theories (Festinger, 1957; Heider, 1958; Newcomb, 1953; Osgood, & Tannenbaum, 1955). Originally, it was thought that consistency was an internal "drive," like the desire to feel safe and secure; a drive that an individual had to obey. More current thinking suggests that consistency is also socially motivated and is as much an attempt to manage face and project a favorable self-image to others as it is an internal force (Greenwald & Ronis, 1978; Scher & Cooper, 1989). Although the individual theories differ somewhat in their approaches, we've integrated the tenets of several theories here to present a more coherent perspective. Though this principle is fairly basic, the recognition that most people strive to remain consistent in their thoughts, words, and deeds reveals a good deal about processes of social influence.

The Inner Peace of Consistency

In the 1994 motion picture *It Could Happen to You,* Nicolas Cage plays a New York City cop who promises a waitress half of his possible lottery ticket winnings in lieu of a tip. As it turns out, he wins $4 million in the lottery. His wife pressures him to lie to the waitress and keep all the money. Cage's character is torn between being an honest person who made a promise and his desire to keep all the money. He tries to lie at first, but the psychological turmoil is too much for him to bear. He agrees to share the money with the waitress.

When harmony exists among our attitudes, beliefs, values, and behavior, life is ducky. When there are inconsistencies in what we think, say, or do, however, we tend to be like Nicolas Cage's character; we experience psychological discomfort. A classic example is that, for smokers, the knowledge that they smoke and that smoking causes cancer, is psychologically uncomfortable. Another example involves children whose parents are undergoing a divorce or separation. The children often experience psychological conflict because they can't understand why two people, both of whom they love, don't want to remain married.

A real-life example of the discomfort resulting from inconsistency faces one of the authors. He applied for and received a General Motors (GM) credit card. Every time he uses the GM card he earns "money" toward the purchase of a new GM car. He's already earned several thousand dollars in credit. Here's the catch, though. The author isn't particularly fond of GM cars. In fact, he owns a foreign car, which he believes is more reliable and fuel-efficient. What will he do when the time comes to replace his present car? If he buys another foreign car, he'll be "throwing away" the money he's earned on the GM card. If he uses the money he's accumulated toward a GM car, he won't be getting the make of car he truly prefers. Thus, his attitudes toward using the money he's earned and buying the brand of car he prefers are incompatible. Holding incompatible attitudes like these can be frustrating.

The amount of psychological discomfort that results from holding incompatible attitudes is not the same in all situations. How much discomfort a person experiences depends on the *centrality* of the attitudes involved. If the issue is relatively minor (a person prefers plastic grocery bags, but knows paper bags are better for the environment) the amount of psychological discomfort will be small. If the issue is major, as when attitudes involve core beliefs or values, then the psychological consequences can be enormous (for example, the mother of a teen-age girl is fervently pro-life but learns that her daughter has just obtained an abortion).

To understand the nature and effects of psychological consistency, attitude theorists have developed a means of graphically depicting compatible and incompatible attitude states. For example, suppose that Muffin thinks of herself as a firm believer in animal rights. However, while out shopping she finds a leather jacket that looks "totally cool." Her attitudes toward animal rights and owning the jacket are in conflict. Her psychological dilemma is depicted in Figure 4.1.

According to consistency theories, Muffin should experience psychological stress no matter what decision she makes. If she buys the jacket she'll be sacrificing her principles; if she doesn't buy the jacket she'll be forgoing an opportunity to look cool. Muffin's case is not unique. We are all confronted with dilemma's involving our attitudes, beliefs, and behaviors on a daily basis. Because psychological inconsistency is unpleasant we are motivated to avoid it, deny it, reduce it, or eliminate it when it occurs.

Methods of Maintaining Consistency

How do people go about reconciling incompatible attitudes when they occur? People don't necessarily preserve or restore psychological consistency in logical ways. They do so in psycho-logical ways, for example, ways that they find psychologically satisfying or comfortable, but which may or may not be strictly logical. Using the example of Muffin above, scholars suggest a number of possible routes for resolving inconsistency.

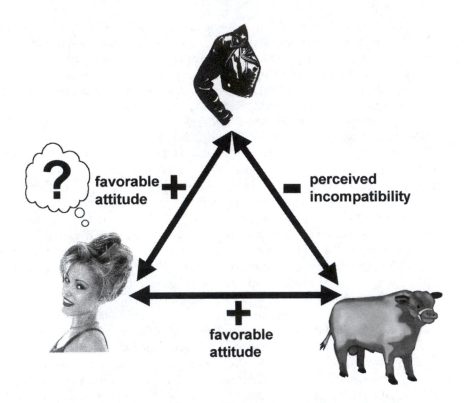

FIGURE 4.1   Muffin's dilemma: Illustration of consistency theory.

1. **Denial**—denying or ignoring any inconsistency. "I really don't like that jacket after all." or "I don't really need a jacket now."
2. **Bolstering**—rationalizing or making excuses. "That cow is already dead, what difference can it make?" or "Sooner or later someone will come along and buy that jacket anyway."
3. **Differentiation**—separating or distinguishing the attitudes that are in conflict. "The jacket is cowhide. Cows aren't an endangered species. It's not as if I'm buying a jacket made from a baby harp seal or a spotted owl."
4. **Transcendence**—focusing on a larger or higher level. "No one is perfect. We all give in to temptation every once in a while."
5. **Modifying** one or both attitudes—altering the attitudes themselves to become more consistent. "I need to be more practical and keep my concern for animal rights in perspective."
6. **Communicating**—trying to convince others to change or convince others one did the right thing. "I'll just have to convince my friends that I'm not a hypocrite when they see me in my new jacket."

Of course, these are just some of the ways people go about reducing cognitive dissonance. Different people go about reducing dissonance in different ways, some of them quite imaginative and elaborate. In trying to gauge what approach a person will use, a good rule of thumb is that a person tends to reduce dissonance in the easiest way possible. That is, he or she tends to follow the path of least resistance in finding a way to restore consistency. Changing an inconsequential attitude to restore consistency, for example, is much more likely than changing a core attitude.

Marketing Strategies: How to Have Your Cake and Eat it Too!

Now that you understand the basic nature of consistency theories, let's look at some examples of how neatly consistency theories apply to persuasion. One example can be found in the "free range" beef and poultry now sold at some supermarkets. A range fed cow or chicken is one that gets to roam around the prairie, forage for its own food and presumably live a happy, carefree life—until it's butchered, that is. Consumers who feel sorry for animals raised in crowded feedlots and cramped cages, but who can't quite bring themselves to become vegetarians, can reconcile their guilt by buying free range meat. The purchase of free range meat preserves psychological consistency. Conscientious consumers can feel good about themselves while sinking their teeth into a nice, juicy steak.

How about another example from the supermarket? Let's say you have a craving for Häagen Dazs ice cream, but you're on a diet. No problem! You can have Häagen Dazs *Light*. Thanks to modern technology you can choose from a whole array of low calorie options from a variety of manufacturers, such as ice milk, frozen yogurt, diabetic ice cream, fruit sorbet, or a non-fat, non-dairy product. Think how many other products at the grocery store rely on the principle of "having your cake and eating it too." There are "light," "fat free," "cholesterol free," "high fiber," "low sodium," and "natural" products on every shelf. The marketing strategy behind such products is to allow consumers to make food purchases that are consistent with their beliefs on health and nutrition. When we buy such foods we are maintaining cognitive consistency.

Brand Loyalty: Accept No Substitute

The concept of brand loyalty offers another useful illustration of psychological consistency. Advertisers want us to experience psychological discomfort if we change brands. By instilling brand loyalty in us, advertisers hope to discourage product switching. We are trained to remain faithful to one motor oil, to be true to one long distance company, to be devoted to one pain reliever, or to cherish a particular make of car. Consider the following slogans:

"Don't leave home without it" (American Express)
"Anything else would be uncivilized" (Right Guard)
"When you're out of Schlitz, you're out of beer" (Schlitz)
"Must see TV" (NBC)
"If it isn't in here, it probably doesn't exist" (GTE Yellow Pages)

All of these slogans are designed to foster brand loyalty on the part of the consumer and feelings of psychological inconsistency if consumers betray their usual brands.

Write and Tell Us Why You Love This Book in 24 Words or Less

Yet another means of reinforcing brand loyalty is through active participation on the part of the consumer. Airlines rely on frequent flyer programs offering free travel for accumulating miles on their carrier to increase passenger loyalty. Manufacturers commonly offer coupons for cash discounts or mail-in rebates for their products. The simple act of cutting out the coupon and presenting it at the cash register or mailing it in reinforces the consumer's relationship to the product. Sometimes a prize is offered for a winning essay about the product; "Why I like (fill in the blank) in 24 words or less." Win or lose, the mere act of writing and submitting an essay to such a contest is bound to increase one's allegiance to the product.

Brand loyalty also can be encouraged through merchandising. Every time you see a Unocal 76 ball or Jack in the Box head on a car antenna, you're witnessing this strategy in action. Every time you hear kids pester their parents for a Happy Meal containing a toy from the latest Disney blockbuster, you're witnessing this strategy

Land O' Lakes mug illustrating merchandising as a means of increasing commitment.

Used with permission of Land O' Lakes, Inc. Photo by Jennifer Nicholson.

as well. Merchandising is a powerful means of promoting products and fostering brand loyalty. That's why the tobacco industry spent $665 million dollars giving away various gear with tobacco logos in 1995, the most recent year for which figures are available (Monmaney, 1997).

An example of how consumers succumb to merchandising pressure involves one of this book's ever-gullible authors. He liked the Indian maiden logo on "Land O' Lakes" © butter. So when he learned he could order two Land O' Lakes © mugs for only $7.95, plus three proof-of-purchase seals from any Land O' Lakes © product, he couldn't resist. He switched from margarine to butter. He bought only Land O' Lakes © butter for the next 3 months (the amount of time it took to accumulate three proof-of-purchase seals). When he found he'd lost one of the proof-of-purchase seals he was despondent. Did he give up? Of course not. He went out and bought another package of Land O' Lakes © butter *he didn't even need,* just to complete the trio of proof-of-purchase seals! The author is now the proud owner of a pair of Land O' Lakes © mugs complete with Indian maiden logo, but let's examine what can be learned from this lesson.

1. The merchandising offer got the author actively involved in the process of reinforcing his own brand loyalty. Since the mugs themselves cost little to manufacture, the author was paying Land O' Lakes for the privilege of becoming a loyal consumer.

2. The merchandising offer secured the author's brand loyalty for a period of 3 to 4 months. Although the author has subsequently switched back to margarine, he still buys the Land O' Lakes © brand, whenever he purchases butter (after all, he has the mugs to remind him of where his loyalty lies).

3. The author bought and used far more butter than he otherwise would have absent the mug offer. In fact, as he was closing in on that elusive third proof-of-purchase seal, he was searching high and low for ways to use up butter!

Admittedly, the author got a little carried away, but that's the beauty of the concept of brand loyalty. We don't necessarily think or act rationally when our allegiance to a particular brand takes over.

Marketing Inconsistency

Of course, other advertising campaigns, typically those for newer products or products with a smaller market share, employ just the opposite strategy. These ads encourage us to switch brands. They realize consumers can be set in their ways. These advertisers try to create psychological inconsistency. They want us to have second thoughts about the products and services on which we've been relying unquestioningly, year after year. They may make "special introductory offers" or provide other incentives to try out their goods and services. Consider the following advertising slogans:

"Think different" (Apple Computers)
"Get out of the old, get into the bold" (Miller Genuine Draft)

"Not Your Father's Oldsmobile" (Oldsmobile)
"I could have had a V8!" (V8 vegetable juice)

Such slogans are based on the recognition that consumers can be set in their ways and seek to overcome this inertia by encouraging *brand-switching*. Many other types of advertising campaigns are based on creating a state of psychological inconsistency. Insurance ads are often designed to make the consumer feel worried or anxious about what would happen to loved ones in the event of the person's death. PBS pledge drives are designed to make the viewer feel guilty for watching public television without making a donation.

Capitalizing on Inconsistency

The use of consistency theory isn't just for advertisers, marketers, and other "professional" persuaders. You, too, can incorporate the principles of consistency theory in your own persuasive messages. One way you can accomplish this is to align your message with your audience's frame of reference. It is much easier to tailor a suit to fit a person than it is to change a person's figure to fit a suit. Similarly, successful persuasion isn't so much a matter of shifting receivers' attitudes over to your position, as it is a matter of adapting your message to the attitudes already held by receivers. The children of one of the authors are quite good at this technique. To postpone their bedtimes they'll ask, "Can we stay up to watch this TV show? It's *educational*." At the supermarket they'll say, "Let's get fruit roll-ups. Fruit is *good* for you." On Saturday mornings they'll plead, "Let's go to the beach today. Swimming is good *exercise*." Clearly, such adaptation is key to persuasion, which is why we'll be discussing this strategy in more detail in Chapter 6, Analyzing and Adapting to Audiences.

Another way you can apply principles of consistency theory is to highlight potential inconsistencies in receivers' attitudes. If you can show that some attitudes held by your receivers are incompatible, you may motivate them to change their attitudes in the direction you are advocating. Be cautious, however, when employing this strategy. If you attempt to drive too big a psychological wedge between your receivers' attitudes, they may simply change their attitudes so as to dislike you.

COGNITIVE DISSONANCE

Now that we've discussed the basic elements of consistency, we turn to one of the more well-known forms of consistency theory, called *cognitive dissonance*. Originated by Leon Festinger (1957), the theory focuses on the self-persuasion that occurs *after* one has made a decision. Hence, cognitive dissonance is sometimes referred to as a *post-decision theory*. The basic idea behind the theory is that, following a decision, a person worries about whether he or she has made the right choice. Because most decisions involve "pros" and "cons," the person worries about the benefits associated with the foregone alternative and the drawbacks associated with the choice that was made. The person is therefore motivated to reduce her or his anxiety by justifying the decision that she or he made. Attempts to justify or reinforce the decision can take place through the individual's thought processes, words, or actions.

Cognitive Dissonance and Buyer's Remorse

An illustration of cognitive dissonance can be found in the phenomenon known as buyer's remorse. Suppose that Biff has been looking for a portable CD player. He likes Sony CD players because he believes they are of high quality. So, after conducting some price comparisons, Biff buys a Sony model at a local electronics chain. According to the theory, after having made the purchase, Biff should experience cognitive dissonance, because he will fret about whether he made the right choice. "Did I get the best price?" he will ask himself. "Is this the most reliable brand?" he will wonder.

According to the theory, Biff also should engage in dissonance reduction attempts, aimed at reducing any lingering regrets. He might re-read a favorable review of a Sony CD player in a consumer magazine. This is referred to by Festinger as *selective exposure,* whereby an individual seeks out only favorable information about the option chosen. He might tell a friend who drops by, "Man, would you listen to that bass?" He might disparage competing brands based on their sound quality, lack of features, or limited warranties. Though his communication may be directed toward others, he is really trying to convince himself that he made the right decision.

Cognitive dissonance isn't an all-or-nothing phenomenon—it occurs in varying degrees. The amount of cognitive dissonance experienced in a particular situation is referred to as the *magnitude of dissonance.* An important decision evokes more dissonance than an unimportant one. Spending $7 to see a movie that was awful wouldn't cause as much dissonance as spending $20,000 on a car that turned out to be a lemon.

Cognitive Dissonance and Self-Image: I've Gotta Be Me

Buyer's remorse isn't the only example of a situation involving cognitive dissonance. Dissonance also can arise when one's self-image is inconsistent with one's actions. For instance, a person who perceives himself or herself to be unprejudiced but who laughs at a racial joke should experience cognitive dissonance. And a person who thinks of himself or herself as honest, but who returns a product, claiming it is defective, when he or she in fact broke it, also should experience cognitive dissonance.

Forced Compliance and External Justifications

The magnitude of dissonance a person experiences hinges on how much freedom he or she has in making a choice or in engaging in a given behavior. When an individual is compelled to engage in behavior contrary to his or her own attitudes or self-image, called a *forced-choice situation,* he or she will not suffer as much cognitive dissonance as when he or she engages in the behavior of his or her own volition. The fact that a person is compelled to do something lets them "off the hook" psychologically. Imagine, for instance, that Trudy is a highly religious person who attends church regularly. Her boss sends her out of town for the weekend on a business trip which requires her to miss church. Because she has no choice in the matter, she should experience less cognitive dissonance over having to miss church than if the choice were her own. According to the theory, however, if Trudy missed church because she chose to go fishing or see a baseball game, she would experience considerably more cognitive dissonance.

External justifications, such as monetary incentives, also affect the magnitude of dissonance experienced by an individual. If there are external inducements for performing acts which are contrary to one's attitudes, the amount of dissonance experienced will be smaller. For example, a "snitch" or police informant who was paid for "ratting" on a friend, wouldn't feel as bad as one who informed on his or her friend without receiving compensation. The more the informant was paid, the easier it would be for him or her to rationalize the act of squealing.

Cognitive Dissonance and Counter-Attitudinal Advocacy

An even better approach to changing another's attitudes is to get the person to persuade him or herself. This can be accomplished by having the person engage in what is called **counterattitudinal advocacy** (CAA). CAA involves having a person create and present (orally or in writing) a message that is at odds with his or her existing attitudes; for example, claiming you favor a tuition hike when, in fact, you favor a tuition decrease. Research demonstrates that after engaging in CAA, the person's attitudes will tend to shift in the direction of the position advocated (Festinger, 1957; Kelman, 1953; Preiss & Allen, 1994). Mind you, the person's attitudes don't undergo a complete reversal. Some degree of attitude change takes place,

DILBERT reprinted by permission of United Feature Syndicate, Inc.

such that the initially counter-attitudinal position becomes somewhat more favorable in the person's mind.

The explanation offered by cognitive dissonance theory for this phenomenon is that CAA causes psychological conflict within the individual. He or she is aware of the inconsistency between his or her privately held beliefs and attitudes and his or her public behavior. One way of resolving the conflict is to make one's private beliefs and attitudes more consistent with one's public behavior; hence, the resultant shift in attitudes. This suggests an effective way of getting another person to persuade him or herself. Simply try to get the person to speak or act in a manner that is contrary to his or her attitudes. This can be accomplished by asking the other to role-play for a few minutes or to play devil's advocate for a while. The research demonstrates that attitude change should follow in the direction of the counterattitudinal position. When using this technique, however, it is important that the other person *choose* to engage in CAA as opposed to being forced to do so. A meta-analysis by Preiss and Allen (in press) revealed that voluntarily engaging in CAA was the key to this strategy's effectiveness.

Cognitive Dissonance and Commitment

Commitment goes hand in hand with cognitive dissonance to produce persuasion. When people become committed to ideas, groups, causes, or decisions they find it difficult to change their minds. By way of example, did you know that once horse racing fans have bet on a horse, they become even more convinced that their horse will win (Knox & Inkster, 1968)? Individuals who volunteer their time to work for political campaigns tend to overestimate the prospects of their candidate winning. The more public the nature of the commitment, the more people tend to become psychologically entrenched and to follow through on that to which they've become committed. For instance, have you noticed that when some people go on a diet, they formally announce their decision to others? Why tell the world? Because the public commitment makes their decision all the more binding which, in turn, increases the likelihood of their remaining on the diet. They don't want others to see them munching on Twinkies or bon bons and asking, "Hey, aren't you supposed to be dieting?" A private or personal pledge to diet, if violated, produces some dissonance. A public commitment, however, arouses considerably more cognitive dissonance if violated.

The social custom of engagements and weddings also illustrates how public commitments can become psychologically binding. When Biff asks Babbs, "Will you marry me?" Biff is making a verbal commitment. If Babbs responds "Yes, I will," she, too, is making a verbal commitment. The engagement announcement involves a public commitment. The purchase of an engagement ring or wedding ring entails a hefty financial commitment. Wedding plans involving photographers, florists, and caterers further compound the commitments. Such commitments make it all the more difficult for either party to subsequently back out of the engagement. Sure, Biff or Babbs *could* still back out, but it wouldn't be easy; considerable cognitive dissonance would be involved. Perhaps that's why, every now and then, a bride or groom doesn't tell anyone, she or he simply fails to show up at the altar!

Many other social customs and rituals are designed to increase a person's sense of psychological commitment to an idea, group, cause, or decision. Fraternity initiation rituals do so. Boot camp in the military serves this purpose. Baptism achieves this goal. As part of a teen chastity program, called "True Love Waits," some teens sign pledge cards promising their parents they will refrain from having sex until they are married. Political rallies, protest marches, and demonstrations accomplish this function for the participants. *Whenever we make public statements or engage in public actions we tend to become bound by our words or deeds.* Yes, we can renege on what we've said or done, but we will pay a psychological toll for doing so. The greater the public commitment, the greater the toll paid.

Speaking of backing out of sizable commitments, you may recall the case of Shannon Faulkner, who became the first woman to enter and exit the Citadel, a previously all-male military academy, all in the same week. On August 13, 1995, following a two and a half year lawsuit, Shannon Faulkner was admitted to the Citadel and hailed by the media as a pioneer and role model. On August 18, less than one week later, she dropped out. She cited mental and physical exhaustion from the legal battle as the reason for leaving. Do you suppose she experienced much cognitive dissonance following her decision to leave? Given the highly public nature of her commitment, and the media attention surrounding it, we suspect she experienced tremendous dissonance.

Commitments Can "Grow Legs"

Robert Cialdini (1993) makes the interesting point that commitments sometimes "grow legs." By this he means that once we become committed to a given course of action, we tend to remain steadfast in our determination, even if the original reason for selecting that course of action is diminished, altered, or eliminated. A story involving friends of one of the author's illustrates this phenomenon. A couple signed their daughter up to play in a citywide soccer league. They paid a fee to the league, bought their daughter soccer shoes, a soccer ball, a uniform, and other equipment. They also signed up to fulfill a number of other responsibilities expected of parents, like participating in bake sales, serving as "linesperson," attending a "kick-a-thon," and so on. Three weeks into the season, however, their daughter decided she hated soccer and didn't want to play another game. What did the couple do? Did they terminate their involvement with soccer? Not in the least! They continued to attend the team's soccer games and fulfill their commitments. Occasionally, they took on extra responsibilities. Once they became committed they found additional reasons for participating in the soccer league beyond their daughter's original interest. Given the time, money, and effort they had put into the endeavor, giving up completely on soccer would have been more psychologically troubling to them.

We all engage in similar behavior from time to time. The owner of an unreliable car keeps spending money on repairs, hoping this brake job or that muffler repair will finally be the last. The repair bills keep mounting, until they may eventually exceed the car's resale value. Does the owner throw in the towel? Nope. The owner becomes even more resolute the next time something breaks. "I've already spent almost two grand on that car. I can't give up now." A gambler bets on a football team, which loses. The next week, he doubles up on the bet, feeling confident they will win the next time around. They lose again. Does he wise up and cut his losses? No sireee. He becomes more determined than ever that the team will win. His commitment actually increases with each loss.

Once we've invested our time and energy or poured our hearts and souls into a cause, a person, an idea, a project, or a group we find it too difficult to let go. We may have second thoughts, but we repress them. We find it easier to remain committed, to redouble our efforts, to allow psychological inertia to take over. We build up layers of rationalizations for remaining true to our original convictions.

Keep in mind that a large initial commitment isn't required in order for persuaders to take advantage of us. Even relatively simple acts such as raising your hand, signing a petition, or filling out a form can be enough. To illustrate, in a now classic study, Deutsch and Gerard (1955) asked three groups of students to estimate the length of a line. The first group was asked to write down their estimates on paper, to sign the paper, and to hand it in to the experimenter. The second group was asked to write down their estimates, but on an erasable pad, and not to hand it in. The third group was asked to simply think about their estimates of the line's length. All three groups were then provided with information that their original estimates were wrong, and all three were given an opportunity to change their estimates. The group members who made a public commitment were the *least* likely to alter their estimates, whereas the group members who simply thought about the line's length were the *most* willing to change.

The fact that commitments can grow legs also means that we are vulnerable to self-persuasion as well. Remember, we manufacture the additional reasons for bolstering our commitment ourselves. Once we become committed, we may become blind to alternative ways of seeing, thinking, or acting. We may see ourselves as displaying determination, but others may regard us as being stubborn and intractable. Thus, we need to remain on guard, not only from others seeking to extract commitments from us, but from ourselves.

Before concluding this section, we wish to note that several worthwhile lessons can be learned from our discussion of commitments and consistency. First, don't allow persuaders to "box you in" by getting you to commit to something when you really don't want to. Feel free to say, "I want to think it over," or "I want to consider some other options first," or "You're not trying to rush me into a hasty decision are you?" Second, don't paint yourself into a corner by making public commitments you really don't want, or intend, to keep. Be willing to say, "Sorry, I'd rather not," or "I have to say 'No' this time." Third, if you do happen to make an ill-advised commitment, admit it, and see what you can do to correct it. Don't be so preoccupied with saving face that you follow through on a really dumb decision. When buying anything, ask about a return or refund policy in advance. Most states have specific laws regarding refunds on items purchased via door-to-door sales pitches or telephone solicitations.

SUMMARY

In this chapter we've seen that attitudes exist in associative networks and that advertisers use these connections to foster favorable images and associations with their products and services. People have a tendency to strive for consistency among their attitudes, beliefs, and behaviors. Persuaders can adapt their messages either to reinforce consistency or to attempt to create inconsistency. Cognitive dissonance, a specialized form of consistency theory, explains how people go about rationalizing decisions after they have made them. Engaging in counterattitudinal advocacy or making commitments, especially public commitments, are two important means of facilitating influence, based on the theory of cognitive dissonance.

ENDNOTES

1. An interesting aside here is that former NBA great Kareem Abdul-Jabbar made a cameo appearance in one of the Coors "Tap the Rockies" commercials. In the commercial, he sank his patented "sky hook" through a hole in a cloud shaped like a basketball hoop. He was chastised by the Islamic Society of North America, however, because alcohol consumption is prohibited by the nation of Islam. Abdul-Jabbar is, himself, a Muslim. A spokesperson for the Muslim society described the former Laker's appearance in the ad as "devastating" (Abdul-Jabbar Gets Heat Over Coors Commercial, 1997). The campaign was subsequently revised, with Abdul-Jabbar endorsing an alcohol-free brand.

REFERENCES

"Abdul-Jabbar gets heat over Coors commercial" (1997, January 18). *Daily Bulletin*, p. C2.

Cialdini, R. B. (1993). *Influence: Science and practice* (3rd ed.). LaPorte, IN: Harper-Collins.

Deutsch, M., & Gerard, H. B. (1955). A study of normative and informational social influence upon judgment. *Journal of Abnormal and Social Psychology, 51*, 629–636.

Festinger, L. (1957). *A theory of cognitive dissonance*. Stanford, CA: Stanford University Press.

Greenwald, A. G., & Ronis, D. L. (1978). Twenty years of cognitive dissonance: Case study of the evolution of a theory. *Psychological Review, 85*(1), 53–57.

Heider, F. (1958). *The psychology of interpersonal relations*. New York: Wiley.

Kelman, H. C. (1953). Attitude change as a function of response restriction. *Human Relations, 6*, 185–214.

Knox, R. E., & Inkster, J. A. (1968). Postdecision dissonance at post time. *Journal of Personality and Social Psychology, 3*, 319–323.

Monmaney, T. (1997, December 12). Study links cigarette gear, youth smoking. *Los Angeles Times*, p. A-1.

Newcomb, T. M. (1953). An approach to the study of communicative acts. *Psychological Review, 60*, 393–404.

Osgood, C. E., & Tannenbaum, P. H. (1955). The principle of congruity in the prediction of attitude change. *Psychological Review, 62,* 42–55.

Preiss, R. W., & Allen, M. (1994). The persuasive effects of incentives to perform counterattitudinal advocacy. In M. Allen & R. W. Priess (Eds.), *Persuasion: Advances through meta-analysis* (pp. 339–361). Dubuque, IA: Brown & Benchmark.

Preiss, R., & Allen, M. (in press). Performing counterattitudinal advocacy: The persuasive impact of incentives. In M. Allen & R. Preiss (Eds.), *Persuasion: Advances through meta-analysis* (pp. 231–239) Cresskill, NJ: Hampton Press.

Salter, S. (1995, March 8). "Tampons on the tennis circuit? Not in this century." *Star Tribune,* Metro Edition, p. 10A.

Scher, S. J., & Cooper, J. (1989) The motivational basis of dissonance: The singular role of behavioral consequences. *Journal of Personality and Social Psychology, 56,* 899–906.

Schudson, M. (1984). *Advertising: The uneasy persuasion.* New York: Basic Books.

Tesser, A., & Shaffer, D. R. (1990). Attitudes and attitude change. In M. W. Rosenzweig & L. W. Porter (Eds.), *Annual review of psychology* (pp. 479–573). Palo Alto, CA: Annual Reviews.

5

CREDIBILITY

John F. Kennedy had it. So did James Dean. Adolf Hitler had it, unfortunately. Dr. Martin Luther King had it, as did both Princess Grace and Lady Di. Sean Connery still has it. So does Colin Powell. Michael Jordan has lots of it. Depending on whom you ask, the Pope, Norman Schwartzkopf, Oprah Winfrey, and Tiger Woods have it. What all these people have, or had, is *charisma*.[1] Charisma is a lay term used to describe someone who possesses a certain indefinable charm or allure. Such a person may be said to have a magnetic personality.

There is a problem with describing people as charismatic, however. The term has no clear, precise meaning. Trying to pinpoint what constitutes charisma is a bit like trying to eat bouillon soup with a fork. It isn't the same as popularity. Nor is it synonymous with leadership. It can't be equated with assertiveness either. Indeed, part of the attraction of charismatic persons may be that their appeal is somewhat magical or elusive.

Because charisma is a fuzzy concept, persuasion researchers tend to avoid it. Instead, they rely on a different but related concept called *ethos* or *credibility*. Ethos bears some similarity to charisma. However, whereas charisma represents an elusive, ineffable quality, ethos can be defined and measured with much greater precision. In this chapter, we examine the concept of ethos or credibility and its relationship to persuasion. First we take a look at credibility as it relates to celebrity endorsers and spokespersons. Next we offer a definition, discuss the basic features, and explore the underlying dimensions that make up credibility. Then we look at how credibility functions according to Petty and Cacioppo's Elaboration Likelihood Model of persuasion (1986), and we examine a phenomenon known as the *sleeper effect*. Finally, we discuss credibility both as it applies to institutions and interpersonal settings.

CELEBRITY SELLING POWER: THE ANSWER IS IN THE STARS

Did you know that 20 percent of all television commercials feature a famous person? Celebrities like Candice Bergen, Bill Cosby, and Michael Jordan head the list.

A decade ago males accounted for nine of the top ten celebrity spokespersons. That situation has changed, however. More recently, women accounted for a majority of the top ten (non-athlete) celebrity endorsers (Goldman, 1995). Why the shift? For one thing, women have more purchasing power than they used to, both in terms of actual dollars and in terms of decision-making authority. For another, female consumers are less willing than they used to be to defer to the say-so of male spokespersons. "Now if you need to speak to a woman, you hire a woman," concludes David Vadehra, president of Video Storyboard Tests (Goldman, 1995).

Catch a Falling Star

There can be a downside to relying on well-known entertainers and athletes to peddle a company's wares. What happens if a celebrity spokesperson becomes embroiled in a scandal or legal proceeding? Such was the case with Michael Jackson (an endorser for Pepsi, accused of child molestation), Tonya Harding (an endorser for Nike, convicted of assault on ice skater Nancy Kerrigan), O. J. Simpson (a spokesperson for Hertz, acquitted of two murders, but found liable in civil court), Mike Tyson (an endorser for Pepsi, convicted of rape and suspended from boxing for biting Evander Holyfield's ear), Kathie Lee Gifford (an endorser for Wal-Mart, associated with clothing manufactured in foreign "sweatshops"), and Marv Albert (NBC Sports commentator, who plead guilty to charges of assault and battery). When a celebrity endorser gets in trouble there can be negative fallout for the company's image as well. Most companies now conduct thorough background checks before signing a celebrity endorser to a contract. Such contracts routinely include a moral turpitude clause. If the entertainer or athlete commits an illegal or immoral act, the contract can be voided (Conrad, 1995).

Of course, selling power only represents *one* kind of credibility. The Pope doesn't do commercials, but he possesses high credibility among Catholics. Nelson Mandela and Yassir Arafat don't appear in TV or magazine ads either, yet they have high credibility among their followers. Family members, friends, and co-workers all possess different levels of credibility in our eyes as well. At this juncture, then, let's examine what comprises credibility in a broader context than that of Madison Avenue.

WHAT IS CREDIBILITY?

O'Keefe (1990) defines credibility as "judgments made by a perceiver (e.g., a message recipient) concerning the believability of a communicator" (pp. 130–131). We would extend this definition to include not only persons as communicators but institutions as well. Private companies and governmental agencies also have images and reputations to protect. They want to be viewed favorably too. In addition, it should be recognized that in face-to-face encounters there are really *two* sources whose credibility is at stake, because each party to the interaction is simultaneously a sender and a receiver of messages. If you try to convince a friend to do you a favor, you must appear credible. If the friend declines by offering an excuse, the friend must try to appear credible while doing so as well.

Credibility Is a Receiver-Based Construct

An important feature of O'Keefe's definition, and virtually every other definition of credibility found in the literature, is the recognition that credibility is a *receiver-based construct.* In other words, credibility exists in the eye of the beholder. For example, Hillary Clinton may be credible to one person, but not to another. One receiver may love Dennis Rodman, the next may hate him. In short, if these folks are credible, it is because we bestow credibility upon them. Modifying a time-worn philosophical question, one might ask, "If a source stood in the middle of a forest and there was no one around to perceive him or her, would there be any credibility?" Our answer is no. Credibility is a perceptual phenomenon. It does not reside in the source.

A bizarre phenomenon following the death of backup musician Jonathan Melvoin of Smashing Pumpkins, illustrates how credibility functions as a receiver-based construct. Melvoin, who played keyboards, died of a heroin overdose in New York City in July 1996. He overdosed after injecting a brand of heroin known as Red Rum. In a macabre twist, demand for that specific brand of heroin *increased* following media reports of Melvoin's death (Goldman, 1996). Why? Credibility: It seems that heroin users concluded from the media reports that Red Rum had unusually high purity. The backup musician's death convinced addicts that Red Rum was the kind of pure, potent fix they were looking for.

Credibility Is a Multidimensional Construct

A second important feature of credibility is that it is not a unidimensional construct, that is, comprised of just one element. Credibility represents a composite of several characteristics that receivers perceive in a source. Thus, credibility is a *multi-dimensional construct.* An analogy may serve to clarify this point. Imagine that you were trying to define "athleticism. It would be difficult to single out just one thing that makes an individual athletic. Athleticism requires, among other things, strength, coordination, stamina, and quick reflexes. In the same way, credibility isn't a single quality, but the product of a number of qualities a source is believed to possess. We'll discuss these qualities shortly.

Credibility is a Situational/Contextual Phenomenon

A third feature of credibility is that it is a *situational* or *contextual phenomenon.* The very qualities that are revered in a communicator in one situation or context may be reviled in another setting. Thus, a persuader's credibility is subject to change as he or she moves from one audience to another, or one setting to another. The editor of *Field and Stream* might be well received when speaking before an audience of hunting and fishing enthusiasts. He might encounter a hostile reception, however, were he or she to speak before a group of animal rights advocates such as People for the Ethical Treatment of Animals. Your own credibility is subject to such situational changes too. You may enjoy more credibility in one context—for example, work, family, friends, and school—than in another.

Credibility Is Dynamic

Credibility also can change over time. Richard Nixon's political career, depicted in an Oliver Stone movie, was marked by hills and valleys from his days as vice president under Dwight Eisenhower, when he gave his famous Checkers speech, to the Watergate scandal, in which he became the first president ever to resign from office, to his later years, when he functioned as the elder statesman of American diplomacy. It is important to recognize, then, that credibility is *dynamic*; it fluctuates from audience to audience, from situation to situation, and from time to time. A source's credibility can change even during the course of a single speech, sales pitch, or boardroom presentation. We further examine the dynamic nature of credibility later in this chapter when we discuss the sleeper effect.

THE FACTOR ANALYTIC APPROACH TO CREDIBILITY

Just as chefs are interested in what ingredients go into award-winning recipes, persuasion researchers have tried to determine the "ingredients" or underlying dimensions of credibility. In fact, as long ago as 380 B.C., Aristotle proclaimed in *The Rhetoric* that the ingredients "which inspire confidence in the orator's character...that induce us to believe a thing apart from any proof of it...[are] good sense, good moral character, and good will" (1378). Aristotle wasn't far off the mark.

In the 1960s and 70s researchers began to use a statistical technique known as factor analysis to uncover the underlying dimensions or ingredients of credibility. Controversy emerged during this period over how many credibility dimensions there were and what they should be called (see Berlo, Lemert, & Mertz, 1969; Cronkhite & Liska, 1976; McCroskey, 1966). Subsequent investigations, though, have clarified the situation considerably, if not completely. There is now general agreement that there are two primary dimensions of credibility, which are almost always relevant to the evaluation of sources, and several secondary dimensions that are more situation-specific. Thus, if you are trying to enhance your own credibility, you always should focus on the primary dimensions. The secondary dimensions may or may not matter depending on your particular situation. We discuss both sets of dimensions next and provide the scale items commonly used to measure these dimensions in Box 5.1.

BOX 5.1   Bipolar Adjectives Used to Measure Credibility with a Semantic Differential Scale

Primary Dimensions

- Expertise (also called competence or qualification)
    experienced/inexperienced
    informed/uninformed
    trained/untrained
    qualified/unqualified
    skilled/unskilled
    intelligent/unintelligent
    expert/inexpert

- Trustworthiness (also called character, safety, goodwill, or personal integrity)
    honest/dishonest
    trustworthy/untrustworthy
    open-minded/close-minded
    just/unjust
    fair/unfair
    unselfish/selfish

Secondary Dimensions

- Extroversion
    timid/bold
    verbal/quiet
    meek/aggressive
    talkative/silent

- Composure
    poised/nervous
    relaxed/tense
    calm/anxious
    excitable/composed

- Sociability
    good-natured/irritable
    cheerful/gloomy
    friendly/unfriendly

Adapted from McCroskey, J. C., & Young, T. J. (1981). Ethos and credibility: The construct and its measurement after three decades. *Central States Speech Journal, 32*, 24–34.

Primary Dimensions of Credibility

The first primary dimension of credibility is *expertise* (Berlo et al., 1969; Hovland, Janis, & Kelly, 1953; McCroskey, 1966). To be credible, a persuader must know his or her stuff or, at least, *appear* to know his or her stuff. Sometimes a title alone, such as M.D., Ph.D., or CPA, can confer credibility upon a source. When tradespersons place ads in the Yellow Pages of the telephone directory, they often state that they are licensed or certified and have been in business for X number of years. They, too, want to bolster their credibility.

To be regarded as an expert, a source needn't possess advanced degrees, specialized training, licenses, or credentials, however. At an Alcoholics Anonymous meeting, for example, a member who had been an alcoholic for 20 years, and who had been sober for the past 10 years, would likely be perceived as having expertise. Such a member would know what he or she was talking about, because he or she had "been there" (Denzin, 1987; Robertson, 1988). Or perhaps you recall seeing a commercial for "The Club," an automobile anti-theft device that attaches to a car's steering wheel. In the commercial, a former car thief claims The Club really works, based on his knowledge and expertise in stealing cars. Even astrologers, fortune-tellers, and psychics make attempts to establish their expertise. "Don't pay for

Perceived expertise is a prerequisite for credibility.

advice from phony psychics," the commercial on the cable TV channel announces, "we have *genuine, certified psychics* waiting to take your call."

Interestingly, a source's expertise doesn't always have to be in the field in which he or she is attempting to persuade. Lindsey Wagner, for example, isn't an expert on automobile engineering. Nor is heavyweight champ George Foreman an expert on muffler repair. Yet both are effective endorsers for those respective products. Endorsements by famous persons enjoy a "halo effect" that allows them to carry over their credibility to new, unrelated fields. An interesting study by Bruce Rind (1992) shows that this phenomenon isn't limited to famous people either.

In Rind's study, a confederate working with the experimenter approached shoppers in the food court of a mall and asked them to buy raffle tickets. In one of the experimental conditions, the confederate amazed the shoppers with phenomenal calculating ability (the confederate was actually wired with a hidden communication device, through which he received the correct answers). In another condition, the confederate made a fool of himself by exhibiting poor calculating skills. In a third control condition, the confederate didn't profess to have any amazing skills. Shoppers bought significantly more raffle tickets when the confederate demonstrated astonishing calculating skills than in either of the other conditions.

It mattered not that the purpose of the raffle was unrelated to the confederate's amazing talent. Expertise, even unrelated expertise, then, can be an asset in persuasion. Bear in mind, however, that purchasing a raffle ticket is a fairly trivial act. We suspect that on a more involving issue, relevant expertise would be valued more highly by receivers.

The second primary dimension of credibility is *trustworthiness* (Applbaum & Anatol, 1972; Berlo et al., 1969; Hovland et al., 1953; McCroskey, 1966). A source may appear knowledgeable, but what if you don't think he or she is being truthful or has your best interests at stake? If your car needs a brake job, you not only want a qualified mechanic, you want an *honest*, qualified mechanic. To be successful, persuaders must therefore convey an impression of honesty and integrity.

Perhaps you've noticed that some advertisements in magazines or newspapers carry the logo "As Seen On TV." The purpose in displaying this logo is to instill trust. Many consumers unthinkingly presume that only reputable companies can afford television commercials. If it says "As Seen On TV" the product must be on the up and up, right? We're sure you recognize the error in this assumption. It wouldn't cost all that much for a fly-by-night company to run a 30-second spot on a local channel at 3 A.M. Furthermore, there is no "As Seen On TV" laboratory that rigorously tests all products bearing this logo. All the logo really signifies is that the product was advertised on television at some point. It is not a guarantee of the manufacturer's integrity.

Or how about ads in the Yellow Pages of the phone directory that feature the *ichthys* logo, the Christian sign of the fish? Isn't the idea behind displaying this symbol that the electrician, plumber, carpenter, or so forth is a Christian and is therefore less likely to rip off his or her customers? Such "sign reasoning" may have merit. But then again, couldn't an unscrupulous tradesperson simply use the ichthys logo to dupe customers into believing he or she was a trustworthy Christian? A grim reminder of why one should exercise caution before placing one's trust in a complete stranger is provided in Box 5.2.

The perceived trustworthiness of witnesses also is crucial to judgments about the veracity of witnesses' testimony in criminal trials. In O. J. Simpson's criminal trial, for example, detective Mark Fuhrman stated under oath that he had never uttered the "N-word" in the preceding 10 years. Fuhrman's credibility was subsequently shattered, however, when the jury learned that he had used the word dozens of times during tape-recorded interviews with screenwriter Laura McKinney.

Secondary Dimensions of Credibility

Researchers have uncovered several other dimensions of credibility that tend to be more situation-specific. One of these, termed *dynamism* by some (Berlo et al., 1966) and *extroversion* by others (Burgoon, 1976; McCroskey & Young, 1981), has to do with how energetic, animated, or enthusiastic the source appears. Obviously, it wouldn't do for the host of an infomercial for exercise equipment to appear sluggish or lethargic. Certain situations call for the source to be "peppy" and full of energy. On the other hand, a person who is too bubbly and effervescent, especially

---

BOX 5.2   Are There Horns Beneath that Halo?

On April 7, 1978, the body of 12-year-old Kimberly Leach was found near Suwannee River State Park in Florida. She was the last of Ted Bundy's victims. The infamous serial killer was executed for the murder of Kimberly Leach and two other women on January 24, 1989. He confessed to killing at least 35 others. Many had been lured to Bundy's car with a seemingly innocent ploy: He feigned an injury and asked his victims to help him carry things to his car. How was it possible that Ted Bundy was able to deceive so many women? According to author Ann Rule (1989), who knew Bundy:

> Ted has been described as the perfect son, the perfect student, the Boy Scout grown to adulthood, a genius, as handsome as a movie idol, a bright light in the future of the Republican party, a sensitive social worker, a budding lawyer, a trusted friend, a young man for whom the future could surely hold only success.

From this description, or from any glance at a picture of Ted Bundy, it is clear that he did not fit the stereotypical image of a serial killer. And that's why he was so dangerous. We often trust people because they appear credible. Good looks and an articulate manner act as a halo that can blind us to the possible horns underneath. Attractiveness and a way with words are not the only halos that can fool us. Sometimes we trust people because of the way they talk, how they dress, or who they know.

How can you avoid the problems associated with the halo effect? Perhaps the best advice we can offer is to heed two pieces of childhood advice: "Don't judge a book by its cover," and "Never talk to strangers."

---

at the wrong times, may lose credibility (Burgoon, 1973). The trick is for a source to match his or her level of dynamism to the demands of the situation.

Another secondary dimension of credibility is *composure* (Miller & Hewgill, 1964). In some situations, we expect a source to remain calm, cool, and collected. The character of James Bond, secret agent 007, exudes this quality. A source who loses his or her composure, or who seems nervous or ill at ease may lose credibility. Receivers may feel that the source is unsure of himself or herself or that the source may be being deceptive.

An additional secondary dimension of credibility has been dubbed *sociability*. This dimension refers to a source's friendliness or likableness. In many situations, a source who relates well to others and who seems personable and outgoing enjoys an advantage. This quality is particularly important in the "people professions," such as sales, law, education, social work, and the like.

Yet another secondary dimension of credibility has been dubbed *inspiring* (Kouzes & Posner, 1993). This quality is similar to dynamism or extroversion. The emphasis, however, is not on how enthusiastic or energetic the source is, but on how enthusiastic or energetic the source makes *others*. We admire sources who inspire us, who motivate us, and who are uplifting. Both presidents Ronald Reagan and Bill Clinton exhibited this dimension. Voters perceived them as forward-looking leaders who had a sense of vision for the country. Retired generals Colin Powell and Norman Schwartzkopf also exhibit these qualities.

THE FACTOR ANALYTIC APPROACH
AND THE REAL WORLD

Given the extraordinary amount of research attention devoted to the study of credibility, how do these dimensions hold up in the real world? The answer is, pretty well. A representative study comes to us from Kouzes and Posner (1993), who examined employee's perceptions of their managers in actual organizational settings. Male and female employees from a variety of organizations were asked to rate their managers on three credibility dimensions—*honesty, expertise,* and *inspiration.* Note that honesty is synonymous with the trustworthiness dimension discussed previously. The employees also were asked to rate their own work attitudes in five areas: their sense of team spirit, the similarity of their own values with those of their organization, pride in their organization, their organizational commitment, and their overall work attitudes. Based on their responses, the employees were then categorized as being "low" or "high" in terms of their overall workplace morale.

The results of the study are displayed in Table 5.1. They reveal a striking chemistry operating between managers and employees. Employees who rated their manager favorably exhibited much higher morale than employees who rated their manager unfavorably. As Kouzes and Posner (1993) observe, "respondents who felt their manager was honest, competent, and inspiring were significantly more likely to feel a strong sense of teamwork, organizational values alignment, and organizational commitment than were those who found their managers less honest, competent, and inspiring" (pp. 282–283). Thus, a manager's credibility tends to "rub off" on his or her employees. A credible manager instills a positive work ethic among employees. The employees feel better and work harder. This only makes sense. It is easier to work for someone who appears to know what he or she is doing. These findings also suggest that the dimensions of credibility identified in laboratory studies are, in fact, generalizable to the real world.

TABLE 5.1 Employee attitudes as a function of perceived managerial credibility.

Employee Attitudes	Low Credibility Manager	High Credibility Manager
Has personal values consistent with company's	4.05	5.11*
Is willing to work long hours	4.01	5.19*
Is proud to tell others where he or she is employed	4.59	5.48*
Feels a sense of ownership in this company	3.39	4.51*
Credits work group with strong sense of team spirit	3.62	4.97*
Feels personally involved with work	4.73	5.27*
Intends to work for this company in two years	2.63	3.90*

*Differences were statistically significant at $p < .001$.

Adapted from Kouzes, J. M., & Posner, B. Z. (1993). *Credibility: How leaders gain and lose it, why some people demand it.* San Francisco: Jossey-Bass, p. 278. Used with permission of Jossey-Bass, Inc. Copyright © 1993 Jossey-Bass, Inc., Publishers.

CREDIBILITY AS A PERIPHERAL CUE

Now that we've explained what credibility is, we turn our attention to how and why it facilitates persuasion. To do so, we return to Petty and Cacioppo's Elaboration Likelihood Model of Persuasion (1986), which was introduced in Chapter 2. Petty and Cacioppo conceptualize credibility as a peripheral cue to persuasion. According to the ELM there are two distinct routes to persuasion, which operate in tandem. One route, which they label the *central route,* involves a focus on the substance or the content of a message. Receivers who process a persuasive message via the central route engage in "cognitive elaboration," which simply means that they think about, and reflect upon, the ideas and information contained in the message. For example, a person who bought *Money* magazine and carefully read the issue to see which mutual funds were performing well would be engaged in central processing. Receivers who process a persuasive message via the *peripheral route,* however, are less inclined to scrutinize the message itself and are more likely to focus on positive or negative cues such as the source or the message environment. For example, a person who bought Paul Newman's spaghetti sauce simply because he or she loved the actor's blue eyes would be basing his or her decision on a peripheral cue.

The ELM acknowledges that in most persuasive situations, persons employ *parallel processing,* that is, they pay attention to *both* the message content and the source of the message. However, Petty and Cacioppo argue that receivers typically tend to favor one route over another. Which route they favor depends, among other things, upon their involvement in the issue. When receivers have a stake in the outcome, their motivation to pay attention to a message is higher. They thus tend to favor the central route. When receivers have little at stake their motivation to pay attention to a message is lower. They therefore tend to favor the peripheral route.

This is where credibility enters the picture. As a general rule, source credibility exerts a greater influence on receivers who aren't highly involved in an issue or topic and lesser influence on receivers who are highly involved. An investigation by William Benoit (1987) illustrates this point well. Benoit wanted to know which of three factors, argument quality, source expertise, or source attractiveness, would play the biggest role in how college students responded to a persuasive message. The persuasive message advocated that all students be required to take a basic computer literacy class. Benoit found that students who read a version of the message containing strong arguments responded much more favorably than those who read a version containing weak ones. However, students who read a version of the message attributed to an expert responded no more favorably than students who read a version attributed to a nonexpert. Similarly, students who read a version of the message presented by an attractive source were no more persuaded than those who read a version by an unattractive source. Why didn't expertise or attractiveness have any effect? The key is that the students were highly involved in the topic. After all, they would be the ones who were required to take the computer class. Hence, they tended to rely on central processing, that is, focusing on the message itself and not on the source's credentials or good looks.

These results thus highlight an important limitation on the persuasiveness of high credibility sources: Credibility matters little if receiver involvement is already high. Instead, credibility tends to work its magic when receiver involvement is low. Receivers with low involvement are more likely to defer to sources because doing so requires less mental effort than concentrating on the substance of a message. To put it bluntly, low-involved receivers are cognitively lazy. This limitation notwithstanding, we mustn't underestimate the importance of credibility. Remember, high credibility didn't inhibit persuasion in Benoit's study, it just didn't enhance the persuasive impact of the message. Credibility may be conceptualized as a peripheral cue, but it is still a big peripheral cue.

You can use this information to your advantage if you are trying to persuade receivers who perceive you as having low credibility. You should do everything you can to increase their involvement in the topic or issue. Explain why the issue is relevant to them. Emphasize how the topic or issue affects them directly. If you can increase your target audience's involvement in the topic or issue, they'll pay more attention to the message and less attention to your credibility.

THE SLEEPER EFFECT

Many of the studies examining the persuasive effects of credibility have been one-shot affairs. That is, a persuasive message is created, the message is then attributed to a high or low credibility source, and any changes in receivers' attitudes are immediately assessed. But what about the effects of credibility over time? Do the benefits conferred by a high credibility source eventually wear off? Do the disadvantages associated with low credibility dissipate over time? Research on the sleeper effect addresses these questions.

The traditional view is that the impact of a persuasive message diminishes over time (Hovland, Lumsdaine, & Sheffield, 1949; Stiff, 1994). Receivers forget what was said or who said it. They become more ambivalent. The sleeper effect, however, suggests that under the right circumstances the delayed impact of a message may be more effective than its initial impact. Specifically, the sleeper effect posits that a message from a low credibility source may increase in persuasiveness as time passes, compared to a message from a high credibility source. Sound unlikely? It is, to some extent. Yet the sleeper effect has been documented by researchers, dating back almost 50 years (Hovland et al., 1949). Just how the sleeper effect works requires some explanation, however.

Imagine that one audience is exposed to a persuasive message from a source with high credibility. A second audience is exposed to the same persuasive message, but from a source with low credibility, by means of a *discounting cue*. A discounting cue consists of a disclaimer containing negative information about the source, the message, or both. For example, let's say the first group heard a message in favor of irradiating fruits and vegetables to kill bacteria before the items are shipped to market. The second group would hear the same message, plus a disclaimer saying the message was drafted by a lobbyist for the agricultural industry whose real concern was agricultural profits not consumer safety. The discounting cue would thus serve as an impediment to the second message's effectiveness, a "ball and chain" so to speak. Afterwards, each group's attitudes toward irradiated produce would be measured.

Initially, the first group's attitudes should be much more favorable toward the topic than the second group's. After all, the first group heard the message from the high credibility source. With the passage of time, however, things might change. The first group's attitudes would gradually decay over time, according to the traditional view. The second group's attitudes, however, might undergo a process known as *disassociation*, whereby the message is separated from its source in the minds of receivers. That is, the second group might remember the message, but forget the discounting cue. If you've ever heard someone say, "I heard somewhere that…" or "I read somewhere that…" you've observed disassociation in action. Once the second group disassociated the message from its source the ball and chain would be removed. The result would be that as the first group's attitudes diminished, the second group's attitudes would become more positive. Voila! The sleeper effect.

Although the sleeper effect has been demonstrated in a number of laboratory studies, it is difficult to produce on a consistent, reliable basis. Only a few studies have demonstrated an *absolute* sleeper effect (see Figure 5.1), of the type we've been discussing (Gruder et al., 1978; Watts & Holt, 1979; Watts & McGuire, 1964). An absolute sleeper effect occurs when a message from a high credibility source loses favor over time, while a message from a low credibility source gains favor over time. Other studies have demonstrated a *relative* sleeper effect (see Figure 5.1), meaning that both messages lose favor over time, but the high credibility message loses more favor than the low credibility message (see reviews by Allen & Stiff, 1989, 1994). Some studies have failed to find a sleeper effect at all (see reviews by Allen & Stiff, 1989, 1994). One study employed the exact same methodology using

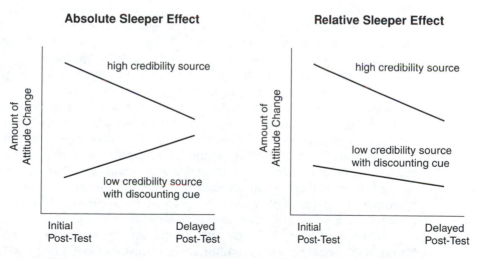

FIGURE 5.1   Illustration of an absolute and a relative sleeper effect.

two different topics to produce the sleeper effect. It worked for one topic (opposing a 4-day work week) but not for the other (allowing right turns on red lights) (Gruder et al., 1978). The sleeper effect, then, can be pretty fickle.

What implications does this hold for you as a persuader? In practice, it would be very difficult for an ordinary persuader, as opposed to a laboratory researcher, to satisfy all of the requirements for obtaining a sleeper effect. We believe there are far too many "ifs" associated with this strategy to recommend it to an ordinary per-suader. The dubious nature of the sleeper effect prompted Petty and Cacioppo (1986) to warn that "although the sleeper effect is of considerable conceptual signif-icance, obtaining it may require conditions that are infrequently present in the 'real world' or in persuasion research" (p. 183). Our advice is that you would be much better off trying to enhance your credibility as much as possible in the first place.

CREDIBILITY AND IMAGE MANAGEMENT

Thus far, we've discussed credibility strictly in connection with people or persons. We believe the concept of credibility can be extended to corporations, organiza-tions, governmental agencies, social movements, and other institutions as well. Such group entities care about how they are perceived by the public and other con-stituencies. They want to project positive images. And to a large extent, their power and ability to influence are tied up in their images and their reputations. For these reasons, we maintain that the credibility construct applies equally well to institutional entities and not just individuals.

By way of illustration, consider the charitable and philanthropic activities of major corporations. McDonald's established Ronald McDonald House to provide assistance to hospital-bound children and their families. The National Football League donates generously to the United Way. Any number of companies con-tribute to the Make-A-Wish Foundation. In so doing, these corporations are dem-onstrating that they are good citizens in their communities. Doing good deeds enhances public perceptions of trustworthiness. We don't mean to imply that cor-porations are disingenuous when they make charitable contributions or that corpo-rate altruism is based entirely on the profit motive. We do wish to point out, however, that it doesn't hurt that philanthropic acts make for good public relations.

So important is image management for corporations, institutions, government agencies, and the like that entire departments, divisions, and staffs exist for just this purpose. Major corporations have large public relations departments whose pri-mary purpose is to feature the corporation in a positive light. Political campaigns employ "spin doctors," that is, political consultants, to offer positive "takes" on events that unfold during a campaign. Industries and organizations employ lobby-ists on Capital Hill to help ensure that their interests are perceived favorably by leg-islators and regulators. Whatever the title of these types of positions, one of their primary missions is to maintain the credibility of the host institution.

On occasion, corporations, institutions, and government agencies commit blunders that damage their credibility. They must then act quickly to restore their image and regain the public's trust. William Benoit (1995) refers to this process as "image restoration" and notes that such efforts are highly persuasive in nature (p. 6). Examples in which circumstances have forced corporations and other institutions to engage in image restoration abound. In 1992 the oil tanker *Exxon Valdez* dumped millions of gallons of oil into Prince William Sound, Alaska, causing an ecological catastrophe in the region and creating a public relations nightmare for Exxon. In 1993 MTV was called to account when the cartoon characters "Beavis" and "Butthead" were accused of inciting children to commit arson. After watching an episode of the show in which the two central characters proclaimed "fire is cool," while lighting matches, a 5 year old set a fire that killed his sister. In 1995 the Bureau of Alcohol, Tobacco, and Firearms (BATF) was roundly criticized for its use of deadly force at Ruby Ridge, Idaho. In the Ruby Ridge incident, BATF agents shot and killed an unarmed woman and her son during a standoff with the father who was holed up with his family in a mountain cabin. In the late 1990's both Denny's, the restaurant chain, and Texaco, the oil company, were sued for racial discrimination. Both companies issued formal public apologies, announced changes in their company policies, and agreed to pay sizable sums as part of their settlements.

Benoit (1995) notes that such defensive campaigns are commonplace. They are undertaken out of a necessity to restore the credibility of the corporation, institution, or agency whose image has been tarnished. Benoit highlights a number of strategies associated with image restoration. These include admissions of regret, pleas for mitigation, announcements of restitution or compensation, and evasions and mystifications, to name only a few. He suggests that all of the strategies used can be broken down into two basic types. The first type is *excuses*, "which attempt to lessen or eliminate the actor's responsibility for the negatively perceived act" (p. 50). The second type is *justifications*, "which attempt to convince the audience that the act is not bad (or as bad) as they initially believed" (p. 50). The specific strategies employed, of course, depend on the nature of the difficulty in which the institution finds itself and the range of available defenses.

We can see, then, that corporations and other institutions, not just individuals, possess credibility in varying amounts. We suspect that the same primary dimensions of credibility that apply to individuals apply equally well to corporations. We suspect that the secondary dimensions of credibility discussed previously, however, might differ. After all, the secondary dimensions don't always appear in studies of individuals' credibility. This would appear to be a fruitful topic for future scholarly inquiry.

INTERPERSONAL CREDIBILITY, IMPRESSION MANAGEMENT, AND FACEWORK

Ordinary folks can't hire their own public relations firm, like corporations do, or employ a publicist, as the rich and famous do, to maintain a positive public image. They do engage in public relations campaigns, nonetheless. Ordinary persons tend to function as their own P. R. departments through impression management and facework.

Impression management theory (Tedeschi & Reiss, 1981) seeks to explain how persons go about trying to project a positive self-image.[2] Individuals want others to form favorable impressions of them. In short, individuals want to be perceived as credible. Individuals attempt to manage others' impressions of themselves by trying to say and do the right things. Engaging in "politically correct" behavior is an example of impression management at work.

Our position is that when an individual is engaging in impression management, he or she is engaging in persuasion. He or she is attempting to influence others' impressions of him or her. At the same time, he or she is vulnerable to influence attempts by others. This is because persons are highly susceptible to persuasive appeals aimed at enhancing the self-image they are trying to project. By way of illustration, a common preoccupation of teenagers, especially younger teens, is "looking cool." If one teen can convince another that dressing a certain way, or acting a certain way, will make him or her "look cool," the other teen is likely to conform to that style of dress or behavior. Most of us need look no further than our high school yearbooks, to realize that we, too, were susceptible to the fads, trends, and fashions of our day.

Impression management also requires that people engage in *facework*, a term coined by Erving Goffman (1967, 1974). A person's "face" refers to his or her social standing in the eyes of others. Facework involves negotiating one's social standing and social worth with others. For example, committing a social faux pas could result in the loss of one's own face. Facework would be required to restore one's face. Threatening or challenging another person could cause the other to lose face. Facework would again be required for the other to regain face.

As with identity management, we suggest that facework is inherently persuasive in nature. Facework involves goal-oriented communication that seeks particular outcomes or ends, namely, "satisfying one's own face wants and the face wants of one's interlocutor" (Cupach & Imahori, 1993, p. 117). For example, consider the related social rituals of asking someone out on a date or declining another's invitation for a date. Both rituals, asking and declining, are persuasive in nature and both are laden with face-saving implications. Although not synonymous with credibility, we see the concepts of face and facework as being closely related to the credibility construct. Maintaining one's face, we believe, is akin to maintaining one's credibility in the eyes of others.

STRATEGIES FOR ENHANCING ONE'S CREDIBILITY

Having gained a better understanding of what credibility is and how it works, what can you do to enhance your credibility when persuading? A number of general guidelines can be offered for improving one's credibility. Keep in mind that because credibility is a receiver-based construct, what works on one listener or audience may not work on the next.

1. **Heed the Boy Scout motto, "Be prepared."** Before making your case be as well prepared and well organized as possible. Think through your position beforehand and anticipate likely objections to your position. Obviously, if you don't seem to know what you are talking about, your credibility will suffer. Research shows that unorganized messages are far less convincing than organized ones (McCroskey & Mehrley, 1969; Sharp & McClung, 1966). Never wing it unless you have to.

2. **Cite evidence for your position and identify the sources of your evidence.** In a review of the effects of evidence usage, Reinard (1988) concluded that in almost all cases, citing evidence and sources significantly enhanced speaker credibility. This advice applies especially to low credibility sources. A low credibility source can hitchhike on the credibility of high credibility sources by citing them in his or her presentation.

3. **Explain your background and expertise on the topic or issue.** Remember, expertise is one of the primary dimensions of credibility. If you have expertise on a topic or issue, let your listener(s) know. Be sure to do so, however, without appearing conceited. If you lack expertise on an issue, don't dwell on your deficiencies. Instead, explain how you came to develop an interest in the subject. Also consider this: If, in fact, you know little or nothing about a topic, then you have no business trying to persuade others about that topic in the first place!

4. **Attempt to build trust by demonstrating to your listener that you have his or her best interest at heart.** Show the other person that you are not operating strictly out of self-interest. One approach is to show how your position is in your own and the other party's mutual self-interest; a win–win scenario.

5. **Adopt a language and delivery style appropriate to the listener(s), topic, and setting.** Your style of speech should be tailored to your particular receiver(s). Different receivers have different needs. In general, nonfluencies, pauses or gaps, and a choppy style of delivery hinder credibility (Berger, 1985; 1994; Miller & Hewgill, 1964). A reliance on "uhms," "ahs," and other fillers impairs credibility as well. An over reliance on slang, colloquialisms, or trite expressions also can compromise credibility.

6. **Avoid a "powerless" style of communication. Use an assertive style of communication instead.** A powerless communication style involves using tag questions ("That was a good movie, don't you think?"), hesitations ("uhm," "uh"), qualifiers ("kind of," "sort of," "perhaps," "maybe"), and negative preambles ("This will probably sound really dumb, but…"). A reliance on powerless language signals to the other party that you perceive yourself as occupying a lower status position in the relationship. For more about this topic, refer to Chapter 8, where we examine the role of language in persuasion.

7. **Emphasizing your similarity to another may indirectly enhance your credibility.** Listeners find it easier to identify with sources they perceive as similar to themselves. O'Keefe (1990) points out two important caveats on similarity and influence. First, he emphasizes that the similarities must be relevant to the topic or issue. Commenting, "Hey, I'm a Libra too!" will probably get you nowhere unless the topic happens to center on astrology, horoscopes, and other similar topics. Second, O'Keefe notes that the perceived similarities must involve positive, rather

than negative, qualities. Stating, "I was arrested for shoplifting once, too" may not enamor you to a new acquaintance, even though he or she may have confessed to a similar mistake.

8. If you think you are perceived as having low credibility, try to increase receiver involvement and emphasize the central route to persuasion. Remember, receivers who are highly involved in a topic place less emphasis on source credibility and more emphasis on the substance of a message. If you suspect that your target audience is skeptical of your credibility, explain how the topic or issue is directly relevant to them, then focus on the substance of the message. That will tend to encourage central processing on the part of your audience.

9. Have another source who is already perceived as highly credible introduce you and/or endorse you. This is a common strategy used in election campaigns. Salespersons also use this strategy when they rely on referrals. The technique allows a source to hitchhike on the established credibility of the person making the introduction or endorsement. Acquiring credibility via endorsements and introductions emphasizes the peripheral route to persuasion.

SUMMARY

As we've seen, credibility is a complex construct. Yet there is one overriding generalization about credibility that persuaders can "take to the bank": *Credibility is a good thing to have if you are a persuader.* So long as we keep in mind that credibility is a perceptual phenomenon, the generalization that high credibility sources are more influential than low credibility sources is as close as one can come to a universal "law" of persuasion.

In advancing this generalization, however, we feel it is important to underscore the point that credibility is a complex, multidimensional, situational communication phenomenon. Credibility can't be bought in a bottle or purchased out of a vending machine. In many persuasive settings, a source who has low or no initial credibility can do little or nothing about it. Low credibility sources tend to be dismissed out of hand; receivers simply fail to attend to their messages. There is an old joke about how to become a multimillionaire: "It's simple: first, get a million dollars, then..." Much the same advice can be offered for using credibility to enhance persuasion: "It's simple: first, get a lot of credibility, then..."

ENDNOTES

1. The term was first coined by German sociologist Max Weber (1968) who defined charisma as "a certain quality of the individual personality by virtue of which he is set apart from ordinary men and women and treated as endowed with supernatural, superhuman, or at least exceptional powers and qualities" (p. 240).

2. Impression management theory also has been referred to as self-presentation strategies or identity management theory (IMT for short) by William Cupach and Todd Imahori (1993).

REFERENCES

Allen, M., & Stiff, J. B. (1989). Testing three models for the sleeper effect. *Western Journal of Speech Communication, 53*(4), 411–426.

Allen, M., & Stiff, J. B. (1994). An analysis of the sleeper effect. In M. Allen & R. W. Preiss (Eds.), *Prospects and precautions in the use of meta-analysis* (pp. 185–204). Dubuque, IA: William C. Brown.

Applbaum, R. L., & Anatol, K. W. E. (1972). The factor structure of source credibility as a function of the speaking situation. *Speech Monographs, 39,* 216–222.

Aristotle. (1954). *The rhetoric* (W. R. Roberts, Trans.) New York: Random House.

Benoit, W. L. (1987). Argumentation appeals and credibility appeals in persuasion. *Southern Speech Communication Journal, 52,* 181–187.

Benoit, W. L. (1995). *Accounts, excuses, and apologies: A theory of image restoration strategies.* Albany, NY: State University of New York Press.

Berger, C. R. (1985). Social power and interpersonal communication. In M. L. Knapp, & G. R. Miller (Eds.), *Handbook of interpersonal communication* (pp. 439–499). Newbury Park, CA: Sage.

Berger, C. R. (1994). Power, dominance, and social interaction. In M. L. Knapp & G. R. Miller (Eds.), *Handbook of interpersonal communication* (2nd ed., pp. 450–507). Newbury Park, CA: Sage.

Berlo, D. K., Lemert, J. B., & Mertz, R. J. (1969) Dimensions for evaluating the acceptability of message sources. *Public Opinion Quarterly, 33,* 563–576.

Burgoon (Heston), J. K. (1973, April). *Ideal source credibility: A re-examination of the semantic differential.* Paper presented at the International Communication Association Convention, Montreal, Quebec.

Burgoon, J. K. (1976). The ideal source: A reexamination of source credibility measurement. *Central State Speech Journal, 27,* 200–206.

Conrad, E. (1995, October 8). Caution: Falling idols. *Pittsburgh Post-Gazette.* p. C1.

Cronkhite, G., & Liska, J. (1976). A critique of factor analytic approaches to the study of credibility. *Communication Monographs, 43,* 91–107.

Cupach, W. R., & Imahori, T. T. (1993). Identity Management Theory: Communication competence in intercultural episodes and relationships. In R. L. Wiseman & J. Koester (Eds.), *Intercultural communication competence* (pp. 112–131). Newbury Park, CA: Sage.

Denzen, N. K. (1987). *The recovering alcoholic.* Newbury Park, CA: Sage.

Goffman, E. (1967). *Interaction ritual essays on face-to-face behavior.* Garden City, NY: Anchor Books, Doubleday.

Goffman, E. (1974). *Frame analysis: An essay on the organization of experience.* Cambridge, MA: Harvard University Press.

Goldman, J. J. (July 16, 1996). "Musician's death spurs heroin demand." *Los Angeles Times,* p. A-5.

Goldman, K. (October 27, 1995). Among celebrity endorsers, women peddling ahead of men. *San Diego Tribune,* p. E4.

Gruder, C. L., Cook, T. D., Hennigan, K. M., Flay, B. R., Alessi, C., & Halamaj, J. (1978). Empirical tests of the absolute sleeper effect predicted from the discounting cue hypothesis. *Journal of Personality and Social Psychology, 36,* 1061–1074.

Hovland, C. I., Janis, I. L., & Kelly, H. H. (1953). *Communication and persuasion.* New Haven, CT: Yale University Press.

Hovland, C. I., Lumsdaine, A., & Sheffield, F. (1949). *Experiments on mass communication.* Princeton, NJ: Princeton University Press.

Kouzes, J. M., & Posner, B. Z. (1993). *Credibility.* San Francisco: Jossey-Bass.

McCroskey, J. C. (1966). Scales for the measurement of ethos. *Speech Monographs, 33,* 65–72.

McCroskey, J. C., & Mehrley, R. S. (1969). The effects of disorganization and nonfluency on attitude change and source credibility. *Speech Monographs, 36,* 13–21.

McCroskey, J. C., & Young, T. J. (1981). Ethos and credibility: The construct and its measurement after three decades. *Central States Speech Journal, 32,* 24–34.

Miller, G. R., & Hewgill, M. A. (1964). The effect of variations in nonfluency on audience ratings of source credibility. *Quarterly Journal of Speech, 50,* 36–44.

O'Keefe, D. J. (1990). *Persuasion: Theory and research.* Newbury Park, CA: Sage.

Petty, R. E., & Cacioppo, J. T. (1986). *Communication and persuasion: Central and peripheral routes to attitude change.* New York: Springer-Verlag.

Reinard, J. C. (1988). The empirical study of the persuasive effects of evidence: The status after fifty years of research. *Human Communication Research, 15,* 3–59.

Rind, B. (1992). Effects of impressions of amazement and foolishness on compliance. *Journal of Applied Social Psychology, 22*(21), 1656–1665.

Robertson, N. (1988). *Getting better: Inside Alcoholics Anonymous.* New York: William Morrow.

Rule, A. (1989). *The stranger beside me.* New York: Signet.

Sharp, H., & McClung, T. (1966). Effects of organization on the speaker's ethos. *Speech Monographs, 33,* 182–183.

Stiff, J. B. (1986). Cognitive processing of persuasive message cues: A meta-analytic review of the effects of supportive information on attitudes. *Communication Monographs, 53,* 75–89.

Stiff, J. B. (1994). *Persuasive communication.* New York: Guilford Press.

Tedeschi, J. T., & Reiss, M. (1981). Identities, the phenomenal self, and laboratory research. In J. Tedeschi (Ed.), *Impression management theory and social psychological research* (pp. 3–22). New York: Academic Press.

Watts. W. A., & Holt, L. E. (1979). Persistence of opinion change induced under conditions of forewarning and distraction. *Journal of Personality and Social Psychology, 37,* 778–789.

Watts, W. A., & McGuire, W. J. (1964). Persistence of induced opinion change and retention of inducing message content. *Journal of Abnormal and Social Psychology, 68,* 223–241.

Weber, M. (1968). *On charisma and institution building.* Chicago: University of Chicago Press.

6

COMMUNICATOR CHARACTERISTICS AND PERSUASIBILITY

How well do you know your boyfriend or girlfriend, husband or wife? Is there anything about that person you don't know? A waist size, perhaps? A secret attitude or ambition? How about gender? Do you know if the person is male or female?

This last question may seem a bit strange until you consider what happened to a man named Bruce Jensen just a few years ago: When Jensen's "wife" of over 3 years was arrested on suspicion of unlawful use of credit cards, authorities discovered that "she" was really a he (Groutage, 1995a, 1995b; "Making sure," 1995). Not surprisingly, upon learning this, Jensen was confused. Officers had to convince him it was true, which, we imagine, was not much fun. Said Grant Hodgson, the detective who broke the news to Jensen, "I've done a lot of death notifications that were easier."

Afterwards, Jensen said, "I feel pretty stupid." Here's his description of what happened: After he met Felix Urioste, who was then posing as a female doctor named Leasa, they dated for a month. When Urioste claimed to be pregnant with twins, they were married, but later Urioste maintained that the twins were stillborn. Jensen claimed he didn't know Urioste was a man because he had never seen Urioste naked, Urioste took hormones to look like a female, and Urioste claimed that normal sex was impossible because of a previous rape (Groutage, 1995a, 1995b; "Making sure," 1995).

Sound unbelievable? If you are at all like we were after hearing this story, you're probably dubious. But authorities claimed, after considerable investigation, that they believed Jensen was just a nice guy who was incredibly naive (Groutage, 1995a). And we suppose when you consider all possible people, it's likely that someone would be gullible enough to fall for such a scheme. (In fact, if you've seen the movie *The Crying Game*, perhaps you can empathize with Jensen.) Most of our students, for example, claim they know at least one person who is very susceptible to persuasion.

However, although it seems that some people are more persuadable than others, the search for a single underlying trait or characteristic that makes people persuadable has not been a successful one. As you may have decided from the chapters you've read so far, persuasion is more complicated than that. And so are people. Even so, the characteristics of the people in a persuasive interaction cannot be ignored. All communicators are unique in terms of gender, age, personality, and background, and such characteristics are important to understanding the nature of social influence.

In this chapter, we explore the role communicator characteristics play in the process of persuasion. Although we don't have room to cover all the communicator characteristics that have been studied, we discuss several that past research has identified as being important to social influence. Then we discuss ways in which a communicator might analyze and adapt to an audience when trying to be persuasive.

Before we begin, however, we note, as we have in earlier chapters, that persuasion is a two-way street. Thus, when we use the term communicator characteristics, we are not limiting our discussion to one person. The characteristics of all the interactants in a persuasive encounter are part of the equation.

DEMOGRAPHIC VARIABLES AND PERSUASION

If someone asked you to use 10 words to describe yourself, there is a good chance you would use demographic information to do so. Demographics include characteristics such as age, gender, ethnicity, and intelligence. In the following sections we discuss how each of these are related to persuasion.

Age and Persuasion: Pretty Please with Sugar on Top

What's the most persuasive sound in the world? Ask any parent and they might tell you "the sound of a baby crying." Indeed, when you stop to think about it, infants are awfully good at getting what they want without uttering a single word. Want some milk? Cry. Hugs? Whine. Attention? Snivel.

Of course, we know some adults whose persuasive strategies differ little from crying infants. Generally, however, as people grow older, their strategies become more complex. Why? Research indicates that as people grow older they become more cognitively sophisticated and are therefore better at seeing the world from the perspective of the person whom they are trying to persuade (Delia, Kline, & Burleson, 1979; Haslett, 1983). For example, when trying to persuade someone to adopt a lost puppy, younger children (e.g., kindergartners and first graders) are more likely to use simple requests such as "Could you keep this dog?" or "Pretty please." In contrast, older children (e.g., seventh to twelfth graders) are more likely to use strategies that adapt to the perspective of their target such as "You look kind of lonely and this dog would be a good companion" (Delia et al., 1979). Not surprisingly, then, as children get older, their persuasive attempts become more sophisticated (Ward & Wackman, 1972).

But what about the other side of the coin? As children grow older, do they also become more difficult to persuade? The expression, "It's like taking candy from a baby," suggests that children are easily taken advantage of, and research in the area of persuasion indicates that this is generally true; children tend to be more vulnerable to persuasive trickery because they lack the ability to understand the nature and intent of persuasive attempts. The implications of such research can be frightening. Indeed, we've all heard stories of children who have been tricked or lured away by criminals (for more on this issue, see Box 6.1).

What we may be less aware of, however, are other types of persuasive messages that may be influencing our children. For instance, considering that most 18-year-old Americans will have spent more time in front of a television set than in school (about 15,000 hours of TV) (Minow & LaMay, 1995), it is clear that the "tube" has a tremendous impact on shaping beliefs and attitudes. Kids between the ages of 2 and 11 spend 20 percent of their TV time watching advertisements (about 25,000 ads a year) (Condra, Berne, & Scheibe, 1988), so you can bet that advertisers pay a great deal of attention to this group of young consumers.

Advertisers know a lot about children and create advertisements accordingly. For instance, have you ever seen a "real life" G. I. Joe or Power Ranger battle look more spectacular than the ones shown on TV? To attract children's attention, advertisers use all kinds of devices, which include shorter messages, continual repetition, realistically executed fantasies, motion, scenes demonstrating how reward results from using a product, and scenes emphasizing the product itself (Hendon, McGann, & Hendon, 1978). What kid wouldn't be persuaded?

What can be done to protect kids from advertisers? At least two variables seem to decrease children's vulnerability to advertising: family influence and getting older. First, research shows that if you interact with children during ads, you can increase their ability to critically examine the ads and provide them with a better understanding of the nature and purpose of advertising (i.e., that ads are biased, intend to persuade, and so forth) (Reid, 1979; Wiman, 1985). Second, as children become older they become more susceptible to peer pressure, but less susceptible to the persuasive appeal of ads. Notice, however, we say *less* susceptible, not immune. For example, Atkin, Hocking, and Block (1984) found that teenagers who were exposed to a greater number of alcohol advertisements consumed larger amounts of alcohol. In addition, despite the fact that eating disorders are a serious problem facing today's youth, Ogletree, Williams, Raffeld, and Mason (1990) argued that advertisements tend to promote them in females. Because food ads tend to feature male actors while appearance ads feature female actors, the ads may be sending the message that it's okay for males to eat but that females should concern themselves with looking good.

From our discussion so far, we've made it clear that young people tend to be very susceptible to persuasion. But what about older people? When you think about people who are retired, you might picture the gullible granny being swindled by someone selling swamp land. In some respects, we imagine the notion of elderly folks being more persuadable is warranted. First, although it is not true of all older people, a certain percentage of the elderly do have diminished mental

BOX 6.1   "Never Take Candy from Strangers"

I was certain it could never happen. After all, I'm a very street-savvy, New York City parent. I write articles advising moms and dads on child safety. Needless to say, I've been so conscientious in teaching my own children that my husband insists I'm paranoid, and my daughter has more than once rolled her eyes heavenward at my often repeated warnings. Which is why I can hardly describe the sick feeling in my stomach as I watched my redheaded little boy and his friend Tahlor march right out of the park one spring afternoon with a total stranger. (Rosen, 1994, p. 108)

Fortunately for Margery Rosen, the scene described above was only part of an informal experiment. To test how well she had trained her children, she had gotten Kenneth Wooden, an expert on the ways in which sex offenders lure children, to see if he could persuade her children to leave the playground with him. He didn't have much trouble. He told the boys he had lost a puppy and would give them money if they would help him find it. They went right with him and so did several other children involved in the experiment (Rosen, 1994).

Many children aren't as fortunate as those involved in Rosen's experiment. Indeed, it's been estimated that one in four girls and one in eight boys is sexually abused by the age of 18 (Wooden, 1988). Clearly, children are especially susceptible to persuasion and sometimes the results are tragic. For that reason, Kenneth Wooden (1988) argued, "Teaching your kids about the tricks that molesters use could save them from grievous harm—even death" (p. 149).

In an effort to prevent children from being molested, Wooden interviewed convicted molesters, pimps, and murderers and discovered 11 lures that are commonly used on children. Of the lures he said, "Knowledge of them is so basic to a child's safety that they should be taught—indeed *must* be taught—by every parent" (Wooden, 1988, p. 149). With this in mind, if you know, are, or plan to be a parent, here is a brief list of the lures and prevention strategies that Wooden identified (1988; see also Rosen, 1994):

1. The assistance lure. The lost puppy example described above is an example of this lure. In it, the molester asks kids for directions, for help carrying packages, or for some other type of assistance. Children should be advised to keep their distance from strangers in cars. Children should tell the assistance seeker to ask another adult for help.

2. The authority lure. Some molesters lure children by posing as a police officer or some other authority figure. If told to "Come with me" by such a person, children should ask an adult to inspect the person's credentials.

3. The affection/love lure. Some molesters lure children by promising them love and affection. Parents should know that 75 to 80 percent of sex crimes are committed by someone a child knows and trusts. Children should beware of *anyone* who wants excessive time alone with them and be encouraged to tell their parents about improper advances. Parents should trust their instincts.

4. The bribery lure. Children are often offered gifts from molesters. Parents should be suspicious of any new toys their children have. The age old saying, "Never take candy from strangers" is still true today.

5. The ego/fame lure. Youngsters are sometimes lured by modeling jobs or beauty contests that should be kept secret from mom and dad. For that reason, parents should accompany kids to such events, encourage openness, and check the credentials of "would-be" modeling agencies.

6. The emergency lure. To catch children off guard and lure them into a car, molesters might trick them by claiming "a house is on fire" or "mommy had to go to the hospital." To prevent falling for this, parents and children should prearrange an emergency plan. Under

BOX 6.1   *Continued*

no circumstance should a child ride with a stranger.

7. The fun and games lure. Molesters sometimes turn tickling, wrestling, and other games into intimate contact. Children need to be taught that there are good and bad touches. Bad touches (e.g., anywhere under a bathing suit) should be reported.

8. The magic and rituals lure. Sometimes, abuse is disguised as magic, sorcery, or satanism in order to fascinate children. Parents, therefore, should discuss with their kids the concepts of good and evil and beware if their kids begin to reject family values.

9. The pornography lure. Molesters have been known to use pornography to destroy their victims' inhibitions. Wooden, therefore, advises parents to keep pornography out of the home so it does not seem legitimate.

10. The hero lure. Because children admire heroes, molesters might pose as Santa, Big Bird, or other characters to obtain children's trust. Children should be taught that bad people can play tricks on children and that real heroes won't do certain things.

11. The jobs lure. Molesters sometimes lure children by promising high paying jobs. When suspicious, parents should accompany children to interviews, especially if the interview is in a secluded or unusual place and ask to see a business license.

Although some psychologists have argued that teaching children about a potential molester only serves to terrify them and prevent the formation of friendships (for a discussion, see "Teaching fear," 1986), Rosen (1994) and others have argued that teaching children to be cautious about potential molesters is little different than teaching them to be safe around stoves or electrical sockets. Education should start at a young age with the goal of making children cautious, not paranoid. As Wooden (1988) noted, children should be taught that most people are good and won't hurt them, but should also realize that some people are bad and sick.

capacity and therefore cannot critically evaluate messages. In addition, elderly people are sometimes lonely, making them "easy" marks for telephone and door-to-door solicitations. Finally, some elderly people have money—a nest egg they've acquired. On the other hand, some research indicates that stereotypes about the "gullible and elderly" are unwarranted. Indeed, Alwin and Krosnick (Alwin & Krosnick, 1991; Krosnick & Alwin, 1989) noted that older Americans, compared to their younger counterparts, may be less persuadable given that their attitudes and beliefs have already been formed and tend to remain stable.

Gender Differences and Persuasion: The Times, They Are a-Changin'

Just as children and adults differ in the persuasive strategies they use, research shows that men and women attempt to persuade in different ways. Compared to females, males tend to be more verbally aggressive (Maccoby & Jacklin, 1974) and are more likely to use coercion and threats early in a compliance-gaining encounter (deTurck, 1985). Interestingly, in one study, although women expressed less confidence than men in their ability to communicate persuasively, men and women performed equally well (Andrews, 1987).

But how do men and women compare when it comes to being persuaded? Early research suggested that women were more easily persuaded than men (e.g., Chaiken, 1979; Janis & Field, 1959; Scheidel, 1963). More recently, however, researchers who have examined and summarized large numbers of studies on the topic have called into question the notion that women are any different from men when it comes to being persuaded (e.g., Becker, 1986; Eagly, 1978; Eagly & Carli, 1981). For example, Eagly (1978) showed that the majority of such studies found no gender differences in persuadability, and Eagly and Carli (1981) found the relationship between gender and persuadability to be weak. As a result, many researchers abandoned the idea of general gender effects, and instead tried to explain *when* gender differences could be expected. For instance, in Eagly's 1978 study, 32 percent of the studies published before 1970 (generally regarded as the onset of the women's movement) found that women were more easily influenced than men, but only 8 percent of the studies published after 1970 found the same result. Thus, evaporating gender differences might be the result of changing times and the attitudes of and toward women.

Another possible reason for the change in research findings was suggested by Eagly and Carli (1981). These researchers hypothesized that earlier studies may have found females to be more persuadable because they used topics that were biased toward men. Results of Eagly and Carli's (1981) study, however, did not support this explanation; the researchers found that male-oriented topics were not overrepresented in earlier studies.

Even so, there is another possible explanation for the change in research findings before and after 1970. Specifically, earlier studies used male rather than female sources (Ward, Seccombe, Bendel, & Carter, 1985), which means that male receivers were being persuaded by members of the same sex while females were being persuaded by members of the opposite sex. That is, in the earlier studies, there may have been a "cross-sex effect," by which people were more easily influenced by members of the opposite sex than by members of the same sex. This effect, however, may be stronger for males persuading females than for females persuading males (Ward et al., 1985). Indeed, even when women exhibit more confidence and appear more powerful and competent, they may be less liked by men and therefore be less persuasive (Carli, 1990). On the other hand, women who are perceived as more likable tend to be more persuasive to male audiences (Carli, LaFleur, & Loeber, 1995).

From our review so far, it is clear that generalizations on gender and persuasion are hard to come by. As Cody, Seiter, and Montagne-Miller (1995) argue, "There is no simple model that links 'gender' or 'sex' to influenceability" (p. 312). Instead, following Miller and Read (1991), these researchers argue that persuadability is not so much related to one's gender as it is to one's goals, plans, resources, and beliefs (Cody et al., 1995). For instance, imagine you are in a shopping mall, looking at clothing. If you don't intend to buy anything (goal), have decided you will look now and buy later (plan), have very little money (resources), and think that all salesclerks are dishonest (beliefs), you will probably be more difficult to influence than if you intend to buy now, have lots of money, and believe salesclerks are honest. In other words, it may not matter so much if you are male or female; how easy you are to influence depends on your goals, plans, resources, and beliefs. Gender only matters to the extent that males and females have different goals, plans, resources, and beliefs. For instance, Cody, Seiter, and Montagne-Miller (1995) found that when shopping for clothes, men and women tend to have different goals and that such goal differences were related to influenceability and the effectiveness of certain sales tactics.

Ethnicity, Culture, and Persuasion: "Me" and "We" Perspectives

Cultural differences play a major role, both in terms of how people fashion influence attempts and how they respond to them. Perhaps the most commonly discussed dimension of cultural variability is known as *individualism–collectivism* (Hofstede, 1983). While collectivist cultures (e.g., China) tend to value harmony, concern for others, and the goals of the group over the goals of the individual, individualistic cultures (e.g., the United States) tend to value independence and the goals of the individual over the goals of a collective.

With that in mind, consider the following list of slogans that were used in magazine advertisements (see Han & Shavitt, 1994) and imagine which you would use to appeal to a collectivistic culture and which you would use to appeal to an individualistic culture:

"The art of being unique."
"She's got a style all her own."
"We have a way of bringing people closer together."
"The dream of prosperity for all of us."
"A leader among leaders."
"Sharing is beautiful."

A study by Han and Shavitt (1994) found that advertisements such as the first, second, and fifth above, which appealed to individual benefits, personal success, and independence, were used more in the United States (an individualistic culture) than in Korea (a collectivistic culture) and were more persuasive in the United States than in Korea. On the other hand, ads such as the third, fourth, and sixth, which appealed to group benefits, harmony, and family, were used more often and were more persuasive in Korea than in the United States.

Gudykunst and Ting-Toomey (1988) also reported that differences in individualism–collectivism are important to the process of persuasion. They noted that while members of collectivistic cultures tend to use persuasive strategies that are appropriate to the context, people from individualistic cultures focus more on whom they are trying to persuade and use strategies that may be less socially appropriate. Similarly, a study by Wiseman, Sanders, Congalton, Gass, Sueda, and Ruiqing (1995) found differences between the persuasive strategies used by people from the United States, China, and Japan. For example, when trying to persuade roommates to be more quiet, people from the United States, who tend to be more individualistic and less concerned with saving face, preferred more direct strategies (e.g., "You are making too much noise. Please be quiet.") and strategies with individually-controlled sanctions ("If you don't quiet down, I'll be as noisy as possible when you are trying to study."). People from China, who tend to be more collectivistic and more concerned with saving face, preferred indirect strategies (e.g., hinting for it to be more quiet.) and strategies with group-controlled sanctions (e.g., "Your noisiness shows a lack of consideration for others."). However, people from Japan hinted less than people from both the United States and China, leading Wiseman and colleagues (1995) to conclude that collectivism and individualism may not be opposite orientations. In other words, the fact that people from Japan sometimes behave consistent with individualistic behavior and sometime behave consistent with collectivistic behavior "suggests that individualism and collectivism are actually two separate continua that may ebb and flow in their significance in influencing communication practices" (Wiseman et al., 1995, p. 12). Thus, depending on the situation, cultures such as Japan may demonstrate either collectivistic or individualistic behaviors.

In addition to affecting the way persuasive messages are sent, culture also influences the way such messages are received. For instance, Burgoon, Hunsaker, and Dawson (1994) argued that because people are more attracted to those who are similar to themselves than to those who are different, because people from different races and ethnic groups are often from different social and economic backgrounds, and because of factors such as prejudice and hostility, "it would seem logical that communication between interactants of the same race or ethnic group would be more effective than communication between people of different races or ethnic groups" (p. 79). However, White and Harkins (1994) reported that past studies have been inconsistent regarding the effect of race on persuasion; for white receivers, past studies have shown that speakers from minority populations have been more persuasive, less persuasive, and as persuasive as white speakers. Even so, a study by White and Harkins (1994) found that whites were more motivated to think about persuasive messages delivered by blacks than messages delivered by whites. This could be because whites are very concerned about not appearing racist and, hence, pay more attention when blacks are speaking (White & Harkins, 1994). The implication may be that when delivering strong speeches to members of a different ethnic group (who are paying more attention), people may be more persuasive than when delivering strong speeches to members of the same ethnic group (who are paying less attention).

Intelligence and Persuasion: Dumb and Dumber

The process of persuasion can be described as occurring in stages. For example, in the late 1950s, Janis, Hovland, and their colleagues argued that for persuasion to be successful, a receiver must first pay attention to the message and then comprehend the message. Next, while being persuaded, a receiver may or may not anticipate the possible rewards and punishments that would go along with being persuaded and critically evaluate the message (Janis et al., 1959). Similarly, William

McGuire (1968a, 1968b, 1985) developed a two-stage model that argued that, in order for persuasion to be successful, a receiver must first receive a message and then yield to the message.

Although common sense might suggest that people of low intelligence are easier to persuade than people with a lot of intelligence, the above approach suggests this might not be the case. Why? Because when it comes to persuasion, intelligence is something of a double-edged sword. Imagine, for a moment, that you're trying to persuade Albert Einstein and Forrest Gump (if you haven't seen the movie, Forrest isn't known for his brains). If persuasion were as simple as comprehending a message, Albert would clearly be easier to persuade than Forrest, who may lack the cognitive abilities to receive the message. On the other hand, Albert has abilities that enable him to critically evaluate a message (e.g., scrutinize the evidence, counterargue if he disagrees), therefore making him less likely to yield than Forrest. Thus, in some respects, intelligent people are easier to persuade, while, in other respects, people of low intelligence are more persuadable. With that said, then, who would you say is the easiest target of persuasion? The above mentioned models predict that people of moderate intelligence should be the easiest to persuade because they are able to comprehend better than Forrest but are more likely to yield than Albert. According to a review of research by Rhodes and Wood (1992), however, there is insufficient evidence to support this conclusion; since most previous studies compared people of high intelligence with people of low intelligence, it is not possible to see how people of moderate intelligence fared.[1] Of the studies reviewed, however, most indicated that people of low intelligence were easier to persuade than people of high intelligence. Sorry Forrest.

PSYCHOLOGICAL AND COMMUNICATION STATES AND TRAITS

Someone once said there are two types of people in the world: those who put everything into categories and those who don't. People who study communicator characteristics and persuasion belong in the first group. As you've probably gathered from our discussion so far, often the goal of these researchers is to classify people based on differences (e.g., age, gender) and then to use those group differences to explain why some people are easy to persuade while others are difficult, or why some people use one strategy to persuade, while others use a different strategy.

One common explanation for why people differ from one another centers around the notion of traits. Unfortunately, not all theorists agree on what a trait is. While some maintain that traits are causes of behaviors, others argue that traits merely describe or summarize behaviors. For instance, theorists in the first group would argue that "shyness" causes people to avoid social situations. On the other hand, theorists in the second group would argue that "shyness" is merely a label for summarizing behaviors. In other words, instead of saying that Bart doesn't date much, avoids parties, and doesn't like to meet people, it is simpler just to say that Bart is shy.

Regardless of which position is taken, Krahé (1992) noted that theorists in this area agree that traits are relatively enduring and stable. Such agreement, however, does not end all the controversies surrounding the notion of traits. To be sure, some theorists, called *situationists*, question the very existence of traits. Mischel (1968), for instance, observed that people's behavior is not as stable as trait theorists claim. Instead, behavior varies considerably from one situation to the next: A person who is aggressive on a football field might be quite gentle when conversing with his grandparents or attending a funeral. Thus, traits, the situationists argue, are of little use. It is the situation that determines how a person behaves.

Of course, it was not long before trait theorists responded to such attacks, and the debate continues still. According to Krahé (1992), the most ambitious response to the situationists' challenge is found in the *interactionist perspective,* which argues that a person's behavior is determined by both traits and situations. In other words, traits and situational variables continually interact to produce behavior.

Related to this perspective is the notion of states. Unlike a trait, which is presumed to be relatively stable across situations, a state varies from situation to situation. For instance, if we conceptualize anxiety as a trait, we would predict that a person possessing the trait would be anxious in practically all situations. On the other hand, if we conceptualize anxiety as a state, we would predict that there are certain situations in which a person becomes anxious. For instance, some people become very anxious when talking with authorities or when meeting people of the opposite sex.

With these issues and definitions in mind, we now turn to a discussion of some specific traits and states that have been the focus of research in the area of persuasion.

Self-Esteem and Persuasion: Feelin' Kinda Low

Are individuals with low self-esteem more susceptible to influence attempts than individuals with high self-esteem? Although the notion that people with a low self-esteem are easy to persuade seems reasonable, it is not supported by research (Perloff, 1994; Rhodes & Wood, 1992). This is because the relationship between esteem and persuasion is very much like that between intelligence and persuasion (see earlier discussion). Recall that, to be persuaded, a person must both receive and yield to a message. However, although people with low self-esteem may feel less confident in themselves and their opinions and be more likely to yield to a message, they may also be too concerned about their appearance and behavior to be receptive to a persuasive message. On the other hand, while people with high self-esteem are more likely to receive a message, they are more confident in themselves and are less likely to change their attitudes and behaviors. Thus, research indicates that people with moderately high self-esteem are easier to persuade than people with either high or low self-esteem (Rhodes & Wood, 1992).

Anxiety and Persuasion: Living in Fear

Unless you've grown up in a closet, you've undoubtedly been exposed to messages about the dangers of global warming, second-hand cigarette smoke, gang violence, and so forth. How do you react to such messages? Do they make you overly nervous or tense? If so, you may be chronically anxious. Research suggests that anxiety, whether chronic or acute, may be related to persuadability, although the relationship is not clear. For instance, Nunnally and Bobren (1959) found that anxious people were more persuadable than nonanxious people, while Janis and Feshbach (1965) found just the opposite. Moreover, research by Lehmann (1970) indicated that anxiety is related to persuasion much as intelligence and self-esteem are. Specifically, anxious people, compared to the nonanxious, may be more likely to yield to a message, but because they may be distracted or overly worried, may be less likely to receive a message. On the other hand, nonanxious people, compared to the anxious, may be more likely to receive a message but less likely to want to do something about it (Lehmann, 1970).

Whatever the relationship between anxiety and persuasion, one thing is clear: When trying to persuade anxious people, be sure to include specific recommendations for avoiding the harms, along with reassurances that if they follow the recommendations, everything will be OK. As you'll see in more detail in Chapter 14, without such reassurances, people who are anxious may not respond well to fear appeals.

Self-Monitoring and Persuasion: Periscope Up

In high school, a sister of one of the authors dated a guy who was a maniac on the dance floor. And we're close to literal when we use the word "maniac." Out of context you'd never have guessed he was dancing. He used to stomp his feet and flap his hands, wild and out of rhythm. Some said he looked badly wounded. Others simply stared. But whatever went on around him, he seemed oblivious, not caring what others thought of him.

The story you've just read is related to a personality trait called *self-monitoring* (Snyder, 1974, 1979). The wild dancer in the story is what people who study personality would call a low self-monitor. If you are a low self-monitor, you tend to be less sensitive to social cues. In addition, you are not that concerned about what others think of your behavior. You are individualistic and may not always act in ways that are considered socially appropriate. You honestly express your thoughts and feelings even though you may not be conforming to other people's expectations.

On the other hand, if you are a high self-monitor, you tend to be very sensitive to social cues. You pay close attention to what's considered appropriate in a given situation and act accordingly. You watch other people's behavior and are good at adapting to different audiences because you have a large repertoire of social skills. You are concerned with appearances and try to "fit in" with others, even when such behavior may contradict what you believe.

As you might expect, high and low self-monitors are persuaded differently. For instance, Becherer, Morgan, and Richard (1982) reported that high self-monitors, because they try to fit in, are more influenced by reference groups than are low self-monitors. In addition, White and Gerstein (1987) conducted a study to investigate how high and low self-monitors might be persuaded to offer help to people with disabilities. Because they knew that high self-monitors want to "look

High self-monitors: Daffodil Queen contestants eavesdropping on contestant interviews.

Reprinted by permission of Steven G. Smith.

good," these researchers suspected that high self-monitors could be persuaded to help if they thought a social reward would result. To test this, high and low self-monitors heard lectures about Kitty Genovese, a woman who was murdered in New York City while many people watched but did not help. In one version of the lecture, subjects learned that people who help receive social rewards. In another version, subjects were told that helping others usually does not result in social rewards. Later, the subjects were phoned and asked to volunteer to help visually impaired people. Of those who'd been told that helping results in social rewards, 80 percent of the high self-monitors volunteered but only 48 percent of the low self-monitors did. On the other hand, when subjects did not expect social rewards, 68 percent of the low self-monitors volunteered, while only 40 percent of the high self-monitors did. In other words, high self-monitors are influenced by situations that make them appear better. Low self-monitors are less susceptible to such appeals.

Similarly, research in advertising suggests that high self-monitors are more influenced by "image-based" advertising. In contrast, low self-monitors are more interested in "product-quality" advertising. For example, Snyder and Debono (1989) found that high self-monitors were willing to pay more money for a product that promised to improve their image (e.g., an ad shows a bottle of Canadian Club resting on a set of house blueprints and reads, "You're not just moving in, you're moving up."), while low self-monitors would pay more for a product that suggests high quality (e.g., an ad for Canadian Club which reads, "When it comes to great taste, everyone draws the same conclusion."). In addition, Becherer and Richard (1978) reported that high self-monitors are more likely to use national brand products over private labels.

Ego-Involvement: Not Budging an Inch

One of the most important explanations of the process by which people are persuaded was presented by Muzafer Sherif, Carolyn Sherif, and Robert Nebergall (Sherif & Sherif, 1967; Sherif, Sherif, & Nebergall, 1965) and is known as *social judgment theory*. We present the theory here because it focuses on receivers and is particularly relevant to a psychological characteristic known as *ego-involvement*.

According to the theory, on any topic, whether it be about abortion, an advertised product, or a favorite movie, there are a range of possible opinions that a person can hold. For example, one topic that has been studied in relation to social judgment theory is what should be done with people who have been found guilty of first degree murder. Here are several positions, some extreme, some moderate, that you might embrace on this topic. Murderers should

1. be rewarded for decreasing the population.
2. be slapped on the hand and sent away.
3. be given a $500 fine.
4. receive a 5-year prison term.
5. receive a 20-year prison term.
6. receive a life sentence with a chance for parole.
7. receive a life sentence with no chance for parole.
8. be put to death.
9. be tortured to death, along with all lawbreakers, jaywalkers included.

Social judgment theory argues that on this continuum of positions we all have a most preferred position called an *anchor*. For instance, imagine that two people, Muffy and Mort, both agree most with position 7, that murderers should spend their lives in prison with no chance for parole. In Figure 6.1, this anchor point is represented by an "X". Of course, the anchor position is not the only position a person might find acceptable. You can see in Figure 6.1, for example, that Muffy also would accept the death penalty as a fitting punishment. Together, with Muffy's anchor, these positions represent Muffy's *latitude of acceptance*. In other words, these are positions she finds tolerable. She would not, however, agree with all positions, for in addition to the latitude of acceptance, social judgment theory describes two other latitudes. The first, called the *latitude of noncommitment*, contains positions about which a person feels neutral or ambivalent. Muffy is neither for nor against murderers receiving life sentences with the possibility of parole; she is neutral. The

✓ second, called the *latitude of rejection*, contains positions that a person would reject. For example, Muffy rejects the idea that murderers be rewarded, slapped, fined or spend 5 to 20 years in prison or that murderers should be tortured.

You will notice in Figure 6.1 that the span of these latitudes is different for different people. Compared to Mort, Muffy has a larger latitude of rejection and narrower latitudes of noncommitment and acceptance. For this reason, Muffy is a good example of an ego-involved person. People are ego-involved when an issue has personal significance to them and their sense of self. Thus, they become strongly committed to their stand on the issue and are more likely to reject other positions. A person might also be ego-involved about one issue and not another. For instance, Muffy might have strong feelings about what happens to murderers, but care less about abortion, gun control, or gasoline prices.

Social judgment theory makes several important predictions about the process of persuasion. First, because people judge everything according to their anchor position, it is difficult, if not impossible, to persuade them to accept a position too

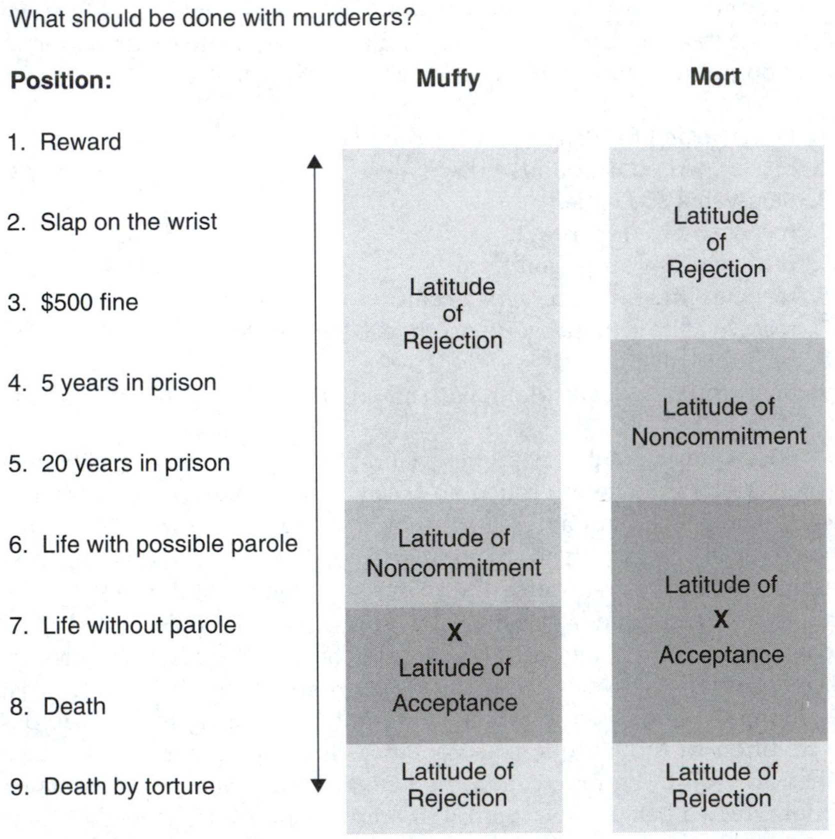

What should be done with murderers?

Position:	Muffy	Mort
1. Reward		
2. Slap on the wrist		Latitude of Rejection
3. $500 fine	Latitude of Rejection	
4. 5 years in prison		Latitude of Noncommitment
5. 20 years in prison		
6. Life with possible parole	Latitude of Noncommitment	Latitude of X Acceptance
7. Life without parole	X Latitude of Acceptance	
8. Death		
9. Death by torture	Latitude of Rejection	Latitude of Rejection

FIGURE 6.1   Illustration of social judgment theory.

far away from that anchor. For instance, if you tried to convince Mort that murderers should be rewarded, you'd be wasting your time (see Figure 6.1); messages falling inside a person's latitude of rejection are bound to fail. In fact, the theory argues that when a message falls too far away from a person's anchor position, the person perceives the message to be further away from the anchor than it really is. This is known as the *contrast effect*. On the other hand, the *assimilation effect* occurs when a message that falls within a person's latitude of acceptance is perceived to be closer to the anchor position than it really is. For example, although Mort would prefer that murderers be severely punished, if you told Mort that murderers should be moderately punished, he might decide that you basically agree and accept your position. Thus, while contrast leads to the rejection of a message, assimilation leads to successful persuasion.

You might have guessed by now that the contrast effect is more likely in ego-involved people than in people who are not ego-involved. Indeed, it's difficult to persuade someone who is ego-involved (e.g., Sherif, Kelly, Rodgers, Sarup, & Tittler, 1973). Because their latitude of rejection is so large (and their latitude of acceptance is so narrow), obviously, they will reject most persuasive messages.

One of the things we like best about social judgment theory is how it suggests that persuasion is not a "one shot deal." We think the theory does a good job of illustrating that persuasion may have to occur over time. For example, imagine trying to persuade Muffy that murderers should merely be spanked (see Figure 6.1). We've already seen that trying to convince her of that will lead to rejection. But aiming messages nearer the anchor point might meet with more success. In other words, you might try to persuade Muffy that life in prison with a chance for parole is a good position. Then, if she agrees to that, later you could try to convince her that 20 years in prison is justified. Get the idea? Anchor positions need to be moved gradually.

Dogmatism and Authoritarianism: You Can't Teach an Old Dog New Tricks

In the movie *A Few Good Men*, Tom Cruise and Demi Moore defend two Marines, who, while following orders from their superior officers, accidentally killed a fellow soldier. Their defense? "We were simply following orders."

History is replete with examples of this excuse, for it was the same one used by Nazi defendants at Nuremberg. It was repeated again during the Vietnam War by soldiers involved in the My Lai massacre and by Ollie North in the Iran–Contragate scandal. "We were following orders" is a timeworn excuse and a reflection of a personality trait known as *authoritarianism*.

Authoritarian people respect authoritative leadership and tend to follow authorities blindly (Adorno, Frenkel-Brunswik, Levinson, & Sanford, 1950; Allport, 1954). According to Narby, Cutler, and Moran's (1993) sources, authoritarians have a deep distrust of human beings, condemn those who question and deviate from conventional norms, and exhibit hostility toward out-group members. In addition, the authoritarian person believes that power and rigid control are acceptable and are

THE FAR SIDE   By GARY LARSON

**Highly involved people are likely to reject
messages they don't want to hear.**

likely to use physical punishment. In fact, if you're on trial, especially for a severe crime like rape or murder, you probably don't want many authoritarians on the jury. A review of research by Narby and colleagues (1993) indicated that authoritarian people, compared to non-authoritarians, are more likely to convict you.

A personality trait that is very much related to authoritarianism is *dogmatism* (Rokeach, 1960). In fact, according to Christie (1991), dogmatism was introduced as a more general type of authoritarianism; although some argue that authoritarianism and dogmatism scales measure the same thing, others claim that the authoritarianism scale tends to identify close-minded conservatives while the dogmatism scale identifies close-minded liberals and conservatives. Moreover, while authoritarianism focuses on people's dispositions with regard to specific ideological positions, dogmatism focuses more on dispositions independent of ideologies (DeBono & Klein, 1993). Whatever the case, dogmatic people, like authoritarians, tend to be deferential to authorities. In addition, dogmatics are close-minded, have difficulty being objective, and tend to believe there is only one right way to do things (i.e., their way). Thus, you won't be surprised when we tell you that dogmatic people are difficult to persuade.

When we say difficult, however, we don't mean impossible. Harvey and Beverly (1961), for instance, reported that high authoritarians, compared to low authoritarians, are more likely to be influenced by a person who is a high-status authority. Similarly, a study by Debono and Klein (1993) found that when dogmatic people received persuasive messages from experts, they did not think much about the messages and regardless of the quality of the messages were more persuaded than people who were not dogmatic. On the other hand, when they received persuasive messages from nonexperts, dogmatics were more persuaded by strong arguments than by weak ones. Thus, it seems that authoritarians and "high dogs," as people who are highly dogmatic are called by researchers, are especially vulnerable to messages from authority figures.

Cognitive Complexity and Need for Cognition

How would you describe your best friend? Fun or boring? Intelligent or stupid? Superficial or disclosive? Even-tempered or moody?

According to a theory known as *constructivism* (Clark & Delia, 1976; Delia & Crockett, 1973; Delia, O'Keefe, & O'Keefe, 1982), people attempt to make sense of their world by using constructs like the ones just mentioned. *Constructs* are perceptual categories (e.g., fat/thin, popular/unpopular, strong/weak) that we use when evaluating everything from professors, to textbooks, to music, to arguments. Constructs can be compared to eyeglasses; just as you see things differently depending on whether you're wearing thick or thin lenses, the constructs you use affect the manner in which you perceive the world. For instance, someone who evaluates you on the sole basis of whether you are Christian or non-Christian will see you much differently than someone who uses more constructs (such as kind or cruel, shy or extroverted, happy or sad, playful or serious, emotional or stoic) to evaluate you. Obviously, everyone has a unique system of constructs, and some people clearly use more constructs than others. People who use a large number of different and abstract constructs that are well integrated are known as *cognitively complex*, while those who use fewer and less abstract constructs are cognitively simple.[2]

People who are more cognitively complex, compared to those who are not, are better at seeing the world from their listener's perspective. As a general rule, they are better at adapting their messages to their listeners and are much more persuasive.

When it comes to *being* persuaded, cognitively complex people may also differ from those who are cognitively simple. For instance, cognitively complex people may be more willing than people low in cognitive complexity to tolerate messages that are inconsistent with their cognitions. At least one study supports this notion. McGill, Johnson, and Bantel (1994) found that managers who were cognitively complex, compared to those who weren't, were more likely to resist the rigid norms of the organization and exhibit creative individualism. The implication is that cognitively complex managers may be better able to help their organizations adapt to changing environments.

In addition to being different in the degree to which they are cognitively complex, research shows that people differ in their *need for cognition* (Cacioppo & Petty, 1982). People who are high in the need for cognition enjoy effortful thinking more than those low in the need. We also bet they like playing chess and torturing themselves with logic puzzles! According to some researchers, need for cognition is one facet of cognitive complexity (McGill et al., 1994). Indeed, we imagine that a person who likes thinking would probably have a good number of perceptual constructs. Whatever the case, research shows that people high in the need for cognition are persuaded differently than their brain-resting counterparts. While people high in the need for cognition pay close attention to messages, evaluating and scrutinizing all the time, people low in the need for cognition are less motivated to attend to messages and are persuaded by peripheral cues instead (Cacioppo & Petty, 1982).[3] Thus, if you're high in the need for cognition, you are persuaded by quality arguments. If you're low in the need for cognition, you may be persuaded by an attractive speaker, a lot of examples, or a snappy-sounding sales pitch even if the arguments used are weak. For that reason, perhaps, once they are persuaded, people high in the need for cognition tend to stay persuaded longer than those who are low in the need for cognition (Haugtvedt & Petty, 1992).

Persuasion and Aggression: Sticks and Stones

Persuasion is not always pretty. Spouse abuse is rampant. Parents beating children as a way to get them to behave is all too common. And who hasn't been called "chicken," "wimp," "bitch," or "brat" by someone wanting to see a change in behavior? Clearly, aggression is the dark side of persuasion. On the other hand, Dominic Infante (1987) argues that aggression is not always bad; aggressive acts can be either constructive or destructive (or both), depending on the type of aggression and how it affects an interpersonal relationship (Infante, 1987; Infante & Rancer, 1982, 1995; Infante, Rancer, & Womack, 1997). According to Infante, the different types of aggressive communication are reflected in four personality traits, two of which are constructive, and two of which are destructive.

First, *assertiveness*, a constructive form of aggression, involves defending your rights and acting in your own best interest while, at the same time, not denying others' rights. Assertive people are not afraid to speak up, express their feelings, and take initiative. How does assertiveness relate to persuasion? According to Infante's (1987) sources, assertive people are likely to refuse unreasonable requests, initiate requests, actively disagree, and provide aggressive leadership.

Second, *argumentativeness*, involves the tendency to defend and refute positions on controversial issues. People who score high on the argumentativeness scale approach arguments, while those scoring low on the scale avoid arguments. Argumentativeness is different from assertiveness because argumentative people are assertive but assertive people are not always argumentative. Even so, argumentativeness, like assertiveness, is a constructive form of aggression. Although we sometimes have negative connotations about the word "argument," research shows that argumentativeness is associated with employee satisfaction (Infante & Gordon, 1991) and success in college (Infante, 1982). Interestingly, research has shown that men tend to be more argumentative than women (Nicotera & Rancer, 1994), but that such differences might be due to social desirability bias (Nicotera, 1996). In other words, women may not want to appear to be argumentative because they are concerned that, if they do, they may be perceived negatively.

The third form of aggression, *hostility,* is the tendency to be angry, and involves the expression of irritability, negativism, resentment, and suspicion (Infante et al., 1997). It is a destructive form of aggression and is related to persuasion. For instance, negativism, one dimension of hostility, refers to a tendency to be noncooperative and antagonistic toward authority, rules and conventions. Thus, a hostile person, in many respects, may be difficult to persuade. Moreover, because hostility is a learned trait, influence tactics can shape a hostile personality. In this regard, Infante and colleagues (1997) noted that parents who use physical punishment as a means of persuasion may make their children more aggressive and hostile. The children learn that "Hitting someone must be a good way to influence people; it certainly worked on me!" (Infante et al., 1997, p. 133).

Finally, *verbal aggressiveness,* involves the tendency to attack someone verbally by using threats, profanity, insults, and teasing, and by insulting their character, competence, background, appearance, and so forth (Infante et al., 1997; Infante, Riddle, Horvath, & Tumlin, 1992; Infante & Wigley, 1986). In short, verbal aggression is aimed at making others feel bad. Verbal aggression is different from hostility because verbally aggressive people are hostile but people can be hostile without being verbally aggressive. Even so, verbal aggressiveness, like hostility, is a destructive form of aggression. As might be expected, compared to nonviolent marriages, violent ones are characterized by higher verbal aggressiveness and lower argumentativeness (Infante, Chandler, & Rudd, 1989). Finally, Lim (1990) found that when partners resist compliance-gaining attempts in an unfriendly manner, verbal aggression is more likely to result.

Although most research on aggressive communication has focused on the ways in which an aggressive trait in *one* person affects communication, Levine and Boster (1996) have argued for a transactional approach to studying traits and communication. Specifically, they argue that to understand the impact of traits on communication, we have to understand that the traits of *all* participants in an interaction help shape the communication. To examine this notion, Levine and Boster (1996) conducted a study in which argumentative *and* nonargumentative people talked with argumentative and nonargumentative partners for 5 minutes about controversial topics (e.g., gun control, drug testing, legalizing drugs). Meanwhile, the researchers watched the conversations and recorded the number of arguments used and how disagreements were resolved. The results of the study were surprising: Although the researchers expected that the most arguments would be generated when argumentative people talked with other argumentative people, that's not what they found. Instead, when argumentative people were paired with nonargumentative people, the debates were more heated (i.e., the greatest number of arguments were generated and the least amount of agreement occurred). The researchers suspected that these results could have occurred because argumentative people may like winning arguments rather than argument for the sake of argument (Levine & Bostner, 1996):

> When paired with a less argumentative partner, such individuals seize on the opportunity to demonstrate superior skill…When dealing with equally argumentative conversational partners, however, highly argumentative individuals may be somewhat frustrated with their inability to dominate, with this frustration being reflected in their less assertive behavior. (p. 355)

Whatever the case, this study is important because it illustrates that an understanding of persuasion and traits may not be as simple as it sometimes seems. To be sure, knowledge of all participants' traits and dispositions may be necessary to fully understand the process of persuasion.

ANALYZING AND ADAPTING TO AUDIENCES

To us, the most entertaining part of Superbowl Sunday is its television advertisements. This, of course, is not surprising when you consider that businesses spend billions of dollars every year analyzing their audiences, trying to determine what will pique interests and sell products. Despite the big bucks, however, when attempting to market products to different cultural groups, businesses have made some pretty big blunders. Copeland and Griggs (1985) list some classic examples:

- Pan Am had to spend a great deal of money redoing and replacing billboards that showed a reclining Japanese woman. The problem? In Japan, only prostitutes recline.
- Latin Americans confused Parker Pen's slogan "Prevent embarrassment—use Parker Ink" for a birth control ad. Why? "Embarazo," the Spanish word for embarrassment, actually means "pregnancy."
- In the United States, the Japanese tried to market a baby soap called "Skina-babe."
- Imagine how those in the auto industry felt when they learned that, in Spanish, Nova means "It doesn't go"; in Portuguese, Pinto is slang for "a small male organ"; and Esso, pronounced phonetically in Japanese, means "stalled car."

The lesson here is simple: if you want to be influential, know who you are talking to and adapt accordingly. This, to us, seems to be what persuasion is all about—adapting a message so that it coincides with the receiver's frame of reference. To be sure, a persuader doesn't move the receiver to where the message is, the persuader moves the message to where the receiver is. It's what's called being "market-driven" in business, "audience-centered" in public speaking, and "listener-oriented" in interpersonal communication. To persuade other people, it helps to know as much as possible about them so you can appeal to their needs and wants, while, at the same time, avoid offending them. Of course, attempting to be too diplomatic can go too far. For example, we once heard a story of some people who asked a politician where he stood on a particular issue. So as not to alienate anyone, the politician replied, "Some of my friends are for it, some of my friends are against it, and I'm for my friends." If we'd have been in the audience, we would not have been impressed. Thus, it's important to adapt to an audience without coming across as insincere, "smooth," or deceptive.

Given that there have been entire books written on audience analysis (e.g., Clevinger, 1966), we cannot give full treatment to the topic here. With that said, however, we have listed a few guidelines that might be useful if you're ever faced with an audience that needs to be analyzed:

Pay attention to the situation. Remember what we discussed earlier in the chapter: Communicator characteristics *and* situations affect how audiences will respond to persuasive messages. Knowing details about some aspects of the situation can be useful when preparing to persuade someone. For instance, will you be talking to one person or a large audience? Will the setting be noisy, hot, colorful? Will the persuasion occur in the morning or evening? Will you be inside or out, in

"Fellow-earthlings . . ."

a church, or on a football field? Might there be hecklers? Are you expected to talk for 5 minutes or can you blab for hours?

Obviously, the number of possible situations is endless. Even so, knowing something about the situation can help you adapt. It's important to try to put yourself in the shoes of your audience. Try to figure out what would persuade and appeal to you if you were in their situation and then adapt your message accordingly.

Keep audience traits, states, and goals in mind. You know by now that communicator traits and states play a large role in persuasion. It's something to keep in mind if you're ever confronted by someone with the traits and/or in the states we've discussed. For example, we noted that anxious people require specific recommendations and reassurances when using fear appeals and that high self-monitors respond well to messages that promise to help them "fit in." People with certain traits may be more difficult to persuade, but if you keep in mind that ego-involved people have narrow latitudes of acceptance, and that dogmatics and authoritarians respond better to people in powerful positions, you'll be better equipped as a persuader.

Don't forget about audience demographics. As you've learned from reading this chapter, demographics play a large role in the process of persuasion. And a person who can adapt to people of different ages, genders, cultures and so forth obviously will be more successful than a person who can't. For example, when speaking to small children, using lots of statistics would probably lead to lots of "ants in the pants." By the same token, a group of senior citizens would probably squirm or snooze if forced to listen to a speech about planning for pregnancy.[4] Moreover, although we noted that there do not appear to be gender differences in persuadability, it doesn't mean a speaker can ignore the gender of *her* audience. Notice, for example, by using the word "her" in the previous sentence, we failed to address males who might be reading this book. In short, we're sure you get the point: Whenever possible, know about your audience's age, gender, socioeconomic status, and so forth. Then adapt.

SUMMARY

In this chapter we discussed several communicator characteristics that affect the process of persuasion. First, we examined demographic variables, noting that some (e.g., age, ethnicity) influence the sending and receiving of persuasive messages, while others (e.g., gender) do not appear to be related to influenceability. Second, we discussed the trait and situationist debate and showed how several psychological and communication states and traits (i.e., self-esteem, anxiety, self-monitoring, ego-involvement, dogmatism, authoritarianism, cognitive complexity, need for cognition, and aggression) influence persuasive communication. Finally, we examined the notion of audience analysis indicating that persuaders, when possible, should attempt to adapt to the needs, wants, backgrounds, and so forth of their audience.

ENDNOTES

1. One of the studies reviewed by Rhodes and Wood (1992) showed support for a curvilinear relationship between intelligence and influence-ability (i.e., moderately intelligent people were more easily persuaded than people of low or high intelligence).

2. Although cognitive complexity may be related to intelligence, it is not the same thing.

3. A person who is very involved in an issue will act similar to a person who is high in the need for cognition. However, need for cognition is a trait and will therefore affect attention to a variety of messages. On the other hand, a person with a lot of involvement will have a high need for cognition only on topics relevant to the issue in which he or she is involved.

4. A study by Hummert and Shaner (1994) found that when people held negative stereotypes towards someone elderly, they tended to use a more patronizing speech style. Thus, attempting to adapt to an audience might also backfire if done inappropriately.

REFERENCES

Adorno, T., Frenkel-Brunswik, E., Levinson, D. & Sanford, N. (1950). *The authoritarian personality.* New York: Harper.

Allport, G. W. (1954). *The nature of prejudice.* Reading, MA: Addison-Wesley.

Alwin, D. F., & Krosnick, J. A. (1991). Aging, cohorts, and the stability of sociopolitical orientations over the lifespan. *American Journal of Sociology, 97*, 169–195.

Andrews, P. H. (1987). Gender differences in persuasive communication and the attribution of success and failure. *Human Communication Research, 13*, 372–385.

Atkin, C., Hocking, J., & Block, M. (1984). Teenage drinking: Does advertising make a difference? *Journal of Communication, 34*, 157–169.

Becherer, R. G., Morgan, F., & Richard, L. M. (1982). Informal group influence among situationally/dispositionally-oriented consumers. *Journal of the Academy of Marketing Science, 10*, 269–281.

Becherer, R. G., & Richard, L. M. (1978). Self-monitoring as a moderating variable in consumer behavior. *Journal of Consumer Research, 5*, 159–162.

Becker, B. J. (1986). Influence again: An examination of reviews and studies of gender differences in social influence. In J. S. Hyde & M. C. Linn (Eds.), *The psychology of gender: Advances through meta-analysis* (pp. 178–209). Baltimore: Johns Hopkins University Press.

Burgoon, M., Hunsaker, F. G., & Dawson, E. J. (1994). *Human communication* (3rd ed.). Thousand Oaks, CA: Sage.

Cacioppo, J. T., & Petty, R. E. (1982). The need for cognition. *Journal of Personality and Social Psychology, 42*, 116–131.

Carli, L. L. (1990). Gender, language, and influence. *Journal of Personality and Social Psychology, 59*, 941–951.

Carli, L. L., LaFleur, S. J., & Loeber, C. C. (1995). Nonverbal behavior, gender, and influence. *Journal of Personality and Social Psychology, 68*, 1030–1041.

Chaiken, S. (1979). Communicator physical attractiveness and persuasion. *Journal of Personality and Social Psychology, 37*, 1387–1397.

Christie, R. (1991). Authoritarianism and related constructs. In J. P. Robinson, P. R. Shaver, & L. S. Wrightsman (Eds.), *Measures of personality and social psychological attitudes* (pp. 501–571). San Diego, CA: Academic Press.

Clark, R. A., & Delia, J. G. (1976). The development of functional persuasive skills in childhood and early adolescence. *Child Development, 47*, 1008–1014.

Clevenger, T., Jr. (1966). *Audience analysis.* New York: Bobbs-Merrill.

Cody, M. J., Seiter, J. S., & Montagne-Miller, Y. (1995). Men and women in the marketplace. In P. J. Kalbfleisch & M. J. Cody (Eds.) *Gender, power, and communication in human relation-ships* (pp. 305–330). Hillsdale, NJ: Erlbaum.

Condra, J., Berne, P., & Scheibe, C. (1988). Nonpro-gram content of children's television. *Journal of Broadcasting and Electric Media, 32,* 255–270.

Copeland, L., & Griggs, L. (1985). *Going interna-tional: How to make friends and deal effectively in the global marketplace.* New York: Random House.

DeBono, K. G., & Klein, C. (1993). Source expertise and persuasion: The moderating role of recip-ient dogmatism. *Personality and Social Psychol-ogy Bulletin, 19,* 167–173.

Delia, J. G., & Crockett, W. H. (1973). Social sche-mas, cognitive complexity, and the learning of social structures. *Journal of Personality, 41,* 413–429.

Delia, J. G., Kline, S. L., & Burleson, B. R. (1979). The development of persuasive communica-tion strategies in kindergartners through twelfth-graders. *Communication Monographs, 46,* 241–256.

Delia, J. G., O'Keefe, B. J., & O'Keefe, D. J. (1982). The constructivist approach to communica-tion. In F. E. X. Dance (Ed.), *Human communi-cation theory* (pp. 147–191). New York: Harper & Row.

deTurck, M. (1985). A transactional analysis of com-pliance-gaining behavior: Effects of noncom-pliance, relational contexts and actor's gender. *Human Communication Research, 12,* 54–78.

Eagly, A. H. (1978). Sex differences in influence-ability. *Psychological Bulletin, 85,* 86–116.

Eagly, A. H., & Carli, L. L. (1981). Sex of research-ers and sex-typed communications as deter-minants of sex differences in influenceability: A meta-analysis of social influence studies. *Psychological Bulletin, 90,* 1–20.

Gudykunst, W. W., & Ting-Toomey, S. (1988). *Cul-ture and interpersonal communication.* Newbury Park, CA: Sage.

Groutage, H. (1995a, July 14). Missing "wife" is a wife not at all. *Deseret News Archives,* p. 2.

Groutage, H. (1995b, July 26). Was fake wife a phony doctor? *Deseret News Archives,* p. 2.

Han, S., & Shavitt, S. (1994). Persuasion and cul-ture: Advertising appeals in individualistic and collectivistic societies. *Journal of Experi-mental Social Psychology, 30,* 326–350.

Harvey, O. J., & Beverly, G. D. (1961). Some per-sonality correlates of concept change through role playing. *Journal of Abnormal and Social Psychology, 63,* 125–130.

Haslett, B. (1983). Preschoolers' communicative strategies in gaining compliance from peers: A developmental study. *Quarterly Journal of Speech, 69,* 84–99.

Haugtvedt, C. P., & Petty, R. E. (1992). Personality and persuasion: Need for cognition moder-ates the persistence and resistance of attitude changes. *Journal of Personality and Social Psy-chology, 63,* 308–319.

Hendon, D. W., McGann, A. F., & Hendon, B. L. (1978). Children's age, intelligence, and sex as variables mediating reaction to TV commer-cials: Repetition and content complexity impli-cations for advertisers. *Journal of Advertising, 7,* 4–12.

Hofstede, G. (1983). Dimensions of national cul-tures in fifty countries and three regions. In J. Deregowski, S. Dzuirawiec, & R. Annis (Eds.), *Explications in cross-cultural psychology.* Lisse, The Netherlands: Swets and Zeitlinger.

Hummert, M. L., & Shaner, J. L. (1994). Patronizing speech to the elderly as a function of stereotyp-ing. *Communication Studies, 45,* 145–158.

Infante, D. A. (1987). Aggressiveness. In J. C. McCroskey & J. A. Daly (Eds.), *Personality and interpersonal communication* (pp. 157–192), Newbury Park, CA: Sage.

Infante, D. A. (1982). The argumentative student in the speech communication classroom: An investigation and implications. *Communica-tion Education, 3,* 141–148.

Infante, D. A., Chandler, T. A., & Rudd, J. E. (1989). Test of an argumentative skill deficiency model of interspousal violence. *Communica-tion Monographs, 56,* 163–177.

Infante, D. A., & Gordon, W. I. (1991). How em-ployees see the boss: Test of an argumentative and affirming model of supervisors commu-nicative behavior. *Western Journal of Speech Communication, 55,* 294–304.

Infante, D. A., & Rancer, A. S. (1995). Argumenta-tiveness and verbal aggressiveness: A review of recent theory and research. In B. R. Burle-son (Ed.), *Communication yearbook 19* (pp. 319–351). Thousand Oaks, CA: Sage.

Infante, D. A., & Rancer, A. S. (1982). A conceptualization and measure of argumentativeness. *Journal of Personality Assessment, 46,* 60–69.

Infante, D. A., Rancer, A. S., & Womack, D. F. (1997). *Building communication theory* (3rd ed.), Prospect Heights, Ill: Waveland Press.

Infante, D. A., Riddle, B. L., Horvath, C. L., & Tumlin, S. A. (1992). Verbal aggressiveness in violent and nonviolent marital disputes. *Communication Quarterly, 38,* 361–371.

Infante, D. A., & Wigley, C. J., III. (1986). Verbal aggressiveness: An interpersonal model and measure. *Communication Monographs, 53,* 61–69.

Janis, I. L., & Field, P. B. (1959). A behavioral assessment of persuadability. In C. I. Hovland & I. L. Janis (Eds.), *Personality and persuadability* (pp. 29–54). New Haven, CT: Yale University Press.

Janis, I. L., & Feshbach, S. (1965). Effects of fear-arousing communications. *Journal of Personality and Social Psychology, 1,* 17–27.

Janis, I. L., Hovland, C. I., Field, P. B., Linton, H., Graham, E., Cohen, A. R., Rife, D., Abelson, R., Lesser, G. S., & King, B. T. (1959). *Personality and persuadability.* New Haven, CT: Yale University Press.

Krahé, B. (1992). *Personality and social psychology: Towards a synthesis.* London: Sage.

Krosnick, J. A., & Alwin, D. F. (1989). Aging and susceptibility to attitude change. *Journal of Personality and Social Psychology, 57,* 23–30.

Lehmann, S. (1970). Personality and compliance: A study of anxiety and self-esteem in opinion and behavior change. *Journal of Personality and Social Psychology, 15,* 76–86.

Levine, T. R., & Boster, F. J. (1996). The impact of self and others' argumentativeness on talk about controversial issues. *Communication Quarterly, 44*(3), 345–358.

Lim, T. (1990). The influences of receivers' resistance on persuaders' verbal aggressiveness. *Communication Quarterly, 38,* 170–188.

Maccoby, E. E., & Jacklin, C. (1974). *Psychology and sex differences.* Stanford, CA: Stanford University Press.

Making sure crime doesn't pay. (1995, September 26). Deseret News Archives, 12.

McGill, A. R., Johnson, M. D., & Bantel, K. A. (1994). Cognitive complexity and conformity:

Effects on performance in a turbulent environment. *Psychological Reports, 75,* 1451–1472.

McGuire, W. J. (1968a). Personality and attitude change: An information-processing theory. In A. G. Greenwald, T. C. Brock, & T. M. Ostrom (Eds.), *Psychological foundations of attitudes* (pp. 171–196). San Diego, CA: Academic Press.

McGuire, W. J. (1968b). Personality and susceptibility to social influence. In E. F. Borgatta & W. W. Lambert (Eds.), *Handbook of personality theory and research* (pp. 1130–1187). Chicago: Rand McNally.

McGuire, W. J. (1985). Attitudes and attitude change. In G. Lindzey & E. Aronson (Eds.), *Handbook of social psychology* (Vol. 2, 3rd ed., pp. 233–346). New York: Random House.

Miller, L. C., & Read, S. J. (1991). Inter-personalism: Understanding persons in relationships. *Advances in personal relationships, 2,* 233–267.

Minow, N. N., & LaMay, C. L. (1995). *Abandoned in the wasteland: Children, television, and the first amendment.* New York: Hill and Wang.

Mischel, W. (1968). *Personality and assessment.* New York: John Wiley & Sons.

Narby, D. J., Cutler, B. L., & Moran, G. (1993). A meta-analysis of the association between authoritarianism and jurors' perceptions of defendant culpability. *Journal of Applied Psychology, 78,* 34–42.

Nicotera, A. M. (1996). An assessment of the argumentativeness scale for social desirability bias. *Communication Research, 9,* 22–35.

Nicotera, A. M., & Rancer, A. S. (1994). The influence of sex on self-perceptions and social stereotyping of aggressive communication predispositions. *Communication Research, 7,* 283–307.

Nunnally, J. C., & Bobren, H. M. (1959). Variables concerning the willingness to receive communications on mental health. *Journal of Personality, 27,* 275–290.

Ogletree, S. M., Williams, S. W., Raffeld, P., & Mason, B. (1990). Female attractiveness and eating disorders: Do children's television commercials play a role? *Sex Roles, 22,* 791–797.

Perloff, R. M. (1994). Attributions, self-esteem, and cognitive responses to persuasion. *Psychological Reports, 75,* 1291–1295.

Reid, L. N. (1979). The impact of family group interaction on children's understanding of television advertising. *Journal of Advertising, 8,* 13–19.

Rhodes, N., & Wood, W. (1992). Self-esteem and intelligence affect influenceability: The mediating role of message reception. *Psychological Bulletin, 111,* 156–171.

Rokeach, M. (1960). *The open and closed mind.* New York: Basic Books.

Rosen, M. D. (1994, August). "Don't talk to strangers." *Ladies Home Journal, 111,* pp. 108, 109, 153, 154.

Scheidel, T. M. (1963). Sex and persuadability. *Speech Monographs, 30,* 353–358.

Sherif, C. W., Kelly, M., Rodgers, H. L., Jr., Sarup, G., & Tittler, B. I. (1973). Personal involvement, social judgment and action. *Journal of Personality and Social Psychology, 27,* 311–328.

Sherif, M., & Sherif, C. W. (1967). Attitudes as the individual's own categories: The social-judgment approach to attitude and attitude change. In C. W. Sherif & M. Sherif (Eds.), *Attitude, ego-involvement, and change* (pp. 105–139). New York: John Wiley & Sons.

Sherif, C. W., Sherif, M., & Nebergall, R. E. (1965). *Attitude and attitude change: The social judgment-involvement approach.* Philadelphia: W. B. Sauders.

Snyder, M. (1974). Self-monitoring of expressive behavior. *Journal of Personality and Social Psychology, 30,* 526–537.

Snyder, M. (1979). Self-monitoring processes. In L. Berkowitz (Ed.). *Advances in experimental and social psychology* (Vol. 12, pp. 85–128). New York: Academic Press.

Snyder, M., & DeBono, K. G. (1989). Understanding the functions of attitudes: Lessons from personality and social behavior. In A. R. Pratkanis, S. J. Brecklet, & A. G. Greenwald (Eds.), *Attitude structure and function* (pp. 339–359). Hillsdale, NJ: Erlbaum.

"Teaching fear" (1986, March 10). *Newsweek, 107,* 62–62.

Ward, D. A., Seccombe, K., Bendel, R., & Carter, L. F. (1985). Cross-sex context as a factor in persuadability sex differences. *Social Psychology Quarterly, 48,* 269–276.

Ward, S., & Wackman, D. (1972). Children's influence attempts and parental yielding. *Journal of Marketing Research, 9,* 316–319.

White, M. J., & Gerstein, L. H. (1987). Helping: The influence of anticipated social sanctions and self-monitoring. *Journal of Personality, 55,* 41–54.

White, P. H., & Harkins, S. G. (1994). Race of source effects in the Elaboration Likelihood Model. *Journal of Personality and Social Psychology, 67,* 790–807.

Wiman, A. R. (1985). Parental influence and children's responses to television advertising. *Journal of Advertising, 12,* 12–18.

Wiseman, R. L., Sanders, J. A., Congalton, J. K., Gass, R. H., Jr., Sueda, K., & Ruiqing, D. (1995). A cross-cultural analysis of compliance gaining: China, Japan, and the United States. *Intercultural Communication Studies, 1,* 1–18.

Wooden, K. (1988, June). "How sex offenders lure our children." *Reader's Digest, 132,* 149–154.

7

CONFORMITY AND INFLUENCE IN GROUPS

Bo, Peep, sheep, and the Hale-Bopp comet may sound like the makings of a good fairy-tale, but, as the saying goes, truth is stranger than fiction, and, unfortunately, the story of Bo and Peep's sheep is a true one. We refer to the people of the Heaven's Gate cult as sheep because it's hard for us to imagine who else but sheep would believe what these people were told—that they should commit mass suicide so they might shed their bodies and be whisked away by an alien spaceship that was flying around in the tail of the Hale-Bopp comet. Whether they believed it or not, they did what their leaders, Bo and Peep, told them to do. In late March of 1997, sheriff's deputies found the corpses of 21 women and 18 men decomposing in a home in Rancho Santa Fe, California. All of the members of the cult had apparently ingested a fatal mixture of phenobarbital, applesauce, pudding, and vodka (Chua-Eoan, 1997; Gleick, 1997b).

As authors who are interested in the process of social influence, we can't help but wonder how and why people like those in the Heaven's Gate cult can be persuaded to such extremes. Clearly, several factors must have contributed to the largest mass suicide in U.S. history. The cult members—though reportedly bright and happy—must have been highly persuadable. Moreover, the leaders of the cult, Marshall Herff Applewhite and Bonnie Lu Nettles (also known as Bo and Peep, Him and Her, and Ti and Do), were highly charismatic and trusted by their followers, who believed that Bo and Peep, like Jesus Christ, were extraterrestrial representatives of the "Kingdom Level Above Humans." But beyond the characteristics of the cult leaders and members, we believe that a strong group dynamic may have contributed to the suicide. Indeed, although from society's perspective the members of the cult were deviants, there seemed to be pressure within the cult to "fit in." For instance, the members of the cult reportedly looked the same, so much so that when the corpses were first discovered, they were believed to be men only. The cult members were described as having an androgynous appearance; the women wore cropped hair and many of the men, including the cult's leader, had been castrated. Finally, the cult members were known to dress the same, wearing what one person described as black pajamas. When the 39 corpses were found, each was dressed in black: black pants, black shirt, and brand-new, black Nike shoes (Gleick, 1997b).

We imagine that, if nothing else, being a member of a cult satisfies a need to belong. Cults often attract new members by providing a seemingly loving environment for their new recruits. Along with this, however, comes pressure to fit in. Cults often have strict rules and regimens on how to behave if you want to be a member. For example, according to Gleick (1997b), in the Heaven's Gate cult:

> *Bo had recruits follow detailed schedules—waking for prayer at precise times, taking vitamins at, say, 7:22 P.M., consuming yeast rolls and liquid protein—and had them do drills, mental and physical, to prepare the flock for outer space. According to a man named Michael, who was with the cult from 1975 to 1988, recruits experimented with their sleeping patterns and their diets, trying to break down their bodies so they would be "under control." The discipline, he said, was "shame based," and when Michael wanted to leave, he was told he was free to go. (p. 35)*

With such pressure to fit in, it's easier to see how a cult member might have been sucked into the suicide. When you identify so strongly with people who are carrying out some action, the action not only seems more "right," it becomes necessary for you to participate if you want to be part of the group. This is true not only in cults, but in other social collectives as well. Families, peer groups, work places, even classrooms, exert strong pressure on their members to behave in certain ways. Groups are a powerful persuasive force. For that reason, this chapter examines the role of groups in the process of social influence. We begin by discussing the topic of conformity and then examine what happens when groups make people less aware of themselves and less responsible for their own actions. Finally, we discuss how groups can affect the decisions that an individual might make.

CONFORMITY AS PERSUASION: IN WITH THE CROWD

During a lecture by a sociology professor, in a classroom that held over 100 people, an undergraduate student, known by both of your authors, removed his shirt, pants, shoes, and socks. Then, almost naked, he stood in the aisle of the classroom waiting to be noticed. The professor, who had been looking down at his notes, did not notice our friend until other people in the classroom began gasping and laughing. When the professor finally did look up, he was stunned. Undaunted, the nearly naked student looked down at himself and asked, "Does this count?"

Apparently, just before the student had disrobed, the professor had been lecturing on the topic of norms and conformity. *Norms* are expectations held by a group of people about what behaviors or opinions are right or wrong, good or bad, acceptable or unacceptable, appropriate or inappropriate (Andrews, 1996). Once norms are understood, we feel pressure to conform to them. Of course, the professor had probably explained to our friend and his other students that some norms are explicit. *Explicit norms* are written or spoken openly. For example, road signs indicate how fast you are permitted to drive, employee manuals may tell you how to dress, and game rules may send you to jail without collecting two hundred dollars. On the other hand, some norms are *implicit* and not so openly stated. For example, most of us don't need be told that it's inappropriate to wave and say hello to everyone we pass on the streets of a big city. We also imagine that when you're a guest in someone's home, you don't put your feet on the dinner table even though you've never read a rule saying you shouldn't. Likewise—and this is what the sociology professor told his class—because we all conform to social norms, no one would take his or her clothes off in the middle of a classroom lecture. Of course, our friend, who prides himself on being a nonconformist, couldn't resist this challenge. The rest is history, and the professor now has a good story to tell whenever he lectures about norms and conformity.

In the Beginning: Early Research on Conformity Effects

Not everyone is like our friend, the student–stripper in the sociology class. As we've noted, in most cases, people know the norms and try to go along with the crowd. One of the first researchers to examine this conformity effect was Muzafer Sherif (1935). Sherif used an optical illusion called the *autokinetic effect* to show how groups can influence an individual's behavior. Here's how the autokinetic effect works: If you are sitting in a dark room and look at a pinpoint of light, the light appears to move even when it is stationary. Try it with your friends or roommates some time. Each will say the light moved, but they may differ in their judgments, some thinking the light moved an inch, others thinking it moved even farther. This is exactly what Sherif found until he brought all of his subjects together and tried the experiment again. This time he allowed his subjects to report out loud how far they thought the light moved. Interestingly, Sherif found that after a while the individuals' judgments began to converge. The individuals began to conform, agreeing on a midpoint of light movement. Moreover, Sherif found that when the subjects went back to being tested alone, the effect of the group stuck; subjects' judgments regarding light movements were closer to the group's judgments than they were to the subjects' original judgments while alone.

Although Sherif's study is frequently cited in the literature on social influence, perhaps the most compelling experiment on the effects of conformity was conducted by Solomon Asch (1956). Here's how his experiment worked: Asch gathered several (7 to 9) college students into a classroom and told them that they would be participating in an experiment in visual judgment. The students were asked to look at two large, white cards like the ones shown in Figure 7.1. As can be seen, a single vertical line appeared on the first card, while three vertical lines, each with differing lengths, appeared on the second card. The students' task was simple: After observing both cards, they were asked to match lines. That is, each student was asked to report out loud, to the rest of the group, which of the three lines on the second card was the same length as the line on the other card.

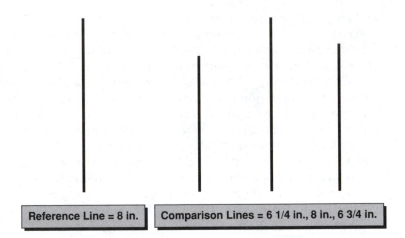

FIGURE 7.1   Example of cards used in Asch's experiment. Subjects are asked which of the three lines on the comparison card (right) match the line on the reference card (left).

According to Asch (1966), the experiment begins uneventfully but changes rapidly:

> The subjects announce their answers in the order in which they have been seated in the room, and on the first round every person chooses the same matching line. Then a second set of cards is exposed: Again the group is unanimous. The members appear ready to endure politely another boring experiment. On the third trial there is an unexpected disturbance. One person near the end of the group disagrees with all the others in his selection of the matching line. He looks surprised, indeed incredulous, about the disagreement. On the following trial he disagrees again, while the others remain unanimous in their choice. The dissenter becomes more and more worried and hesitant as the disagreement continues in succeeding trials; he may pause before announcing his answer and speak in a low voice, or he may smile in an embarrassed way. (p. 320)

What the dissenting student in Asch's study did not know was that all of the other students in the group were confederates; they were planted in the group by Asch and told beforehand to give the wrong answers in 12 of the 18 trials that were used in the experiment. In other words, Asch was really interested in what a person would do when he or she was giving correct answers that are contrary to the answers of a near-unanimous group decision. Would the person give what he or she believed to be the correct answer, or would he or she refuse to rock the boat and choose to go along with the crowd? What Asch found was that conformity was common; under group pressure, 75 percent of the subjects gave the wrong answer in at least one of the trials.

In short, then, Asch's experiment illustrates the tremendous power of groups to exert influence. Even when subjects believed they knew the right answer, they gave what they believed was a wrong answer in order to fit in. Even so, not all of Asch's subjects behaved in the same way. For instance, about 25 percent remained fairly independent, rarely conforming to the group's answers. Moreover, about 10 percent of the subjects agreed with the group on almost every trial. Thus, it is probably true that some individuals are more prone to conformity than others. In addition, some situations may produce more conformity than others. In the following sections, we examine some of the variables that lead to more or less conformity.

Variables Related to Conformity

Does Group Size Affect Conformity?:
The More the Scarier?

One perspective on conformity, called *social impact theory* (Latané, 1981; Latané, & Wolf, 1981), suggests that as a group becomes larger, its members are more likely to conform, although each new member has less impact than the person that was added just before him or her. In short, it doesn't matter how many people we add; each new member will increase pressure to conform.

An alternative perspective, called the *social influence model* (Tanford & Penrod, 1984), suggests that the first person added to a group does not have the most impact, because with only one other person, the dissenter is not in the minority. Instead, the second or third person influences conformity the most. After three or four people are added, the pressure to conform levels off, perhaps because as group size increases, complete agreement among all members becomes less believable; thus, a dissenter in a group may "smell a rat," begin to suspect collusion among the other group members, and be less likely to conform (see Insko, Smith, Alicke, Wade, & Taylor, 1985).

Empirical results and meta-analyses on which is the better of these two perspectives are mixed (see Bond & Smith, 1996; Latané & Wolf, 1981; Tanford & Penrod, 1984); some studies support one perspective, some the other, and some neither. After reviewing the literature, we suspect that both models have found support because both models may be accurate. The models only seem contradictory until you consider an additional variable. Specifically, Campbell and Fairey (1989) argued that when you are making a decision in a group, you are motivated by two things: You want to be right and you want to be liked (see also Insko et al., 1985). According to these authors, sometimes we conform to a group because the group has *informational influence*. That is, we have a desire to be right and we conform to the group because we think the group may be correct. On the other hand, sometimes we conform to a group because it has *normative influence*. This means that even when we know the group is wrong, we may conform so that we gain rewards (e.g., liking) and avoid punishments (e.g., scorn) that are associated with agreement and disagreement.

What does this have to do with group size? According to Campbell and Fairey (1989), increasing the number of people in a group affects informational and normative processes differently. Specifically, the first person added to the group provides the most information. Additional people have less informational value because their judgments may be redundant. In contrast, each person added to a group substantially increases the group's normative influence. Obviously, it's more uncomfortable disagreeing with four people than it is disagreeing with one person. With this in mind, Campbell and Fairey (1989) argued that in contexts in which people are mostly concerned about being right, social impact theory is most accurate in predicting the effects of size on conformity (i.e., the first person added to a group exerts the most influence). On the other hand, in contexts where people are concerned with being liked, the social influence model is most accurate in predicting the effects of size on conformity (i.e., the second and third members added to a group have the most impact). In a research study, these hypotheses were tested and confirmed (Campbell & Fairey, 1989) (for more on size on conformity, see Box 7.1).

Security in Numbers: The Effect of More than One Dissenter

In the classic movie *Twelve Angry Men*, a jury is asked to decide whether a young Puerto Rican boy is innocent or guilty of stabbing his abusive father to death. The decision seems to be an easy one, at least for 11 of the jury members; they all believe that the defendant is guilty. Only one of the jurors, played by Henry Fonda, believes there is a reasonable shadow of doubt regarding the defendant's guilt. As you can probably imagine, Henry has a rough time of it—at least to begin with. The other members of the jury deride and ridicule, trying to make him conform. Finally, he asks for a vote. If the vote is 11 to 1 against him, he promises to go along with the rest of the jury. When the vote is taken, however, it ends up being 10 to 2. Henry has convinced an older man that the defendant is innocent, and as you might have guessed, with an ally, Henry is much more confident in his judgment. He goes on to convince the rest of the jury that the accused man is truly innocent.

BOX 7.1   Majority Rules?: How to Influence When You're Alone In A Group

So far this chapter has discussed the ways in which a majority of people can influence a minority. As many minority groups have illustrated throughout history, however, influence is not always so simple. Sometimes the minority can influence the majority.

According to a review of research by Tanford and Penrod (1984), two strategies that a minority can try are to first conform with the group and then deviate and to consistently disagree with the group. The first tactic involves accumulating what might popularly be known as brownie points. Specifically, by going along

with the group on most issues, you are more favorable in the group's eyes when you disagree. As a result, you may actually convince the group to go along with your point of view. In contrast, the second tactic involves disagreeing with the group consistently. By doing this, whoever holds the minority point of view looks more confident and may get the group's attention (Moscovici & Faucheux, 1972; Moscovici, Lage, & Naffrechoux, 1969). Of course, these two tactics involve opposite behaviors, so if you're in the minority, don't try both; pick one tactic and stick to it.

How likely is this to happen outside of Hollywood? Although we're not sure about convincing an entire jury, research indicates that having an ally helps a person resist conforming to a group. For example, Allen and Levine (1969) found that a single subject is likely to conform when he or she is faced with four other people who disagree, but if one of those four side with the subject, the subject continues to dissent. Asch (1966) reported similar findings, noting that the presence of a supporting partner caused his subjects to conform only one fourth as often as when faced with a unanimous majority. Interestingly, this seems to be the case even when the supporting partner's judgments are questionable. For example, Allen and Levine (1971) found that when trying to make judgments about visual stimuli, even a supporting partner who seemed visually impaired (e.g., wore thick glasses and seemed to have a hard time seeing) prevented subjects from conforming. Moreover, Asch (1966) reported that even when the partner's judgment was clearly inaccurate, conformity decreased. Specifically, in a study where the partner disagreed with both the subject and the majority by choosing a line that clearly did not match a comparison line, the subject was more likely to disagree with the majority.

Thus, it appears that having an ally, whether that ally is one that completely agrees with you or not, can help you resist the pressures of a majority. This is most likely because an ally provides reassurance. Indeed, Asch (1966) noted that when his subjects had support from one other person, they felt warm and close to the person, crediting him with inspiring confidence.

Initiation and Identification: Attractive Groups Promote Conformity

Past research makes it clear that attractive people tend to be more persuasive than unattractive ones. This same principle holds true for groups; attractive groups are more influential than unattractive ones. Thus, we tend to conform to groups that

we value and consider attractive. But what makes a group attractive? Two factors that affect how much you value a group include the nature of your initiation into the group and how much you identify with the group.

The only time one of your authors was formally initiated into a group, his high school's Varsity Club, he had to wear a dress and sing Christmas carols in a shopping mall (it wasn't even Christmas time!). Of course, there are more severe initiations than this. For instance, a gang in Southern California initiates its new members by allowing the rest of the gang to beat the new members. We also once heard the story of a fraternity hazing that resulted in a death; the initiate was forced to drink so much alcohol that he passed out, was thought to be asleep, and was not discovered to be dead until the next afternoon when he was still laying on the frat house's floor. And finally a story that aired on CNN discussed "blood pinning," a sadistic way in which some Marines are initiated into the military. Apparently, after completing 10 training jumps, Marine paratroopers receive a golden-winged pin with two large points on the back. To congratulate them, other Marines "take turns punching, pounding and grinding the gold pins into the bloody chests of the new initiates, who scream and writhe in pain" (Gleick, 1997a, p. 30). As brutal as the ritual sounds, Gleick (1997a) noted that it has a long history in the corps and that many "jarheads" insist that it is an important part of Marine bonding. Interestingly enough, this may be true. Research suggests that we value a group more if our initiation into the group is severe (e.g., Aronson & Mills, 1959). The reasoning goes something like this: If we have to pay a large price to get into a group, we convince ourselves that the pain was worth it by valuing the group more. Without such a rationalization, we'd feel pretty dumb about tolerating such a painful or humiliating initiation.[1] After singing Christmas carols in a dress, your author was as loyal as could be to his club and is convinced that part of the reason is the humiliation he suffered as a result of the initiation.

In addition to the ways in which we are initiated into a group, identification, or the degree to which we identify with a group, also determines how much we value it. The notion of identification is central to Kenneth Burke's (1950) conceptualization of rhetoric. According to Burke, identification occurs when people are united in substance (e.g., when they share attitudes, activities, ideas, possession, and so forth). Burke argued that although humans are fundamentally divided, they are motivated to communicate with one another to create identification. The notion of identification is important here because the more a person identifies with a group, the more power that group has to influence that person.

A group that has the power to influence us through the process of identification is known as a *reference group*. Of course not all groups are reference groups. For example, you might get together with several other students to study for a test. It's unlikely that such a group would exert much influence on the way you think and behave on a daily basis. On the other hand, a group of people whom you admire and want to be like might have a strong impact on you, oftentimes without your even knowing it. Because we identify with reference groups, we tend to dress the way they dress, think the way they think, and act the way they act. With this in mind, it's not surprising that a considerable amount of research indicates that we tend to conform more to a group of people who are similar to us than to a group of people who are not (Abrams, Wetherell, Cochrane, Hogg, & Turner, 1990; Bond & Smith, 1996; Lott & Lott, 1961). Friends, for example, probably foster conformity more than strangers. Moreover, we imagine that groups such as Alcoholics Anonymous owe much of their success to the degree of identification that exists between their members. In particular, it seems to us that sitting around and listening to a lot of nonalcoholics preach about setting one's life straight would not have the same impact as participating in a group in which other alcoholics discuss the importance of not drinking and demonstrate their successes.

In the case of Alcoholics Anonymous and other groups, it's apparent that identification can be a good thing. On the other hand, Seiter (1998) argued that although a great deal of instruction in the field of communication promotes identification, fitting in, and getting along with others (see also Redding, 1985), we must be cautious in doing so precisely because identification and the conformity it fosters can lead to negative consequences in a variety of communication contexts. For example, in intercultural contexts, *ethnocentrism*, or the belief that one's culture is the standard by which all others should be evaluated, occurs when members of a culture identify too strongly with their own culture. In small group contexts, *groupthink* (Janis, 1972) occurs when the members in a group are so concerned with achieving consensus and getting along with each other that they don't disagree when they should. In organizational communication contexts, too much identification can lead to what Tompkins and his colleagues (Bullis & Tompkins, 1989; Tompkins & Cheney, 1985) called "strong culture." Strong cultures exist when employees identify so much with their organization that they conform to the organization's values and actions.

As you might imagine ethnocentrism, groupthink, and strong culture can result in some seriously negative consequences. For instance, ethnocentrism can lead to intolerance, hatred, discrimination, and violence toward members of another culture (Gudykunst & Kim, 1997; Parrillo, 1985). Moreover, groups and organizations characterized by groupthink and strong culture are notorious for bad decision making because they involve collectives of people that are all think-ing in the same way. Seiter (1995), for example, showed how a lumber company with a strong culture had difficulty communicating with people outside of the organization. That's because inside the company, everyone thought things were rosy, and as a result, the organization found itself threatened in the face of environ-mentalist attacks. Clearly, organizations and groups need members who will occa-sionally "rock the boat" (Redding, 1985). For instance, in the Heaven's Gate cult, we wonder what might have happened if two or three of the members argued against the mass suicide.

In short, then, it is clear that identification, by enabling us to communicate, organize, and decrease division, can be a worthwhile goal. On the other hand, we must be moderate in promoting it because too much identification can be "too much of a good thing" (Seiter, 1998).

Communicator Characteristics and Conformity

In Chapter 6, we discussed in some detail the ways in which communicator char-acteristics are related to persuasion. Many of the same characteristics examined there have also been studied by researchers interested in the topic of conformity.

Gender.   In a recent analysis of a large number of studies examining the relation-ship between gender and conformity, Bond and Smith (1996) concluded that females are more likely to conform than males. This seems to be the case regardless of when the studies were conducted (i.e., gender differences have not narrowed over time) or whether the participants in the studies were in the presence of the other group members. A study consistent with these findings examined 115 men and 111 women in a cafeteria line (Guarino, Fridrich, & Sitton, 1994). The research question was this: If the person you are dining with selects a dessert before you do, are you more likely to select a dessert yourself? The study revealed that 77 percent of the women conformed to the dessert-selecting behavior of the person ahead of them in line while only 43 percent of the men did. In addition, the gender of the person who selected the dessert first made a difference. Specifically, if the first per-son to select a dessert was a female, 75 percent of the women also selected a des-sert, while only 27% of the men did. Men were more likely to conform when following a male dessert eater than when following a female dessert eater. What-ever the case, here's our suggestion after reading this study: If you're on a diet, make sure you're the first person in line!

Peer-suasion.   Peer pressure exerts strong pressures on teens to comply (see Cos-tanzo & Shaw, 1966). Indeed, according to McCoy (1991), one study conducted on over 3,000 teenagers found that over two-thirds of them felt substantial peer pres-sure to have sex, drink, and take drugs. Gordon (1986) found that peer pressure is the most important factor in determining whether teens begin smoking. Moreover, because teens so desperately want to be accepted by their peers, for those who do not feel that they fit in with groups that pressure them, the consequences can be severe. For instance, not fitting in can lead to depression, the number one risk factor for teen suicide (Royte, 1994). According to Karlsberg (1991), each year more than 100,000 people between the ages of 10 and 24 attempt to kill themselves, and if unreported cases were included in the statistics, suicide would be the number one cause of death for people in this age group.

However, we should note that it is simply not true that adolescents follow their peers without question. For instance, Hoving, Hamm, and Galvin (1969) found that older children may be more likely to conform to peers when faced with a difficult or ambiguous problem, but when the problem is unambiguous, conformity decreases with age. Moreover, in their review, Walker and Andrade (1996) failed to find the "inverted U" relationship between age and conformity and suggested that the willingness of adolescents to conform may have decreased in recent times. Whatever the case, we must keep in mind that peer pressure is not always a bad thing. While parents must communicate openly with their children about what is right and wrong and be cautious of negative peer pressure, they shouldn't forget that peers also can praise, encourage, teach compromise, and help a child develop a sense of morality (Hoyt, 1995).

Personality.　Several studies have identified various aspects of personality that are related to conformity. First, McGill, Johnson, and Bantel (1994) found that managers with high cognitive complexity (i.e., those that have a large number of diverse and integrated mental constructs for interpreting the world) tend to perform best in turbulent environments largely because they conform less than managers with low cognitive complexity. Second, Burger (1987) found that people high in the desire to control events in their lives react negatively to group pressure and are therefore less likely to conform than people with a low desire for control. Third, high self-monitors, who pay close attention to social cues on appropriate behavior, are more likely to conform than low self-monitors (Snyder, 1987). Finally, Rose, Shoham, Kahle, and Batra (1994) found that people who are high in the need for affiliation and group identification conform more than people without such needs. Interestingly, those with needs for affiliation and group identification prefer clothing with popular brand names and styles, while those without such needs prefer clothing that is comfortable and durable.

Culture.　After surveying over 100,000 people in 40 different cultures, Hofstede (1984) identified four different dimensions of values along which any culture can be placed. He labeled these dimensions *power distance, uncertainty avoidance, masculinity–femininity,* and *individualism–collectivism.* Recently, Lustig and Cassotta (1996) argued that each of Hofstede's value dimensions can be applied to the study of persuasion to determine which cultures are more likely to conform than others.

First, people from cultures that score high on power distance value hierarchy and obedience to authority, while those that score low on power distance prefer equality and participative decision making. For that reason, Lustig and Cassotta

(1996) argued that people from cultures with low power distance scores (e.g., Israel, Australia, and Western European countries) are less likely to conform than those cultures with high power distance scores (e.g., The Philippines, Mexico, Venezuela, India, and Singapore).

Second, people from some cultures avoid uncertainty and have little tolerance for ambiguity, while people from other cultures are more at ease with the unknown. Because, ambiguous stimuli foster conformity more than unambiguous stimuli, Lustig and Cassotta (1996) argued that cultures that are uncomfortable with ambiguous situations (e.g., Greece, Portugal, Japan, Peru, Chile, and Spain) should conform more than cultures that are comfortable with ambiguity (e.g., The U.S., Singapore, India, England, and Sweden).

Third, some cultures can be characterized as "masculine" because they value competition, strength, assertiveness, and achievement, while others can be characterized as "feminine" because they value cooperation, affection, intuition, and nurturance. As such, members from masculine cultures (e.g., Japan, Italy, Austria, Mexico, England, Venezuela) should conform less than members from feminine cultures (e.g., Scandinavian countries, Portugal, the Netherlands).

Finally, while individualistic cultures value personal goals and self-autonomy, collectivistic cultures emphasize the importance of group goals and harmony. For that reason, Lustig and Cassotta (1996) argued that individualistic cultures (e.g., the United States, England, Australia, Canada, Italy, and Denmark) are less conforming than collectivistic cultures (e.g., Columbia, Korea, Peru, Taiwan, Pakistan, and Chile). A recent meta-analysis by Bond and Smith (1996) supports this conclusion. Conformity was much higher in collectivistic cultures than it was in individualistic cultures.

The "Whys" of Conformity

Up to this point, we've discussed the "whats," "wheres," and "whens" of conformity, but perhaps a more important question concerns the "whys" of conformity. That is, why is it that people are motivated to conform to the majority's behavior or point of view? According to Insko and Schopler (1972), past scholars have suggested at least five different reasons why conformity occurs. These include the following:

- **The group locomotion hypothesis**—This view suggests that members of a group are motivated to achieve the group's goals. When a member of the group believes that going along with the group will help achieve those goals, he or she is motivated to conform.
- **Social comparison theory**—How do you decide if you are attractive, tall, weird, or good at something? This theory suggests that you determine such things by comparing yourself to others (usually others who are similar to you). Clearly, doing so can lead to conformity. For instance, if, as a parent, you spank your children but learn that none of your friends spank their children, it may lead you to stop spanking your kids.

- **Consistency (or balance) theory**—This theory suggests that it is uncomfortable to disagree with a group that you like and find attractive. Thus to restore balance you are motivated to go along with the group and perhaps even convince yourself that the group was correct all along.
- **Epistemological weighting hypothesis**—This view suggests that we gain knowledge in two ways: personally, through trial and error and perceptual observation and socially, through observations and communication with others. When our view differs from a group's view, these two modes of knowledge compete with one another. For instance, in Asch's experiment, subjects thought they were seeing one thing (personal knowledge) but the group convinced them that they were seeing something else (social knowledge). The epistemological weighting hypothesis suggests that the degree to which a person conforms depends on how much weight is given to personal and social knowledge. Clearly, this weighting differs for different people, which is why some people conform more than others.
- **The hedonistic hypothesis**—This view argues that we conform to avoid pain (e.g., rejection, censure, scorn) and gain pleasure (e.g., acceptance, love, approval).

Social Proof: Using the Sheep Factor to Persuade Others

"But, Mom, *everybody's* doing it," is a familiar childhood refrain. Even so, children are not the only ones who pattern their behavior after others. Much of adult behavior is based on what Cialdini (1993) has termed *social proof:*

> *The tendency to see an action as more appropriate when others are doing it normally works quite well. As a rule, we will make fewer mistakes by acting in accord with social evidence than contrary to it. Usually when a lot of people are doing something, it is the right thing to do. This feature of the principle of social proof is simultaneously its major strength and its major weakness. Like the other weapons of influence, it provides a convenient shortcut for determining how to behave, but, at the same time, makes one who uses the shortcut vulnerable to the attacks of profiteers who lie in wait along its path. (p. 116)*

One of the authors once met a person who makes money by playing a guitar and singing in subways and on street corners. The person explained that, even before she starts singing, she throws some of her own money into the open guitar case. Why? When people pass by, they think others have contributed and are more likely to do the same.

A study by Cody, Seiter, and Montagne-Miller (1995) found that when people are buying gifts for others, social proof is one of the most effective tactics that a salesclerk can use. In fact, when salesclerks told their customers that a particular product was "the most popular," "the best selling," or "selling faster than we can bring them in," customers spent more money than when clerks used other tactics

such as praising the customer, doing favors for the customer, and trying to demonstrate expertise and trustworthiness (Cody et al., 1995). In short, people are sheep
and social proof works.

DEINDIVIDUATION AND SOCIAL LOAFING: GETTING LOST IN THE CROWD

In the previous section we saw how people can be pressured to conform to a group.
This, however, is not the only way that groups can influence an individual. In this
section we examine how groups can affect a person's behavior by causing the person to lose his or her sense of self or by making the person feel less responsible for
his or her actions.

What a Riot: An Examination of Deindividuation

In our opinion, one of the worst jobs you can have is as a referee or umpire for a
sporting event. Sure, refs and umps get to see some games up close without buying
tickets, but can you think of any other profession that takes more abuse? Who else
is the target of so much hostility, profanity, and screaming from complete strangers?
The point is, crowds influence people's behavior; once we get lost in them, we tend
to do things that we would never do alone. If you don't believe us, ask our friend
who was one of the 500,000 people at the Woodstock concert in 1969. She won't say
whether she was one of the people running around naked, but she admits to doing
things she wouldn't have done if she had not been lost in the crowd.

This tendency "to get lost in the crowd," was first labeled *deindividuation* by
Festinger, Pepitone, and Newcomb (1952). Deindividuation is said to occur when
being in a group causes people to become less aware of themselves and less concerned with how others will evaluate them (Diener, 1980). Because being in a large
group makes a person both more aroused and anonymous, the person focuses less
on him or herself and behaves less rationally and more impulsively.

Although shouting at refs and running around naked at concerts may sound
harmless enough, it is clear that deindividuation can have much more severe consequences. For example, one of the authors lived near and was a student at the University of Southern California when the L. A. riots broke out in 1992. Seeing
firsthand the trashed storefronts and burnt buildings of the riot's aftermath made
the potentially cruel nature of deindividuation all too real. The riots made it clear
to everyone how powerful the effects of a crowd can be—when one person starts
looting and vandalizing, others may be likely to follow.

A classic study by Diener, Fraser, Beaman, and Kelem (1976) illustrates how
deindividuation can lead to antisocial behavior. The researchers suspected that if
any night of the year would lead to deindividuation, it was Halloween. To be sure,
children usually trick-or-treat in groups and, because they wear costumes, are
more anonymous than usual. To see if deindividuation would affect children's
behavior, these researchers gave 1,352 trick-or-treaters, who were either trick-or-

treating alone or in groups, the opportunity to steal candy or money from 27 homes in Seattle. How did the experiment work? When trick-or-treaters came to the door, an experimenter greeted them, commenting on their costumes. The experimenter asked some of the children their names, while other children were allowed to remain anonymous. The experimenter then left the room after telling the trick-or-treaters they could take one of the candies that was in a bowl near the door (there was also a bowl full of nickels and pennies). Unbeknownst to the children, a hidden observer watched how much candy (and money) the children really took, and here's what the observer saw: When children were trick-or-treating alone, 7.5 percent of them took more candy than they were supposed to. When they were in groups, however, the thievery increased substantially; 20.8 percent stole candy. Moreover, when the children remained anonymous, they stole more candy and money than they did when the experimenter asked their names. In short, deindividuation led the trick-or-treaters to a night of petty crime.

Unfortunately, the negative effects of deindividuation do not stop with vandalism and stealing as illustrated by a number of laboratory studies which demonstrate that people who think they are delivering electric shocks to other people tend to be much more aggressive (i.e., administer more shocks) when in a deindividuated state than when they are not. Such aggressiveness is true of both deindividuated males and females, although males tend to be more aggressive then females when deindividuation is not present (Lightdale & Prentice, 1994).

Perhaps the most disturbing research on the relationship between deindividuation and aggression focused on violent behaviors perpetrated outside of the laboratory. First, in one study, Mann (1981) examined over 150 newspaper accounts of what happened when people threatened to kill themselves by jumping from a building. Mann found that in some cases people who had gathered on the streets below actually baited the potential jumpers, encouraging them to leap to their deaths. Can you guess what one of the factors was determining whether the crowd engaged in such behavior? According to Mann, when the crowds contained more than 300 people, baiting was more common then it was in smaller crowds. This, of course, is consistent with the notion that larger crowds produce more deindividuation.

Second, in an even more disturbing study, Mullen (1986) examined the relationship between the size of lynch mobs and the severity of atrocities committed by such mobs. To do so, he analyzed over 300 newspaper reports to determine the following: (1) the number of people in each lynch mob; (2) whether the lynchings included violent acts such as hanging, shooting, burning, lacerating, and dismembering the victims; and (3) whether the lynchings happened quickly or were prolonged and tortuous. Results of the study indicated that victims suffered more when the lynch mobs were larger. Mullen (1986) concluded that "these results support the contention that lynchers become less self-attentive, and thereby more likely to engage in acts of atrocity, as the lynchers become more numerous relative to the number of victims" (p. 191).

Considering the above studies, an important question concerns how deindividuation might be attenuated. Because deindividuation results from low self-awareness, the answer may lie in making people more aware of themselves.

According to Prentice-Dunn and Rogers (1982), however, there are two types of self-awareness and only one is related to deindividuation. First, *public self-aware-ness* refers to how we view ourselves as social objects and our concerns about such things as our appearance and the impression we are making on others. *Private self-awareness* refers to our focus on hidden aspects of ourselves such as our thoughts, feelings, and perceptions (see Buss, 1980). Prentice-Dunn and Rogers (1982) have found that deindividuation is decreased only when a person's private self-aware-ness is increased. This suggests, then, that to attenuate deindividuation, the object is to get people to focus on their own thoughts and feelings. Thus, rather than stating that people will get in trouble for their actions or look bad for doing something, it may be better to have them reflect on their personal views on what is right and wrong in a given situation.

Social Loafing: Not Pulling Your Own Weight

Have you ever had to push a stalled car or move a heavy piece of furniture with several other people? If so, be honest for a moment—did you give it your all? Did you work your hardest, exerting all of your energy? Or, because there were others to share the burden, did you slack off a bit? If you're at all like the average research participant, you probably did not work as hard as you could have. Indeed, research suggests that when working in groups, people may not try as hard as they do when working alone (e.g., Harkins, Latané, & Williams, 1980; Karau & Williams, 1993; Latané & Darley, 1970). In short, like a lot of other people, you may be a social loafer.

According to Karau and Williams (1993), "social loafing is the reduction in motivation and effort when individuals work collectively compared with when they work individually or coactively" (p. 681). Like deindividuation, *social loafing* is another way of "getting lost in the crowd." There's often a diffusion of responsibility; people either don't do their fair share or are not certain whether to get involved in the first place because, when there's a crowd, it's easier to assume that someone else will take responsibility for whatever should be done.

Unfortunately, like deindividuation, social loafing can also have disastrous effects. If you've ever seen the movie *The Accused*, you'll know what we mean. The movie is a true story about a woman (played by Jodie Foster) who is raped in a bar room. If that's not bad enough, several people in the bar watch what is happening but don't get involved. The story is both infuriating and all too common. For example, in another well-known case in the 1960's, a woman named Kitty Genovese was beaten and stabbed for over 30 minutes outside her New York apartment. While this happened, over 30 people watched from their windows without helping or without even calling the police. Finally, this same type of behavior has been repeated again and again in the laboratory. For instance, in a study by Latané and Darley (1970) subjects were led into a room, given earphones and a microphone, and told that they would be having a conversation over an intercom with other subjects in the study. Some were told they would be talking with one other person, while others were told they would be talking with either two or five other people.

In reality, there were no other subjects. The only true subject was listening to tape recorded messages. At some point during the conversation, one of the phony subjects (i.e., the tape recorder), who had previously claimed to have epilepsy, began choking and gasping as if having a seizure. Did the supposed victim receive help? The answer is "it depends." When subjects thought they were in groups with five other people, only 30 percent of them went to help the supposed victim. With two other people, 62 percent went to help. It was only when the subjects thought they were alone with the victim that 85 percent went to help. In short, the larger the group, the less likely people are to get involved.

Although the above studies and examples have to do with social loafing as it relates to physical behaviors, some research indicates that social loafing also occurs when performing cognitive tasks. For example, Petty, Harkins, and Williams (1980) wanted to see what would happen when students were asked to evaluate persuasive messages either alone or in groups of 10. All of the subjects heard a message arguing that seniors should have to take comprehensive exams to graduate, but some subjects heard strong arguments, some heard weak arguments, and some heard a combination of strong and weak arguments in favor of the exams. Results of the study indicated that subjects evaluated the strong message more favorably when they were alone than when they were in groups and evaluated the weak message less favorably when they were alone then when they were in groups. Thus, because solo subjects were better at recognizing which arguments were strong and which were weak, it suggests that solo subjects put more cognitive effort into evaluating the messages than subjects who were in groups (to examine the implications of social loafing, see Box 7.2).

Whatever the case, it is clear that social loafing can have severe, negative consequences. With that in mind, you might be wondering how social loafing can be decreased. According to Karau and Williams (1993), social loafing can be reduced or overcome by:

> ...providing individuals with feedback about their own performance or the performance of their work group, monitoring individual performance or making such performance identifiable, assigning meaningful tasks, making tasks unique such that individuals feel more responsibility for their work, enhancing the cohesiveness of work groups, and making individuals feel that their contributions to the task are necessary and not irrelevant. (p. 700)

HOW GROUPS AFFECT DECISION MAKING: TAKING IT TO THE EXTREME

In the previous sections, we've seen that it is easy to get lost in groups and how groups can cause us to do things that we would never do by ourselves. The same is true when making decisions. To illustrate this, consider the following example: Imagine that you're the parent of a small child, a daughter, with a terrible heart

BOX 7.2   "We the Jury": Does the Number of Jurors Make a Difference?

Ever wonder why juries usually consist of 12 members? According to Saul Kassin and Lawrence Wrightsman (1988):

> Although the Constitution says nothing about the proper size of a jury, some have imbued the number 12 with an almost mystical quality. There were 12 tribes of Israel, Christ had 12 apostles, our calendar is divided into 12 months, our school system has 12 grades, and there are 12 units to a dozen. Maybe we are wedded to that tradition only because the jury has worked as such since the *twelfth* century. And maybe, the number 12, in the U. S. Supreme Court's words, "is a historical accident, unnecessary to effect the purposes of the jury system and wholly without significance 'except to mystics.'" (pp. 195–196)

Whatever the reason for 12 person juries, we might ask ourselves whether they are really necessary. That's the exact question that was asked in *Williams v. Florida,* a 1970 case involving a defendant convicted of armed robbery (cited in Kassin & Wrightsman, 1988). On being charged, Williams had asked the judge for a 12-person jury, but instead was given a 6-person jury, which was the usual in Florida. He was sentenced to life in prison, but appealed to the U.S. Supreme Court, claiming that a 6 person jury was not constitutional. Ultimately, the court ruled against him, arguing that, in essence, 6- and 12-member juries behaved in the same way. Interestingly, however, another case placed the court in a predicament. In 1978 Claude Ballew was convicted by a 5-person jury in Atlanta for showing an allegedly obscene film in the adult movie theater he managed. Because the court feared that it would

eventually be faced with smaller and smaller juries, it halted the shrinkage by declaring that 6-person juries were the minimum size for a criminal jury (Hans & Vidmar, 1986; Kassin & Wrightsman, 1988). Following the decision, critics were quick to point out that the Supreme Court had used the same evidence for apparently contradictory decisions.

Whatever the case, the debate over the proper size of juries continues, and since that time more studies have been conducted. In one review, for instance, Kerr and MacCoun (1985) noted at least 12 studies concluding that juries of different sizes did not reach significantly different verdicts. With this in mind, it's easy to see why smaller juries might be preferred: They are easier to organize, cost less money, deliberate for less time, and have fewer "hung" decisions (Hans & Vidmar, 1986; Kerr & MacCoun, 1985). Moreover, considering the research on social loafing, Petty and Cacioppo (1986) argued that "as jury size increases people may be less motivated to participate in the group" (p. 95). Indeed, according to their sources, in 12-member juries, 25 percent of the jurors remain silent, while in 6-member juries, only 4 percent of jurors fail to participate. The implication, they note, is that larger juries are less critical. Thus, to larger juries, weaker evidence seems stronger than it really is and vice versa.

Despite such research, critics are quick to point out the disadvantages of allowing smaller juries. For instance, juries should represent the divergent views of society, but with fewer members, juries are less representative (Hans & Vidmar, 1986). Clearly, this is true. But considering the effects of groups on decision making, social loafing, and conformity, we must decide what aspects of juries we most desire.

condition. Because of the condition, your daughter has to refrain from any activity that might put too much strain on her. Your child's doctor, however, presents you with some interesting news: There's a new surgery your child can have that will make her completely normal. There's a catch, however; the doctor tells you that there is a 1 percent chance your child will die from the surgery. What would you do? Would you allow the doctor to perform the surgery? If you thought "yes," imagine that the odds are different; instead of a 1 percent chance, what if there were a 50 percent chance your child would die? Or worse, yet, what if the chances of death were 80 or 90 percent?

Interestingly, research has shown that when selecting between alternatives like the ones above, groups and individuals make different decisions. The first study on this subject was conducted by Stoner (1961, cited in Brauer, Judd, & Gliner, 1995), who found that individuals made riskier decisions when they were in groups than they did when alone. In other words, while an individual might decide to allow the surgery when there was a 1 percent chance of death, a group might allow it when there was a 50 percent chance. Following Stoner's study, several other researchers confirmed these results, and soon this effect became known as the *risky shift phenomenon.* Not all studies, however, confirmed this phenomenon. In fact, some later studies found just the opposite effect. Sometimes groups made decisions that were *less* risky than decisions made by individuals (e.g., Knox & Safford, 1976; Myers & Arenson, 1972). How might such results be explained? According to Myers and Arenson (1972), instead of a risky shift phenomenon, what actually occurs is a *group polarization phenomenon.* In short, groups cause people to become more extreme in their decisions. Thus, if you are predisposed to making a slightly risky decision, being in a group may cause you to make a riskier decision; if you are predisposed to make a conservative decision, being in a group may cause you to make an even more conservative decision.

Ever since the group polarization phenomenon was identified, at least 200 studies have been conducted to examine it (Brauer et al., 1995). Many of these have been devoted to identifying why group polarization occurs. Although there are many explanations, two are most prominent (see Boster, 1990; Brauer et al., 1995; Pavitt, 1994). The first, social comparison theory, was mentioned earlier in this chapter. Recall that according to this theory, we learn about ourselves by comparing ourselves to others. Because most people are average, when they compare their view to the view of others, they don't find much difference. Interestingly, however, because most people want to see themselves in a positive light, they don't want to be average; they want to be "better than average." Thus, according to this theory, when people learn that their position is the same as everyone else in the group, they shift their position so that it is more extreme. Because everyone tends to do this, group polarization occurs.

A second perspective, *persuasive arguments theory,* asserts that, before entering a group discussion, each member has one or more arguments that support his or her own position. If you consider all of these arguments together there will be more supporting one position than another (e.g., there may be more support for a risky decision than there is for a conservative one). Persuasive arguments theory asserts that the position that has the best and largest number of arguments supporting it is the position toward which members shift.

Recently, several authors have argued that these theories are not contradictory (Boster, 1990; Isenberg, 1986; Pavitt, 1994). In other words, *both* social comparison and persuasive arguments might contribute to group polarization. In addition,

Brauer and colleagues (1995) have argued that a third process might contribute to the extreme decisions made by groups. They noted that although social comparison and persuasive arguments explanations both focus on interpersonal processes (e.g., what we hear from other group members), *intra*personal processes also may affect polarization. Specifically, they argued that when making decisions in groups, we not only hear from other group members, we state our own opinion and defend it several times. Such repetition, they argued, also moves us toward polarization. To test this notion, they conducted a study in which group members repeated their own positions on a topic often or very little. Moreover, members also heard arguments from other group members. Results indicated that all three processes (i.e., social comparison, persuasive arguments, and repeated expressions) may contribute to group polarization.

Before concluding this section, we wish to point out that, like the other topics we've discussed in this chapter, group polarization can have disastrous effects. For instance, imagine being on the front lines in a hopeless battle. Who would you want deciding whether you should take a hill, one military leader or a group of them? How about if a decision were being made to start a war or send a missile? Or imagine an innocent person accused of a crime. Would he or she be better off with or without a jury deciding on a verdict? You get the idea. As frequent members of groups, it is important to remember the effects they can have on us. Only then might we hope to be less vulnerable to their influence.

SUMMARY

In this chapter we examined several topics related to influence in groups. First, we discussed early research on conformity and saw that several perspectives explaining why people tend to conform. In addition, several factors (i.e., group size, having an ally, the degree to which we find a group attractive, communicator characteristics, and culture) influence how likely we are to conform. We also saw that social proof can be a powerful persuasive tactic because it relies on people's tendencies to conform. We then saw that because people are less aware of themselves in groups or because people feel less responsible in groups, deindividuation and social loafing can result. Finally, for various reasons, groups tend to make more extreme decisions than do individuals (group polarization).

Before concluding, we wish to note that although this chapter has often discussed group influence in a negative light, without some degree of conformity, we could not communicate. If everyone did whatever they wanted to whenever they wanted to do it, chaos would reign. Imagine a classroom or business meeting in which everyone talked at the same time or a freeway on which cars went in all directions and never yielded to one another. Clearly, without norms and some conformity, we could never get anything done. On the other hand, this chapter underlines the potentially dire consequences of group influence and illustrates the importance of balancing conformity and independence. As Asch (1966) stated:

Life in society requires consensus as an indispensable condition. But consensus, to be productive, requires that each individual contribute independently out of his experience and insight. When consensus comes under the dominance of conformity, the social process is polluted and the individual at the same time surrenders the powers on which his functioning and feeling and thinking being depends. That we have found the tendency to conformity in our society so strong that reasonably intelligent and well-meaning young people are willing to call white black is a matter of concern. It raises questions about our ways of education and about the values that guide our conduct. (p. 324)

THE FAR SIDE   By GARY LARSON

"Wait! Wait! Listen to me! . . . We don't HAVE to be just sheep!"

ENDNOTES

1. The notion of rationalizing a behavior that contradicts our beliefs is consistent with the predictions made by cognitive dissonance theory, discussed in Chapter 4.

REFERENCES

Abrams, D., Wetherell, M., Cochrane, S., Hogg, M. A., & Turner, J. C. (1990). Knowing what to think by knowing who you are: Self-categorisation and the nature of norm formation, conformity and group polarisation. *British Journal of Social Psychology, 29,* 97–119.

Allen, V. L., & Levine, J. M. (1969). Consensus and conformity. *Journal of Experimental and Social Psychology, 5,* 389–399.

Allen, V. L., & Levine, J. M. (1971). Social support and conformity: The role of independent assessment of reality. *Journal of Experimental Social Psychology, 4,* 48–58.

Andrews, P. H. (1996). Group conformity. In R. S. Calthcart, L. A. Samovar, & L. D. Henman, *Small Group Communication* (7th ed., pp. 184–192). Madison, WI: Brown & Benchmark.

Aronson, E., & Mills, T. (1959). Effects of severity of initiation on liking for a group. *Journal of Abnormal and Social Psychology, 59,* 177–181.

Asch, S. E. (1956). Studies of independence and conformity: A minority of one against a unanimous majority. [Special Issue] *Psychological Monographs, 70.*

Asch, S. E. (1966). Opinions and social pressure. In A. P. Hare, E. F. Borgatta, & R. F. Bales (Eds.), *Small groups: Studies in social interaction* (pp. 318–324). New York: Alfred A. Knopf.

Bond, R., & Smith, P. B. (1996). Culture and conformity: A meta-analysis of studies using Asch's (1952b, 1956) line judgment task. *Psychological Bulletin, 119*(1), 111–137.

Boster, F. J. (1990). Group argument, social pressure, and the making of group decisions. In J. A. Anderson (Ed.), *Communication yearbook 13* (pp. 303–312). Newbury Park, CA: Sage.

Brauer, M., Judd, C. M., & Gliner, M. D. (1995). The effects of repeated expressions on attitude polarizations during group discussions. *Journal of Personality and Social Psychology, 68* (6), 1014–1029.

Bullis, C. A., & Tompkins, P. K. (1989). The forest ranger revisited: A study of control practices and identification. *Communication Monographs, 56,* 287–306.

Burger, J. M. (1987). Desire for control and conformity to a perceived norm. *Journal of Personality and Social Psychology, 35*(2), 355–360.

Burke, K. (1950). *A rhetoric of motives.* New York: Prentice-Hall.

Buss, A. H. *Self-consciousness and social anxiety.* San Francisco: W. H. Freeman.

Campbell, J. D., & Fairey, P. J. (1989). Informational and normative routes to conformity: The effect of faction size as a function of norm extremity and attention to the stimulus. *Journal of Personality and Social Psychology, 57*(3), 457–468.

Chua-Eoan, H. (1997, April 7). Imprisoned by his own passions. *Time, 149*(14), 40–41.

Cialdini, R. B. (1993). *Influence: The psychology of persuasion* (Rev. ed.). New York: William Morrow.

Cody, M. J., Seiter, J. S., & Montagne-Miller, Y. (1995). Men and women in the marketplace. In P. Kalbfleisch & M. Cody (Eds.) *Gender, power and communication in human relationships* (pp. 305–329). Hillsdale, NJ: Erlbaum.

Costanzo, P. R., & Shaw, M. E. (1966). Conformity as a function of age level. *Child Development, 37,* 967–975.

Diener, E. (1980). Deindividuation: The absence of self-awareness and self-regulation in group members. In P. B. Paulus (Ed.), *The psychology of group influence* (pp. 209–242). Hillsdale, NJ: Erlbaum.

Diener, E., Fraser, S. C., Beaman, A. L., & Kelem, R. T. (1976). Effects of deindividuation variables on stealing among Halloween trick-or-treaters. *Journal of Personality and Social Psychology, 33*(2), 178–183.

Festinger, L., Pepitone, A., & Newcomb, T. (1952). Some consequences of deindividuation in a group. *Journal of Abnormal Social Psychology, 47,* 382–389.

Gleick, E. (1997a, February 10). "Marine blood sports." *Time, 149,* 30.

Gleick, E. (1997b, April 7). "The marker we've been waiting for." *Time, 149,* 28–36.

Gordon, N. P. (1986). Never smokers, triers and current smokers: Three distinct target groups for school-based antismoking programs. *Health Education Quarterly, 13,* 163–179.

Guarino, M., Fridrich, P., & Sitton, S. (1994). Male and female conformity in eating behavior. *Psychological Reports, 75,* 603–609.

Gudykunst, W. B., & Kim, Y. Y. (1997). *Communicating with strangers: An approach to intercultural communication* (3rd ed.). Reading, MA: Addison-Wesley.

Hans, V. P., & Vidmar, N. (1986). *Judging the jury.* New York: Plenum Press.

Harkins, S. G., Latané, B., & Williams, K. (1980). Social loafing: Allocating effort or taking it easy? *Journal of Experimental Social Psychology, 16,* 457–465.

Hofstede, G. (1984). *Culture's consequences: International differences in workrelated values.* Beverly Hills, CA: Sage.

Hoving, K. L., Hamm, N., & Galvin, P. (1969). Social influence as a function of stimulus ambiguity at three age levels. *Developmental Psychology, 1,* 631–636.

Hoyt, C. (1995, October). When peer pressure is good for your child. *Good Housekeeping, 221,* 233–235.

Insko, C. A., & Schopler, J. (1972). *Experimental social psychology.* New York: Academic Press.

Insko, C. A., Smith, R. H., Alicke, M. D., Wade, J., & Taylor, S. (1985). Conformity and group size: The concern with being right and the concern with being liked. *Personality and Social Psychology Bulletin, 11*(1), 41–50.

Isenberg, D. J. (1986). Group polarization: A critical review and metaanalysis. *Journal of Personality and Social Psychology, 50,* 1141–1151.

Janis, I. L. (1972). *Victims of groupthink.* Boston: Houghton Mifflin.

Karlsberg, E. (1991, April). Teen suicide: Real-life stories. *'Teen, 35,* 24.

Kassin, S. M., & Wrightsman, L. S. (1988). *The American jury on trial: Psychological perspectives.* New York: Hemisphere.

Karau, S. J., & Williams, K. D. (1993). Social loafing: A meta-analytic review and theoretical integration. *Journal of Personality and Social Psychology, 65*(4), 681–706.

Kerr, N. L., & MacCoun, R. J. (1985). The effects of jury size and polling method on the process and product of jury deliberation. *Journal of Personality and Social Psychology, 48,* 349–363.

Knox, R. E., & Safford, R. K. (1976). Group caution at the racetrack. *Journal of Experimental Social Psychology, 12,* 317–324.

Latané, B. (1981). The psychology of social impact. *American Psychologist, 36,* 343–356.

Latané, B., & Darley, J. M. (1970). *The unresponsive bystander: Why doesn't he help!* New York: Appleton-Century-Crofts.

Latané, B., & Wolf, S. (1981). The social impact of majorities and minorities. *Psychological Review, 88,* 438–453.

Lightdale, J. R., & Prentice, D. A. (1994). Rethinking sex differences in aggression: Aggressive behavior in the absence of social roles. *Personality and Social Psychology Bulletin, 20*(1), 31–44.

Lott, A. J., & Lott, B. E. (1961). Group cohesiveness, communication level, and conformity. *Journal of Abnormal and Social Psychology, 62,* 408–412.

Lustig, M. W., & Cassotta, L. L. (1996). Comparing group communication across cultures: Leadership, conformity, and discussion processes. In R. S. Calthcart, L. A. Samovar, & L. D. Henman, *Small Group Communication* (7th ed., pp. 316–326). Madison, WI: Brown & Benchmark.

Mann, L. (1981). The baiting crowd in episodes of threatened suicide. *Journal of Personality and Social Psychology, 30,* 729–735.

McCoy, K. (1991, May). "Help your child beat peer pressure." *Reader's Digest, 138,* 67–70.

McGill, A. A., Johnson, M. D., & Bantel, K. A. (1994). Cognitive complexity and conformity: Effects on performance in a turbulent environment. *Psychological Reports, 75*(2), 1451–1472.

Moscovici, S., & Faucheux, C. (1972). Social influence, conforming bias, and the study of active minorities. In L. Berkowitz (Ed.), *Advances in experimental social psychology* (Vol. 6, pp. 149–202). New York: Academic Press.

Moscovici, S., Lage, E., & Naffrechoux, M. (1969). Influence of a consistent minority on the responses of a majority in a color perception task. *Sociometry, 32*, 365–379.

Mullen, B. (1986). Atrocity as a function of lynch mob composition: A self-attention perspective. *Personality and Social Psychology Bulletin, 12*(2), 187–197.

Myers, D. G., & Arenson, S. J. (1972). Enhancement of dominant risk tendencies in group discussion. *Psychological Reports, 30*, 615–623.

Parrillo, V. N. (1985). *Strangers to these shores* (2nd ed.). New York: John Wiley & Sons.

Pavitt, C. (1994). Another view of group polarizing: The "reasons for" one-sided oral argumentation. *Communication Research, 21*(5), 625–642.

Petty, R. E., & Cacioppo, J. T. (1986). *Communication and persuasion: Central and peripheral routes to attitude change.* New York: Springer-Verlag.

Petty, R. E., Harkins, S. G., & Williams, K. D. (1980). The effects of group diffusion of cognitive effort on attitudes: An information-processing view. *Journal of Personality and Social Psychology, 38*, 81–92

Prentice-Dunn, S., & Rogers, R. W. (1982). Effects of public and private self-awareness on deindividuation and aggression. *Journal of Personality and Social Psychology, 43*(3), 503–513.

Redding, W. C. (1985). Rocking boats, blowing whistles, and teaching speech communication. *Communication Education, 34*, 247–276.

Rose, G. M., Shoham, A., Kahle, L. R., & Batra, R. (1994). Social values, conformity, and dress. *Journal of Applied Social Psychology, 24*(17), 1501–1519.

Royte, E. (1994, Nov/Dec). They seemed so normal. *Health, 8*, 76–80.

Seiter, J. S. (1995). Surviving turbulent organizational environments: A case study of a lumber company's internal and external influence attempts. *Journal of Business Communication, 32*(4), 363–382.

Seiter, J. S. (1998). *When identification is too much of a good thing: An examination of Kenneth Burke's concept in organizational, intercultural, and small group communication contexts.* Journal of the Northwestern Communication Association, 26(1), 39–46.

Sherif, M. (1935). A study of some social factors in perception. *Archives of Psychology, 27*, 187.

Snyder, M. (1987). *Public appearances private realities: The psychology of self-monitoring.* New York: W. H. Freeman and Company.

Tanford, S., & Penrod, S. (1984). Social Influence Model: A formal integration of research on majority and minority influence processes. *Psychological Bulletin, 95* (2), 189–225.

Tompkins, P. K., & Cheney, G. E. (1985). Communication and unobtrusive control. In R. McPhee & P. Tompkins (Eds.), *Organizational communication: Traditional themes and new directions* (pp. 179–210). Beverly Hills, CA: Sage.

Walker, M. B., & Andrade, M. G. (1996). Conformity in the Asch task as a function of age. *Journal of Social Psychology, 136*(3), 367–372.

8

LANGUAGE AND PERSUASION

When Frankie Valle and the Four Seasons sang, "Walk like a man, talk like a man," we're certain their advice applied to males. But what about females? Should women talk like men? Or should they at least be capable of talking like men when the situation calls for it? Some people seem to think so. For example, Dr. Gail Reisman, an organizational consultant, helps women who are new to the executive world by teaching them to communicate more like men. This idea is not new as evidenced by popular books such as *Games Mother Never Taught You: Corporate Gamesmanship for Women,* which asserts that, among other things, women must learn the language of men (e.g., sports and military metaphors) if they hope to survive in the corporate world (Harragan, 1977). It's an idea that is based in part on the notion that when communicating, men project more power than women, therefore, to succeed in business, women must learn to fit in and act as men do (Rizzo & Mendez, 1990).

In our opinion, the problem with such an approach is that it portrays women as deficient (see also Eisenberg & Goodall, 1993) when, in many ways, women may be more competent businesspersons than men. For instance, while the communication patterns of female managers tend to be more positive, relational, facilitative, empowering, and cooperative, the communication patterns of male managers tend to be more authoritative, directive, depersonalizing, and commanding (see Byers, 1997). Moreover, some organizations have adopted a more feminist culture because it is believed to promote organizational excellence (Byers, 1997). In short, then, some might argue that the "women as deficient" view should be reversed; in other words, men should be trained to communicate more like women.

From our perspective, there is nothing wrong with men and women learning to communicate in a variety of ways as long as it is for the right reasons. The deficiency model is deficient, yet, any communicator, male or female, should benefit by building a large repertoire of communication skills and patterns. A larger repertoire provides more choices, which is important when you consider that the way you communicate, or more specifically, the language that you use, affects the way you are perceived. For that reason and others, language is persuasive. Indeed, the maxim, "The pen is mightier than the sword," is correct. Words are the primary means of persuasion. They not only affect our perceptions, attitudes, beliefs, and emotions, they create reality. In fact, U.S. author Philip K. Dick (cited in Columbia, 1993) wrote, "The basic tool for the manipulation of reality is the manipulation of words. If you can control the meaning of words, you can control the people who must use the words" (p. 28).

Because words are so important in the process of persuasion, the purpose of this chapter is to examine words and their effects on social influence. We begin by discussing the nature of symbols and of meaning, which are integral to understanding the relationship between language and persuasion. Then we turn our attention to connotative and denotative meanings in words and how persuaders, by using certain terms, labels, euphemisms, and doublespeak can shape beliefs and attitudes. Finally, we examine the ways in which several language variables—including vividness, intensity, offensiveness, and powerlessness—affect the process of persuasion.

SYMBOLS, MEANING, AND PERSUASION: THE POWER OF BABBLE

What distinguishes humans from other animals? According to Kenneth Burke (1966), humans are the "symbol-using, symbol-misusing, and symbol-making animal" (p. 16). We invent symbols, and through their use and misuse, we create meaning, define what's real, and persuade others. Obviously, then, to understand humans and how they influence one another, it is important to understand the nature of symbols.

What is a *symbol*? A very basic definition is that a symbol is something that represents something else. Your name is a good example. It represents the thing that is you, just as the word "pig" represents an animal with a curly tail and slimy snout.

One important characteristic of symbols is that they are arbitrary. In other words, symbols have no necessary connection to what they represent, although we sometimes seem to forget this. For example, S. I. Hayakawa (cited in Adler, Rosenfeld & Towne, 1995) told the story of a little boy who thought that pigs were called pigs because they are so dirty. The word "pig," however, has no direct connection to the curly-tailed animal, just as your name, although it may seem to fit, has no necessary connection to you. That is, when your parents were trying to decide what to call you, there was nothing written in stone that said you had to be given a certain name. You could just as easily been called Binky or Unga Bunga. Don't laugh—the singer Frank Zappa named his children Moon Unit and Dweezil, and when tax authorities told a Swedish couple that they had to give their 5-year-old son a name or pay a fine, the couple named the child "Brfxxccxxmnpcccclllmmn-prxvclnmckssqlbb11116" ("The best and worst," 1996). As wrong as such names might seem, however, they're not. When it comes to finding representations of things, there's not one "right" word or symbol.

Because they are arbitrarily connected to what they represent, a second characteristic of symbols is that they are conventionalized, which means that if we want to use a symbol to communicate to someone else, we have to agree on the symbol's meaning. Without some measure of agreement on the meanings of words, communication and persuasion would be difficult, if not impossible. If you've ever tried to communicate with someone who speaks a different language, you know this is true.

Connotative and Denotative Meaning: That's Not How I See It

Up to this point, we've noted how important it is for communicators to agree on the meaning of the symbols they use. With that said, however, we are certain that, without telepathy, total agreement on the meaning of symbols is impossible. Of course, the degree to which people agree may depend on the type of meaning with which we're concerned. There are at least two meanings for every word. The first, the denotative meaning, is a word's direct, explicit dictionary definition. Although denotative meanings can be problematic for communicators (e.g., when the dictionary meaning changes, as it did for the word "gay"), agreement on the denotative meaning of a word is likely.

The second type of meaning, connotative, refers to the thoughts and emotions associated with a word. As you might expect, the connotations associated with words vary widely from person to person. To illustrate, let's return to pigs. While all of us might agree on the denotative meaning of the word "pig" (i.e, curly-tailed animal with snout, etc.), our attitudes associated with the word may be quite different. For instance, compared to a farmer's child who grew up sloppin' hogs, a person who grew up reading books or watching movies about cuddly, talking pigs such as Wilbur from *Charlotte's Web* or Babe from the movie *Babe* would probably have a different view of pigs. Moreover, if tested, the authors, one a vegetarian and the other an avid meat-eater, would probably respond quite differently to words such as pork, bacon, ham, Hormel, Oscar-Mayer, and Farmer John. Likewise, in contrast to the members of some religious groups, Jews and Muslims are forbidden from eating pork, which is perceived as unclean. Recently, in fact, a woman in Israel was sentenced to 50 years for depicting Allah as a pig.

As persuaders, it is important to recognize that the meanings of words are subjective. As scholars in the field of communication are fond of saying, "Meanings are in people, not in words." Effective persuaders are aware of this and attempt to adapt their messages accordingly.

Ultimate Terms: Speak of the Devil

Although connotative meanings tend to be more subjective than are denotative meanings, sometimes the connotations associated with certain words are shared by large groups of people (i.e., societies and cultures). As a result, such words can be powerful persuasive tools for motivating people. This is especially true of what

Richard Weaver (1953) labeled *Ultimate Terms,* which are words or phrases that are highly revered, widely accepted, and carry special power in a culture. According to Weaver, there are three types of Ultimate Terms. The first, *God Terms,* carry the greatest blessing in a culture and demand sacrifice or obedience (see Hart, 1997; Foss, Foss, & Trapp, 1985). When Weaver wrote, he used terms such as "fact" and "progress" as examples of God Terms. Modern-day God Terms include "family values," and "balanced budget."

In contrast to God Terms, Weaver argued that some terms, which he labeled *Devil Terms,* are perceived by a culture as associated with that which is absolutely abhorrent and disgusting. Examples of past Devil Terms include "Communism," "Nazi," and "Fascist" (Foss et al., 1985). Today, terms such as "dead-beat dad," "racist," "gang member," "sweat shop," and "sexual harassment" might be considered Devil Terms. Because such terms represent what is evil or detestable to a culture, they can also be extremely persuasive (Hart, 1997).

Finally, Weaver labeled a third type *Charismatic Terms.* Unlike God and Devil Terms, which are associated with something observable, Charismatic Terms, much like a charismatic person, have a power which in some way is mysteriously given (Foss et al., 1985):

> *"Freedom" and "democracy" are charismatic terms in our culture. We demand sacrifice in the name of these terms, yet the referents most of us attach to them are obscure and often contradictory. In fact, Weaver says, we may resist the attempt to define such terms, perhaps fearing that a term defined explicitly will have its charisma taken away. (p. 66)*

What becomes clear, then, is that although God, Devil, and Charismatic Terms have power, their ability to persuade is not stable; the connotations associated with such terms may change over time. For instance, calling someone a communist today would not have the same impact as it did in the days of Senator Joseph McCarthy. Similarly, for some people, the term *political correctness* has shifted meanings from God Term to Devil Term. Indeed, political correctness, once a term of positive evaluation, referring to a position of humanitarian concerns for the poor, homeless and disenfranchised groups of society (Whitney & Wartella, 1992), has changed to a derisive term surrounded by controversy (Frye, 1992).

In addition to politicians, people in the business world are fond of using Ultimate Terms as persuasion devices as well. For instance, the word "empowerment" is a modern-day Charismatic Term upon which marketers and advertisers have capitalized. Products and services that promise to *empower* people have become unavoidable. For instance, as a former suit salesman, one of the authors was regularly asked by customers where the "power ties" could be found or what was the "power color" for ties this year. The Hotel del Coronado in Southern California offers its guests "power walks" in the morning. Athletes now have an alternative to Gatorade: Powerade! And one of our colleagues told us about a seminar his sister attended that teaches its clients how to take "power naps."

Other terms that seem to have appeal these days are *extreme* and *alternative.* Indeed, these words are popular now as "rebel" labels for things. There are, of course, alternative music and alternative clothing (e.g., flannel hooded shirts, Doc Martin shoes, etc.). There are also extreme sports, like extreme snowboarding, extreme skateboarding, and extreme mountain biking. But does placing words in front of something necessarily make it cooler or more "edgy"? Is "alternative golf" really alternative just because the people playing it have goatees and tennis shoes (instead of golf shoes) on?

What is clear from this discussion is that words, when widely accepted as representing what is good or evil in a culture, have incredible persuasive potential. As we've noted, being labeled a communist in the 1950s was hazardous. In the late 1600s, being labeled a witch in Salem, Massachusetts, was deadly. In the next section we explore more thoroughly the power of such labeling.

The Power of Labeling: Sticks and Stones

Earlier, we stated that names such as "Dweezil" and "Brfxxccxxmnpcccclllmmn-prxvclnmckssqlbb11116" were not wrong, but we might have lied to you. As arbitrary symbols they work just fine, but pragmatically, how would you like to be saddled with such a name? Perhaps you wouldn't mind, but, whatever the case, one thing is clear: The name you use affects the way people respond to you. In fact, we know a person who changes his name every decade because he says that people respond differently to him depending on whether he's a Richard, a Jay, or a Hank. And research supports the idea that our friend is not just a kook. For instance, according to the sources of Adler and colleagues (1995), compared to names like Percival, Elmer, Isadore, and Alfreda, common names such as John, Michael, Karen, and Wendy are rated as more likable, active, and stronger. Moreover, when such names were placed on essays and evaluated by teachers, the more common names tended to receive higher grades than the less common ones.

The power of such labels extends far beyond the names that people are given. To be sure, the labels we use to describe people or things reflect our attitudes about and affect others' reactions to, the people and things labeled. For example, many years ago, children with divorced parents came from a "broken home." Talk about stigmatization! Nowadays, we say children belong to "single-parent" or "blended" families.

Another good example of the power of labeling comes from the chastity movement. Teenage girls refer to themselves as "secondary virgins," meaning they have had sex in the past, but they won't again until they are married. There are also "technical virgins." This refers to females who have not had vaginal intercourse, but have had sex in other ways.

Another example of the power that labels carry comes from a study that one of the authors worked on with Caltrans (California Transportation) in an effort to warn motorists driving near the California/Mexico border about Mexican pedestrians who might be crossing U.S. roads. As it turns out, there was considerable controversy about what to call the pedestrians—illegal aliens, undocumented workers, or illegal immigrants. Notice that some of the labels are more pejorative than others.

The notion that the labels we use affect our attitudes about what we label lies at the heart of criticisms aimed at sexist language. For example, if a professor refers to all of his male students as "men" or "sir" and to all of his female students as "girls," "broads," or "dear," it not only says something about the professor's attitudes toward men and women, it has the power to shape attitudes. According to what is commonly known as the *Sapir-Whorf hypothesis*, the language we use determines the way we understand the world (Sapir, 1949; Whorf, 1956). Thus, when women are wrongly described in ways that make them seem inferior to men, people begin to believe that women truly are inferior.

The same dynamics are at work when people use racist language, which perpetuates the illusion that one racial group is superior to another. Ethnic/cultural references carry vastly different meanings. For example, Americans with an African heritage have been identified by terms such as African Americans, blacks, Negroes, coloreds, and by more derogatory terms as well. Such derogatory terms, whether racist or sexist, have the power to shape perceptions. Indeed, the media illustrated its sensitivity to the power of naming when reporting about Mark Fuhrman's testimony in the O. J. Simpson trial; instead of using a more derogatory term, the media replaced it with the term "the N-word." On the other hand, rappers use the word to describe close friends and to show solidarity (see Holloway, 1997) (for more on race and language, see Baker, 1981; Davis, 1969; Moore, 1995).

Euphemisms and Doublespeak: Making the Worse Appear the Better and Vice Versa

In the fifth century B.C., a group of teachers known as the Sophists created private schools in Athens, Greece. Students who wanted to learn from the Sophists were charged fees and were taught, among other subjects, oratory and persuasion. Soon, however, being a Sophist was so profitable that the occupation attracted a number of charlatans, who gave the Sophists a bad reputation (today, "sophistry" means deceitful or fallacious reasoning). In fact, Plato argued that the Sophists were more interested in lies than truths and more interested in dazzling audiences than in instructing them. Sophists, Plato argued, were skilled at making the "worse cause appear the better" (Corbett, 1971).

The practice of using words to make the worse appear the better (and vice versa) is still alive and well. Modern-day Sophists commonly use *doublespeak* (ambiguous or evasive language) and *euphemisms* (inoffensive terms substituted for offensive ones) to create messages with less sting. For example, in the business world, no one gets fired or laid-off anymore. Instead, companies engage in "downsizing," "right-sizing," or even "bright-sizing." Mercedes doesn't sell used cars anymore; it sells "pre-owned automobiles." (Try asking the Mercedes dealer, "Was this car previously used, or just owned?"). To appear more "healthy," Kentucky Fried Chicken has taken the "fried" right out of their name; now they're simply KFC. And when companies want to make what they're describing sound more important, they can do that too. Disneyland, for instance, refers to its customers as "guests." Small businesses may refer to themselves as "boutiques" or "shoppes." Other companies give their employees job titles that sound more important or grandiose than they really are. A garbage collector is now a "sanitation engineer." Salespersons and seamstresses have become "marketing representatives" and "clothing consultants."

The use of doublespeak and euphemisms is rampant in other places as well. For example, civilian casualties, killing selected targets, and combat operations are referred to by the military as "collateral damage," "neutralizing," and "peacekeeping missions," respectively. Police no longer interrogate people who are suspects, they "interview" people who "haven't been ruled out as suspects." In the medical field, terms such as assisted suicide, transsexual surgery, and cancer might instead be labeled "hastening death" (or "death with dignity"), "gender reassignment," and "a growth." Politicians don't raise taxes, they adopt "revenue enhancing measures." In education, students at Stanford University do not fail their classes; instead, their report cards say "NP" (not passing). And one of our friends is not allowed to have parties in her high school classes, so, instead, has "reinforcement for desirable behavior days." In the world of undertakers and funeral directors, people "pass away" rather than die, are "interred" rather than buried, and are called "cases" or "patients" rather than corpses. Instead of saying "No," parents are fond of saying "We'll see," or "Maybe later." And finally, in the abortion controversy, the words you use probably depend on the side you take. For example, "pro-life" is more value-laden than "anti-abortion" or "anti-choice." "Pro-choice" avoids the term "abortion" altogether and sounds much nicer than "anti-life" or "anti-anti-abortion." Whatever the case, all of these examples illustrate how language not only reflects the attitudes of the language-user, but also how language can be manipulated to shape attitudes. Clearly, as persuaders, we must be careful about how we use words, and, as persuadees, we must be cautious of the effect that words can have on us.

DILBERT reprinted by permission of United Feature Syndicate, Inc.

LANGUAGE INTENSITY, VIVIDNESS, AND OFFENSIVENESS

So far, we've examined the nature of symbols and how they relate to the notion of meaning and the process of persuasion. We now turn to a discussion of specific variables related to language and persuasion. Three of these include language intensity, vividness, and offensiveness. These three variables are closely related. For example, when studying intense language, some authors include reviews of research on profanity, which, of course, has the potential to be quite offensive. On the other hand, it is possible to use intense language without being offensive. Moreover, while some definitions imply that vividness is a component or outcome of intense language (e.g., see Hamilton & Stewart, 1993), others do not (e.g., see Bowers, 1964). Because these three topics are so closely related, we examine them together in this section. We then turn to a discussion of several theories that have been used to explain the relationship between intense language and persuasion.

##@**!!!!##: Profanity and Persuasion

In 1961 night club comedian Lenny Bruce was arrested on stage and jailed for using obscenities in his act. Afterwards, he was more careful about what he said to his audiences—sort of. Pointing out law officers who stood in the crowd and monitored his monologue, Bruce simply explained to his audience that he needed to "cool his act," and proceeded to substitute well-known profanities with something else (e.g., "You're full of blah," and "Have you ever blahed a blah?"). Bruce claimed that the act with substituted words was the dirtiest show he'd ever done in his life. He also illustrated one of the themes running throughout this chapter: Symbols are arbitrary, yet people react to them as if they were the real thing.

Even though profanity, like any symbol, is arbitrary, it clearly plays a role in the process of persuasion, mostly because such strong connotations are associated with swearing. Perhaps this is why ancient rhetoricians like Quintilian advised against using profanity (Rothwell, 1971). Despite such advice, however, empirical research indicates that the use of profanity may be quite common. For instance, one study found that profanity accounted for 8.1 percent of the words used in conversations between college students, 3.5 percent of the words used by adults at work, and 12.5 percent of the words used by adults at leisure (Cameron, 1969).[1] Because profanity is so common, some authors have asserted that it merits more attention as a form of persuasion. For instance, J. Dan Rothwell (1971) argued:

> Despite centuries of negative criticism, verbal obscenity has become a more frequent rhetorical device. It is successful in creating attention, in discrediting an enemy, in provoking violence, in fostering identification, and in providing catharsis. Its effects are governed by a variety of circumstances which need to be understood more fully. It has precipitated a police riot, brutal beatings, and even death. Hoping it will go away will not make it so. It is time to accept verbal obscenity as a significant rhetorical device and help discover appropriate responses to its use. (p. 242)

To explore more thoroughly people's perceptions of profanity, E. Scott Baudhuin (1973) gave students "swear word" booklets and asked the students to evaluate several words according to how offensive they were. Based on the students' perceptions, he found that the words could be categorized into one of three categories: religious, excretory, and sexual. Which type of profanity did students find most offensive? The results of the study indicated that sexual words received the most negative responses. Religious profanities were perceived to be the least offensive.

If profanity is perceived to be offensive, are people who use it perceived negatively and are they less persuasive? Several studies have been conducted to test this question and most indicate that if you want to be perceived as attractive, credible, and persuasive, you should clean up your language. For example, a study by Powell and his colleagues asked students to evaluate applicants who either did or did not cuss during a job interview. The researchers found that applicants with filthy mouths, regardless of their gender, were perceived as significantly less attractive than their counterparts (Powell et al., 1984). Similarly, Bostrom, Baseheart, and Rossiter (1973) found that in general using profanity damages a speaker's credibility. Finally, research in psychology indicates that when counselors swore, their clients were not only less likely to seek them out for help (Kottke & MacLeod, 1989), their clients were also less compliant (Kurklen & Kassinove, 1991; Sazer & Kassinove, 1991).

Political Correctness

Obviously, using profanity is not the only way to be verbally offensive. Earlier we discussed the notion of political correctness, which, in many ways, is all about being nonoffensive. Indeed, political correctness refers to issues of inclusive speech and advocacy of nonracist, nonageist, nonsexist terminology (Hoover & Howard, 1995).

DILBERT reprinted by permission of United Feature Syndicate, Inc.

Although political correctness is relevant to a wide range of contexts and topics including issues of gender, race, ethnicity, age, socioeconomic status, and so forth, a study by Seiter, Larsen, and Skinner (1998) focused on political correctness as it related to speaking about people with disabilities. In the study, college students read one of four hypothetical scenarios, each involving a person seeking donations who portrayed people with disabilities as either "normal" (e.g., "uses a wheelchair"), "heroic" (e.g., "handicapable"), "disabled" (e.g., confined to a wheel chair"), or "pathetic" (e.g., "abnormal"). After reading the scenarios, participants rated the speakers on scales measuring credibility and persuasiveness. Results of the study showed that, compared to communicators who portrayed people with disabilities as "pathetic," communicators who portrayed such people as "normal," "heroic," and "disabled" were perceived as significantly more trustworthy and competent (Seiter et al., 1998). On the other hand, only communicators portraying people with disabilities as "heroic" and "disabled" were perceived as more persuasive than the communicator portraying such people as "pathetic." How did the authors interpret these results? Perhaps by trying *not* to portray people with disabilities as victims, the communicator using "normal" language also did not demonstrate as urgent a need to help people with disabilities as the communicators using "disabled" and "heroic" language did (e.g., a child described as "being confined to a wheelchair," or one that is pandered to may be perceived as requiring more help than a child described as "using a wheelchair"). Whatever the case, the results of this study suggest that individuals seeking donations for people with disabilities face a dilemma: How can a person raise money to help people with disabilities while at the same time describe people with disabilities in a politically correct and dignified manner?

The Effects of Vividness: A Picture's Worth a Thousand Words

If there is one thing we've learned as parents, it's this: Little kids judge the worth of a book by examining the book's picture to word ratio. When you're 3 or 4 years old, books with lots of words aren't much fun. But the same may also be true of adults. Advertisers know that pictures are more vivid than words and, as a result, are an effective means of capturing attention, as the Qualcomm ad in Figure 8.1 illustrates. Of course, just because a persuader uses words does not mean that he or she cannot be vivid. Obviously, some words have more vividness than others. According to Nisbett and Ross (1980), vivid information captures and holds our attention and excites our imagination because it is "emotionally interesting, concrete and imagery-provoking, and proximate in a sensory, temporal, or spatial way" (p. 45). By way of example, it's more vivid to say "the glass crashed and shattered into pieces" than it is to say "the glass broke." It's more vivid to display the name of every person killed in the Vietnam war than it is to give us statistics. It's more vivid to show pictures of starving children covered with flies than it is to explain in words how much those children are suffering.

FIGURE 8.1   **This Qualcomm advertisement demonstrates the effective use of vivid images.**

Advertisement and photography courtesy of PGWB Advertising and Tony Stone Images.

Although vivid words or pictures may be more effective than pallid information (bland, plain descriptors) at holding our attention, provoking our emotions, and helping us recall information (Childers & Houston, 1984; Reyes, Thompson, & Bower, 1980), evidence that vivid information is more persuasive than pallid information is questionable (see Ralston & Thameling, 1988; Taylor & Thompson, 1982). Even so, there are some circumstances that may increase the vividness effect. First, if vividness is conceptualized as "live or videotaped broadcasts" as opposed to "written media," highly credible and likeable sources are most persuasive on videotapes and least persuasive in writing. It's just the opposite for low credible and unlikable sources (Andreoli & Worchel, 1978). People recall and are more persuaded by complex information when they read it than when they see and/or hear it on audio or videotapes (Chaiken & Eagly, 1976). Finally, Kisielius and Sternthal (1986) argued that the degree to which vividness affects persuasion depends, in part, on how much it makes the receiver engage in cognitive elaboration. Recall from our discussion of the Elaboration Likelihood Model in Chapter 2 that people attend to and scrutinize messages when they have the motivation and ability to do so. Vividness may stimulate receivers' ability and motivation to comprehend a message. Thus, when messages are vivid, receivers may think about them more and thereby internalize more of their content.

Language Intensity

"You are shockingly stupid" versus "You are not real smart."

"The lumber industry is raping our forests" versus "The lumber industry is cutting down a lot of trees."

In the pairs of phrases above, which phrase has the strongest connotative meaning? Obviously the first phrase in each pair. The terms *shockingly* and *raping* are more intense than terms found in the other phrases. Language that is intense is emotional, metaphorical, opinionated, specific, forceful, and evaluative. For that reason, perhaps, Bowers (1964) defined *language intensity* as "the quality of language which indicates the degree to which the speaker's attitude deviates from neutrality" (p. 215). Clearly, someone who compares "cutting down trees" to "rape" is far from neutral in his or her attitudes about the lumber industry. But is a person who uses such language persuasive? The best answer to that question may be "it depends." To be sure, several variables have been found that affect the persuasiveness of intense language. With that said, let's examine four different theories that attempt to explain when and why intense language does or does not persuade.

First, *reinforcement theory* assumes that people are motivated to avoid pain and seek pleasure. Bradac, Bowers, and Courtright (1979, 1980) assumed that the same is true when people are being persuaded. If a person generally agrees with the position advocated by a source, the person will find it rewarding and evaluate the source positively. The reverse is true if the person generally disagrees with the position advocated by the source. Language intensity is believed to enhance this effect. Specifically, if the listener generally agrees with the speaker, when the speaker throws some forceful language at the listener, the listener is even more motivated to agree. On the other hand, a listener who generally disagrees will react even more negatively than he or she normally would when the speaker uses intense language (Bradac et al., 1980).

A second perspective on language intensity is found in *language expectancy theory* (Burgoon, 1989, 1995). This theory assumes that we have expectations about what types of language are normal to use when trying to persuade other people. For example, we may not think it is normal for a speaker to use intense words like "rape" and "shockingly." Of course, our expectations may differ depending on who is using the language. For instance, Burgoon (1989, 1995) argued that in our culture, while men are expected to use intense language, women are not. Men and high credible sources have freedom to choose from a larger number of persuasive strategies than women and low credible sources do. Whatever the case, according to language expectancy theory, when persuaders violate our expectations concerning normal language, those violations can either help or hurt the effectiveness of the persuasive message. It all depends on whether the violations are positive or negative. For example, Burgoon, Jones, and Stewart (1975) found that when women used intense language, therefore violating expectations in a negative way, they were less persuasive than women who used language that was not intense. Just the opposite was true for men. Similar results were found for low and high credible sources. That is, low credible sources were more effective when using less intense language, while high credible sources were more effective when using more intense language.[2]

Third, Hamilton and Stewart (1993) have extended **information processing theory** (McGuire 1968, 1989) to explain the effects of intensity on persuasion. The theory argues that to be persuaded you must first attend to and comprehend a persuasive message. If you attend to and comprehend the message, you then compare your own position on the message to the position that's being argued by the source. Ultimately, you may either accept or reject the source's position. According to Hamilton and Stewart (1993), language intensity affects this process by making a source's position on an issue seem more extreme compared to your own position. This can be good, up to a point. In general, some discrepancy between a persuader and a receiver's positions leads to increased attention and therefore more attitude change. On the other hand, as we noted in our discussion of social judgment theory in Chapter 6, too much discrepancy may lead a receiver to reject a message or to scrutinize a message so much that he or she fails to attend to all of the message's content. In addition, intense language tends to be more specific and vivid.

Finally, **communication accommodation theory** (Giles & Wiemann, 1987; Street & Giles, 1982) argues that when we communicate with others we adjust our style of speaking to their style in order to gain approval and increase communication efficiency. For example, we may try to talk the same way others talk so that they will like us better. Aune and Kikuchi (1993) conducted a study to see if this theory would predict the effectiveness of messages that either were or were not intense. Specifically, speakers delivered intense and nonintense messages to people whose language style could be categorized as either intense or nonintense. Results of the study supported communication accommodation theory. Specifically, speakers using intense language were most persuasive with people who use intense language, while speakers using non-intense language were most persuasive with people who use nonintense language. Speaker's who "matched" the style of their audience also were perceived as more credible.

POWERLESS LANGUAGE AND PERSUASION: "UMS" THE WORD

As a student, one of the authors had two speech professors who did not like the utterance "um" too much. One called "ums" social burps. The other, when listening to speeches, smacked her pencil on a desk whenever the author said, "um." It was not fun, but it beat electrical shocks. In retrospect, the author supposes he should be grateful to these professors, because "ums," as well as a number of other utterances, prevent people who use them from being persuasive. Why? Because such utterances create the perception of *powerlessness.* In case you want to avoid using them when you talk, here is a list of such speech mannerisms with some examples in italics (also see Bradley, 1981; Erickson, Lind, Johnson, & O'Barr, 1978; Lakoff, 1973, 1975; Lowenberg, 1982; Newcombe & Arnkoff, 1979; O'Barr, 1982):

- **Hesitations** (signal uncertainty or anxiety): "*Well,* I, *uh, you know, um,* would like to borrow a dollar."
- **Hedges** (qualify the utterance in which they occur): "*I guess I sort of* like you and *kind of* want to know you."
- **Intensifiers** (fortify the utterance): "I *really* believe that and agree with you *very* much."
- **Polite forms** (indicate deference and subordination): "*Excuse me, if you wouldn't mind too much, I'd appreciate* if you'd *please* shut the door. *Thank you.*"
- **Tag questions** (lessens the force of a declarative sentence): "This is fun, *don't you think*? Much more fun than yesterday, *isn't it*?"
- **Disclaimers** (utterances offered before a statement that anticipate doubts, signal a problem, or ask for understanding): "I know this is a *really dumb question,* but...?"
- **Deictic phrases** (phrases indicating something outside the speaker's vicinity): "That man *over there* is the one who stole my wallet."

As noted above, a considerable amount of research indicates that using these powerless forms of speech can prevent you from being persuasive (Erickson et al., 1978; Newcombe & Arnkoff, 1979). For example, Adkins and Brashers (1995) conducted a study in which groups of people were asked to make a decision on teaching evaluations at a university. While the decision was being made, the people were not allowed to see one another. They only communicated via computer.

Moreover, two of the group members were confederates, planted by the researchers and instructed to communicate in either powerful or powerless language. Later the other group members were asked to evaluate the powerful and powerless communicators. Results of the study showed that the confederate who used more powerful language was perceived as more attractive, credible, and persuasive than the one who used powerless language. Similarly, a study by Haleta (1996) found that teachers who use powerless language were perceived as significantly less dynamic and credible than teachers who did not.

One problem with some research on powerless language is that it has lumped together all of the powerless forms discussed above. However, some research indicates that this may not be the best idea because not all of the forms may be detrimental to a speaker. For instance, in one study, Bradac and Mulac (1984) found that using polite forms actually enhanced speakers' credibility. Moreover, the type of language that is most effective may depend on who is using it. Carli (1990), for instance, found that females were persuasive with men when they used powerless forms of speech, but persuasive with females when using powerful speech. For males speakers, it did not matter what form of speech was used.[3] This may mean that women, compared to men, need to be more sensitive about the style of speech they decide to use when trying to be persuasive. Clearly, along with the topics we've discussed earlier, the results of this study suggest that men have negative stereotypes about women who use powerful speaking styles.

SUMMARY

In this chapter, we examined the role of language in the process of persuasion. We began with an examination and definition of the term *symbol*. Symbols are arbitrary but have the power to shape perceptions and construct social reality. Symbols also have connotative and denotative meanings, both of which affect persuasion. For example, we examined Ultimate Terms, which, because of their strong connotations, have incredible persuasive power in a culture. We also examined the power of labels and how, oftentimes, through the use of euphemisms and doublespeak, persuaders attempt to lessen (or strengthen) the connotative impact of a word. Finally, we discussed several language variables that affect persuasion. By making their words more vivid, intense, offensive, and powerless/powerful, persuaders affect the way audiences respond to their messages.

ENDNOTES

1. Students preferred using sexual profanities to religious and excretory profanities, while adults preferred religious profanities over sexual and excretory profanities.

2. Language expectancy theory argues that we not only have expectations about how intense language should or should not be. We also have expectations concerning the use of fear appeals, verbal aggression, and other types of persuasive language.

3. Erickson and colleagues (1978) found that males rate males who use powerless speech low in credibility.

REFERENCES

Adkins, M., & Brashers, D. E. (1995). The power of language in computer-mediated groups. *Management Communication Quarterly, 8*(3), 289–322.

Adler, R. B., Rosenfeld, L. B., & Towne, N. (1995). *Interplay: The process of interpersonal communication* (6th ed.). Fort Worth, TX: Harcourt, Brace.

Andreoli, V., & Worchel, S. (1978). Effect of media, communicator, and message position on attitude change. *Public Opinion Quarterly, 42,* 59–70.

Aune, R. K., & Kikuchi, T. (1993). Effects of language intensity similarity on perceptions of credibility, relational attributions, and persuasion. *Journal of Language and Social Psychology, 12*(3), 224–237.

Baker, R. (1981). "Pricks" and "chicks": A plea for "persons." In M. Vetterling-Braggin (Ed), *Sexist language: A modern philosophical analysis* (pp. 161–182). Totowa, NJ: Rowman and Littlefield.

Baudhuin, E. S. (1973). Obscene language and evaluative response: An empirical study. *Psychological Reports, 32,* 399–402.

"The best and worst of everything." (1996, December 29). *Parade Magazine,* pp. 6, 7, 10.

Bostrom, R. N., Baseheart, J. R., & Rossiter, C. M. (1973). The effects of three types of profane language in persuasive messages. *Journal of Communication, 23,* 461–475.

Bowers, J. W. (1964). Some correlates of language intensity. *Quarterly Journal of Speech, 50,* 415–420.

Bradac, J., Bowers, J., & Courtright, J. (1979). Three language variables in communication research: Intensity, immediacy, and diversity. *Human Communication Research, 5,* 257–269.

Bradac, J., Bowers, J., & Courtright, J. (1980). Lexical variations in intensity, immediacy, and diversity: An axiomatic theory and causal model. In R. W. St. Clair & H. Giles (Eds.). *The social psychological contexts of language* (pp. 193–223). Hillsdale, NJ: Lawrence Erlbaum.

Bradac, J. J., & Mulac, A. (1984). A molecular view of powerful and powerless speech styles: Attributional consequences of specific language features and communicator intentions. *Communication Monographs, 51,* 307–319.

Bradley, P. H. (1981). The folk-linguistics of women's speech: An empirical evaluation. *Communication Monographs, 48,* 73–90.

Burgoon, M. (1995). Language Expectancy Theory: Elaboration, explication, and extension. In C. R. Berger & M. Burgoon (Eds.) *Communication and social influence processes* (pp. 29–51). East Lansing, MI: Michigan State University Press.

Burgoon, M. (1989). The effects of message variables on opinion and attitude change. In J. Bradac (Ed.), *Messages in communication sciences: Contemporary approaches to the study of effects* (pp. 129–164). Newbury Park, CA: Sage.

Burgoon, M., Jones, S., & Stewart, D. (1975). Toward a message-centered theory of persuasion: Three empirical investigations of language intensity. *Human Communication Research, 1,* 240–256.

Burke, K. (1966). *Language as symbolic action: Essays on life, literature, and method.* Berkeley, CA: University of California Press.

Byers, P. Y. (1997). *Organizational communication: Theory and behavior.* Boston: Allyn and Bacon.

Cameron, P. (1969). Frequency and kinds of words in various social settings, or what in the hell's going on? *Pacific Sociological Review, 12,* 101–104.

Carli, L. L. (1990). Gender, language, and influence. *Journal of Personality and Social Psychology, 59,* 941–951.

Chaiken, S., & Eagly, A. H. (1976). Communication modality as a determinant of message persuasiveness and message comprehensibility. *Journal of Personality and Social Psychology, 34,* 605–614.

Childers, T. L., & Houston, M. J. (1984). Conditions for a picture-superiority effect on consumer memory. *Journal of Consumer Research, 11,* 643–654.

Columbia Dictionary of Quotations (1993). New York: Columbia University Press.

Corbett, E. P. J. (1971). *Classical rhetoric for the modern student* (2nd ed.). New York: Oxford University Press.

Davis, O. (1969). The language of racism: The English language is my enemy. In N. Postman, C. Weingartner, & T. P. Moran (Eds.), *Language in America* (pp. 73–79), New York: Bobbs-Merrill.

Eisenberg, E. M., & Goodall, H. L., Jr. (1993). *Organizational communication : Balancing creativity and constraint*. New York: St. Martin's Press.

Erickson, B., Lind, E., Johnson, A., & O'Barr, W. M. (1978). Speech style and impression formation in a court setting: The effects of "powerful" and "powerless" speech. *Journal of Experimental Social Psychology, 14,* 266–279.

Foss, S. K., Foss, K. A., & Trapp, R. (1985). *Contemporary perspectives on rhetoric.* Prospect Heights, IL: Waveland Press.

Frye, M. (1992). Getting it right. *Signs, 17,* 781–793.

Giles, H., & Wiemann, J. M. (1987). Language, social comparison, and power. In C. R. Berger & S. H. Chaffee (Eds.), *The handbook of communication science* (pp. 350–384). Newbury Park, CA: Sage.

Haleta, L. L. (1996). Student perceptions of teachers' use of language: The effects of powerful and powerless language on impression formation and uncertainty. *Communication Education, 45*(1), 16–28.

Hamilton, M. A., & Stewart, B. L. (1993). Extending an information processing model of language intensity effects. *Communication Quarterly, 41*(2), 231–246.

Harragan, B. L. (1977). *Games mother never taught you: Corporate gamesmanship for women.* New York: Warner Books.

Hart, R. P. (1997). *Modern rhetorical criticism* (2nd ed.). Boston: Allyn and Bacon.

Holloway, L. (1997, January 9). Hip-hop slang finds a literary homey. *The Orange County Register (Accent),* p. 1.

Hoover, J. D., & Howard, L. A. (1995). The political correctness controversy revisited. *American Behavioral Scientist, 38*(7), 963–975.

Kisielius, J., & Sternthal, B. (1986). Examining the vividness controversy: An availability-valence interpretation. *Journal of Consumer Research, 12,* 418–431.

Kottke, J. L., & MacLeod, C. D. (1989). Use of profanity in the counseling interview. *Psychological Reports, 65,* 627–634.

Kurklen, R., & Kassinove, H. (1991). Effects of profanity, touch, and subject's religiosity on perceptions of a psychologist and behavioral compliance. *The Journal of Social Psychology, 131*(6), 899–901.

Lakoff, R. (1973). Language and woman's place. *Language Society, 2,* 45–79.

Lakoff, R. (1975). *Language and woman's place.* New York: Harper and Row.

Lowenberg, I. (1982). Labels and hedges: The metalinguistic turn. *Language and Style, 15,* 193–207.

McGuire, W. J. (1968). Personality and susceptibility to social influence. In E. F. Borgotta & W. W. Lambert (Eds.), *Handbook of personality theory and research* (pp. 1130–1187). Chicago: Rand McNally.

McGuire, W. J. (1989). Theoretical foundations of campaigns. In R. E. Rice & C. K. Atkin (Eds.), *Public communication campaigns* (2nd ed., pp. 43–65). Newbury Park, CA: Sage.

Moore, R. B. (1995). Racist stereotyping in the English Language. In K. S. Verderber (Ed.), *Voices: A selection of multicultural readings* (pp. 9–17), Belmont, CA: Wadsworth.

Newcombe, N., & Arnkoff, D. B. (1979). Effects of speech style and sex of speaker on person perception. *Journal of Personality and Social Psychology, 37,* 1293–1303.

Nisbett, R., & Ross, L. (1980). *Human inference: Strategies and shortcomings in social judgment.* Englewood Cliffs, NJ: Prentice-Hall.

O'Barr, W. M. (1982). *Linguistic evidence: Language, power, and strategy in the courtroom.* New York: Academic Press.

Powell, L., Callahan, K., Comans, C., McDonald, L., Mansell, J., Trotter, M. D., & Williams, V. (1984). Offensive language and impressions during and interview. *Psychological Reports, 55,* 617–618.

Ralston, S. M., & Thameling, C. A. (1988). Effect of vividness of language on the information value of reference letters and job applicants' recommendations. *Psychological Reports, 62,* 867–870.

Reyes, R. M., Thompson, W. C., & Bower, G. H. (1980). Judgmental biases resulting from differing availabilities of arguments. *Journal of Personality and Social Psychology, 39,* 2–12.

Rizzo, A., & Mendez, C. (1990). *The integration of women in management.* New York: Quorum Books.

Rothwell, J. D. (1971). Verbal obscenity: Time for second thoughts. *Western Speech, 35,* 231–242.

Sapir, E. (1949). *Culture, language and personality.* Berkeley, CA: University of California Press.

Sazer, L., & Kassinove, H. (1991). Effects of counselor's profanity and subject's religiosity on content acquisition of a counseling lecture and behavioral compliance. *Psychological Reports, 69,* 1059–1070.

Seiter, J. S., Larsen, J., & Skinner, J. (1998). "Handicapped" or "Handi-capable?": The effects of language describing people with disabilities on perceptions of source credibility and persuasiveness. *Communication Reports 11*(1), 21–31.

Street, R. L., Jr., & Giles, H. (1982). Speech accommodation theory: A social cognitive approach to language and speech behavior. In M. Roloff & C. R. Berger (Eds.), *Social cognition and communication* (pp. 193–226). Beverly Hills, CA: Sage.

Taylor, S. E., & Thompson, S. C. (1982). Stalking the elusive "vividness" effect. *Psychological Review, 89,* 155–181.

Weaver, R. M. (1953). *The ethics of rhetoric.* Chicago: Henry Regnery.

Whitney, D. C., & Wartella, E. (1992). Media coverage of the "political correctness" debate. *Journal of Communication, 42* (2), 83–93.

Whorf, B. L. (1956). *Language, thought, and reality.* New York: John Wiley & Sons.

9

NONVERBAL INFLUENCE

Shelley's boyfriend was probably frowning as he watched one of this book's authors reach out and take Shelley's hand. At the time, the author was not thinking about Shelley's boyfriend, though; he was thinking about how pretty Shelley was. He remembers leaning toward her and gazing into her eyes. In response, she blinked once or twice. Her lips tightened into a grin as she squeezed the author's hand. He'd never talked to her before this and was nervous, but even so, he had no trouble finding words. They came out smooth and suggestive. "Pass the salt," he whispered. And, after swallowing hard and leaning even closer, he repeated those words—"Pass the salt, pass the salt"—again and again.

Don't get the wrong idea. Even after writing a book about persuasion, neither author is even close to Don Juan status. When one of us met Shelley years ago, he was a sophomore in college, where he, Shelley, and Shelley's boyfriend were taking an acting class. As part of an exercise, the instructor paired each of us students up with a stranger and asked us to convince the rest of the class that we were deeply and passionately in love. "Pass the salt," however, was the only phrase we were allowed to use.

In retrospect, the author is not sure how persuasive an actor he was, but he did learn something that day: The words "I love you" are not all they are cracked up to be. Sure, it's nice to hear those words, but if you can convey the same meaning with "pass the salt," who needs them? By the same token, we're sure you can imagine someone saying, "I love you," with complete insincerity (e.g., perhaps while never looking up from a newspaper). The point here is that, when we are trying to interpret meaning, there is a lot more involved than just words. As the old saying goes, "it's not what a person says, it's *how* the person says it that's important," which is why it is crucial that we understand something about nonverbal communication—how we say things through the use of gestures, body movements, touch, spatial behavior, appearance, eye contact and so forth.

While this underlines the important role that nonverbal cues play in the overall process of communication, in this chapter, we are interested in focusing on one particular question about nonverbal communication. That is, in what way does nonverbal communication influence the process of persuasion? We know, for example, that when people are trying to be persuasive, they change their nonverbal behavior by increasing their eye contact, nodding, gesturing, facial activity, and speech volume and rate (Mehrabian & Williams, 1969). But are these nonverbal changes effective? Can some behaviors make you more influential than others? Or perhaps a more interesting question centers on whether some behaviors can make you more persuadable (see Box 9.1).

According to Burgoon (1994), nonverbal communication plays an important role in the process of social influence for several reasons. First, nonverbal behaviors can impact our perceptions of a person's dominance, power, status, authority, credibility, and attractiveness, that in turn can make the person more persuasive. Second, through the use of nonverbal communication, people can establish intimate relationships. In other words, nonverbal cues like touch can be helpful in developing rapport. Third, nonverbal behaviors can heighten or distract attention from persuasive messages that are likely to reinforce learning. For example, a teacher can use nonverbals to get his or her students to pay more attention to a message while a heckler can use such tactics to distract listeners. Fourth, through nonverbals, a person can be reinforced to imitate a model's behavior. Fifth, nonverbal cues can be used to signal a person's expectations and to elicit behavior that conforms to those expectations. For example, a simple frown can inform a child that he or she is not behaving appropriately. And finally, nonverbal behaviors can be used to violate peoples' expectations for normal behavior so as to distract the people. Later in the chapter, for instance, we'll see that standing too close to another person can, under some circumstances, make that person more compliant.

BOX 9.1   The Way You Sit Affects Your Attitudes: Self-Persuasion and Nonverbal Communication

Did you know that the nonverbal behavior of people receiving messages can affect how likely they are to be persuaded? Over the years, researchers have found that when people are highly involved with a topic, it affects how persuaded they are by messages about that topic (Petty & Cacioppo, 1986; Roser; 1990; Roser & Thompson, 1995). People who are highly involved tend to be less persuaded by opposing arguments than uninvolved people are. But Petty, Wells, Heesacker, Brock, and Cacioppo (1983) found that even when people are not involved with a topic, their nonverbal behavior can fool them into thinking so. The researchers hypothesized that when people are standing, they are more prone to agitation and attack than when they are relaxing. Thus, the researchers suspected that standing might pre-

dispose people to respond more negatively to a message with which they already disagreed. To test this notion, the researchers had people listen to counterattitudinal messages while either standing or lying comfortably. Results confirmed the hypothesis. Standing participants were less persuaded than relaxing ones. In a similar study, researchers found that people who listened to messages while nodding their heads (a sign of agreement) were more persuaded than those who moved their heads back and forth horizontally (Wells & Petty, cited in Petty & Cacioppo, 1986).

The moral of the story, then, is that when someone is trying to persuade you, you need not only monitor the persuader's behavior, you need to keep an eye on your own as well!

Of course, we do not have the space needed in one chapter to discuss every aspect of nonverbal communication. We have, therefore, chosen to focus on those areas that we find the most important and intriguing. We begin by looking at several different types of nonverbal communication and how each type impacts the process of social influence.

TYPES OF NONVERBAL COMMUNICATION

Although researchers have identified several different types or "codes" of nonverbal communication, there is some disagreement about how many or what kinds of nonverbal codes exist. For example, while Burgoon (1994) identified seven codes, Knapp (1978) and Argyle (1988) identified eight, and Leathers (1986) identified nine. Rather than argue for the superiority of any one typology over the other, we believe that it is more important to recognize that regardless of the codes one identifies, nonverbal behaviors are interdependent. By way of illustration, we should probably tell you that the "Shelley story" is not yet over. There's still the part about Shelley's boyfriend, Louis, who responded to the "pass the salt" line by attacking the author after class. With eyes wide and fists clinched, Louis called the author a "lousy something-or-other" and then slugged him. In response, the author merely chuckled, because he could see that Louis was only having fun; Louis was smiling, and the punch was only a playful "tap."

As it turns out, Louis's behavior was probably not all that uncommon. Indeed, like us, you may have seen people (probably men) play fighting as a means of greeting one another. But how do we know that they are just playing? We know because we don't see *just* their punches or *just* their eyes; we see other cues that help us interpret their messages. In other words, although there are many types of nonverbal communication, they do not occur in isolation. Nonverbal behaviors occur simultaneously and how we interpret one behavior can affect our interpretations of other behaviors. Thus, although we discuss each of the following codes separately, it is important to realize that each code rarely operates alone. As Burgoon, Buller, and Woodall (1989) noted, "Discussing them [codes] as separate entities is a matter of convenience and tradition, as well as a way of providing a foundation for understanding the processes and functions of nonverbal communication" (p. 35).

With that said, we now examine seven types of nonverbal communication that are important in the process of persuasion. These types include kinesics, haptics, proxemics, chronemics, artifacts, physical appearance, and paralinguistics.

Kinesics: Head, Shoulders, Knees and Toes, Knees and Toes

The word *kinesics* was derived from the Greek term *kinein* that means "to move" and refers to the study of eye contact, facial expressions, gestures, and body movements and posture. We start by taking a look at eye contact.

The Eyes Have It

Ralph Waldo Emerson once claimed that "The eyes of men converse as much as their tongues." And when you think of all the expressions we use to discuss the communication potential of eyeballs (e.g., "evil eyes," "bedroom eyes," "shifty eyes," "laughing eyes," "lying eyes," "Bette Davis eyes"), Emerson's claim does not seem so far-fetched. Besides being an important means of expressing interest, attraction, and intimacy, eye contact has been found to convey dominance, persuasiveness, aggressiveness, and credibility (Burgoon & Dillman, 1995). In a study by Beebe (1974), for instance, participants were asked to rate how qualified, dynamic, and honest they perceived speakers to be. Although eye contact did not affect perceptions of dynamism, the study revealed that speakers were seen as more honest and qualified when they gazed more. Similarly, a study by Exline, Ellyson, and Long (1975) found that, in general, dominant people gaze longer and avert their gaze less than submissive people do.[1] In short, then, eye contact might have an indirect impact on persuasiveness by influencing peoples' perceptions of credibility, dominance, and power.

As potential targets of persuasion, we need to keep in mind that everyday persuaders are well aware of the power of eye contact and use it to their advantage. One of the authors, for instance, was involved in a study that investigated the influence strategies used by beggars when attempting to get money from strangers (Robinson, Seiter, & Acharya, 1992). As part of the study 36 beggars were interviewed, and several claimed that before even asking for money, the first thing they tried to do was establish eye contact with whoever was passing by. Without eye contact, the beggars argued, it was easier for their "targets" to ignore them and walk on by.

If eye contact helps beggars get more money, does it also help public speakers to be more persuasive? Some evidence seems to support this notion. For example, Birk, Pfau, and Burgoon (cited in Burgoon et. al., 1989) found that speakers who engaged in more eye contact, exhibited more facial pleasantness, and used certain types of gestures (i.e., illustrators) were more persuasive than speakers who did not.

Speakers who do not use eye contact to their advantage may have problems gaining trust. During speeches, for instance, Ronald Reagan and Bill Clinton, who have/had reputations for being effective communicators, were also well known for their direct and sincere eye contact. On the other hand, Richard Nixon, who had to be tutored to minimize his problems with making eye contact, was advised to place his speeches right on top of the camera so that he would be forced to make eye contact with the camera (Webbink, 1986). In his debates with Kennedy, Nixon also had problems with being perceived as "shifty eyed."

Before concluding this section, we should note that using more eye contact does not always mean that you will be more persuasive. A study by Kleinke (1980), for instance, illustrates that the effectiveness of eye contact may depend on other factors, for example, the legitimacy of the request you make. In Kleinke's study, persuaders were instructed to approach people in an airport and ask them for money. Some of the targets were told that the money would be used to make an important phone call (a legitimate request), while others were told that the money would be used to pay for a candy bar or gum (an illegitimate request). It turned out that people who thought the persuader needed to make a phone call gave more money, but only when the persuader looked at them. Interestingly, however, eye contact actually decreased compliance when the persuader made an illegitimate request (see Table 9.1). Perhaps, as the researcher suggested, looking away while making an illegitimate request makes a person seem more humble or embarrassed, thereby increasing his or her persuasiveness by winning the sympathy of others (Kleinke, 1980).

About Face

Has anyone ever told you that you have an amazing face? According to some estimates (Birdwhistell, 1970), your face may be capable of producing 250,000 different expressions! And that's without saying a single word.

Despite the face's capacity to communicate a large number of messages, there has been very little research examining the role of facial expressions in social influence. Heslin and Patterson (1982) suspected that this may be because the complexity and subtlety of facial expression makes such research extremely difficult. Ekman and Friesen (1975), for instance, found that there are eight different positions for the eyes alone. Even so, there is some research that helps us understand the relationship between facial expressions and persuasion. In general, research tends to show that when a person is sociable (e.g., extroverted, likable, and involved in the conversation) and relaxed (i.e., pleasant, positive, and not nervous), he or she tends to appear more credible. Thus, by smiling and/or nodding, waitresses earn more tips (Tidd & Lockard, cited in Heslin & Patterson, 1982), therapists are judged to be warmer and more competent (Leathers, 1986), job interviewees create positive impressions of themselves (Washburn & Hakel, 1973) and are more likely to get jobs (Forbes & Jackson, 1980), and teachers inspire students to pay more attention and achieve higher IQ scores (Saigh, 1981).

We do not, however, want to give you the impression that influence is always as easy as a smile. As noted in the credibility chapter (Chapter 5), persuaders need

TABLE 9.1   Illustration of Kleinke's (1980) results.

	Legitimate Request	Illegitimate Request
Eye contact	Persuadee complies with request.	Persuadee does not comply with request.
No eye contact	Persuadee does not comply with request.	Persuadee complies with request.

Adapted from Kleinke, C. L. (1980). Interaction between gaze and legitimacy of request on compliance in a field setting. *Journal of Nonverbal Behavior, 5,* 3–12.

to come across as trustworthy and sincere. People who smile too much may not always be perceived that way, however. A case in point is former president Jimmy Carter, who had a reputation for smiling a lot. In fact, he smiled so much that when talking about serious topics, he often had a problem appearing sincere. Similarly, in situations in which a dominant demeanor would be most persuasive, positive and likable facial expressions could be counterproductive. For instance, a study by Mehrabian and Williams (1969) found that although smiling and nodding were more persuasive when used by people of equal status, dominant behaviors are more effective in established hierarchies. Moreover, Kaplan, Greenfield, and Ware (cited in Buller & Street, 1992) found that patients were healthier in follow-up visits when their doctors expressed negative emotions in prior visits. The expression of positive emotions did not have this effect.

The situational nature of facial expressions is even more apparent if you consider research that has been done on the subject of "mirroring." Such research indicates that rather than using any one type of nonverbal behavior, a persuader should try to build rapport with others by mimicking their nonverbal cues. In other words, smile when people smile and frown when people frown. The basic assumption is that people like those who are similar to them and are persuaded by those whom they like. Thus, if you behave as others behave, you should be more persuasive.

Mirroring is often advised in self-help publications as a means of improving sales or rapport (DePaulo, 1992). One example is in Anthony Robbins's (1986) best-seller, *Unlimited Power:*

> So how do you mirror another person's physiology? What kinds of physical traits can you mirror? Start with his voice. Mirror his tonality and phrasing, his pitch, how fast he talks, what sort of pauses he makes, his volume. Mirror his favorite words or phrases. How about posture and breathing patterns, or eye contact, body language, facial expressions, hand gestures, or other distinctive movements… What if you could mirror everything about another person? Do you know what happens? People feel as though they've found a soulmate, someone who totally understands, who can read their deepest thoughts, who is just like them. But you don't have to mirror everything about a person to create a state of rapport. If you just start with the tone of voice or similar facial expressions, you can learn to build rapport with anyone. (p. 235)

Although we are not sure that mirroring is as easy or effective as Robbins claims, some research suggests that it is persuasive. Graham (cited in DePaulo, 1992), for instance, found that in negotiations, mutual facial expressions were associated with positive outcomes.

From the Neck Down: Persuasion and Body Language
Some of the principles of persuasion that we discussed in relation to the eyes and the face also apply to communication with the body. For example, just as you can mirror a person's facial expressions, you can mirror his or her gestures and body

movements. Moreover, we mentioned that certain behaviors such as eye contact and nodding can make people more persuasive by indicating that they are more involved in a conversation. Such involvement can be signaled via the body as well. For example, people who lean forward when communicating tend to be more persuasive than those who do not. In addition to these findings, research shows that people are more persuasive when they are pictured using open body positions (i.e., when their arms and legs are positioned away from their bodies) rather than neutral or closed positions (McGinley, LeFevre, & McGinley, 1975).

Perhaps most of the research on body movement and persuasion, however, has focused on the use of gestures. Although various researchers have discussed a number of different gestures, Argyle (1988) argued that it has been found most useful to focus on three: emblems, illustrators, and self-touching.

Emblems. According to Ekman and Friesen (1969), *emblems* are nonverbal behaviors, usually hand movements, with precise verbal meaning. Thus, emblems can substitute for words. Although traffic cops, referees, baseball catchers, and scuba divers are well-known emblem users, we use them all the time. Think of all the words for which we have gestures: hello, good-bye, come here, crazy, peace, I don't know, good luck, and shame on you, not to mention the ever popular middle finger gesture used by motorists.

Emblems are an important part of communication and serve many functions, persuasion included. But what part do emblems play in social influence? Several scholars have argued that a prerequisite for persuasion is attention to and retention of a message (e.g., McGuire, 1968; Petty & Cacioppo, 1986), and it seems that by providing more visual information, emblems play a large role in fostering attention and retention in persuadees. Woodall and Folger (1981), for example, found that people recalled 34 percent of a verbal message when it was accompanied by an emblem compared to only 11 percent when other types of gestures were used. Saigh (1981) found that the more teachers gesture, the more their students learn.

Illustrators. While emblems have meaning independent of verbal communication, *illustrators*, a second type of gesture, accompany speech (Ekman & Friesen, 1969). Like their name implies, illustrators illustrate, emphasize, or repeat what is being said. A child saying she loves you "this much" while spreading her arms wide is using an illustrator. Likewise, we can use illustrators to give directions, show our excitement, follow a rhythm, demonstrate a shape, and so forth. Interestingly, some research indicates that such gesturing may help us produce speech (Ekman & Friesen, 1972). Why else would we gesture while talking on the phone?

Several studies indicate that the use of illustrators increases a speaker's persuasiveness. In one study, for instance, actors who used more forceful and rhythmic gestures were more persuasive than those who did not (Maslow, Yoselson & London, 1971). Moreover, Mehrabian and Williams (1969) found that speakers were rated as more persuasive when they used more illustrators.

Self-Touching Behaviors (Adaptors). Although emblems and illustrators seem to increase people's persuasiveness, *self-touching behaviors* (e.g., scratching your arm, rubbing your cheek, picking your nose, stroking your hair), also known as *adaptors* (Ekman & Friesen, 1969), may decrease persuasiveness (unless, of course, you're Michael Jackson or Madonna). For example, several studies have found that the use of adaptors was associated with less persuasion (Maslow et al., 1971; Mehrabian & Williams, 1969). But why?

Earlier in this chapter, we mentioned that behaviors indicating relaxation generally are more persuasive than those indicating anxiety. People often interpret self-touching behavior as a sign of anxiety. For example, in Chapter 13, we note that adaptors are fairly reliable indicators of deception because deception is often accompanied by feelings of anxiety. For now, though, we conclude our examination of gestures and turn to a discussion of haptics, the next category of nonverbal communication.

Haptics: Reach Out, Reach Out and Touch Someone

If touching yourself makes you less persuasive, does touching other people have the same effect? Several years ago, three researchers interested in the topic of *haptics* (or touch) conducted a simple yet classic study to explore this question. In the study, library clerks did one of two things when they handed library cards back to university students who were checking out books: Either they did not touch the students or they made light physical contact by placing a hand over the students' palm. After their cards were returned, students were asked to rate the quality of the library, and, interestingly, those who were touched evaluated the library much more favorably than those who were not (Fisher, Rytting, & Heslin, 1976).

But you do not have to be a librarian to observe the persuasive effects of touch. For example, if you are or know a waiter or waitress, you might be interested in a study conducted by Jacob Hornick (1992), who wanted to know if being touched caused diners to leave bigger tips. To find out, Hornick had attractive and unattractive waiters and waitresses either touch diners on the arm or not touch them at all when asking "if everything was okay with their meals." The results of the study showed that touching not only increased tips significantly, it also caused customers to evaluate the servers and restaurants more favorably. Although the gender of the servers did not affect tips, the gender of the customer and the attractiveness of the server did. Specifically, attractive servers received larger tips, and attractive waitresses who touched female customers received the highest tips of all.

The persuasive impact of touch has been demonstrated in other contexts as well. For example, touch has been found to increase the number of people who volunteered to score papers (Patterson, Powell, & Lenihan, 1986), sign petitions (Willis & Hamm, 1980), and return money that had been left in a telephone booth (Kleinke, 1977). Similarly, Hornick (1992) found that touching bookstore customers on the arm caused them to shop longer (22.11 minutes vs. 13.56 minutes), purchase more ($15.03 vs. $12.23), and evaluate the store more positively than customers who had not been touched. Hornick (1992) also found that supermarket customers who had been touched were more likely to taste and purchase food samples than non-touched customers. Finally, Nannberg and Hansen (1994) found that people who had already agreed to participate in a lengthy and difficult survey completed more survey items if they had been touched.

Considering this research, it seems, then, that all the stuff we learned as kids about "the Midas touch" may not be such a fairy tale. Touching people seems to be persuasive. Touch may put people in a good mood, making them more likely to comply with requests (Hornick, 1992; Nannberg & Hansen, 1994). Another explanation is that people who touch create more favorable impressions of themselves and, therefore, are more persuasive (Hornick, 1992; Nannberg & Hansen, 1994). Burgoon, Walther, and Baesler (1992), for example, found that touch carries with it favorable interpretations of immediacy, affection, similarity, relaxation, informality, and task orientation. Finally, people who touch may be more persuasive because, through touch, they augment their image of power (Nannberg & Hansen, 1994; Patterson et al., 1986).

Whatever the reason for the persuasive impact of touch, one thing is clear: The use of touch for persuasive purposes is tricky because touch is so ambiguous. What one person may interpret as "friendly," for example, another may see as "flirtatious." Can the "brushing" of one employee against another be interpreted as accidental or as a form of sexual harassment? Is a pat on the back a sign of encouragement or an attempt to demonstrate dominance? Clearly, interpretations of touch depend on a vast array of factors, including context, gender, and culture. It is not yet clear, for example, who is more influenced by touch, males or females. Similarly, although some research shows that greater compliance should be apparent between a man and a woman (Brockner, Presman, Cabitt, & Moran, 1982; Patterson et al., 1986), others find that compliance is most likely in same gender pairs (Willis & Hamm, 1980).

It is apparent, then, that touch can communicate many messages and, because of its ambiguity, can easily be misused. In most of the studies we've just discussed, touching generally occurred on the hands or arms. We suspect that too much touching or touching other parts of a person might actually backfire, making persuasion less likely. As would-be persuadees, it is important for us to realize that even touches like those enacted in most of the studies we discussed wield tremendous persuasive power. Such touches may be so subtle that we might not even be aware that they are being used for persuasive purposes. But do not be fooled. Touch is persuasive, as is the use of space—our next topic.

Keep your Distance? Proxemics and Persuasion

The study of *proxemics,* or how we use space to communicate, covers a variety of topics such as the spatial arrangement of furniture, architecture, territoriality, and dominance. We know, for example, that dominant people are given more space and that people try to communicate dominance by taking up more space. In organizations, superiors are given bigger offices, larger desks, and seats at the heads of tables. As children grow older and less dependent on their parents, they require more space. Violent prisoners have larger body-buffer zones than nonviolent ones (22 sq. ft. vs. 7 sq. ft.) (Kinzel, 1970). And men, in general, tend to take up more

Touch, along with just about all forms of nonverbal communication, is ambiguous and, therefore, difficult to interpret.

THE BORN LOSER reprinted by permission of Newspaper Enterprise Association, Inc.

space than women. For example, when you go to a movie with someone of the opposite sex, who gets the armrest?

In this chapter, however, we are less concerned with research on territoriality and dominance. Instead, we focus our discussion on the topic of *personal space*, which refers to what might be considered an invisible bubble that surrounds us. An obvious case in point is that a door-to-door salesperson should not stick his nose in a potential customer's face. However, there is some evidence that indicates that the opposite is the case. That is, violating a person's space may be more persuasive. Heslin and Patterson (1982) for instance, explained how spatial invasion is common during police interrogations:

> *Texts on police methods recommend that the suspect not be placed behind a desk or even a desk chair. An obstruction of any sort gives the subject a feeling of relief and confidence not otherwise attainable. Although the officer may start the interrogation 2 or 3 feet away from the suspect, he [she] is instructed to move his [her] chair in close so that ultimately one of the suspect's knees is just about in between the interrogator's two knees. It is the clear implication that such close proximity makes the suspect more likely to yield to the officer's pressure to confess. Further, it is assumed that the close proximity will make guilty persons squirm as they*

sense they will not be able to hide the behavioral manifestations of guilt from the
intense (and close) examination of the police officer. (p. 58)

Empirical research also suggests that space invasion can be an effective tool of
persuasion. In a study by Baron and Bell (1976), for instance, diners in a cafeteria
were approached by an experimenter and asked to volunteer for a survey for a
period of 30 minutes to 2 hours and 30 minutes. The experimenter stood close to
some diners (12 to 18 in.) and farther away from others (3 to 4 ft.). Results of the
study showed that diners volunteered to participate for longer periods of time
when they were approached at closer distances. Similarly, research by Milgram
(1965) found that people were more likely to perform cruel acts (i.e., research participants believed that they were administering dangerous levels of electric shock
to other people) when an experimenter stood closer rather than farther away.

How can we explain these findings? First, because people tend to stand closer
to people they like (Argyle, 1988), persuadees may simply be reciprocating the liking by complying with the violator's requests (Baron & Bell, 1976). In addition,
because people find spatial invasion uncomfortable, those invaded may perceive
persuaders as more demanding, desperate, and needful (Baron & Bell, 1976).

As with other forms of nonverbal communication, some caution should be
taken when making generalizations about the role of proxemics in persuasion.
Indeed, at least two studies indicate that closer distances may not encourage compliance. For instance, Smith and Knowles (1979) found that pedestrians who had
their space invaded without justification were less likely to return a lost object than
those who had not had their space invaded. Moreover, a study by Albert and
Dabbs (1970) found that speakers were more persuasive the farther they were from
other people (i.e., speakers were more persuasive when standing 4–5 or 14–15 feet
from their audience than they were when standing 1–2 feet from their audience).[2]

If the conflicting results of these studies seem confusing, you might be interested in a theory presented by Judee Burgoon and her colleagues (Burgoon, 1978,
1992, 1994; Burgoon & Hale, 1988; Burgoon & Le Poire, 1993). It is called *expectancy
violations theory,* and we think it provides a strong and elegant explanation for the
ways in which space violations affect the process of social influence.[3]

According to the theory, we all have expectations about how close other people
should stand to us. When people violate those expectations and get either too close
or too far away, we experience arousal and may become distracted. How we react
to the violation, however, depends on several factors, perhaps the most important
being the "reward value" of the violator. If he or she is attractive, has the power to
reward or punish us, or is just plain likable, the violation is perceived as a pleasant
surprise and we are more likely to be persuaded. On the other hand, if the violator
has low reward value, the violation will be perceived as negative and compliance
will be less likely. In addition, the theory states that if violations are so extreme that
they are perceived as threatening, they also will decrease compliance.

The theory has received a considerable amount of support and implies several
practical suggestions for those interested in persuading others. First, if you think
the person you are trying to persuade sees you as attractive, powerful, or credible,

it is best to stand a litter farther or a little closer to that person than would be expected. Second, if you think you are perceived by someone as powerless and icky, you should maintain appropriate distances. Finally, never overdo it. If you stand too close or too far away, you will probably not be persuasive.

Chronemics: All Good Things to Those Who Wait?

In science, the concepts of space and time are often discussed together. However, in the study of persuasion, although considerable research has examined the topic of proxemics, little attention has been paid to *chronemics*, or the study of how time is used to communicate. Even so, we know that time can be an important commodity, especially in a culture like ours.

A common expression in the military, especially among soldiers with lower ranks, is "hurry up and wait." Oftentimes, it seems that such soldiers are expected to be on time although their superiors can show up whenever they want to. The point is, the higher your status, the more power you have over other people's time.

This is true in other contexts as well. For instance, how much time have you spent waiting in doctor's offices? Do you have to make appointments to see some professors or to get interviewed for a job? And don't be fooled, if you are a subordinate and show up more than a few minutes late to a business meeting, do you think you'll be very persuasive? We suspect not.

Practically speaking, then, you might be wondering whether it is okay to be late if you have a lot of status. Our suggestion is "be careful." Indeed, a study mentioned in the work of Burgoon and colleagues (1989) found that people who arrive 15 minutes late are considered dynamic, but much less competent, composed, and sociable than people who arrive on time. Plus, we think making people wait is rude.

Time not only affects perceptions of people, it can be used as a persuasive ploy. For instance, for people in a hurry, drive-through banking or fast food restaurants may have appeal. The success of establishments such as Jiffy Lube and 1Hour Photo also illustrate the effectiveness of this ploy.

Strategies related to chronemics sometimes are based on what Cialdini (1993) calls the *principle of scarcity*. According to Cialdini and others (e.g., Brehm, 1966; Brehm & Brehm, 1981), people love freedom, and when that freedom is threatened or limited, people experience something called *psychological reactance*. For example, a person in a store may decide that she likes a certain dress. If a salesperson explains to the customer that there is only one more dress like that in her size (i.e., that the dress is scarce), the woman, who might have thought that she was free to buy the dress at any time, may now react psychologically by wanting the dress more than she did in the first place (Cialdini, 1993). As you well know, persuaders also attempt to use psychological reactance in their favor by making time scarce. For instance, by telling us that we must "act now" or that there is a "limited time offer," advertisers are relying on the principle of scarcity. By limiting our time, they hope to make us more likely to purchase their product or service.

Interestingly, perhaps it's because psychological reactance is so uncomfortable that some persuaders have found that a "non-urgency" tactic is more successful.

In other words, because people don't want to be rushed and pressured, sometimes coming across as if time is *not* an issue can be very persuasive. Messages such as "90 days same as cash," "no payments or interest for a full year," and "free 30 day trial offer" facilitate sales by removing time pressures.

↖ comparative studies?

The Effect of Artifacts: Dress for Success

While talking about the notion of time, did we mention that an expensive watch with a gold wristband couldn't hurt your image much? Obviously, the clothes and makeup we wear, the cars we drive, the furniture we own, and other physical objects, also known as *artifacts,* can communicate a great deal about our credibility and status. In our society, material goods are viewed as an extension of oneself. Why else would color analysts be getting rich by telling people whether to wear summer, autumn, winter, or spring colored makeup? And why else would some-one pay thousands of dollars for an Armani suit?

Speaking of suits, we know a good story about how artifacts can affect people's perceptions. Many years ago, one of the authors sold men's suits for commission. Because he obviously did not earn anything unless he sold merchandise, when given a choice, the author tried to help customers who appeared as if they would spend a lot of money. One day a customer entered the store wearing a greasy tee-shirt, jeans, no socks, and filthy tennis shoes. Because at the time, there were plenty of other people shopping, the author decided to pick a more "profitable-looking" customer on whom to wait. One of the new employees, however, decided to help the greaseball. Much to the author's surprise, however, that "greaseball" ended up buying six very expensive suits. It seems that he was not a greaseball at all; he was a high-paid executive who had just lost all of his suits in a fire. He was restocking his wardrobe. Of course, the old saying "you can't judge a book by its cover" took on a whole new meaning that day!

In addition to clothing, other artifacts can be influential. For instance, one of our favorite studies examined how the appearance of professors' offices influenced the ways students perceived those professors (Teven & Comadena, 1996). In the study, 97 students went one at a time to meet a professor in his office. Upon arriving for the meeting, however, they found no professor and were asked to wait 5 minutes for him. Some of the students waited in a disorganized and untidy office, while others waited in a clean and neatly arranged office. After the 5 minutes were up, the students were told that the professor could not make the meeting. Later, however, they saw the professor lecture and then rated him on several scales. The results of the study showed that the professor's office had a significant influence on students' perceptions. Specifically, compared to students who visited the tidy office, those who visited the untidy one perceived the professor to be less authoritative, less trustworthy, less open, less relaxed, less concerned about making a good impres-sion, less animated, and less friendly. Interestingly, however, the "untidy" professor was seen as the most dynamic, perhaps because the disheveled office created the impression of a busy and energetic person (Teven & Comadena, 1996). Whatever the case, after reading this study, we'll be working on our cleanliness.

In addition to the studies and experiences we've mentioned so far, there is considerable evidence that shows that artifacts can not only make people appear more (or less) credible, they can make them more persuasive. Most of this research has focused on the impact of clothing. Lawrence and Watson (1991), for example, found that individuals asking for contributions to law enforcement and health-care campaigns earned more money when wearing sheriffs' and nurses' uniforms than when they did not. In another study, Bickman (1974) had young men, dressed as either civilians (i.e., wearing coats and ties), milkmen, or uniformed guards (with a badge and no gun), approach pedestrians on the streets of New York and ask them to do one of three things. In one situation, pedestrians were shown a bag lying on the ground and were told, "Pick up this bag for me!" In another condition, the experimenter pointed at a man standing near a parked car and said, "This fellow is over-parked at the meter but doesn't have any change. Give him a dime!" In the final condition, a person standing at a bus stop was told, "Don't you know you have to stand on the other side of the pole? The sign says, 'No Standing'." Results of the study showed that, in all three conditions, people complied more with the guard than they did the milkman or civilian. In other words, something about a uniform tends to make us obedient.

Fancy suits and uniforms, however, might not always be necessary tools of persuasion. In some cases, it may also be possible to influence people by wearing clothing that makes them identify with a persuader. When visiting local factories or appearing on MTV, for instance, politicians are often seen without their usual suits and neckties. Moreover, Hensley (1981) found that well-dressed people were more persuasive in airports but casually dressed people were more persuasive at bus stops.

In short, it appears that artifacts, particularly clothing, make a difference when trying to seek compliance. Of course, artifacts also can affect your appearance or attractiveness, which, in turn, can affect your persuasiveness. We now turn our discussion to this topic.

Physical Appearance: Of Beauties and Beasts

Beauty may only be skin deep, but it is persuasive. And the people out there trying to influence us know this. Beauty sells. For example, if Cindy Crawford had a big nose and warts with hair growing out of them, do you think you would see her face spread across the pages of makeup and shampoo ads? It seems, in fact, that the products being endorsed by attractive spokespersons do not even have to be connected with making us more attractive. Indeed, beautiful people are trying to sell us everything from milk, to law firms, to dog food.

Not surprisingly, plenty of research indicates that physical attractiveness is persuasive in contexts other than advertising. For instance, compared to their less attractive counterparts, attractive people are judged to be happier, more intelligent, friendlier, stronger, and kinder and are thought to have better personalities, better jobs, and greater marital competence (Knapp & Hall, 1992). Attractive

Dressing like your audience may make it identify with you more.

Photograph reprinted by permission of Reuters/Erik de Castro/Archive Photos.

women get more dates, higher grades, and lighter court sentences than unattractive people (see Box 9.2). Moreover, Norman (1976) found that although experts were more persuasive when providing supporting arguments for their position, attractive speakers were persuasive with or without the supporting arguments. Cialdini (1993) argued that these results may be due to a halo-effect, in which one positive characteristic of a person causes us to see everything about the person in a positive light. In other words, if the person is attractive, he or she must also be trustworthy, competent, and so forth. On the other hand, Bettinghaus and Cody (1994) argued that attractive people may be persuasive because we want to be like them, want them to like us, and because they are more self-confident and fluent than unattractive people. We suspect these results apply primarily in situations in which receiver involvement is low (à la Petty & Cacioppo, 1986). Involved receivers are more motivated to focus on the issues or the substance of a message and less on peripheral cues such as attraction.

Whatever the case, given the above findings, perhaps you are wondering what physical characteristics are related to attractiveness. Although we know that standards for beauty change over time (for instance, did you know that in medieval times, pale and plump people were perceived as the most attractive?) and that

BOX 9.2   Nonverbals in the Courtroom

You can probably imagine the ways a lawyer might use nonverbals in the courtroom. Although he or she may not be allowed to tell a witness, "That's the stupidest thing I've ever heard," the point can be illustrated with a simple facial expression. Likewise, during cross-examination, a lawyer's voice can reflect sarcasm or a long silence might provoke more testimony. To those who understand the subtle aspects of nonverbal communication, however, it should come as no surprise that nonverbals are at work in other corners of the courtroom. For example, in one study (Stewart, 1980), 73 defendants who had been rated on physical attractiveness went to trial. Results showed that the more attractive defendants received significantly lighter sentences. In addition, research shows that trial judges, who are supposed to appear fair and impartial, can and do influence the outcome of trials because of their nonverbals. Blanck and Rosenthal (1992) for instance, tell this true story:

> an appellate court reversed a burglary conviction when the trial judge, hearing the defendant's brother testify that the defendant was at home watching television when the alleged burglary occurred, without saying a word, placed his hands to the sides of his head, shook his head negatively, and leaned back, swiveling in his chair 180 degrees away from the jury (pp. 107–108).

Research also indicates that a judge's behavior can affect trial verdicts as well. A study by Dorsch and Fontaine (1978), for instance, found that when judges gazed more at defendants during a trial, defendants received higher fines if found guilty.

beauty is supposedly in the eye of the beholder, research tells us that some of the following characteristics are related to perceptions and/or persuasiveness:

1. **Body shape:** Arnold Schwarzeneggar, Kate Moss, and John Goodman represent the three basic body shapes. The first, a *mesomorph,* is athletic and muscular; the second, an *ectomorph* is thin and frail; and the third, an *endomorph*, is fat and round. Findings summarized by Argyle (1988) show that while mesomorphs are rated as, among other things, strong and adventurous, ectomorphs are seen as tense, pessimistic, and quiet, and endomorphs are seen as warm, sympathetic, agreeable, and dependent. Endomorphs are less likely to get jobs, less likely to earn high salaries and are less likely to be accepted into colleges than are thinner people with the same IQs.

2. **Facial appearance:** According to Argyle (1988), faces are perceived as more attractive when they have wide cheek bones, narrow cheeks, high eyebrows, wide pupils, large smiles, noses that are not too long or too short, and eyes not too far or too close together. Baby-faced women are perceived as more attractive but immature by men (Berry & McArthur, 1986) and, while baby-faced people are cast into commercials that want to portray trustworthiness, mature-faced people are cast into commercials that want to emphasize expertise (Brownlow & Zebrowitz, 1990). Interestingly, because baby-faced speakers may look more honest, they are more persuasive when their trustworthiness is questioned, while mature-faced speakers are more persuasive when their expertise is questioned (Brownlow, 1992).

3. Hair: Perceptions associated with body-hair obviously change over time. Although the hippies of the sixties rebelled by growing their hair long, today's skinheads do the same by befriending their razors. The same may be true of facial hair. For example, Disneyland, still striving for the clean-cut image, does not allow its employees to wear beards or moustaches, even though some research indicates that men with beards are regarded as more masculine and mature (Argyle, 1988). And finally, although men supposedly prefer blondes, research shows that any color hair may be better than none. For instance, a recent study comparing hair loss among governors and members of Congress to the general public found that elected politicians are more likely to have a full head of hair than would be expected of men their age (Sigelman, Dawson, Nitz, & Whicker, 1990).

4. Height: Although little research has examined how height affects perceptions of women, we know that tall men seem to have an advantage. According to Argyle's (1988) sources, the taller candidate usually becomes president, taller men are more likely to get jobs, and men over 6 feet 2 inches receive higher salaries.

Paralinguistics and Persuasion: Pump Up the Volume?

Paralinguistics or *vocalics* is the study of vocal stimuli aside from spoken words. It includes such elements as pitch, rate, pauses, volume, tone of voice, silences, laughs, screams, sighs, and so forth. We know from prior research that the *way* in which persons speak affects not only their credibility (Addington, 1968, 1971; Pearce & Conklin, 1971), but their ability to persuade as well. Mehrabian and Williams (1969), for instance, found that people who spoke faster, louder, and more fluently and who varied their vocal frequency and intensity were perceived as more persuasive than those who did not. Similarly, Miller, Maruyama, Beaber, and Valone (1976) found that speeches delivered at fast speeds were more persuasive than those at slow or moderate speeds, perhaps because persuaders who speak faster appear more competent and knowledgeable or because, at faster rates, receivers are not able to mentally engage in counterarguing. Hall (1980) and Buller and Aune (1988), however, argued that the optimal rate may depend on both the encoding ability of the sender and the decoding ability of the receiver. Specifically, although good decoders were more likely to comply with speeches delivered at fast rates, poor decoders preferred slower rates.

SUMMARY

In this chapter we learned that persuasion is not as simple as what you say. How you say something may be just as, if not more, important. We also learned that there are many categories of nonverbal communication that affect the process of communication. In our examination of kinesics, for instance, we saw that people are generally more persuasive when they (1) make eye contact, (2) use facial expressions and body movements that signal relaxation and sociability, and (3) use more emblems and illustrators but less adaptors. Similarly, we noted that people tend to be more compliant when they are touched or approached at distances that violate their expectations, as long as the touch and distances are not perceived as too inappropriate. Moreover, people can make themselves appear more credible, dominant, or powerful and, in turn, affect their persuasiveness through the use of time, artifacts, or physical appearance. Those who control others' time, wear the right clothing at the right time, and are attractive tend to be more persuasive than their counterparts. Finally, various features of the voice, particularly its rate, influence how persuasive one tends to be.

ENDNOTES

1. Dominant people actually gaze less when listening to subordinates (Exline et al., 1975).

2. Interestingly, people sitting 4 to 5 feet from the speaker paid more attention to the contents of the speech, while those sitting 1–2 or 14–15 feet away paid more attention to the appearance of the speaker.

3. Recently, expectancy violations theory has also been applied to other areas of nonverbal communication such as touch and gaze (e.g., Burgoon, Coker, & Coker, 1986; Burgoon et al., 1992).

REFERENCES

Addington, D. W. (1968). The relationship of selected vocal characteristics to personality perception. *Speech Monographs, 35,* 492–503.

Addinton, D. W. (1971). The effect of vocal variations on ratings of source credibility. *Speech Monographs, 38,* 242–247.

Albert, S., & Dabbs, J. M., Jr. (1970). Physical distance and persuasion. *Journal of Personality and Social Psychology, 15,* 265–270.

Argyle, M. (1988). *Bodily communication,* (2nd ed.). Madison, CT: International Universities Press.

Baron, R. A., & Bell, P. A. (1976). Physical distance and helping: Some unexpected benefits of "crowding in" on others. *Journal of Applied Social Psychology, 6,* 95–104.

Beebe, S. A. (1974). Eye contact: A nonverbal determinant of speaker credibility. *Speech Teacher, 23,* 21–25.

Berry, D. S., & McArthur, L. Z. (1986). Perceiving character in faces: The impact of age-related craniofacial changes on social perception. *Psychological Bulletin, 100,* 3–18.

Bettinghaus, E. P., & Cody, M. J. (1994). *Persuasive communication* (5th ed.). New York: Harcourt Brace.

Bickman, L. (1974). The social power of a uniform. *Journal of Applied Social Psychology, 4,* 47–61.

Birdwhistle, R. L. (1970). *Kinesics and context.* Philadelphia: University of Pennsylvania Press.

Blanck, P. D., & Rosenthal, R. (1992). Nonverbal behavior in the courtroom. In R. S. Feldman (Ed.), *Applications of nonverbal behavioral theories and research* (pp. 89–118). Hillsdale, NJ: Erlbaum.

Brehm, J. W. (1966). *A theory of psychological reactance.* New York: Academic Press.

Brehm, S. S., & Brehm, J. W. (1981). *Psychological reactance: A theory of freedom and control.* New York: Academic Press.

Brockner, J., Pressman, B., Cabitt, J., & Moran, P. (1982). Nonverbal intimacy, sex, and compliance: A field study. *Journal of Nonverbal Behavior, 6,* 253–259.

Brownlow, S. (1992). Seeing is believing: Facial appearance, credibility and attitude change. *Journal of Nonverbal Behavior, 16,* 101–115.

Brownlow, S., & Zebrowitz, L. A. (1990). Facial appearance, gender, and credibility in television commercials. *Journal of Nonverbal Behavior, 14,* 51–60.

Buller, D. B., & Aune, R. K. (1988). The effects of vocalics and nonverbal sensitivity on compliance: A speech accommodation theory explanation. *Human Communication Research, 14,* 301–332.

Buller, D. B., & Street, R. L., Jr. (1992). Physician–patient relationships. In R. S. Feldman (Ed.), *Applications of nonverbal behavioral theories and research* (pp. 119–142). Hillsdale, NJ: Lawrence Erlbaum.

Burgoon, J. K. (1978). A communication model of personal space violations: Explications and an initial test. *Human Communication Research, 4,* 129–142.

Burgoon, J. K. (1992). Applying a comparative approach to nonverbal expectancy violation theory. In J. Blumler, K. E. Rosengren, & J. M. McLeod (Eds.), *Comparatively speaking: Communication and culture across space and time* (pp. 53–69). Newbury Park, CA: Sage.

Burgoon, J. K. (1994). Nonverbal signals. In M. L. Knapp & G. R. Miller (Eds.), *Handbook of interpersonal communication* (2nd ed, pp. 229–285). Thousand Oaks, CA: Sage.

Burgoon, J. K., Buller, D. B., & Woodall, W. G. (1989). *Nonverbal communication: The unspoken dialogue.* New York: Harper and Row.

Burgoon, J. K., Coker, D. A., & Coker, R. A. (1986). Communicative effects of gaze behavior: A test of two contrasting explanations. *Human Communication Research, 12,* 495–524.

Burgoon, J. K., & Dillman, L. (1995). Gender, immediacy, and nonverbal communication. In P. J. Kalbfleisch & M. J. Cody (Eds.), *Gender, power, and communication in human relationships* (pp. 63–82). Hillsdale, NJ: Lawrence Erlbaum.

Burgoon, J. K., & Hale, J. L. (1988). Nonverbal expectancy violations: Model elaboration and application to immediacy behaviors. *Communication Monographs, 51,* 193–214.

Burgoon, J. K., & Le Poire, B. A. (1993). Effects of communication expectancies, actual communication, and expectancy disconfirmation on evaluations of communicators and their communication behavior. *Human Communication Research, 20,* 75–107.

Burgoon, J. K., Walther, J. B., & Baesler, E. J. (1992). Interpretations, evaluations, and consequences of interpersonal touch. *Human Communication Research, 19,* 237–263.

Cialdini, R. B. (1993). *Influence: Science and Practice* (3rd ed.). New York: HarperCollins.

DePaulo, P. J. (1992). Applications of nonverbal behavior research in marketing and management. In R. S. Feldman (Ed.), *Applications of nonverbal behavioral theories and research* (pp. 63–88). Hillsdale, NJ: Lawrence Erlbaum.

Dorsch, E., & Fontaine, G. (1978). Rate of judges' gaze at different types of witnesses. *Perceptual and Motor Skills, 46,* 1103–1106.

Ekman, P., & Friesen, W. V. (1969). The repertoire of nonverbal behavior: Categories, origins, usage, and coding. *Semiotica, 1,* 49–98.

Ekman, P., & Friesen, W. V. (1972). Hand movements. *Journal of Communication, 22,* 353–374.

Ekman, P., & Friesen, W. V. (1975). *Unmasking the face.* Englewood Cliffs, NJ: Prentice-Hall.

Exline, R. V., Ellyson, S. L., & Long, B. (1975). Visual behavior as an aspect of power role relationships. In P. Pliner, L. Krames, & T. Alloway (Eds.), *Nonverbal communication of aggression* (pp. 21–52). New York: Plenum Press.

Fisher, J. D., Rytting, M., & Heslin, R. (1976). Hands touching hands: Affective and evaluative effects of an interpersonal touch. *Sociometry, 39,* 416–421.

Forbes, R. J., & Jackson, P. R. (1980). Non-verbal behaviour and the outcome of selection interviews. *Journal of Occupational Psychology, 53,* 65–72.

Hall, J. A. (1980). Voice tone and persuasion. *Journal of Personality and Social Psychology, 38,* 924–934.

Hensley, W. E. (1981). The effects of attire, location, and sex on aiding behavior: A similarity explanation. *Journal of Nonverbal Behavior, 6,* 3–11.

Heslin, R, & Patterson, M. L. (1982). *Nonverbal behavior and social psychology.* New York: Plenum Press.

Hornick, J. (1992). Tactile stimulation and consumer response. *Journal of Consumer Research, 19,* 449–458.

Kinzel, A. F. (1970). Body-buffer zones in violent prisoners. *American Journal of Psychiatry, 127,* 59–64.

Kleinke, C. L. (1977). Compliance to requests made by gazing and touching experimenters in field settings. *Journal of Experimental Social Psychology, 13*, 218–223.

Kleinke, C. L. (1980). Interaction between gaze and legitimacy of request on compliance in a field setting. *Journal of Nonverbal Behavior, 5*, 3–12.

Knapp, M. L. (1978). *Nonverbal communication in human interaction* (2nd ed.). New York: Holt, Rinehart and Winston.

Knapp, M. L. (1992). *Nonverbal communication in human interaction* (3rd ed.). New York: Holt, Rinehart and Winston.

Knapp, M. L., & Hall, J. A. (1992). *Nonverbal communication in human interaction*. Fort Worth, TX: Harcourt Brace Jovanovich.

Lawrence, S., & Watson, M. (1991). Getting others to help: The effectiveness of professional uniforms in charitable fund raising. *Journal of Applied Communication Research, 19*, 170–185.

Leathers, D. G. (1986). *Successful nonverbal communication*. London, England: Collier Macmillan.

Maslow, C., Yoselson, K., & London, H. (1971). Persuasiveness of confidence expressed via language and body language. *British Journal of Social and Clinical Psychology, 10*, 234–240.

McGinley, H., LeFevre, R., & McGinley, P. (1975). The influence of a communicator's body position on opinion change in others. *Journal of Personality and Social Psychology, 31*, 686–690.

McGuire, W. J. (1968). Personality and susceptibility to social influence. In E. G. Borgatta & W. W. Lambert (Eds.), *Handbook of personality theory and research* (pp. 1130–1187). Chicago: Rand McNally.

Mehrabian, A., & Williams, M. (1969). Nonverbal concomitants of perceived and intended persuasiveness. *Journal of Personality and Social Psychology, 13*, 37–58.

Milgram, S. (1965). Some conditions of obedience and disobedience to authority. *Human Relations, 18*, 57–76.

Miller, N., Maruyama, G., Beaber, R. J., & Valone, K. (1976). Speed of speech and persuasion. *Journal of Personality and Social Psychology, 34*, 615–624.

Nannberg, J. C., & Hansen, C. (1994). Post-compliance touch: An incentive for task performance. *Journal of Social Psychology, 134*, 301–307.

Norman, R. (1976). When what is said is important: A comparison of expert and attractive sources. *Journal of Experimental Social Psychology, 12*, 294–300.

Patterson, M. L., Powell, J. L., & Lenihan, M. G. (1986). Touch, compliance and interpersonal affect. *Journal of Nonverbal Behavior, 10*, 41–50.

Pearce, W. B., & Conklin, F. (1971). Nonverbal vocalic communication and perceptions of a speaker. *Communication Monographs, 38*, 235–241.

Petty, R. E., & Cacioppo, J. T. (1986). *Communication and persuasion: Central and peripheral routes to attitude change*. New York: Springer-Verlag.

Petty, R. E., Wells, G. L., Heesacker, M., Brock, T., & Cacioppo, J. T. (1983). The effects of recipient posture on persuasion: A cognitive response analysis. *Personality and Social Psychology Bulletin, 9*, 209–222.

Robbins, A. (1986). *Unlimited power*. New York: Fawcett Columbine.

Robinson, J. D., Seiter, J. S., & Acharya, L. (February, 1992). *"I just put my head down and society does the rest." An examination of influence strategies among beggars*. Paper presented at the Annual Meeting of the Western Speech Communication Association, Boise, ID.

Roser, C. (1990). Involvement, attention and perceptions of message relevance in the response to persuasive appeals. *Communication Research, 17*, 571–600.

Roser, C., & Thompson, M. (1995). Fear appeals and the formation of active publics. *Journal of Communication, 45*, 103–121.

Saigh, P. A. (1981). Effects of nonverbal examiner praise on selected WAIS subtest performance of Lebanese undergraduates. *Journal of Nonverbal Behavior, 6*, 84–86.

Sigelman, L., Dawson, E., Nitz, M., & Whicker, M. L. (1990). Hair loss and electability: The bald truth. *Journal of Nonverbal Behavior, 14*, 269–283.

Smith, R. J., & Knowles, E. S. (1979). Affective and cognitive mediators of reactions to spatial invasions. *Journal of Experimental Social Psychology, 15*, 437–452.

Stewart, J. E., Jr. (1980). Defendant's attractiveness as a factor in the outcomes of trials. *Journal of Applied Social Psychology, 10*, 348–361.

Teven, J. J., & Comadena, M. E. (1996). The effects of office aesthetic quality on students' perceptions of teacher credibility and communicator style. *Communication Research Reports, 13*(1), 101–108.

Washburn, P. V., & Hakel, M. D. (1973). Visual cues and verbal content as influences on impressions formed after simulated employment interviews. *Journal of Applied Psychology, 58,* 137–141.

Webbink, P. (1986). *The power of the eyes.* New York: Springer.

Willis, F. N., & Hamm, H. K. (1980). The use of interpersonal touch in securing compliance. *Journal of Nonverbal Behavior, 5,* 49–55.

Woodall, W. G., & Folger, J. P. (1981). Encoding specificity and nonverbal cue context: An expansion of episodic memory research. *Communication Monographs, 48,* 39–53.

10

STRUCTURING AND ORDERING PERSUASIVE MESSAGES

The study of persuasion and the study of rhetoric, if not one and the same, are closely related. Aristotle, for instance, defined rhetoric as "the faculty of discovering all the available means of persuasion." Although, today the term "rhetoric" is often used in conjunction with words like "empty" or "meaningless," the connotations surrounding the term did not always used to be so negative. The ancient Greeks and Romans, for example, considered rhetoric an essential ingredient in a good education. By the time the great Roman orator, Cicero, wrote about rhetoric, its study was divided into five parts. Four were called *inventio, elocutio, memoria,* and *pronuntiatio*, which focused on finding and inventing arguments, speaking with style, remembering arguments, and delivering speeches effectively. The last part, *dispositio*, focused on selecting the most important arguments and ideas and on the effective and orderly arrangements of those ideas and arguments (Corbett, 1971). Quintilian, another Roman rhetorician, noted the significance of strategically planning and organizing a persuasive message. As Corbett (1971) wrote:

> *Quintilian hints at the more important concern of disposition when he says that it is to oratory what generalship is to war. It would be folly to hold a general to a fixed, predetermined disposition of his forces. He must be left free to distribute his troops in the order and proportion best suited to cope with the situation in which he may find himself at any particular moment. So he will mass some of his troops at one point on the battle line, thin them out at other points, keep other troops in reserve, and perhaps concentrate his crack troops at the most crucial area. Guided by judgment and imagination, the general stands ready to make whatever adjustments in strategy eventualities may dictate. (pp. 299–300)*

Clearly, when planning a persuasive message, we are often confronted with questions of strategy such as: "What should I leave in, and what should I leave out?," "How should I arrange my arguments?," and "Should my strongest arguments come first or last?" However, in addition to questions concerning the order of arguments within persuasive messages, there is the issue of the sequencing of messages when more than one persuader is involved. For example, imagine that you are about to speak to a large audience and want to convince that audience to lower tuition at your school. You know that after you've spoken, another person will argue just the opposite: Tuition should be raised. Is there anything you can do to make your opponent's arguments less powerful? In this chapter we examine these issues.

IMPLICIT AND EXPLICIT CONCLUSIONS: THE WRITING'S ON THE WALL

According to Kardes, Kim, and Lim (1994), one of the key decisions facing advertisers is whether a hard-sell or a soft-sell strategy is best. One type of hard-sell strategy is to draw explicit conclusions for your audience. In other words, when employing an "explicit conclusions approach," any claim that is made in a message is directly stated by the person sending the message (e.g., you should buy our product, our product is simply the best, etc.). In contrast, one type of soft-sell strategy involves the use of implicit conclusions. Here the persuader is more subtle, allowing persuadees to reach their own conclusions without being told what to do or believe (Kardes et al., 1994). For example, consider the following ad discussed by Sawyer (1988):

> *A commercial...begins when a perky young woman comes on the screen and says, "I've got a question. Pay attention, there will be a quiz later. People prefer their hamburgers at home and flame-broiled. Now, if McDonald's and Wendy's fry their hamburgers and Burger King flame-broils theirs...where do you think people should go for a hamburger? (p. 159)*

In this advertisement, an "implicit conclusions approach" is used because customers are allowed to make their own inferences (in this case, "People should go to Burger King!"). Had the spokesperson said, "People should go to Burger King!," the ad would have been an example of one using an "explicit conclusion approach."

An obvious question facing persuasion researchers concerns whether there is an advantage to using one approach over the other (i.e., do implicit conclusions work best or vice versa?). According to Kardes and colleagues (1994), both approaches have potential risks and benefits. For instance, although explicit conclusions involve the use of very simple and straightforward claims, receivers could resent being told what to believe and might distrust the message. On the other hand, while people may perceive implicit conclusions as more valid because they came up with the conclusions by themselves, they might fail to draw the conclusions or might draw the wrong conclusions (Kardes et al., 1994).

Until recently, persuasion scholars have argued that explicit conclusions are more effective than implicit ones. For example, at least two studies (Fine, 1957;

Hovland & Mandell, 1952) revealed that messages with explicit conclusions were more persuasive than those that led subjects to draw their own conclusions. Based on such evidence, McGuire (cited in Sawyer, 1988, p. 164) made this (explicit) claim:

> *It may well be that if the person draws the conclusion for himself he is more persuaded than if the source draws it for him; the problem is that in the usual communication situation the subject is either insufficiently intelligent or insufficiently motivated to draw the conclusion for himself, and therefore misses the point of the message to a serious extent unless the source draws it for him. In communication, it appears it is not sufficient to lead a horse to water; one must also push its head underneath to get him to drink.*

McGuire's statement suggests that although explicit conclusions may be more prudent to use in general, sometimes implicit conclusions may be more effective. For instance, consistent with Petty and Cacioppo's (1986) Elaboration on Likelihood Model, Sawyer and Howard (1991) argued that when a message is personally relevant to a person, that person should be more motivated to draw his or her own conclusions. Thus, compared to people who are not personally involved with a topic, those who are should be more persuaded by an implicit conclusions approach. To test this hypothesis, Sawyer and Howard asked subjects to look at advertisements that used either implicit or explicit claims about disposable razors and toothbrushes. To make the ads more personally relevant, some of the subjects viewing toothbrush ads were told that as a free gift for their participation they would be allowed to choose from several brands of toothbrushes, including one shown in the ad. On the other hand, to make the ads less personally relevant, other subjects viewing the toothbrush ads were told that they would get to choose a free razor. (Similarly, subjects watching razor ads were told they'd be choosing either razors or toothbrushes, depending on whether they were in the "relevant" or "non-relevant" conditions.) The results of the study confirmed the researchers' hypothesis. Specifically, when subjects viewed ads that were personally relevant, they were more persuaded by implicit conclusions. For those watching ads that were not relevant, it did not matter whether implicit or explicit conclusions were used.

In a similar study, Kardes and colleagues (1994) found that it is better to let receivers draw their own conclusions about a product when the receivers have a lot of knowledge about that type of product (i.e., compact disc players). On the other hand, for people with little knowledge about the product type, it is more persuasive to include explicit conclusions in a message. In short, when trying to decide whether to draw conclusions for an audience, it is most important to know what type of person is in the audience.

QUANTITY VERSUS QUALITY OF ARGUMENTS: THE MORE THE MERRIER?

What are you going to have for your next dinner? If given the choice between an all you can eat buffet and a fancy French restaurant, which would you pick? We imagine your answer depends on whether you like to treat your taste buds or fill your belly. Indeed, buffets usually offer lots of mediocre food, while a good French restaurant typically promises small portions of really tasty food. What appeals to you more than likely depends on your priorities.

The same is probably true of persuasive messages. For some people, it is the *quantity* of arguments presented that counts. A "kitchen sink" approach in which an advocate throws in every available argument works best. For other people, it is the *quality* of arguments that counts. For such people, the number of arguments is inconsequential. They require "gourmet" arguments. To illustrate this notion, we return briefly to Petty and Cacioppo's (1986) Elaboration Likelihood Model which we discussed in more detail in Chapter 2.

Recall that, according to the ELM, there are two routes to persuasion, the peripheral route and the central route. First, when people are persuaded by a message that they have carefully scrutinized, they are being persuaded via the central route (of course, after scrutinizing a message, they may also remain unpersuaded). Sometimes, however, people do not scrutinize the persuasive messages they receive. For example, they may not have the ability or the motivation to think about the message. Even if that happens, however, they may still be persuaded via the peripheral route. For example, if there is some easy way for them to decide to be persuaded, they may very well change their attitude or behavior. If there is no "easy" cue, however, they will not be persuaded (Petty & Cacioppo, 1986).

According to Petty and Cacioppo (1984), one type of peripheral cue may be the number of arguments that a persuader uses. These researchers reasoned that some people might decide that a persuasive message containing a lot of arguments must be a lot better than one that does not ("It must be a good argument! Look at all those reasons!"). Of course, not all people would be persuaded by a lot of weak arguments. People who carefully scrutinized the arguments, they hypothesized, would not be fooled.

To test their hypothesis, these researchers asked several university students to read a message proposing that at some future date all students would have to complete comprehensive examinations before they graduated. Some students were told that the exam policy would be implemented in 1 year, meaning that they would all have to take the exams themselves. The remaining students, however, were told the exam policy would take 10 years to be implemented. Thus, some of the students were highly involved with the topic and others were not. Petty and Cacioppo suspected that, compared to the uninvolved students, the involved students would be more motivated to scrutinize the message. (Wouldn't you be?) In addition, Petty and Cacioppo had the students read one of four different versions of the persuasive messages: One version contained three weak arguments, one contained nine weak arguments, one contained three strong arguments, and one contained nine strong arguments.

Results of the study confirmed the researchers expectations and supported the ELM. Specifically, for the students who were not involved in the topic, the quality of the arguments did not matter. Quantity did though. This group was much more persuaded that comprehensive exams would be a good thing after they heard nine arguments than after they heard three arguments. On the other hand, the students who were involved in the topic were not taken in by a lot of weak arguments. They were only persuaded when strong arguments were used, especially when there were a lot of strong arguments (Petty & Cacioppo, 1984) (see Figure 10.1). The moral of this study, then, is the following—if you think your audience will scrutinize your message, use strong arguments, but if your audience does not seem involved in the topic, a smorgasbord of arguments may be quite effective.

REPETITION AND MERE EXPOSURE: YOU CAN SAY THAT AGAIN

Although we've just seen that using a lot of arguments in a message can sometimes make you more persuasive, what happens if you use the *same* argument or message a lot of times? Stated differently, can repeating your message make you more persuasive? Several researchers have argued that repetition can be an effective tactic, although there is some disagreement concerning why. One perspective argues that in order to be persuaded, a person must first *attend to* and *comprehend* the persuasive message (McGuire, 1968, 1969). Obviously, when a message is repeated, it increases the odds that it will be attended to and comprehended, thereby increasing the chances of successful persuasion.

Another perspective that has received considerable attention by persuasion scholars is known as the *mere exposure theory* (Zajonc, 1968). According to Sawyer

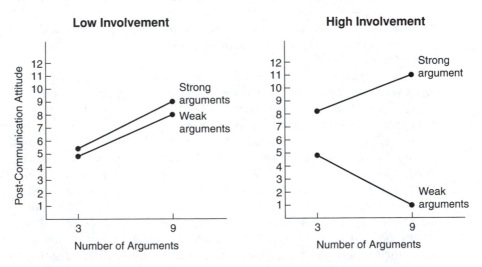

FIGURE 10.1   Results of Petty & Cacioppo's 1984 study.

From Petty, R. E., & Cacioppo, J. T. (1984). The effects of involvement on responses to argument quantity and quality: Central and peripheral routes to persuasion. *Journal of Personality and Social Psychology, 46,* 69–81. Copyright © 1984 by the American Psychological Association. Reprinted with permission.

(1981), "This theory hypothesizes that familiar objects are more liked than less familiar ones, and that by merely being repetitively exposed, something initially unfamiliar will be looked upon more favorably" (p. 238). In other words, mere exposure theory suggests that we really do "*acquire* tastes," that things can "grow on us," and that "familiarity does *not* breed contempt." By way of example, you might have noticed that some songs seem to get better and better the more you hear them, or that some people seem more likeable the longer you know them. In a now classic study, Zajonc (1968) found that repeated exposure even made the Chinese language more likeable to people who didn't know how to read or speak it. In the study, subjects saw pictures of Chinese characters anywhere from one to twenty-five times. Afterwards, the subjects were asked to guess the meanings of the characters. Interestingly, the characters that were seen the most often were "defined" in much more positive ways than were the characters that were seen less often. With this in mind, it's not surprising to us that politicians pepper front yards, telephone poles, bumpers, and just about anything they can get their paws on with their names and faces.

Although research has shown that mere and repeated exposure to songs, people, languages, and messages may increase attention, comprehension, and likeability, there is considerable evidence suggesting that too much repetition can backfire. For example, in one study (Miller, 1976), a group of people were exposed to a poster campaign trying to convince them to stop foreign aid. One group of people just read a questionnaire concerning the topic. Another group of people read the questionnaire and then was exposed to 30 posters concerning the topic. A final group read the questionnaire and was exposed to 200 posters. Thus, for some groups, the message was repeated much more often. Results of the study showed that people were most persuaded when repetition was moderate. In other words, one exposure to the persuasive message did not seem to be enough, but 200 posters were too many, causing people to react negatively to the message.

Consistent with the findings of this and other studies is Petty and Cacioppo's (1986) notion that message repetition affects reactions to a persuasive message in a two-stage process. First, message repetition increases a person's ability to comprehend the arguments in a message. Second, after a person has grasped the meaning of the message, repeating the message leads to tedium or reactance, causing the person to reject the message. To test this model, Cacioppo and Petty (1979) conducted an experiment. They told 193 undergraduates to listen to and judge the sound quality of some audiotapes. The researchers weren't interested in judgments of sound quality, however; they really wanted to see how the students would react to the audiotaped message after hearing it either one, three, or five times. The tapes contained a message recommending that the university increase expenditures and argued that the money should come from one of two sources— a visitor's luxury tax, or from raising students' tuition. Not surprisingly, results of the study showed that students agreed less with arguments in support of higher tuition than with arguments in support of a luxury tax. Regardless of the message, however, students agreed most when they heard the message three times (rather than one or five times). Moreover, when the researchers examined the thoughts that students recorded while listening to the tapes, they found that the thoughts became more favorable up to three repetitions, but that favorable thoughts decreased at five repetitions. In short, some repetition is good, but don't overdo it.

Although the research we've discussed so far makes it fairly clear that a moderate amount of repetition/exposure is most effective, you should also be aware that some factors make repetition much more or much less tolerable (see Sawyer, 1981). For example, you've heard the saying, "No one likes to hear the same joke twice." That's because we tend to be less tolerant of messages that repeat humorous material than we are of those that don't (although we'd obviously much rather hear a funny message twice then a message with no appeal whatsoever). In addition, we may be more tolerant of complex or abstract messages that are repeated since they take longer to figure out. Finally, messages with stronger arguments may be tolerated longer than those with weak arguments. In general, then, three repetitions might be considered a "golden mean"; sometimes fewer repetitions is better, sometimes more, but three repetitions strikes the best balance if the persuader is unsure about other issues such as receiver involvement, attitudes toward the topic, and so forth (for more on the effects of repetition, see Box 10.1).

ORDER EFFECTS AND PERSUASION: FIRST THINGS FIRST

In the preceding sections, we've seen that strong arguments are not always the most persuasive and that people are generally more willing to hear a strong argument repeated rather than a weak one. Sometimes, however, it is not so easy to separate

---

BOX 10.1   "Not Again!": Repetition and Commercials

The research findings regarding mere exposure and repetition do not apply solely to pictures, written and audiotaped messages. Anyone who has watched more than an hour of television has probably had the experience of seeing the same commercial at least twice, maybe more. "We just saw this!" or "Not *this* one again!" may sound familiar to you avid TV watchers. But if these are common reactions from television audiences, why do advertisers repeat their commercials? It's got to be because repetition works. Indeed, air time is expensive. Advertisers know that repetition can be effective, but they have to be careful. For example, one of the authors is so tired of seeing a particular little pink bunny that he wishes it would keep "going and going" and never come back.

This raises an important question for advertisers: How much will viewers tolerate be-

fore they become impatient or bored? Although several studies have examined this question, one of our favorites was conducted by Gorn and Goldberg (1980). Here's how the study worked. While watching the Flintstones, several boys (8 to 10 years old) saw from 1 to 5 identical or different commercials for the same product: Danish Hill ice cream. Results of the study showed that the boys who had seen three commercials had greater recall for the product than the boys who saw the commercial only once. Recall, however, did not get better if the commercial had been seen five times. In addition, the boys who had seen three commercials said they preferred the product more than the boys who had seen one or five. This was particularly true of the boys who had seen three different commercials.

strong from weak arguments. In other words, persuasive messages often contain many arguments, some stronger than others. When that happens, whoever is delivering the persuasive message must decide how he or she should arrange the arguments. For example, imagine you're planning to give a persuasive speech. Should you begin with your strongest argument to create a favorable first impression? Or would it be better to dazzle your audience at the end of your speech so that the audience leaves feeling motivated? Of course, there's always a third option. You could compromise and put your strongest argument in the middle of your speech.

When strong arguments come first, a message is said to have an *anticlimax order.* When they come last, a message has a *climax order.* A message with a *pyramidal order* has strong arguments in the middle. But which order works best? Most research on this subject suggests that putting your strongest argument either first *or* last is the best strategy (Gilkenson, Paulson, & Sikkink, 1954; Gulley & Berlo, 1956; Sikkink, 1956). Both seem to work better than sandwiching strong arguments in the middle of a speech, but beyond that, strong arguments seem effective at either the beginning or end of a message.

Of course, other variables may determine whether strong or weak arguments should go first or last. For example, Unnava, Burnkrant, and Erevelles (1994) argued that the means or channel by which a message is transmitted should determine whether strong arguments go first or last. Their study found that when groups were visually exposed to information about the characteristics of a book bag, their attitudes about the bag were the same whether they were exposed to strong or weak arguments about the bag's quality first. On the other hand, if they received auditory messages about the bag, they had more favorable attitudes when strong arguments came before weak arguments. Thus, when information is presented for people to hear, order is important.

PRIMACY AND RECENCY EFFECTS: THE FIRST SHALL BE LAST AND THE LAST SHALL BE FIRST

Up to this point, we've been looking at how arguments should be selected and organized within a single speech. The issue of what goes first and what goes last extends beyond single speeches, however. It is also possible to consider whether *who* goes first and *who* goes last affects the process of persuasion. Nowadays, it is quite common for political candidates to be involved in debates that are not very interactive. A coin is flipped, one candidate speaks, and then the other takes a turn. When that happens, is there any advantage to speaking first, or do all good things come to those who wait? As with research on climax and anticlimax, results in this area are mixed; some studies support a *primacy effect* (i.e., the first speaker has an advantage) but others support a *recency effect* (i.e., the second speaker has an advantage). On the other hand, several studies have investigated whether some circumstances favor primacy while others favor recency. We consider two such circumstances now.

First, a classic study by Miller and Campbell (1959) demonstrated that the passage of time determines whether primacy or recency prevails. Primacy, they found, works best when you hear two opposing messages, back to back, and then have to wait a while before deciding what to do about the messages. For instance, a primacy effect is likely when you hear one candidate speak right after another and then wait a week before voting for one of the candidates. Why should this scenario work to the advantage of the candidate who speaks first? According to Miller and Campbell (1959), with time we tend to remember information we receive first. In other words, first impressions may be lasting impressions.

On the other hand, Miller and Campbell (1959) found that the recency effect is more likely when you hear one message, wait some time before hearing the opposing message, and then decide immediately after the second message what you are going to do. For instance, a recency effect is likely if you hear one candidate give a speech, and then, just before voting, hear the opposing candidate give a speech. Why, in this situation, should the second candidate prevail? The researchers argued that because we tend to forget information rapidly, we'll have forgotten most of the first message by the time we vote. On the other hand, voting immediately after hearing the second message should enable us to remember most of the candidate's message, giving him or her an advantage[1] (see Figure 10.2).

In addition to time delay, the content of the message may determine whether first messages are more persuasive then second messages or vice versa. For instance, some research indicates that material that is relatively unsalient, noncontroversial, uninteresting, and unfamiliar to the audience tends to produce a recency effect. On the other hand, salient, interesting, controversial and familiar material tends to produce a primacy effect, perhaps because an audience starts with a high level of interest that decreases over time (Furnam, 1986; Rosnow, 1966; Rosnow & Robinson, 1967). Thus, if given the choice to speak first or last, you may want to base your decision on the nature of your material[2] (see Box 10.2)

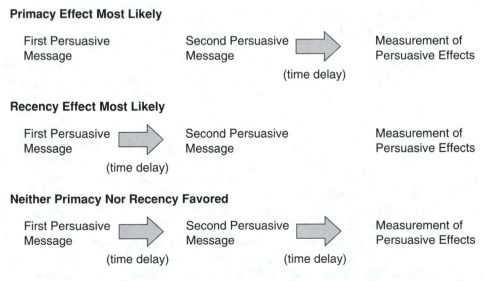

Primacy Effect Most Likely

First Persuasive Message   Second Persuasive Message   Measurement of Persuasive Effects

(time delay)

Recency Effect Most Likely

First Persuasive Message   Second Persuasive Message   Measurement of Persuasive Effects

(time delay)

Neither Primacy Nor Recency Favored

First Persuasive Message   Second Persuasive Message   Measurement of Persuasive Effects

(time delay)   (time delay)

FIGURE 10.2   **Primacy versus recency effects in persuasion.**

BOX 10.2   Copycatter, Dirty Ratter: Should You Be First or Second to Market a Product?

What do IBM, Burger King, and Pepsi have in common? You might say they are copycatters. When it comes to personal computers, fast food, and colas, when these three companies came along, someone (or some other company) was already there first. But is there an advantage to being the first company to market a product? Is there something analogous for businesses to the primacy/recency effect for speakers? According to Haines, Chandran, and Parkhe (1989), there are definite advantages and disadvantages to being either the leader or the follower where marketing is concerned. So if you have considered starting your own business, here are some things that Haines and colleagues (1989) suggest you think about.

When pioneering your own product or service, there are several advantages. First, the product or service that is on the market first becomes entrenched in the consumer's mind. People may be more receptive to the product that does not compete with others, and once they've become accustomed to the product will be less likely to switch. For example, why risk trying Powerade when you know you already like Gatorade? Second, pioneering a new product does not require the dollars that marketing a copycat product might. For instance, to lower the risk of trying a new product you have to give free samples and coupons. Moreover, it costs a lot in advertising to show that a copycat product has noticeable advantages over the pioneer product. Third, pioneer products tend to sustain a market share advantage over new products. Fourth, pioneers get experience quicker and can cut costs more effectively than

the new competitions. Finally, the pioneer company can establish an image and reputation before competitors come along. Imagine, for example, trying to steal the market from companies and products such as Xerox, Band-Aids, Kleenex, and Jell-O, whose names have become synonymous with the actual products (Haines et al., 1989).

Although being a pioneer can be an advantage in the business world, being a follower also can have benefits. First, if you start a follow-up company, you know that a market already exists for your product. Second, a follow-up company can use newer manufacturing technologies and may have access to the knowledge and experience of the customers and suppliers of the company that they are trying to imitate. Third, a new company can redesign a product to better meet the needs of a consumer. For example, after interviewing Volkswagen owners to discover VW weaknesses, the makers of Toyota took over the market by making better heated cars with bigger backseats and more attractive interiors (Haines et al., 1989).

Of course, there are disadvantages to both pioneering and following strategies as well. For example, many pioneers find that a market they thought existed really does not. Similarly, many copycatters learn that a company they thought they could elbow out of the market might not budge. From the perspective of Haines and colleagues (1989), then, once you know you have a great product, "the key to success is not to be there too late, or too early" (p. 69).

ONE-SIDED VERSUS TWO-SIDED MESSAGES: BOTH SIDES NOW

In the last section we saw that when speaking against an opponent, sometimes it's better to go first and sometimes it's better to go last. Obviously, though, when you are the only one delivering a message, your opponent's perspective is inconsequential. Or is it? A considerable amount of past research has examined whether a one-sided message, presenting arguments in favor of a single proposition, is more or less persuasive than a two-sided message, which presents arguments in favor of one proposition while also considering opposing arguments. In other words, when trying to persuade an audience, is it best to address your opposition or to ignore them?

The first empirical study to investigate this issue was conducted by Hovland, Lumsdaine, and Sheffield (1949) at the request of the War Department during World War II. The study's purpose was to determine the best way to convince American soldiers that the war in Japan would last for a considerable amount of time. The researchers asked their subjects to listen to one of two messages. One presented arguments that supported the war with Japan and argued that the war would be a long one. The other message included the same arguments as the first in addition to a brief description of opposing arguments. Results of the study found that the effectiveness of one- or two-sided arguments depended on two factors: education level and initial attitude. First, the one-sided message was more effective for persuading subjects with little education, while the two-sided message was more effective for persuading subjects who had at least a high school education.[3] Second, when the subjects initially agreed with the argument presented, they were more persuaded by the one-sided argument. Just the opposite was true of subjects who initially disagreed with the argument presented.

In addition to studying the effects of message-sidedness on persuasion, early research also examined whether one-sided or two-sided messages matter when people are judging a speaker's credibility. The general idea is that people who present both sides of an issue may seem more competent, fair-minded, and trustworthy than those who don't. That is, people who present both sides are not only expert enough to know the opposing arguments, they are honest enough to share them. For example, we imagine that a salesperson who points out possible weaknesses in his or her product would seem more trustworthy.

Although the large number of studies examining the effects of one- and two-sided messages have produced some contradictory findings, recent work by Mike Allen and his colleagues (Allen, 1991, 1993; Allen et al., 1990) has demonstrated that such findings are not contradictory when you consider the type of two-sided messages that have been used in past studies. Specifically, they argue that some studies have used two-sided messages that are *nonrefutational*. In these messages, opposing arguments are mentioned, but not argued against. On the other hand, some studies have used two-sided messages that are *refutational*. In these messages, opposing arguments are not only mentioned, they are shown to be inferior to the position advocated by the speaker.

Allen and his colleagues suspected that two-sided messages that are refutational would be much more persuasive than those that merely mention opposing arguments. In fact, they suspected that two-sided arguments that did not refute opposing arguments might make a speaker less persuasive than would one-sided arguments. Hence, the contradictions of past research.

To test their idea, Allen and his colleagues (Allen, 1991, 1993; Allen et al., 1990; Jackson & Allen, cited in Allen et al., 1990) examined a large number of previous studies on message-sidedness, this time taking into account both types of two-sided messages. What they found confirmed their hypothesis—two-sided messages were always more persuasive than one-sided messages, as long as the two-sided messages were refutational. When they were not refutational, they were less persuasive than one-sided messages. Moreover, speakers who used two-sided refutational messages were more credible than those who used one-sided messages, and speakers who used two-sided nonrefutational messages were the least credible of all (see Table 10.1).

A study by Hale, Mongeau, and Thomas (1991) provides some insight into why two-sided refutational messages may be so effective. Results of these researchers' study found that although both types of two-sided messages cause an audience to have more favorable thoughts, this is especially so if the message is refutational. However, this does not explain why one-sided arguments are more persuasive than two-sided nonrefutational messages. Whatever the case, the practical implications of this research are clear—When delivering a message, present the opponent's perspective, but make sure you "go all the way" by refuting your opponent's position.

INOCULATION THEORY: OF NEEDLES AND ARGUMENTS

When parents make cliches out of phrases like "and if your friends told you to jump off a cliff, would you do that too?" they may succeed in making their children feel stupid for succumbing to peer pressure, but, truth be told, the act has already been done. Indeed, we're sure that parents would much rather prevent their children from being persuaded to engage in dangerous or unethical behaviors than deal with the problem after the fact. Likewise, governments have and still wish to prevent their citizens from adopting certain political viewpoints. For instance, did you know that members of the former Soviet Union were not supposed to play Monopoly, a clearly capitalistic game? Moreover, after the Second World War, there was widespread paranoia in the United States that Americans would be brainwashed by communist propaganda. In short, although most of this book has been devoted to examining how people persuade other people, oftentimes a more immediate concern centers around how to *prevent* people from being persuaded.

TABLE 10.1   Hierarchy of effectiveness for message sidedness.

Type of Message	Effectiveness
Two-sided refutational message	*Most effective* (20% more effective than a one-sided message)
One-sided message	*Second most effective* (20% more effective than a two-sided nonrefutational message)
Two-sided nonrefutational message	*Least effective*

Inoculation theory, an approach to persuasion proposed by William McGuire (1961a, 1961b, 1964), is devoted to this issue.

Inoculation theory might best be understood by using a biological analogy. Specifically, if you want to keep your body healthy, what should you do? One strategy is to eat your Wheaties and Flinstones chewables, avoid fats and sugars, stay rested, and exercise. This is what is known as a *supportive strategy* or *treatment.* The rationale here is that a stronger body will be more effective at fending off diseases and viruses. A second way to stay healthy is through inoculation. Perhaps your rear end has forgotten all of those needles it encountered in your youth (e.g., small-pox immunizations), but if you've ever had a flu shot or treated your dog or cat to a rabies booster, you're familiar with the reasoning behind such injections. The idea is that if you or Fido are exposed to a small dose of a disease virus, your bodies are better able to defend themselves against the virus later. This is because a dose that is too small to give you the disease often stimulates your body's defenses. Thus, if exposed to a stronger dose of the virus later, your body can overpower it.

According to McGuire (1964), this metaphor can also be applied to situations involving persuasion. For example, imagine you are a lawyer hired to defend someone who is accused of murder, but is innocent. You realize that after you have a chance to present your case, another lawyer will argue against you, presenting evidence that he or she hopes will hang your client. With that in mind, what might you do? First, you could use a supportive strategy, making the jury's belief in your client's innocence as "healthy" as possible by spending a lot of time discussing reasons why the client is not guilty. On the other hand, you could inoculate the members of the jury by exposing them to weak doses of the other lawyer's arguments and by showing how such arguments might be refuted.[4] The hope is that jurists exposed to weak doses of the opposition's argument will be less persuaded.

In a classic test of inoculation theory, McGuire, and Papageorgis (1961) focused on the support and refutation of *cultural truisms.* A cultural truism is a belief whose truth is taken for granted. For example, the idea that "it is good to brush your teeth after every meal if possible" is a cultural truism because it is generally accepted in our culture. According to McGuire and Papageorgis, however, cultural truisms should also be especially vulnerable when attacked. This is most likely because they have never been questioned. Returning to the biological metaphor for a moment, imagine that you were raised in a plastic bubble all of your life, breathing only the purest, germ-free air. What would happen if you stepped out of the bubble? Your body, having never been exposed to germs before, would be especially vulnerable to them. Indeed, huge numbers of Native Americans died this way when missionaries brought with them unfamiliar European viruses. According to McGuire and Papageorgis, the same thing can happen with cultural truisms. Unlike beliefs on such topics as capital punishment and the legalization of drugs that may have been challenged frequently, cultural truisms have been raised in what amounts to hermetically sealed bubbles; they've never been questioned, they've never required defense, and, therefore, they are sitting ducks when attacked. Even so, McGuire and Papageorgis (1961) argued that inoculation could help defend such beliefs.

To test this notion, these researchers exposed participants in their study to several messages that attacked cultural truisms (e.g., brushing your teeth too much damages the teeth's protective enamel). Two days before hearing the attacking messages, however, the participants were provided with one of two defenses against the attacks. One group of participants was equipped with a *supportive defense*; that is, they were presented with several arguments which supported the cultural truisms. A second group of participants received an *inoculation defense* against the attacking message; they heard weak messages attacking a cultural truism in addition to arguments that refuted the attacks. A third group of participants was not provided with any defense. After hearing the attacking messages, the participants rated the degree to which they believed the cultural truisms were true or false. Results of the study supported the researchers' expectations. Specifically, both the supportive and inoculation defenses were better than no defense at all at making participants more resistant to persuasion. Moreover, the group that had been inoculated was the most resistant to the attacking messages.

Although research exploring messages that attack cultural truisms shows that inoculation may be more effective than supportive strategies at inducing resistance, research exploring beliefs that are less generally accepted does not. To be sure, considerable research suggests that when messages are not attacking cultural truisms, supportive strategies are just as effective as inoculation strategies at inducing resistance to persuasion (e.g., Adams & Beatty, 1977; Pryor & Steinfatt, 1978). As might be expected, however, just as *both* supportive treatments and inoculation work best for keeping a body healthy, research indicates that a combination of supportive treatments and inoculation are more effective at making people resistant to persuasion than either one is alone (McGuire, 1961a).

In addition, research suggests that inoculating people against one particular argument may make them resistant to other, different arguments that attack a cultural truism (Papageorgis & McGuire, 1961). This might be analogous to a flu shot that also protects you from polio or smallpox. For example, imagine you hold the belief that a person should drink eight glasses of water a day. A counterargument might be that too much water neutralizes acids that you need for proper digestion. To get you to resist such a counterargument, we might inoculate you by providing weak doses and refutations of the "neutralize acid" argument. In doing so, the research shows that you will become more resistant to other, new arguments to which you weren't originally exposed. For instance, you will be more resistant to a message that says drinking too much water now can wear out your bladder and lead to incontinence in old age.

Why would such generalized immunization work? According to Papageorgis and McGuire (1961), inoculation causes people to think of more arguments that support their beliefs, thereby making subsequent attacking arguments less credible. Thus, once a cultural truism has been defended, it is easier to defend again later, even if the arguments attacking it are different from the initial arguments.

Finally, inoculation may work better on some people than others. For instance, Michael Pfau and his colleagues (Pfau, Lee, Godbold, Hong, Tusing, Koerner, Penaloza, & Yang, 1996) noted that people who are ego-involved in a topic (i.e., people for whom a topic has a lot of personal relevance) may benefit from inoculation more than those who are not ego-involved. This is because of the way inoculation works. First it threatens people by making them aware that their existing attitudes are vulnerable to attack, then it provides ammunition against the attack. Because ego-involved people find a topic more personally relevant, Pfau and colleagues (1996) suspected that ego-involved people would feel more threatened by inoculation and therefore be more motivated to think about arguments that would bolster their attitudes. To test this notion, Pfau and colleagues inoculated college students against arguments regarding gun control, the legalization of marijuana, and nationwide legalization of gambling. Results of the study supported the researchers' hypothesis; in general, following inoculation, ego-involved students were more resistant to persuasion (for more on inoculation, see Box 10.3).

FOREWARNING: YOU'D BETTER WATCH OUT

In the Oscar nominated film *A Few Good Men*, Kevin Bacon and Tom Cruise play lawyers who are prosecuting and defending two marines accused of murder. At the beginning of the trial, Bacon's character, the prosecutor, tells the jury to beware; the defense, he warns, "will try a little misdirection, astonish you with stories of rituals, and dazzle you with official sounding terms like 'code red.'" A similar tactic was used in the 1996 presidential campaign when Bob Dole warned elderly voters that Bill Clinton would try to scare them about issues such as social security. In each of these cases, the warnings were not effective (both Bacon and Dole lost), but considerable research indicates that *forewarning* an audience of a persuasive message can be an effective way of making the audience resistant to that message. Of course, this line of research is related to inoculation, although the two tactics are distinct; while inoculation exposes people to a weakened dose of the attacking message, forewarning only makes people aware of a possible counterattitudinal attack.

According to Papageorgis (1968), there are two types of forewarning messages. First, you can simply warn people that they will hear a message intended to persuade them. Second, you can warn people by telling them about the topic and position taken in the persuasive message. Research indicates that both tactics are moderately effective at inducing resistance to persuasion (see Benoit, in press). Even so, the process by which each tactic works may be different. For instance, when people are warned about a topic and position, it permits them to arm themselves with counterarguments before the attack. If forewarning about a persuasive topic and position works by making people counterargue, Freedman and Sears (1965) thought that the amount of time between the warning and the persuasive speech might be an important variable moderating the effect of forewarning. They hypothesized that people who were given more time between the warning and the persuasive message would be able to think of more counterarguments and should therefore be more resistant to persuasion than those who were given little time. To test this hypothesis, the researchers told high school students that they would hear

BOX 10.3   When Smoke Gets in Your Eyes: Inoculation Theory Applied

It's clear from our discussion of inoculation theory that inoculation works effectively with messages that attack cultural truisms in laboratory settings. But how does the theory pan out when tested in "real life" settings? Several studies by Pfau and his colleagues (Burgoon, Pfau, & Birk, 1995; Pfau & Burgoon, 1988; Pfau, Kenski, Nitz, & Sorenson, 1990; Pfau & Van Bockern, 1994; Pfau, Van Bockern, & Kang, 1992) attempt to address this question.

First, Pfau and colleagues (1992) argued that inoculation might be a good strategy to use if you want to prevent young adolescents from smoking cigarettes. According to these researchers' sources, more than 3,000 teenagers become smokers each day and, as a result, millions die of smoke-related diseases later in life. Because more than half of all smokers become regulars before high school, Pfau and colleagues (1992) conducted their study using seventh graders. The students were shown videos that (1) warned them that peer pressure might cause them to change their minds about smoking and (2) presented and refuted arguments that challenged the students' attitudes about smoking (e.g., smoking is cool). Results showed that inoculation helped students resist smoking, but only if the students had low self-esteem. Interestingly, however, a follow-up study 2 years later found just the opposite; inoculation worked for students with high self-esteem, but not for those with low self-esteem (Pfau & Van Bockern, 1994). Thus, inoculation may wear off for those with low self-esteem while there may be a sleeper effect for those with high self-esteem. Whatever the case, the authors argue that inoculating children against smoking must occur between elementary school and high school. After that, resistance strategies do not seem to work (Pfau & Van Bockern, 1994).

Second, Pfau and colleagues (1990) examined inoculation in political campaigns. These researchers noted that negative advertisements, in which one politician attacks another, are becoming more common and that one third to one half of all political ads may be negative. With that in mind, what should a politician do? One possibility is to inoculate voters. Another is to wait until you are attacked and then refute the attacks. To test which strategy works best, Pfau and colleagues sent messages to voters during the 1988 presidential campaign. Voters received messages attacking their preferred candidate. Some of the voters were inoculated before being exposed to the attack message. Other voters, after being exposed to the attack message, received a message that refuted it. Results of the study found that an inoculation strategy worked the best. Those voters who had been inoculated were the least affected by the attack message. Similar results were reported in a related study by Pfau and Burgoon (1988).

Finally, Burgoon and colleagues (1995) investigated the ways in which corporate advertising can work to inoculate audiences. They noted that the Mobil Oil Corporation spends huge amounts of money on advertisements expressing the corporation's positions on issues that are controversial and publicly important (e.g., the environment). Although some have argued that such advertising can change the public's attitudes about a corporation, Burgoon and colleagues found that such ads are more useful for maintaining attitudes. In general, their study found that such advertisements helped people resist messages that attacked the credibility of Mobil. People who had not been inoculated were more likely to "slip" when Mobil was attacked, viewing the corporation as less credible.

a message arguing that teenagers were a menace on the road and should not be allowed to drive. After being warned, some of the students were exposed to the message immediately, although others did not hear the message for 2 or 10 minutes. Results of the study confirmed the hypothesis; the high schoolers who waited 10 minutes were most resistant to the message. Those who were exposed to the message immediately were least resistant. Similar studies (e.g., Petty & Cacioppo, 1977) have found that when warned and given time before hearing a message, people can think of and list more counterarguments and are more resistant to persuasion.

Despite these findings, some scholars have questioned the notion that forewarning leads to counterarguing and then resistance. A meta-analysis (i.e., an overall assessment of studies using advanced statistical analysis) by Benoit (in press), for instance, found that the presence of a delay between a warning and a message did not matter. Thus, there is some question as to whether counterarguing is really necessary for developing resistance.

To examine this issue further, Romero, Agnew, and Insko (1996) conducted a study. These researchers argued that if forewarning leads people to counterargue, then we should notice two things. First, people who are more motivated to counterargue should be more affected by forewarning than those who are not. And second, people who have the ability to counterargue should be more affected by forewarning than those who do not have the ability.

To test this notion, Romero, Agnew, and Insko (1996) forewarned college students who either did or did not have the motivation or ability to counterargue with a persuasive message. The researchers motivated some of the students to counterargue by making the topic of the message more personally relevant to them. Specifically, they told some of the students that the message they were about to be exposed to argued that they all should be required to take comprehensive exams before graduation. The remaining students were told that the comprehensive exams would not be required for 10 years, long after they had left the university. Thus, this second group of students was not that motivated to counterargue. In addition, the researchers hindered some students' ability to counterargue by distracting them. Specifically, after they were warned, some students simply waited 3 minutes before being exposed to the message about comprehensive exams. Other students, however, were distracted during the 3 minutes with difficult letter and number puzzles. Thus, their ability to counterargue was hampered. Results of the study confirmed the researchers' suspicions; compared to students without the motivation and ability to counterargue, the students who found the topic personally relevant and who were not distracted by puzzles were more resistant to the persuasive message (for more on distraction and persuasion, see Box 10.4). In short, it seems that forewarning of topic and position makes people more resistant *by* encouraging counterarguing.

Although warning people about a topic and position provides them an opportunity to think of and rehearse counterarguments, it is clear that the other type of warning—a warning about persuasive intent—does not. Indeed, if people don't know what the topic will be, how can they think of counterarguments? But if coun-

---

BOX 10.4 Distraction and Persuasion

Did you know that it is not unheard of for people working on political campaigns to send hecklers to wherever their opponent is speaking? The practice is known as *bracketing* (Pinocchio Index, 1996). It almost certainly is designed to fluster the heckled candidate. What bracketers may not be aware of, however, is that heckling may actually benefit the heckled speaker. Indeed, a study by Beatty and Kruger (1978) found that when an audience identifies with a heckled speaker, the speaker is more persuasive and is perceived as more credible. But how is it possible that the effects of heckling can be exactly opposite of those intended? According to one perspective, distraction, whether caused by hecklers, flashing lights, eating, static, loud noises, or other things, prevents people from scrutinizing a counterattitudinal message. And if they cannot scrutinize the message, people are more likely to be persuaded by it.

Although considerable research supports this explanation (e.g., Festinger & Maccoby, 1964; Keating & Brock, 1974; Osterhouse & Brock, 1970), Buller (1986) examined several studies and found more support for a different perspective. Specifically, learning theory (McGuire, 1969) argues that to be persuaded, people must first comprehend a message. Because distraction hinders comprehension, distraction also should decrease the persuasiveness of a message. Buller's (1986) work supports this notion by indicating that distraction generally reduces the effectiveness of a persuasive message. This may depend, however, on the type of distraction being examined. For instance, in addition to distraction that is external to a communicator (like hecklers and loud noises), a second type of distraction can be initiated by the communicator. For example, you might be distracted by someone who stands too close or who uses intense language. According to Buller (1986), when a distraction is initiated by a communicator, our reaction depends not so much on comprehension or counterarguments, but rather on the communicator's credibility. Specifically, when distracted by a high credible source, we tend to be more persuaded, when distracted by a low credible source, we tend to be less persuaded. Thus, if you are a high credible source and want to be persuasive, feel free to distract your audience.

---

terarguing is not responsible for the effectiveness of this type of warning, what is? As noted in Chapter 9, Brehm (1966) and Brehm and Brehm (1981) argued that when people feel that their freedom to behave or think in a certain way is restricted, they experience *psychological reactance* and attempt to restore their freedom. If you've ever tried reverse psychology on a child, you are familiar with how psychological reactance works. For instance, the other day, one of the authors was having trouble getting his preschooler to pack up his toys, leave his pals, and get in the car to go home. The child, of course, thought he had the freedom to choose: stay with his pals or get in the car. However, when dad pretended he was leaving without his son, the child gathered his toys and hurried into the car. Why? His freedom to choose the ride home was being taken away. He was reacting to the loss of freedom.

According to some writers (see Fukada, 1986; Hass & Grady, 1975), this phenomenon occurs when you are warned that someone intends to persuade you. It's like a comedian who tells you he or she will make you laugh before telling a joke. We like to feel free to laugh or to be persuaded, and if we feel that freedom is in jeopardy, we experience psychological reactance; we don't laugh or we resist persuasion. To illustrate this principle, Fukada (1986) told one group of people that they would be exposed to a message intended to make them afraid and to change their attitude. Another group did not receive the warning. Later, both groups received a message that tried to persuade them to be tested for syphilis. Results indicated that the warned group not only experienced more psychological reactance, it was also less persuaded than the unwarned group.

Because it is apparent that forewarning makes people more resistant to persuasion, you might be wondering what you should do if you ever want to persuade an audience that has been warned or is aware of your intent to persuade them. With that question in mind, Benoit (in press) offered the following advice:

> In these cases, the persuader may wish to attempt to compensate for the inhibiting effects of forewarning. The persuader could stress a lack of bias, emphasize that the audience's best interests were considered (and not just the persuader's own selfish interests), explain that both sides of the issue were carefully considered before a position was taken, or simply ask the audience to keep an open mind. At the very least, persuaders should moderate their expectations for success, keeping in mind that their persuasive task is more difficult when the audience is forewarned. (pp. 146–147)

SUMMARY

In this chapter, we examined the topic of message selection and organization. First, we saw that, depending on the characteristics of the audience, that it's sometimes better for a persuader to tell the audience what to believe, but at other times it's best to let the audience members draw their own conclusions. Second, we saw that when selecting arguments to use for persuasion, quality arguments matter with audiences that will scrutinize the message, but that quantity works for less discerning audiences. Third, we examined message repetition, and noted that a message that is repeated, but not repeated too much, can be much more persuasive than one that is not repeated. Fourth, we discussed the ways in which arguments might be ordered or arranged in a speech and indicated that the most effective order depends on several variables. Similarly, our examination of primacy and recency effects showed that when two people are giving opposing speeches, under some circumstances the first speaker may have the advantage, while under others, the last speaker may have the advantage. Even when there is only one speaker, however, research shows that he or she is more persuasive when presenting both sides of an issue than when presenting only one side. Finally, we explored the ways in which people may be more resistant to persuasion, either by being inoculated with a weak dose of an opposing argument or by being warned about the possibility of an attacking argument.

ENDNOTES

1. Miller and Campbell (1959) also found that if there is a time delay between both messages and between the second message and the measurement of attitude, neither primacy nor recency works better. Moreover, if there are no time delays between messages and the measurement of attitudes, neither primacy or recency works better.

2. Of course, an additional advantage to speaking first is that you have the opportunity to inoculate your audience against your opponent's messages or at least warn your audience that opposing messages are forthcoming. The topics of inoculation and forewarning are discussed later in this chapter.

3. Subsequent studies have not always supported the notion that educational level interacts with message sidedness.

4. Notice that inoculation, which may be used to refute opposing arguments, is similar to the definition of a two-sided argument discussed earlier in the chapter. The main difference is that research on two-sided messages exposes subjects to both sides of an argument in a single-exposure. Research on inoculation exposes subjects to messages sequentially. That is, *after* being exposed to the inoculating message, subjects are then exposed to counterarguments.

REFERENCES

Adams, W. C., & Beatty, M. J. (1977). Dogmatism, need for social approval, and the resistance to persuasion. *Communication Monographs, 44,* 321–325.

Allen, M. (1991). Comparing the persuasiveness of one-sided and two-sided messages using meta-analysis. *Western Journal of Speech Communication, 55,* 390–404.

Allen, M. (1993). Determining the persuasiveness of one and two sided messages. In M. Allen & R. Preiss (Eds.), *Prospects and precautions in the use of meta-analysis* (pp. 101–125). Dubuque, IA: Brown and Benchmark.

Allen, M., Hale, J., Mongeau, P., Berkowitz-Stafford, S., Stafford, S., Shanahan, W., Agee, P., Dillon, K., Jackson, R., & Ray, C. (1990). Testing a model of message sidedness: Three replications. *Communication Monographs, 57,* 275–291.

Beatty, M. J., & Kruger, M. W. (1978). The effects of heckling on speaker credibility and attitude change. *Communication Quarterly, 26*(2), 46–50.

Benoit, W. L. (in press). Forewarning and persuasion. In M. Allen & R. Preiss (Eds.), *Persuasion: Advances through meta-analysis* (pp. 139–154). Creskill, NJ: Hampton Press.

Brehm, J. W. (1966). *A theory of psychological reactance.* New York: Academic Press.

Brehm, S. S., & Brehm, J. W. (1981). *Psychological reactance: A theory of freedom and control.* New York: Academic Press.

Buller, D. B. (1986). Distraction during persuasive communication: A meta-analytic review. *Communication Monographs, 53,* 91–114.

Burgoon, M., Pfau, M., & Birk, T. S. (1995). An Inoculation Theory explanation for the effects of corporate issue/advocacy advertising campaigns. *Communication Research, 22,* 485–505.

Corbett, E. P. J. (1971). *Classical rhetoric for the modern student* (2nd ed.). New York: Oxford University Press.

Festinger, L. & Maccoby, N. (1964). On resistance to persuasive communications. *Journal of Abnormal and Social Psychology, 68,* 359–366.

Fine, B. J. (1957). Conclusion-drawing, communicator credibility, and anxiety as factors in opinion change. *Journal of Abnormal and Social Psychology, 54,* 369–374.

Freedman, J. L., & Sears, D. O. (1965). Warning, distraction, and resistance to influence. *Journal of Personality and Social Psychology, 1,* 262–266.

Fukada, H. (1986). Psychological processes mediating the persuasion inhibiting effect of forewarning in fear arousing communication. *Psychological Reports, 58,* 87–90.

Furnham, A. (1986). The robustness of the recency effect: Studies using legal evidence. *The Journal of General Psychology, 113* (4), 351–357.

Gilkenson, H., Paulson, S. F., & Sikkink, D. E. (1954). Effects of order and authority in an argumentative speech. *Quarterly Journal of Speech, 40,* 183–192.

Gorn, G., & Goldberg, M. (1980). Children's responses to repetitive TV commercials. *Journal of Consumer Research, 6,* 421–425.

Gulley, H. E., & Berlo, D. K. (1956). Effect of intercellular and intracellular speech structure on attitude change and learning. *Speech Monographs, 23,* 288–297.

Haines, D. W., Chandran, R., & Parkhe, A. (1989). Winning by being the first to market…or second? *Journal of Consumer Research, 6,* 63–69.

Hale, J., Mongeau, P. A., & Thomas, R. M. (1991). Cognitive processing of one- and two-sided persuasive messages. *Western Journal of Speech Communication, 55,* 380–389.

Hass, R. G., & Grady, K. (1975). Temporal delay, type of forewarning, and resistance to influence. *Journal of Experimental Social Psychology, 11,* 459–469.

Hovland, C. I., Lumsdaine, A., & Sheffield, F. (1949). *Experiments on mass communication.* Princeton, NJ: Princeton University Press.

Hovland, C. I., & Mandell, W. (1952). An experimental comparison of conclusion-drawing by the communicator and by the audience. *Journal of Abnormal and Social Psychology, 47,* 581–588.

Kardes, F. R., Kim, J., & Lim, J. S. (1994). Moderating effects of prior knowledge on the perceived diagnosticity of beliefs derived from implicit versus explicit product claims. *Journal of Business Research, 29,* 219–224.

Keating, J. P., & Brock, T. C. (1974). Acceptance of persuasion and the inhibition of counterargumentation under various distraction tasks. *Journal of Experimental Social Psychology, 10,* 301–309.

McGuire, W. J. (1961a). The effectiveness of supportive and refutational defenses in immunizing defenses. *Sociometry, 24,* 184–197.

McGuire, W. J. (1961b). Persistence of the resistance to persuasion induced by various types of prior defenses. *Journal of Abnormal and Social Psychology, 64,* 241–248.

McGuire, W. J. (1964). Inducing resistance to persuasion: Some contemporary approaches. In L. Berkowitz (Ed.), *Advances in experimental social psychology* (pp. 191–229). New York: Academic Press.

McGuire, W. J. (1968). Personality and susceptibility to social influence. In E. F. Borgatta & W. W. Lambert (Eds.), *Handbook of personality theory and research.* (pp. 1130–1187). Chicago: Rand McNally.

McGuire, W. J. (1969). The nature of attitudes and attitude change. In G. Lindzey & E. Aronson (Eds.), *The handbook of social psychology* (2nd ed., pp. 136–314). Reading, MA: Addison-Wesley.

McGuire, W. J., & Papageorgis, D. (1961). The relative efficacy of various types of prior belief—defense in producing resistance to persuasion. *Public Opinion Quarterly, 62,* 327–337.

Miller, N., & Campbell, D. T. (1959). Recency and primacy in persuasion as a function of the timing of speeches and measurements. *Journal of Abnormal and Social Psychology, 59,* 1–9.

Miller, R. L. (1976). Mere exposure, psychological reactance and attitude change. *Public Opinion Quarterly, 40,* 229–233.

Osterhouse, R. A., & Brock, T. C. (1970). Distraction increases yielding to propaganda by inhibiting counterarguing. *Journal of Personality and Social Psychology, 15,* 344–358.

Papageorgis, D. (1968). Warning and persuasion. *Psychological Bulletin, 70,* 271–282.

Papageorgis, D., & McGuire, W. J. (1961). The generality of immunity to persuasion produced by pre-exposure to weakened counterarguments. *Journal of Abnormal and Social Psychology, 62,* 475–481.

Petty, R. E., & Cacioppo, J. T. (1977). Forewarning, cognitive responding, and resistance to persuasion. *Journal of Personality and Social Psychology, 35,* 645–655.

Petty, R. E., & Cacioppo, J. T. (1979). Effects of forewarning of persuasive intent and involvement on cognitive responses and persuasion. *Personality and Social Psychology Bulletin, 5,* 173–176.

Petty, R. E., & Cacioppo, J. T. (1984). The effects of involvement on responses to argument quantity and quality: Central and peripheral routes to persuasion. *Journal of Personality and Social Psychology, 46,* 69–81.

Petty, R. E., & Cacioppo, J. T. (1986). *Communication and persuasion: Central and peripheral routes to attitude change.* New York: Springer-Verlag.

Pfau, M., & Burgoon, M. (1988). Inoculation in political campaign communication. *Human Communication Research, 15,* 91–111.

Pfau, M., Kenski., H. C., Nitz, M., & Sorenson, J. (1990). Efficacy of inoculation strategies in promoting resistance to political attack messages: Application to direct mail. *Communication Monographs, 57,* 1–12.

Pfau, M., Lee, W., Godbold, L. C., Hong, Y., Tusing, K. J., Koerner, A. F. Penaloza, L. J., & Yang, V. S. (1996). *Nuances in Inoculation: The role of inoculation approach and receiver ego-involvement, message processing disposition, and gender in the process of resistance.* Paper presented at the Annual Speech Communication Association, San Diego, CA.

Pfau, M., & Van Bockern, S. (1994). The persistence of inoculation in conferring resistance to smoking initiation among adolescents: The second year. *Human Communication Research, 20,* 413–430.

Pfau, M., Van Bockern, S., & Kang, J. G. (1992). Use of inoculation to promote resistance to smoking initiation among adolescents. *Communication Monographs, 59,* 213–230.

Pinocchio Index (1996, Sept. 3). *Time,* p. 22.

Pryor, B., & Steinfatt, T. M. (1978). The effects of initial belief level on inoculation theory and its proposed mechanisms. *Human Communication Research, 4,* 217–230.

Romero, A. A., Agnew, C. A., & Insko, C. A. (1996). The cognitive mediation hypothesis revisited: An empirical response to methodological and theoretical criticism. *Personality and Social Psychology Bulletin, 22,* 651–665.

Rosnow, R. (1966). Whatever happened to the "Law of Primacy." *Journal of Communication, 16,* 10–31.

Rosnow, R., & Robinson, E. (1967). *Experiments in persuasion.* New York: Academic Press.

Sawyer, A. G. (1981). Repetition, cognitive responses, and persuasion. In R. E. Petty, T. M. Ostrom, & T. C. Brock (Eds.), *Cognitive responses in persuasion* (pp. 237–261), Hillsdale, NJ: Lawrence Erlbaum.

Sawyer, A. G. (1988). Can there be effective advertising without explicit conclusions? Decide for yourself. In S. Hecker & D. W. Stewart (Eds.), *Nonverbal communication in advertising* (pp. 159–184). Lexington, MA: Lexington Books.

Sawyer, A. G., & Howard, D. J. (1991). Effects of omitting conclusions in advertisements to involved and uninvolved audiences. *Journal of Marketing Research, 28,* 467–474.

Sikkink, D. (1956). An experimental study of the effects on the listener of anticlimax order and authority in an argumentative speech. *Southern Speech Journal, 22,* 73–78.

Unnava, H. R., Burnkrant, R. E., & Erevelles, S. (1994). Effects of presentation order and communication modality on recall and attitude. *Journal of Consumer Research, 21,* 481–495.

Zajonc, R. B. (1968). Attitudinal effects of mere exposure. *Journal of Personality and Social Psychology Monographs, 9* (2, Pt. 2), 1–27.

11

COMPLIANCE GAINING

Do you remember Felix, the cartooned cat with the bag of tricks, a veritable warehouse of gizmos and gadgets? It seems that whenever he had that polka-dotted bag, Felix could get himself out of any jam. The funny thing is, sometimes our students remind us of that cat. Take any exam week, for example. Some of the stories we hear are astounding. The only thing is, our students don't need a bag of tricks; they do a fine job of coming up with reasons for missing tests on their own. By far, the most popular reason, at least for our students, is sick or dying grandparents. We don't want to sound unsympathetic here, but there's no denying that during midterms and finals this excuse runs rampant. In fact, a colleague of ours jokes that he hates giving his students exams because in the process he kills too many grandmothers. We've heard of other tactics as well. One colleague, for instance, told us that a student was serious about missing a test merely because "it was her birthday." Another student tried to avoid an exam because he thought his house might be robbed if he came to school. One of our students explained that she could not take a test because she had been subpoenaed to testify against her boss in court, while another was reluctant to take exams because of a foreboding horoscope. Who knows what we might hear next term?

Whatever reasons our students might muster, one point is clear: When faced with a situation requiring persuasion, people can come up with any number of strategies or tactics. But what types of strategies are available to people who are seeking compliance. What specific kinds of strategies are people most likely to use? Do the strategies that people use vary across situations? Do different types of people use different types of strategies? What methods are used to study strategy selection?

All of these issues have been explored by researchers who are interested in a very broad topic area that is often labeled compliance gaining and that is considered by many to be one of the most important subjects in the study of interpersonal influence. Indeed, by 1994, Seibold, Cantrill, and Meyers (1994) estimated that at least 124 studies on compliance gaining had been conducted and, recently, Boster (1995) argued that "in the last 15 years, the study of compliance-gaining message behavior has held the attention of communication scholars as much as, if not more than, any other single topic in the discipline" (p. 91).

Because of the significance and prominence of compliance gaining in our field, we devote this chapter to an examination of compliance-gaining issues and research. Before proceeding, though, a few definitions are in order.

ACTIONS SPEAK THE LOUDEST: A DEFINITION OF COMPLIANCE GAINING

We used to know a guy who liked to say, "I don't care if you hate me, as long as you're nice to me." We think that this maxim is a fine illustration of the distinction between thoughts and actions that undergirds the primary difference between compliance and other forms of persuasion. As we mentioned in Chapter 2, it is useful to distinguish between the terms *persuasion* and *compliance.* Persuasion, an umbrella term, is concerned with changing beliefs, attitudes, intentions, motivations, and behaviors. The term compliance is more restrictive, typically referring to changes in a person's overt behavior. For example, a mother might tell her 10-year-old son, "Take out the trash." If the child says, "I don't want to," the mother might respond, "I don't care what you want. Take out the trash!" In this case the mother is not concerned with belief or attitude change. She doesn't care if the child likes taking out the trash, believes in recycling, or so on. She just wants compliance, or behavior change (i.e., the trash taken out). In short, research examining compliance gaining generally focuses on persuasion aimed at getting others to do something or to act in a particular way.

We should also note that compliance gaining differs from more traditional notions of persuasion in a number of important ways. First, for the most part, studies of compliance gaining have concentrated on influence in interpersonal, face-to-face contexts rather than in one-to-many contexts. Moreover, the emphasis has primarily been on "senders" rather than on "receivers." That is, while traditional research has concerned itself with identifying what strategies are most effective, studies on compliance gaining have attempted to identify which strategies are most likely to be used by a persuader. In other words, compliance-gaining research focuses on what people do when they want to get something.

With these distinctions in mind, we now turn to a discussion of compliance gaining. We start by examining how compliance-gaining research got started and then discuss some of the situational and individual difference factors that influence compliance-gaining behavior. We then identify some of the problems facing compliance-gaining research and finish up by illustrating the importance of compliance-gaining goals.

IN THE BEGINNING: THE ROOTS OF COMPLIANCE-GAINING RESEARCH

Imagine you were failing a course and wanted a friend to tutor you. What would you do to ask for help? Or imagine that it was not you, but your teenage son, a high school student, who was getting lousy grades because he wouldn't study. What would you do to get him to crack the books? Or better yet, what if you were trying to sell encyclopedias to a father who didn't care if his children studied? Or what if you'd sold so much merchandise that you felt you deserved a promotion? How would you try to be persuasive? Can you think of a couple of different approaches? If not, read on—you might find a few tactics to add to your repertoire.

Although scholars in the field of communication have produced the most research on the topic of compliance gaining, two sociologists, Gerald Marwell and David Schmitt, first got the ball rolling in 1967. After examining past research and theory in the areas of power and influence, these two researchers developed a taxonomy of 16 different tactics that might be used to gain compliance (These tactics are presented in Table 11.1). Afterwards, they told people to imagine themselves in the four scenarios mentioned above (i.e., requesting a tutor, more studying, a purchase, and a promotion) and asked the people how likely they would be to use each of the 16 tactics in each of the four scenarios. Finally, based on the peoples' responses, Marwell and Schmitt grouped the tactics in terms of their commonalities,[1] ultimately identifying five basic types of compliance-gaining strategies:

Rewarding activity: involves seeking compliance in an active and positive way (e.g., using promises).

Punishing activity: involves seeking compliance in an explicitly negative way (e.g., making threats).

Expertise: involves attempts to make a person think that the persuader has some special knowledge (e.g., trying to appear credible).

Activation of impersonal commitments: involves attempts to appeal to a person's internalized commitments (e.g., telling the person he or she will feel bad about him/herself if he/she does not comply).

Activation of personal commitments: relies on appeals to a person's commitment to others (e.g., pointing out that the person is indebted and should therefore comply to repay the favor).

Marwell and Schmitt's (1967) study showed that there are a wide range of tactics available to persuaders. It was an important study because it became the springboard for the compliance-gaining studies that followed. Even so, as is often the case with research on human communication, the study made compliance gaining appear more simple than it really is. We will see later in this chapter the ways in which this study was criticized and improved upon. First, however, we

TABLE 11.1   Marwell and Schmitt's (1967) compliance-gaining tactics with examples of how you might get your teenager to study.

1. **Promise:** If you comply, I will reward you. For example, you offer to increase Dick's allowance if he studies more.
2. **Threat:** If you do not comply, I will punish you. For example, you threaten to forbid Dick to use the car if he doesn't start studying more.
3. **Expertise (positive):** If you comply, you will be rewarded because of the "nature of things." For example, you tell Dick that if he gets good grades he will be able to get into college and get a good job.
4. **Expertise (negative):** If you do not comply, you will be punished because of the "nature of things." For example, you tell Dick that if he does not get good grades he will not be able to get into a good college or get a good job.
5. **Liking:** Act friendly and helpful to get the person in a "good frame of mind" so that he or she will comply with the request. For example, you try to be as friendly and pleasant as possible to put Dick in a good mood before asking him to study.
6. **Pregiving:** Reward the person before requesting his or her compliance. For example, you raise Dick's allowance and tell him you now expect him to study.
7. **Aversive stimulation:** Continuously punish the person, making cessation contingent on his or her compliance. For example, you forbid Dick the use of the car and tell him he will not be able to drive until he studies more.
8. **Debt:** You owe me compliance because of past favors. For example, you point out that you have sacrificed and saved to pay for Dick's education and that he owes it to you to get good enough grades to get into a good college.
9. **Moral appeal:** You are immoral if you do not comply. You tell Dick that it is morally wrong for anyone not to get as good grades as possible and that he should study more.
10. **Self-feeling (positive):** You will feel better about yourself if you comply. For example, you tell Dick that he will feel proud if he gets himself to study more.
11. **Self-feeling (negative):** You will feel worse about yourself if you do not comply. For example, you tell Dick that he will feel ashamed of himself if he gets bad grades.
12. **Altercasting (positive):** A person with "good" qualities would comply. For example, you tell Dick that because he is a mature and intelligent person he naturally will want to study more and get good grades.
13. **Altercasting (negative):** Only a person with "bad" qualities would not comply. For example, you tell Dick that he should study because only someone very childish does not study.
14. **Altruism:** I need your compliance very badly, so do it for me. For example, you tell Dick that you really want very badly for him to get into a good college and that you wish he would study more as a personal favor to you.
15. **Esteem (positive):** People you value will think better of you if you comply. For example, you tell Dick that the whole family will be very proud of him if he gets good grades.
16. **Esteem (negative):** People you value will think the worse of you if you do not comply. For example, you tell Dick that the whole family will be very disappointed in him if he gets poor grades.

Adapted from Marwell, G., & Schmitt, D. R. (1967). Dimensions of compliance-gaining behavior: An empirical analysis. *Sociometry, 30,* 350–364.

Calvin and Hobbes   by Bill Watterson

turn to a discussion of some of the factors that affect the selection of compliance-gaining strategies.

SITUATION: THE "IT DEPENDS" OF COMPLIANCE-GAINING BEHAVIOR

Before this chapter was written, one of the authors was faced with two different situations requiring persuasion. In the first, the author's 2-year-old son tried to provoke a food fight at the dinner table by throwing a chunk of roast beef, gravy and all, at his older brother. There was quite a splat. The 2 year old then proceeded to reach for a second chunk, at which point the author intervened, explaining that any more "beef bombs" would result in a time-out (i.e., 2 minutes of sitting alone in the bedroom). Fortunately, the next hunk of beef found its way into the kid's mouth.

In the second situation, the same author needed to ask his boss to hurry up and look over some paperwork that needed the boss's signature. The deadline for the paperwork was nearing and, admittedly, threatening the boss with something like a time-out had appeal but, quite obviously, would not have been appropriate. Instead, the author tapped lightly on the boss's door, smiled, and asked ever so politely whether the boss had "had a chance to look over that paperwork yet?"

The point is that even though we can isolate a specific number of compliance-gaining strategies, not all strategies are appropriate in all situations. To be sure, even when trying to persuade the same person, different contexts require different strategies. For instance, trying to keep a 2 year old from repeatedly playing near electrical outlets may require a different strategy than trying to get the child to try tasting a horrible-looking vegetable. Or getting a friend to spend more time with you may require a different approach than getting the friend to stop smoking. Obviously, selecting a compliance-gaining strategy depends a lot on the situation.

For quite some time now, communication scholars have argued that compliance-gaining behavior can vary greatly from one situation to the next. By way of example, imagine that Trudy wants to persuade Bubba, his neighbor, that Bubba's dog is making too much noise at night and needs to be shut up. What can Trudy do? One option is to threaten to call the police. But what are the chances Trudy will use such a strategy? According to Sillars (1980), such a decision would depend on three things. First, how important does Trudy think it is to get compliance? If Trudy is planning on moving out of the neighborhood in a few days, threats may not be as likely as they would be if she was staying put. Second, the decision to use a strategy may depend on how much persuaders think that the strategy will affect their relationship with a persuadee. If, for instance, Trudy enjoys going to Bubba's parties and believes that a threat would prevent her from receiving any more invitations, she might be less inclined to use such a strategy. Finally, the likelihood that a strategy will be used may depend on how successful the persuader thinks the strategy will be. For instance, if Trudy knows that Bubba is hot tempered and might very well turn around and buy a pitbull if threatened, she will be more likely to search for an alternative strategy.

Margaret McLaughlin, Michael Cody, and their colleagues (Cody & McLaughlin, 1980; Cody, Woelfel, & Jordan, 1983; Cody, Greene, Marston, O'Hair, Baaske, & Schneider, 1986) would agree with Sillars (1980) that the compliance-gaining strategy a person uses depends on situational factors. However, these researches argued that an even larger number of situational factors affect strategy choice. Specifically, their research showed that, when trying to decide which compliance-gaining strategy to use, there are seven situational dimensions that affect our decisions. These dimensions include the following:

Dominance: The level of control or power in a relationship. For example, because a boss generally has more power to influence a subordinate than vice versa, a boss's strategies may differ from a subordinate's.

Intimacy: The level of emotional attachment or knowledge one has of a partner's affect. For example, because they are more intimate and more concerned with the relationship, spouses may use different strategies than strangers.

Resistance: The degree to which the persuader thinks a strategy will be resisted. For example, strategies that are more likely to be resisted will probably not be used as readily as those that are less likely to be resisted (for more information on resisting compliance, see Box 11.1).

Personal benefits: The extent to which the self or the other is benefited by compliance. For example, strategies that are perceived to produce the greatest benefits are most likely to be used.

Rights: The extent to which a persuader thinks the request is warranted. For example, a persuader may feel that complaining about a barking dog and losing sleep is justified, although complaining about someone else's hair style is not.

BOX 11.1   Just Say No?: A Look at Strategies for Resisting Compliance and Resisting Resistance

In our opinion, a lot of advertising these days makes persuasion seem pretty simple. For example, Nike's "Just Do It," campaign suggests that we should forget all about reasoning and weighing pros and cons. The "If It Feels Good Do It" maxim had a similar appeal. On the other side of the coin, you're probably familiar with the popular slogan for keeping kids off of drugs; "Just Say No," it advises. But is resisting compliance really all that easy? Whatever the case, some research shows that just saying no is not the only option available to us when trying to resist the compliance-gaining attempts of others. For instance, a study by McLaughlin, Cody, and Robey (1980) identified four possible strategies you might use to resist persuasion:

Nonnegotiation: You overtly refuse to comply (say, "No.").

Identity management: You resist by manipulating images of the other person. (You say, "I would never make such an awful request.").

Justifying: You justify noncompliance by pointing to negative outcomes. (You say, "If I comply with your request I might lose my job.").

Negotiation: You engage in an alternative behavior that you propose. (Rather than turn off the stereo, you offer to turn it down.)

Rather than look at resistance strategies, perhaps a more important issue centers on situations in which people find themselves wanting to resist compliance. Indeed, considering contemporary issues associated with the spread of AIDS and the prevalence of date rape, researchers have started to examine strategies that can be used to resist sexual advances. An interesting study by Byers and Wilson (1985) examined men's and women's perceptions of the different ways in which women refuse sexual advances by men. In the study, subjects watched a videotape of a man and woman engaged in romantic physical behavior. At some point in the tape, the woman refuses to go any further by (1) simply saying, "No"; (2) saying "No" and offering an excuse (i.e., "someone's coming over"); or (3) saying "No" and offering an explanation (i.e., "we don't know each other well enough"). Results of the study showed that most of the males in the study would comply with all of the requests, but several said they would be reluctant to do so. Moreover, both male and female subjects interpreted the simple "No" and the "No" with an explanation as meaning the man should stop with his advances, but interpreted the "No" with an excuse as meaning that the man should try making more advances later that day.

One possible problem with messages meant to resist sexual advances centers around the stereotype that "when women say 'no,' they really mean 'yes'" (see Metts & Spitzberg, 1996). Muehlenhard and Hollanbaugh (1988), for example, found that nearly 40 percent of women in their study claimed to have said "no" when they meant "yes" because they did not want to appear promiscuous, wanted to show concern for religious issues, and so forth. Perper and Weis (1987) argued that such token resistance can cause problems by encouraging males not to take "no" for an answer. With this in mind, when faced with such situations, it is important to say what you mean. Indeed, research shows that direct, verbal messages, compared to indirect messages, are the best for avoiding sexual advances (Christopher & Frandsen, 1990). A possible problem, however, is that sexual rejection messages that are moderately direct are perceived to be more comfortable and "save face" more than very direct messages (Metts, Cupach, & Imahori, 1992).

It is apparent from this discussion so far that resistance strategies, in and of themselves, may not be as important as *how* people respond

BOX 11.1 *Continued*

to those resistance strategies. For instance, deTurck (1985) found that in interpersonal relationships people who have met with noncompliance tend to follow up with more reward and punishment strategies than they did initially. Moreover, in some situations, noncompliance is likely to be met with physical aggression (deTurck, 1987). A related study by Rudd and Burant (1996) found that, compared to women in nonviolent relationships, women in violent relationships (i.e., abused women) use more indirect/submissive strategies (ingratiation, promise, allurement, and deceit) followed by more aggressive strategies (threats and warnings). According to Rudd and Burant (1996), these findings support the "violence cycle" phenomena by which a wife first tries to smooth over the conflict, but, on failing, resorts to more aggressive strategies in order "to escalate the inevitable violence so that the conflict will end" (p. 141).

According to Wilson, Cruz, Marshall, and Rao (1993), the way people react to noncompliance depends, in part, on the excuses given for noncompliance. For example, in one study, students were asked to telephone people who had previously agreed to participate in an experiment. The students were instructed to remind the people about their agreement and to dissuade anyone who tried backing out. What they did not know was that the people they phoned were part of the study and had been told not to comply with the students' requests. Results of the study showed that the students' reactions depended on what they perceived to be the causes for noncompliance. For instance, when people said they couldn't comply for *external reasons over which they had no control* (e.g., "I won't be able to make it because my boss scheduled me to work."), students were more persistent in their persuasive attempts than when people said they couldn't comply for *internal reason that they could control* (e.g., "I knew I had a test later this week, but I still put it off and now I have to study") (Wilson et al., 1993). In other words, what you say can determine whether your resistance strategies are resisted.

So, what happens if your resistance meets with resistance? For example, what if you're a kid who has just refused a cigarette and ends up getting more pressure to smoke despite it? To study what would happen in such a situation, Reardon, Sussman, and Flay (1989) asked 268 adolescents what they would do to resist a peer who asked them to smoke twice. Results of the study showed that teenagers' rejections became more intense when they were pressured a second time and when there was more than one person doing the pressuring. "Just say no" was found to be a strategy reserved for people who were in less intimate relationships with the teenagers.

Relational consequences: The degree to which a strategy will have long-term or short-term effects on the persuader's relationship with the persuadee. For example, a threat that may lead to divorce may be less likely than one that merely leads to an argument.

Apprehension: The degree to which a persuader perceives nervousness in the situation. For example, situations filled with anxiety may lead to different strategies than those without anxiety.

It is clear, then, that compliance-gaining behavior depends a great deal on the situation in which it is used. In the following sections, we discuss some research findings on several of these situational dimensions.

Seeking Compliance from Strangers and Intimates

In what is now considered a classic study, Gerald Miller, Frank Boster, Michael Roloff, and David Seibold (1977) examined the effects of intimacy on compliance-gaining behavior. These researchers imagined that compliance gaining in interpersonal relationships would be different from compliance gaining in noninterpersonal relationships. Specifically, because people in interpersonal relationships know their partners well, they can tailor their messages to appeal to their partners' specific wants, needs, interests, and so forth. The same is not true in noninterpersonal relationships where little is known about the other person. In addition, Miller and colleagues (1977) thought that the type of compliance-gaining strategy a person decided to use would depend on whether a situation had short-term or long-term consequences.

To test their hypotheses, these researchers asked people how likely they would be to use each of Marwell and Schmitt's (1967) strategies to persuade others in four different situations:

1. **Noninterpersonal; short-term consequences**—You want to get a car dealer, whom you barely know, to give you a $1,000 trade-in on your old car.
2. **Noninterpersonal; long-term consequences**—You want your new neighbors, who are planning to cut down a shade tree that adds value to your home, to leave the tree standing.
3. **Interpersonal; short-term consequences**—You have a close relationship with a man or woman and want to cancel a date with him or her in order to visit an old acquaintance who is passing through town.
4. **Interpersonal; long-term consequences**—You have a close relationship with a man or woman and want to persuade him or her to move to another geographical location so you can take a better job.

Results of this study showed that the situation strongly affected strategy choice. In general, people preferred "friendly," socially acceptable strategies (e.g., liking) in all the situations, but said they were more likely to use different tactics in different situations. For instance, threat tactics were more likely in short-term, noninterpersonal contexts. Finally, in noninterpersonal situations, people picked a greater variety of strategies, perhaps because, without knowing much about the person they were trying to persuade, more trial and error was necessary (Miller et al., 1977).

Thus, compliance-gaining strategies may differ depending on whether a relationship is interpersonal or noninterpersonal. But are all interpersonal relationships the same? One of our favorite studies shows that they are not. Specifically, Witteman and Fitzpatrick (1986) argued that husbands and wives can be categorized into three different couple-types, which include *Traditionals, Separates,* and *Independents.* They explained that:

> *Traditionals hold conventional values about the relationship. These values empha-size stability as opposed to spontaneity. Traditionals exhibit interdependence, both*

physically and psychologically, and tend not to avoid conflict. Separates hold ambivalent views on the nature of relationships, report having the least interdependence, and avoid open marital conflict. Independents hold fairly nonconventional relational values and maintain some interdependence, yet not with respect to some of the physical and temporal aspects of their lives. Also Independents report some assertiveness and tend to engage in conflict. (p. 132)

Because couples differed in the ways they interacted, Witteman and Fitzpatrick suspected that couples also would differ in the ways they sought compliance. To test this hypothesis, these researchers separated 51 couples into one of the three marital categories (i.e., Traditional, Separate, and Independent). Then, each couple was brought into a living room and asked to participate in a simulated conflict about one of two topics: spending more time together or bringing new friends into the relationship. The conflicts revealed that different compliance-gaining strategies were used by the different couple types. First, Traditionals sought compliance by discussing what they expected to be the positive and negative outcomes of a proposed course of action. They tended to be open and used their relationship as a basis of power. Separates, on the other hand, did not attempt to identify with their partners or to use their relationship to seek compliance. Instead, Separates focused on the negative consequences of noncompliance and tried to constrain the behavior of their spouses. According to Witteman and Fitzpatrick (1986), "Separates are not without affect in their interactions, but instead have a guerrilla-like communication style that demands acquiescence from the spouse" (p. 141). Finally, Independents, compared to other couple types, used a wider variety of power bases when seeking compliance. They also tended to discount and refute their partners more than other couple types, indicating that Independent couples debate one another relatively intensely. In short, then, our use of compliance-gaining strategies not only depends on how intimate our relationship is, but also on the type of intimate relationship in which we are involved.

The Effects of Perceived Benefits: What's in It for Me?

Although people prefer to use "friendly," socially acceptable tactics for gaining compliance, they don't always choose to use such tactics. But, besides the relationship type, what other factors determine the use of more negative approaches? According to Boster and Stiff (1984), it is possible to distinguish between compliance-gaining situations on the basis of who benefits if compliance is gained. For example, if you get a friend to loan you her car, you have benefited. On the other hand, getting your friend to stop smoking would more likely benefit her. Research by Boster and Stiff (1984) found that if there is a perceived benefit, regardless of who benefits, we become more willing to use negative tactics for gaining compliance. Similarly, Dillard and Burgoon (1985) found that people are more likely to use verbal aggression when self-benefit is high. It seems that the presence of some benefit acts to justify the use of negative tactics or to motivate the persuader, thereby making such tactics more likely to be used.

Power, Legitimacy, and Politeness

Our earlier illustration about trying to influence a child and a boss makes it clear that power plays a large role in the selection of compliance-gaining strategies. In what is now considered a seminal work, French and Raven (1960) argued that there are five bases of power that people can use to influence others:

1. A person with *reward power* has control over some valued resource (e.g., promotions and raises).
2. A person with *coercive power* has the ability to inflict punishments (e.g., fire you).
3. *Expert power* is based on what a person knows (e.g., you may do what a doctor tells you to do because he or she knows more about medicine than you do).
4. *Legitimate power* is based on formal rank or position (e.g., you obey someone's commands because he or she is the vice president in the company for which you work).
5. People have *referent power* when the person they are trying to influence wants to be like them (e.g., a mentor often has this type of power).

Regardless of the type of power that's at work, one thing remains clear: Power affects compliance-gaining behavior. For example, although managers are more successful when using consultation, inspirational appeals, rational persuasion, and nonpressure tactics (Yuki, Kim, & Falbe, 1996), because they often believe that their power adds legitimacy to their requests, they may not provide justifications or explanations when seeking compliance. Their influence strategies therefore may tend to be more direct than the influence strategies used by their less powerful subordinates (see Hirokawa, Mickey, & Miura, 1991).

But what happens when a request is not perceived as legitimate? In other words, when the tables are turned, how does a less powerful person try to persuade a more powerful person? To address this question, several researchers (e.g., Baxter, 1984; Craig, Tracy, Spisak, 1986; Hirokawa, Mickey, & Miura, 1991) have applied Brown and Levinson's (1978) *politeness theory* to the study of compliance-gaining behavior.

According to politeness theory, all people are motivated to maintain two kinds of face: positive and negative. We maintain *positive face* when others like, respect and approve of us. We maintain *negative face* when we do not feel constrained or impeded by others. According to Brown and Levinson (1978), when making a request of someone else, both types of face may be challenged. First, the request may constrain the other person's freedom, thereby challenging his or her negative face. By way of illustration, asking someone to pick you up at the airport is challenging because it keeps a person from doing something else that he or she might rather be doing. Second, the request may imply that the other person is being taken advantage of, thereby challenging his or her positive face. For example, in our opinion, the stereotypical sports slob who shouts to his wife, "Bring me another beer!", does not convey much respect.

So, how does the issue of power fit into the picture? According to Brown and Levinson (1978), a person is less likely to comply if his or her face is threatened. Thus, to keep from threatening a person's positive or negative face, we try to be polite when making requests. Moreover, when trying to persuade someone who is more powerful than us, we may have to be extra polite because it is not as likely that our requests will be perceived as legitimate.[2] Research so far has supported this conclusion. For example, in one study, Leslie Baxter (1984) found that compared to less powerful others (i.e., group members), more powerful others (i.e., group leaders) were less polite when making requests. Considering the above, you might be wondering which types of strategies are polite and which are not. Most would agree that threats are not as polite as hints. On the other hand, threats may be more efficient than hints. To test this notion, Kellerman and Shea (1996) asked people to rate how polite and efficient they perceived several different strategies to be. Interestingly, threats, while impolite, were not considered efficient, and hints, while inefficient, were not considered polite. Perhaps the best way to get compliance is by using direct requests (i.e., explicitly asking for what you want); such requests were among the most efficient strategies and were not considered impolite (Kellerman & Shea, 1996).

Whatever strategy you decide to use, it is apparent from our discussion so far that compliance-gaining behavior depends, to a large extent, on several situational dimensions (to learn about compliance-gaining behavior in a *specific* context, see Box 11.2). The situation, however, is not the only factor that affects compliance-gaining behavior. In the next section we explore the impact of individual differences on interpersonal influence.

WHO ARE YOU?: INDIVIDUAL CHARACTERISTICS AND COMPLIANCE-GAINING BEHAVIOR

Up to this point we've talked about the whats and whens of compliance-gaining. That is, we've shown that past research has pointed to a number of situational dimensions (e.g., interpersonal/noninterpersonal, short-term/long-term consequences) that influence strategy choice. According to Hunter and Boster (1987), however, there is but one factor that determines what types of compliance-gaining strategies will be used in a given situation. These researchers argued that when trying to decide what strategy we will use, we try to determine what the emotional impact of the message will be. For example, if you tried to persuade your friend to study more, the friend might become angry and resentful. On the other hand, the friend could be grateful that you cared enough to say something. According to Hunter and Boster, we prefer using strategies that have a positive emotional impact.

But how do we decide which strategies will have a positive emotional impact and which will have a negative emotional impact? Hunter and Boster (1987) argued that each of us has a perceptual "threshold" that helps us make decisions about what strategies are acceptable and what strategies are not. Threatening

---

BOX 11.2   Take Two Aspirin and Call Me in the Morning: Compliance Gaining Between Doctors and Patients

If you are at all like us, you almost certainly have a weakness for some type of food that's probably not all that good for you. It might be pizza, or Doritos, or ice cream. For us, it's chocolate. To be sure, if there is a Nutrageous candy bar within walking distance, then "diets be damned" (one of us, who, for integrity's sake, will remain nameless, ate seven Nutrageous bars in a 24-hour period!).

We imagine that people with limited taste bud control like ourselves pose serious concerns for people in the medical profession. Indeed, physicians are not only confronted with the task of persuading patients to stay on diets, they are constantly trying to get patients to comply with requests to take medication, return for regular checkups, modify their behaviors, and so forth. When one considers the personal and economic costs of not complying with doctors' requests, the study of persuasion in medical contexts is of obvious significance.

According to Burgoon and Burgoon (1990), compliance gaining in medical contexts is unique because, unlike most compliance-gaining situations, patients visit physicians voluntarily, pay for physicians' compliance-gaining directives, perceive physicians as experts, and believe that compliance will benefit themselves rather than the physician. Unfortunately, however, Burgoon, Birk, and Hall's (1991) sources indicate that patient noncompliance is the most significant problem facing medicine today and that patient noncompliance is as high as 62 percent with prescribed drug regimens, 50 percent with medical appointment keeping, and 92 percent with health promotion and life-style changes.

For these reasons, researchers have attempted to determine not only what types of compliance-gaining strategies physicians use, but also what types of strategies are the most effective. For example, a review of literature by Burgoon and Burgoon (1990) found that physicians prefer to use strategies that appeal to authority, knowledge, and expertise and tend to avoid threatening and antisocial strategies. Indeed, Schneider and Beaubien (1996) found that positive expertise, legitimacy, and liking (see strategies discussed earlier) accounted for 83.5 percent of all the compliance-gaining strategies used by doctors on patients. Physicians report that their strategies tend to become more verbally aggressive, however, when patients have not complied with previous requests and have more severe medical problems (Burgoon and Burgoon, 1990).

In addition to issues about strategy use, researchers also have tried to determine what types of strategies are most effective. Some research, for instance, has found that patients are more likely to comply with doctors who express similarity (i.e., indicate that they share things in common with the patient) and are more satisfied with doctors who communicate a willingness to listen, affection, composure, similarity, formality, and nondominance (Burgoon, Pfau, Parrot, Birk, Coker, & Burgoon, 1987). Compliance, however, might be affected by other factors such as physician gender. For instance, Burgoon and colleagues (1991) found that when male doctors deviated from their normally aggressive strategies and use more affiliative tactics, compliance increased. The same was not true for female doctors.

---

someone, for example, may exceed the threshold while promising something may not. Strategies that do not cross the threshold are more likely to be used.

A major implication of this model, of course, is that these thresholds are idiosyncratic, varying from one person to the next. Biff, for example, may be perfectly comfortable threatening others, while Babbs may not. Obviously, then, individual differences are important in determining the types of compliance-gaining messages that are used. For that reason, considerable research has examined several "sender" characteristics that affect strategy choice. Some of these characteristics include Machiavellianism (O'Hair & Cody, 1987), dogmatism (Roloff & Barnicott, 1979), self-monitoring (Smith, Cody, Lovette, & Canary, 1990; Snyder, 1979), Type A personality (Lamude & Scudder, 1993), verbal aggressiveness and argumentativeness (Boster, Levine, & Kazoleas, 1993; Infante, Trebing, Shepherd, & Seeds, 1984; Infante & Wigley, 1986), gender (Dallinger & Hample, 1994; deTurck & Miller, 1982; Fitzpatrick & Winke, 1979), culture (Burgoon, Dillard, Doran, & Miller, 1982; Hirokawa & Mirahara, 1986; Lu, 1997), and age (Haslett, 1983). Many of these characteristics were detailed in Chapter 6.

PROBLEMS FACING COMPLIANCE RESEARCH: TROUBLE IN PARADISE

Up to this point, the things we have said about compliance gaining probably seem fairly simple; when trying to persuade people, we have a number of strategies at our disposal, and the strategies we use are determined in part by the situation and in part by our personal characteristics. Despite this rather straightforward description, however, compliance-gaining research has not been so simple. To be sure, there has been a lot of confusion and argument about what is the best way to study compliance-gaining behavior. Although some of these concerns can get a bit complex and tedious, we believe it is important to mention at least some of them here. Indeed, if we hope to understand the nature of compliance gaining, it is essential that we know about the appropriateness of the methods used to study it. In this section we discuss some of the more visible methodological concerns.

Problems with Typology Development: Here a Strategy, There a Strategy

Earlier we talked about Marwell and Schmitt's (1967) typology of 16 compliance-gaining strategies. Although a considerable amount of research resulted from that study, it wasn't long before their typology met with criticism. In 1981 Wiseman and Schenck-Hamlin argued that, among other problems, the original typology was flawed because it left out many significant strategies that people might use when seeking compliance. Marwell and Schmitt, they argued, had derived their strategies only from previous theory (e.g., "on the drawing board"), and, therefore, the strategies may not correspond with those used by people in real life. To overcome this problem, Wiseman and Schenck-Hamlin (1981) developed a new typology. This time, instead of using past theory to derive strategies, the researchers presented people with persuasive situations and asked them to *generate* a list of strategies they would use in the situations.[3] As a result, Wiseman and Schenck-Hamlin came up with a different typology that distinguished 14 compliance-gaining strategies, many of which differed from Marwell and Schmitt's original typology.

Since that time, typology development has been a popular undertaking. Indeed, after a review of literatures on linguistic devices, interpersonal communication, clinical psychology, child psychology, social psychology, organizational communication, education, marketing, consumer research, and sexual behavior, Kellerman and Cole (1994) identified no less than 74 typologies of compliance-gaining messages! What's more, an integration of these studies resulted in a new "super" typology of 64 distinct compliance-gaining strategies. (We won't identify all 64 of these strategies here, or your instructor might test you on them).

After noting several problems with existing typologies,[4] Kellerman and Cole (1994) argued that the traditional search for a typology of strategies should be scrapped. Instead, they argued that research should focus on "features" of compliance-gaining messages. In other words, instead of trying to come up with the "right list of strategies," or a "comprehensive list of strategies" (see O'Keefe, 1994), research would address questions regarding "features" of messages, such as how polite a compliance-gaining message was. For example, a research study might attempt to determine whether the level of intimacy in a relationship affected the degree of politeness in the compliance-gaining strategies used. Telling a visiting relative not to smoke in your home, for instance, might require a different strategy than telling a stranger sitting under a no smoking sign in a restaurant to "extinguish the butt."

Creating Versus Selecting and Other Methodological Problems

If you could listen to any song right now, what would it be? Can you think of three songs? How about three songs from last year? Depending on how much music you listen to, coming up with songs off the top of your head might not be all that easy. But imagine, for a moment, that you are standing in front of a jukebox and can shuffle through a list of titles before deciding what to pick. Would picking be easier? Do you think the songs you selected would be different than if you couldn't see the titles? We suspect they might.

But what does all of this have to do with compliance-gaining research? If you stop to think about it, the Marwell and Schmitt (1967) study we discussed earlier is not entirely different from our jukebox example. Only, instead of asking their research participants to select from a list of song titles, Marwell and Schmitt asked people to select from a list of preestablished compliance-seeking strategies. The problems with such an approach, however, have been pointed out by numerous researchers (e.g., Burleson, Wilson, Waltman, Goering, Ely, & Whaley, 1988; Cody, McLaughlin, & Jordan, 1980; Seibold et al., 1994; Wiseman & Schenck-Hamlin, 1981). By way of illustration, let's return to the jukebox example. Let's say your favorite Partridge Family song was not a jukebox selection so you settle for a Liberace number (a favorite of jukebox lovers). Obviously, your choice has been constrained by the songs that are available on the jukebox. You can't pick a song if it's not available. Researchers who provide their subjects lists of compliance-gaining strategies constrain their subjects' choices in the same way. That is, lists of strategies often leave things out. In other words, a checklist may force you to use a strategy you normally would not use.

Second, imagine that you notice an old song that you had forgotten about and would not have selected if you'd never seen it listed. If I heard you listening to the song, I might guess that the song is more popular than it really is. In other words, seeing the song title made you more likely to listen to it. In the same way, strategies selected off of a list can artificially "cue" participants. When participating in a study, it's possible that we see a strategy on a list and think, "Oh yeah, that seems like a good one." But in real life, we might never entertain using such a strategy. Thus, the list makes some strategies seem more popular than they truly are.

Finally, imagine that you hate country music but are with a group of friends who love the stuff. To fit in, you two-step over to the jukebox and play some Willie Nelson. Researchers have argued that the same type of thing can happen when participating in research. Specifically, in order to "fit in" or "look good," we may not report what we would do in real life, but rather what makes us look the most socially desirable. Thus, while Biff may go around threatening people in real life, he may tell researchers that he uses more prosocial compliance-gaining tactics. Having a list of tactics to choose from may make this *social desirability bias* more likely to occur.

In an attempt to overcome these problems, some researchers have indicted "selection" in favor of "construction" procedures (e.g., Wiseman & Schenck-Hamlin, 1981). The argument goes like this: If people are presented with a situation requiring persuasion and are asked to describe the strategy they would use (i.e., construct the strategy from scratch rather then select it from a list), the strategy will better reflect true behavior, not misrepresent strategies that are not typically used, and be less prone to a social desirability bias.

As neat as this sounds, research indicates little difference in the results of studies using these two techniques (Boster, 1988; Plax, Kearney, & Sorenson, 1990). What may be of even greater importance, though, are the findings of a study by Dillard (1988). To determine which of several methods for assessing compliance-gaining behavior was the best,[5] Dillard asked people to rate, on paper, how likely they would be to use 16 different compliance-gaining messages in persuasive situations. He then observed these people in actual compliance-gaining situations but found that, regardless of the method he used to assess compliance-gaining behavior, there was no correspondence between the paper–pencil measures and actual behavior. In other words, what people *said* they would do was not the same as what they actually *did*.

When we consider the implications of this study, it reminds us of a story we once heard about a man who exits a cab late at night and sees a drunk on his hands and knees snooping around a street light. The man asks, "Is anything wrong?," to which the drunk replies, "Yeah, I lost my keys." The man says, "Did you lose them here?" The drunk answers, "Naw, I lost them over there in the dark, but the light is much better here." In the same vein, Dillard's (1988) study illustrates that investigators have been looking very hard at compliance gaining, but perhaps not in the right way. Rather than examining compliance gaining in artificial laboratory settings using hypothetical situations, investigators should look for compliance gaining as it occurs in more naturalistic contexts.

NEW DIRECTIONS: THE STUDY OF COMPLIANCE-GAINING GOALS

If we told you that the most effective strategy for getting something was to make threats, would you start threatening people every time you wanted something?

"Loan me twenty bucks or I'll break your nose!"
"If you want to keep your job, get me some coffee!'"
"Keep it up and you can stand in the corner for the next hour."
"Let me get a tattoo or I'll run away from home!"

We suspect that, for most of you, the answer to this question would be "no." But why? If threats really were so effective, why not throw them around a little? Because, you might be thinking to yourself, if I made threats every time I wanted something, I might not have many friends. Plus, you probably wouldn't like yourself too much. And if the other party still refused, you might be forced to follow through with the threat.

The issue here is that when we are seeking compliance, compliance is not the only thing about which we are concerned. Indeed, most of the time we are concerned with pursuing multiple goals at the same time. For instance, research by Kellerman and Kim (1991) distinguished 49 different goals in compliance-gaining situations. Similarly, Canary and Spitzberg (1987, 1989) found that when seeking compliance in conflict situations, people are not only concerned with being *effective*, they also want to behave *appropriately*.

In recent years, the study of compliance-gaining goals has received an increasing amount of attention by communication scholars. In fact, Canary, Cody, and Marston (1986) argued that our goals for interaction may be more important than anything else in helping us distinguish between different compliance-gaining situations. For that reason, we discuss the notion of compliance-gaining goals in the following sections.

Primary and Secondary Goals: Wanting and Eating Your Cake

According to James Dillard and his colleagues (Dillard, 1989; Dillard, Segrin, & Harden, 1989), people pursue different types of goals when they are trying to influence someone. These goals are important because they determine the types of strategies that people use when trying to gain compliance. To identify these goals Dillard and colleagues (1989) asked students to imagine themselves in a compliance-gaining situation and to state why they would or wouldn't use particular influence strategies in that situation. Results of the study indicated that one primary goal, to influence the other person, is the most important in determining the type of strategy that a person uses. For example, a person may decide not to use a strategy because he or she thinks it won't work or because it is irrelevant.

In addition, Dillard (1989) found that four secondary goals influenced people's choices in compliance-gaining situations. First, *identity goals* are concerned with maintaining one's moral standards and principles for living. Thus, people might decide to ignore a strategy that seems immoral. Second, *interaction goals* are concerned with creating a good impression and behaving in appropriate ways. For instance, people motivated by this goal might refuse to use a strategy that would make them look bad. Third, *resource goals* are concerned with maintaining a relationship and increasing personal rewards. Thus, using a strategy that would end a friendship would not be likely. Finally, *arousal goals* are concerned with maintaining levels of arousal (e.g., nervousness) within an acceptable range. Thus, people with this goal would not use a strategy that would make them too anxious (Dillard et al., 1989).

In short then, compliance-gaining situations are not as simple as they may seem. People do not only select tactics that they think will help them gain compliance, but ones that will help them achieve other goals as well. Oftentimes, these goals conflict so that people are faced with complex decisions about which strategies to use. Dillard and colleagues (1989) note that the primary goal plays the strongest role in initiating and maintaining social action, while secondary goals set boundaries which limit the actions taken.

Goals and Rules

Why do people differ so much in the ways they seek compliance? Why, for example, might one person yell and threaten while another begs and pleads? Clearly, the above discussion shows that the answer to this question might be that people's goals differ. Obviously, besides wanting compliance, a person who threatens has different goals than one who begs. According to O'Keefe (1988, 1990), however, differing goals do not play the only role in determining the types of messages we produce. O'Keefe argued that people produce different messages not only because they have differing goals, but also because they think differently about what communication is and does. In other words, people have different beliefs about the nature of communication, and these beliefs affect what they say, how they act, what strategies they use, and so forth. O'Keefe called these different beliefs about communication *design logics* and argued that they are threefold:

1. **Expressive design logic:** A person with this design logic believes that communication is a process by which people merely express what they think and feel. Such people fail to realize that communication can be used to achieve other goals (e.g., see earlier discussion) and therefore "speak from the gut," dumping whatever they think and feel without any regard for what might be appropriate in the given situation. For that reason, O'Keefe argued that such people's messages tend to be "primitive." For instance, a person with an expressive design logic might say

something like the following: "You **##&*@ jerk. You've had it. I'm going to get you fired for this!"

2. Conventional design logic: A person with this design logic believes that communication is a game played cooperatively, according to social conventions and procedures (O'Keefe, 1990, p. 91). Thus, people using this logic express their thoughts and feelings, but believe that they must also follow rules for appropriate social behavior in the given situation. For instance, a person with a conventional design logic might say something like the following: "You missed our meeting today and I don't appreciate this irresponsibility. If you miss one more meeting, you're fired."

3. Rhetorical design logic: People with a conventional design logic believe that the given context determines what type of communication is appropriate, while people with a rhetorical design logic believe the opposite—Context is created by communication. Rhetorical design logic assumes that communication's purpose is to negotiate character, attitude, selves, and situations. The process involves repeatedly solving and coordinating problems, consensus, and harmony. Thus, someone with this logic pursues multiple goals, tends to be proactive, and uses rational arguments. Here's an example: "You have been coming back late from lunch and we need to reach some kind of understanding about this. I don't want to have to force you to follow the rules, but I will if I have to. But surely you can appreciate why we have rules and what function they serve. I know if you just think about the situation you will see how your behavior could be creating a problem in this office" (O'Keefe, 1988, p. 103).

According to O'Keefe (1988, 1990), as they gain more experience, people develop more complex and sophisticated design logics. Rhetorical design logics are the most sophisticated, followed by conventional and then expressive logics. Presumably, design logics influence the types of influence messages that are sent. Moreover, research has found that messages that reflect rhetorical design logics are rated as more competent, favorable, and persuasive than messages reflecting the other design logics (Bingham & Burleson, 1989; O'Keefe & McCornack, 1987).

SUMMARY

This chapter focused on the study of compliance gaining. Early research in this area attempted to discover the different types of strategies that people use to get other people to behave in certain ways. Early research also focused on the ways in which situations and individual characteristics affected the use of compliance-gaining strategies. In this chapter we showed that compliance-gaining research has been plagued by several problems, including concerns about typology development and difficulties surrounding the measurement of compliance. Finally, we discussed the notion of compliance-gaining goals and how differing goals influence the choice of compliance-gaining strategies.

ENDNOTES

1. There is a statistical test called factor analysis that can determine whether several separate measures or, in this case, tactics, can be combined into fewer or more basic items. This is the method used by Marwell and Schmitt (1967).

2. Other factors that cause people to be more or less polite are relational intimacy, cost of compliance, deservingness of aid, directness of the request, and the magnitude of the request (see Baxter, 1984; Clark, 1993).

3. Because Marwell and Schmitt's (1967) typology was based on previous theory, it is often said that their typology was "deductively derived." One the other hand, Wiseman and Schenck-Hamlin's typology, generated by responses from research participants, was "inductively derived."

4. According to Kellerman and Cole (1994), existing typologies of compliance-gaining strategies are problematic for several reasons. First, current typologies are not exhaustive. In other words, any given typology may leave out strategies that persuaders might use. Second, there are no clear distinctions between different types of categories so that some categories are confused while others seem to overlap. Finally, Kellerman and Cole (1994) argued that definitions and examples of strategies found in prior research are often incomplete, not understandable, not representative, and irrelevant. In short, a few decades of research have produced nothing but an atheoretical, hodge-podge of strategies (Kellerman & Cole, 1994).

5. Three prior methods have been used to assess compliance-gaining behavior, each using a different dependent variable. First, the technique approach treats each individual compliance-gaining tactic as a separate dependent variable and assumes that the correspondence between selected tactics (selected from a checklist) and used tactics will be high. Second, the strategy approach treats groups of tactics as dependent variables and assumes that correspondence between strategy choice and use will be high. Finally, the summed-tactic approach argues that a single dependent variable is indicative of some global compliance-gaining attempt and assumes that the summed tactic-selection score will correspond to the frequency of compliance-gaining messages (see Dillard, 1988).

REFERENCES

Baxter, L. (1984). An investigation of compliance-gaining as politeness. *Human Communication Research, 10,* 427–456.

Bingham, S. G., & Burleson, B. R. (1989). Multiple effects of messages with multiple goals: Some perceived outcomes of responses to sexual harassment. *Human Communication Research, 16,* 184–216.

Boster, F. J. (1995). Commentary on compliance-gaining message behavior research. In C. Berger & M. Burgoon (Eds.), *Communication and social influence processes* (pp. 91–113). East Lansing, MI: Michigan State University Press.

Boster, F. J. (1988). Comments on the utility of compliance-gaining message selection tasks. *Human Communication Research, 15,* 169–177.

Boster, F. J., Levine, T. R., & Kazoleas, D. C. (1993). The impact of argumentativeness and verbal aggressiveness on strategic diversity and persistence in compliance gaining behavior. *Communication Quarterly, 41,* 405–414.

Boster, F. J., & Stiff, J. B. (1984). Compliance gaining message selection behavior. *Human Communication Research, 10,* 539–556.

Brown, P., & Levinson, S. (1978). Universals in language usage: Politeness phenomena. In E. N. Goody (Ed.), *Questions and politeness: Strategies in social interaction* (pp. 56–289). New York: Cambridge University Press.

Burgoon, M., Birk, T., & Hall, J. R. (1991). Compliance and satisfaction with physician–patient communication: An expectancy theory interpretation of gender differences. *Human Communication Research, 18,* 177–208.

Burgoon, M. H., & Burgoon, J. K. (1990). Compliance-gaining and health care. In J. P. Dillard

(Ed.), *Seeking compliance: The production of interpersonal influence messages* (pp. 161–188). Scottsdale, AZ: Gorsuch-Scarisbrick.

Burgoon, M., Dillard, J. P., Doran, N. E., & Miller, M. D. (1982). Cultural and situational influences on the process of persuasive strategy selection. *International Journal of Intercultural Relations, 6,* 85–100.

Burgoon, J. K., Pfau, M., Parrott, R., Birk, T., Coker, R., & Burgoon, M. (1987). Relational communication, satisfaction, compliance-gaining strategies, and compliance in communication between physicians and patients. *Communication Monographs, 54,* 307–324.

Burleson, R. R., Wilson, S. R., Waltman, M. S., Goering, E. M., Ely, T. K., & Whaley, B. B. (1988). Item desirability effects in compliance-gaining research: Seven studies documenting artifacts in strategy selection procedure. *Human Communication Research, 14,* 429–486.

Byers, E. S., & Wilson, P. (1985). Accuracy of women's expectations regarding men's responses to refusals of sexual advances in dating situations. *International Journal of Women's Studies, 8,* 376–387.

Canary, D. J., Cody, M. J., & Marston, P. J. (1986). Goal types, compliance-gaining and locus of control in managing interpersonal conflict. *Journal of Language and Social Psychology, 5,* 249–269.

Canary, D. J., & Spitzberg, B. H. (1987). Appropriateness and effectiveness perceptions of conflict strategies. *Human Communication Research, 14,* 93–118.

Canary, D. J., & Spitzberg, B. H. (1989). A model of the perceived competence of conflict strategies. *Communication Research, 15,* 630–649.

Christopher, F. S., & Frandsen, M. M. (1990). Strategies of influence in sex and dating. *Journal of Social and Personal Relationships, 7,* 89–105.

Clark, R. A. (1993). The impact of cost of compliance, deservingness of aid, and directness of a request on reactions to the request. *Southern Communication Journal, 58,* 215–226.

Cody, M. J., Greene, J. O., Marston, P. J., O'Hair, H. D., Baaske, K. T., & Schneider, M. J. (1986). Situation perception and strategy selection. In M. L. McLaughlin (Ed.), *Communication yearbook 9* (pp. 391–420). Beverly Hills, CA: Sage.

Cody, M. J., & McLaughlin, M. L. (1980). Perceptions of compliance-gaining situations: A dimensional analysis. *Communication Monographs, 47,* 132–148.

Cody, M. J., McLaughlin, M. L., & Jordan, W. J. (1980). A multidimensional scaling of three sets of compliance-gaining strategies. *Communication Quarterly, 28,* 34–46.

Cody, M. J., Woelfel, M. L., & Jordan, W. J. (1983). Dimensions of compliance-gaining situations. *Human Communication Research, 9,* 99–113.

Craig, R. T., Tracy, K., & Spisak, F. (1986). The discourse of requests: Assessment of a politeness approach. *Human Communication Research, 12,* 437–468.

Dallinger, J. M., & Hample, D. (1994). The effects of gender on compliance gaining strategy endorsement and suppression. *Communication Reports, 7,* 43–49.

deTurck, M. (1985). A transactional analysis of compliance-gaining behavior: Effects of noncompliance, relational contexts and actor's gender. *Human Communication Research, 12,* 54–78.

deTurck, M. (1987). When communication fails: Physical aggression as a compliance–gaining strategy. *Communication Monographs, 54,* 106–112.

deTurck, M. A., & Miller, G. R. (1982). The effect of birth order on the persuasive impact of messages and the likelihood of persuasive message selection. *Communication, 11,* 78–84.

Dillard, J. P. (1988). Compliance-gaining message-selection: What is our dependent variable? *Communication Monographs, 55,* 162–183.

Dillard, J. P. (1989). Types of influence goals in personal relationships. *Journal of Social and Personal Relationships, 6,* 293–308.

Dillard, J. P., & Burgoon, M. (1985). Situational influences on the selection of compliance-gaining messages: Two tests of the predictive utility of the Cody-McLaughlin typology. *Communication Monographs, 52,* 289–304.

Dillard, J. P., Segrin, C., & Harden, J. M. (1989). Primary and secondary goals in the production of interpersonal influence messages. *Communication Monographs, 56,* 19–38.

Fitzpatrick, M. A., & Winke, J. (1979). You always hurt the one you love: Strategies and tactics in interpersonal conflict. *Communication Quarterly, 27,* 3–11.

French, J. P. R., Jr., & Raven, B. (1960). The bases of social power. In D. Cartwright & A. Zander (Eds.), *Group dynamics* (pp. 607–623). New York: Harper and Row.

Haslett, B. (1983). Preschoolers' communication strategies in gaining compliance from peers: A developmental study. *Quarterly Journal of Speech, 69,* 84–99.

Hirokawa, R. Y., Mickey, J., & Miura, S. (1991). Effects of request legitimacy on the compliance-gaining tactics of male and female managers. *Communication Monographs, 58,* 421–436.

Hirokawa, R. Y., & Mirahara, A. (1986). A comparison of influence strategies utilized in American and Japanese organizations. *Communication Quarterly, 34,* 250–265.

Hunter, J. E., & Boster, F. (1987). A model of compliance-gaining message selection. *Communication Monographs, 54,* 63–84.

Infante, D. A., Trebing, D. W., Shepard, P. E., & Seeds, D. E. (1984). The relationship of argumentativeness to verbal aggression. *Southern States Speech Journal, 50,* 67–77.

Infante, D. A., & Wigley, C. J. (1986). Verbal aggressiveness: An interpersonal model and measure. *Communication Monographs, 53,* 61–69.

Kellerman, K., & Cole, T. (1994). Classifying compliance gaining messages: Taxonomic disorder and strategic confusion. *Communication Theory, 4,* 3–60.

Kellerman, K., & Kim, M. S. (1991). *Working within constraints: Tactical choices in the pursuit of social goals.* Paper presented at the annual meeting of the International Communication Association, Miami, FL.

Kellerman, K., & Shea, B. C. (1996). Threats, suggestions, hints, and promises: Gaining compliance efficiently and politely. *Communication Quarterly, 44*(2), 145–165.

Lamude, K. G., & Scudder, J. (1993). Compliance-gaining techniques of Type-A managers. *Journal of Business Communication, 30,* 63–78.

Lu, S. (1997). Culture and compliance gaining in the classroom: A preliminary investigation of Chinese college teachers' use of behavior alteration techniques. *Communication Education, 46*(1), 11–43.

Marwell, G., & Schmitt, D. R. (1967). Dimensions of compliance-gaining behavior: An empirical analysis. *Sociometry, 30,* 350–364.

McLaughlin, M. L., Cody, M. J., & Robey, C. S. (1980). Situational influences of the selection of strategies to resist compliance-gaining attempts. *Human Communication Research, 7,* 14–36.

Metts, S., Cupach, W. R., & Imahori, T. T. (1992). Perceptions of Sexual compliance-resisting messages in three types of cross-sex relationships. *Western Journal of Communication, 56,* 1–17.

Metts, S., & Spitzberg, B. H. (1996). Sexual communication in interpersonal contexts: A script-based approach. In B. R. Burleson (Ed.), *Communication Yearbook 19* (pp. 49–92). Thousand Oaks, CA: Sage.

Miller, G. R., Boster, F., Roloff, M., & Seibold, D. (1977). Compliance-gaining message strategies: A typology and some findings concerning effects of situational differences. *Communication Monographs, 44,* 37–51.

Muehlenhard, C. L., & Hollanbaugh, L. C. (1988). Do women sometimes say no when they mean yes? The prevalence and correlates of women's token resistance to sex. *Journal of Personality and Social Psychology, 55,* 872–879.

O'Hair, D., & Cody, M. J. (1987). Machiavellian beliefs and social influence. *Western Journal of Speech Communication, 51,* 279–303.

O'Keefe, B. J. (1988). The logic of message design: Individual differences in reasoning about communication. *Communication Monographs, 55,* 80–103.

O'Keefe, B. J. (1990). The logic of regulative communication: Understanding the logic of message designs. In J. P. Dillard (Ed.), *Seeking compliance: The production of interpersonal influence messages* (pp. 87–106). Scottsdale, AZ: Gorsuch-Scarisbrick.

O'Keefe, B. J., & McCornack, S. A. (1987). Message logic and message goal structure: Effects on perceptions of message quality in regulative communication situations. *Human Communication Research, 14,* 68–92.

O'Keefe, D. J. (1994). From strategy-based to feature-based analyses of compliance gaining message classification and production. *Communication Theory, 4,* 61–69.

Perper, T., & Weis, D. L. (1987). Proceptive and rejective strategies of U.S. and Canadian college women. *Journal of Sex Research, 23,* 455–480.

Plax, T., Kearney, P., & Sorensen, G. (1990). The strategy selection-construction controversy II: Comparing pre- and experienced teachers' compliance-gaining message constructions. *Communication Education, 39,* 128–141.

Reardon, K. K., Sussman, S., & Flay, B. R. (1989). Are we marketing the right message?: Can kids "just say 'no' to smoking?" *Communication Monographs, 56,* 307–324.

Roloff, M. E., & Barnicott, Jr., E. F. (1979). The influence of dogmatism on the situational use of pro- and anti-social compliance-gaining strategies. *Southern Speech Communication Journal, 45,* 37–54.

Rudd, J. E., & Burant, P. A. (1996). A study of women's compliance-gaining behaviors in violent and non-violent relationships. *Communication Research Reports, 12* (2), 134–144.

Schneider, D. E., & Beaubien, R. A. (1996). A naturalistic investigation of compliance gaining strategies employed by doctors in medical interviews. *Southern Communication Journal, 61*(4), 332–341.

Seibold, D. R., Cantrill, J. G., & Meyers, R. A. (1994). Communication and interpersonal influence. In M. L. Knapp & G. R. Miller (Eds.), *Handbook of interpersonal communication* (2nd ed., pp. 542–588). Thousand Oaks, CA: Sage.

Sillars, A. L. (1980). The stranger and the spouse as target persons for compliance gaining strategies: A subjective expected utility model. *Human Communication Research, 6,* 265–279.

Smith, S. W., Cody, M. J., Lovette, S., & Canary, D. J. (1990). Self-monitoring, gender, and compliance-gaining goals. In M. J. Cody & M. L. McLaughlin (Eds.), *The psychology of tactical communication* (pp. 91–135). Philadelphia: Multilingual Matters.

Snyder, M. (1979). Self-monitoring processes. In L. Berkowitz (Ed.), *Advances in experimental social psychology* (Vol. 12, pp. 85–128). New York: Academic Press.

Wilson, S. R., Cruz, M. G., Marshall, L. J., & Rao, N. (1993). An attributional analysis of compliance-gaining interactions. *Communication Monographs, 60,* 352–372.

Wiseman, R. L., & Schenck-Hamlin. W. (1981). A multidimensional scaling validation of an inductively-derived set of compliance-gaining strategies. *Communication Monographs, 48,* 251–270.

Witteman, H., & Fitzpatrick, M. A. (1986). Compliance-gaining in marital interaction: Power bases, processes and outcomes. *Communication Monographs, 53,* 130–143.

Yuki, G., Kim, H., & Falbe, C. M. (1996). Antecedents of influence outcomes. *Journal of Applied Psychology, 81,* 309–317.

12

SEQUENTIAL PERSUASION

"If you're a door-to-door salesperson," we're told by a friend of ours who once made his living selling encyclopedias, "half your job is getting into people's houses. Once you're inside," he informed us, "they're yours, all yours."

According to our friend, most door-to-door salespeople have sneaky ways of getting their feet into your doorway. Some mention your neighbors by name. Some ask for a glass of water. Our pal had a whole spiel based largely on deception. He's not proud of it now, he admitted, but when he greeted prospective customers, he was trained to look like anything but a salesperson.

"After introducing myself to the customers," he told us, "I promised I was not going to try to sell them anything. I was just in the neighborhood conducting surveys. I asked them if they would give me their opinions about their family's educational needs and told them that, if they did, I would repay them with 'educational materials.' That usually got me inside."

Once our friend was in the door, he asked his customers to respond to a phony "opinion survey" (e.g., "Do your kids use the library?," "Do your kids go to the library after dark?") and then showed them a set of encyclopedias that he was "willing to give them, for promotional reasons, if they promised to keep the set up to date." How could they do that? Simply by purchasing one yearbook for the next 10 years.

Many of the customers agreed to this seemingly unbelievable offer. What they did not realize was that the amount of money they paid for the yearbooks actually covered the cost of the encyclopedias and then some. They'd been "schmoozed" into buying something they thought they were getting for free.

This example shows that oftentimes persuasion is not as simple as making a single request or giving one speech. Persuasion, quite frequently, is a process that requires that a number of steps be enacted in the right order. Indeed, before making his pitch, our friend had to get himself into the customer's house. And for reasons we'll discuss later in this chapter, by getting customers to agree to the survey, our friend probably increased his chances of making a sale.

In this chapter we discuss the notion of "sequential persuasion." We'll explore research that shows how people increase their persuasiveness, often at the expense of others, by saying or doing something before actually making their request. We begin with a strategy known as *pregiving*.

PREGIVING: THE OLD "I'LL SCRATCH YOUR BACK IF YOU'LL SCRATCH MINE" APPROACH

While writing this chapter, one of the authors received a package in the mail. The package contained two unused rolls of film and a letter explaining that the film was a gift. The letter went on to explain how, after using the film, the author could mail it to the company to be processed. And the funny thing is, the author did, even though the cost of the processing was more expensive than taking the film to Wal-mart. Why was the author persuaded to spend more money? Because the ploy used by the processing company is a well-known and effective tactic of persuasion known as pregiving (see Kellerman & Cole, 1994; Marwell & Schmitt, 1967; Wiseman & Schenck-Hamlin, 1981). Pregiving entails trying to get someone to comply by acting nice or doing favors for them in advance. When supermarkets offer free samples of foods to taste, they are employing this strategy. A study by Lammers (1991) demonstrated that free samples did promote buying, but not necessarily the same brand as the sample.

Tactics such as pregiving are effective because of the "norm of reciprocity," which says that "we should try to repay, in kind, what another person has provided us" (Cialdini, 1993, p. 19). Greenberg (1980) argued that feeling indebted makes us feel uncomfortable because it threatens our independence. Thus, as we become more indebted, we are more motivated to repay the debt (Greenberg, 1980).

A classic study done by Dennis Regan (1971) showed how effective the pregiving strategy can be. In the study, freshmen at Stanford University who had been asked to participate in an experiment on "aesthetics" were seated in a room with another student. What the freshmen had not been told was that the other student was a confederate who had been planted there by the researcher. After a few minutes, the confederate left the room. When he returned, he was either empty-handed or was carrying two Coca Colas. If he was empty-handed, he simply sat back down. But if he had sodas, he offered one to the research subject and said, "I bought one for you too."

Seems nice enough, but there's a catch; later, the plant informed the subject that he was selling raffle tickets for a new high school gym and would appreciate it if the subject would do him a favor and buy some tickets. Not surprisingly, the results of the study revealed that subjects who had been given a soda ahead of time bought almost twice as many raffle tickets as those who had been given nothing. In other words, the motivation to reciprocate was strong enough to get the subjects to comply.

Whether or not they are consciously aware of the reasons behind the pregiving tactic, it is clear that many real world persuaders are not shy about putting this tactic into use. In Los Angeles and New York City, for instance, panhandlers have figured out a tricky way to make commuters feel indebted. Armed with a sponge and a pail of dirty water, these "squeegee guys," as they are called, are frequently seen wading into traffic to wash unsuspecting motorists' windshields. It is not uncommon, for example, to receive one of these uninvited cleanings while stopped at a red light. A slap of a wet sponge, a little elbow grease, and a squeegee typically make the motorist feel indebted enough to repay the favor with some cash.

The pregiving tactic works in other contexts as well. For instance, as a suit salesman, one of the authors was trained to ask customers if they would like to have their jackets pressed while they were shopping. Very few refused the favor and even those that did were cheerfully surprised at the offer. What they did not understand was that there was a hidden rationale behind the gesture; asking if they'd like their jackets pressed was not only an effective means of getting customers to spend more time looking at merchandise, it also made them feel indebted. And when it came to purchasing a suit, who better to buy from than that nice salesman who had already done them a favor?

Our final example of the pregiving strategy is, to us, perhaps the most disturbing. Specifically, the next time a man asks if he can by you a drink, women beware; a study by George, Gournic, and McAfee (1988) found that if women allow men to buy them drinks, both men and women perceive the women to be more sexually available than if the drinks are refused.[1] In other words, and once again, there seems to be an assumption that pregiving makes one obligated to return favors.

Finally, we should note that if you decide to try the pregiving strategy yourself, you should be careful. It does not always succeed. Groves, Cialdini, and Couper (1992) argue that people do not feel obligated to reciprocate positive behaviors "when the earlier behavior received is not viewed as a gift or a favor but as a bribe or an undue pressure to comply" (p. 480). In fact, when pregiving is perceived as a bribe or a pressure tactic, it actually decreases compliance (Groves et al., 1992). Hence, the pregiving must be perceived by the target as an altruistic act, not as a self-serving act.

FOOT IN THE DOOR: THE "GIVE ME AN INCH AND I'LL TAKE A MILE" TACTIC

Not too long ago, one of the authors and a friend were leaving a shopping mall when they were approached by a woman. She was about 30 years old, nicely dressed, and had a small child with her.

"Excuse me," she said to the author, "would you please tell me what time it is?"

The author was nice enough to oblige.

"I was wondering if you could also spare a few dollars?" the woman added. She claimed that her car had run out of gas, she had forgotten her purse, and, if the author would give her his address, she would be happy to return the money to him.

Once again, the author obliged, giving her three or four dollars. He never heard from the woman again. The author's friend, however, saw the same woman several weeks later, using the same scam but at a different mall.

In retrospect, there were probably several things that made the woman more successful in her attempt to gain compliance. The fact that she was well-dressed made her story seem more believable. She gave a plausible reason for needing the money. And having a small child with her probably created more sympathy. Interestingly, however, having nice clothes, good reasons, and a small child may not have been the only keys to her success. A considerable amount of research shows that the woman might have increased her chances of compliance by asking for the time *before* she asked for money (Hmm. Maybe there is a good reason then for not giving a stranger "the time of day.").

The tactic we have just described is often referred to as the *foot in the door technique,* hereafter called FITD. The tactic involves making a small request first and then making a second larger request. Of course, it is the second, larger request that most interests the persuader. The first, small request is merely a setup. For instance, the encyclopedia salesman we talked about earlier used this tactic when he asked people if they would answer a short survey before he asked for a sale. He didn't really care about their responses to the survey, he just wanted to soften them up. For reasons we will talk about later, when people comply with a smaller request, it often makes them more likely to comply with a second, larger request.

The first study to demonstrate the effectiveness of the FITD technique was conducted by Jonathan Freedman and Scott Fraser (1966) at Stanford University. These researchers were interested in finding out if they could get housewives to agree to a very large request. Specifically, they asked housewives to allow a team of five or six men into their homes for 2 hours. The men, they were told, would have complete freedom in the house to go through the cupboards and storage spaces in order to classify all of the household products that were there. Before being approached with this request, however, some of the women were set up with a smaller initial request. That is, 3 days before making the large request, the researchers called some of the housewives and asked if they would participate in a survey about household products (e.g., "What brand of soap do you use?"). Surprisingly, about 50 percent of the housewives who agreed to answer the survey also agreed to let complete strangers rifle through their houses. On the other hand, when the researchers had not approached housewives with a smaller request first, only about 25 percent of the housewives agreed to the subsequent larger request (Freedman & Fraser, 1966).

According to Dillard (1991) over 43 articles have been published on the FITD technique. Recent reviews of these studies suggest that, given the right conditions, the strategy is effective (Beaman, Cole, Preston, Klentz, & Steblay, 1983; Dillard, Hunter, & Burgoon, 1984; Fern, Monroe, & Avila, 1986)[2] and has increased compliance for a variety of requests such as those asking people (1) to put large signs on their front lawns (Freedman & Fraser, 1966), (2) to make contributions to charities (Pliner, Hart, Kohl, & Saari, 1974), and (3) to participate in research (Snyder & Cunningham, 1975; Wagener & Laird, 1980). But why does the tactic work? In the following section we discuss what makes the FITD such a powerful tool of persuasion. We then turn to a discussion of some variables that influence the tactic's effectiveness.

Why Is a Foot in the Door So Persuasive?

The most common explanation for the effectiveness of the foot in the door tactic is based on Bem's (1972) *self-perception theory* (see DeJong, 1979; Freedman & Fraser, 1966). According to this theory, people come to know about their attitudes, emotions, and other internal states by inferring them from their own behavior (Bem, 1972). For example, if you notice yourself eating a lot of Nutrageous candy bars, you are likely to come to the conclusion that you have a favorable attitude toward chocolate. In other words, you use your behavior to infer your attitude.

As an explanation for the FITD effect, self-perception theory says this: When you agree to comply with a small request, you see yourself as an altruistic person who is likely to help. Once you form that impression, you are motivated to behave in a way that is consistent with that impression. Thus, when a larger request is made, you are more easily persuaded. (A similar argument is made to explain the effectiveness of the foot in the mouth tactic, another sequential approach to persuasion that is discussed in Box 12.1).

Although early research pointed to the viability of self-perception theory as an explanation for the effectiveness of the FITD tactic, recent evidence is not so

---

BOX 12.1 "How Are You Today?": The Foot in the Mouth Effect

The next time someone greets you by asking, "How are you?," you might want to grumble and tell them you're feeling terrible. If you don't, you might be setting yourself up for what Howard (1990) calls the "foot in the mouth effect." That is, by telling someone that you're feeling wonderful, you may make yourself feel committed to behave in a way that is consistent with that declaration. Thus, you may be more likely to comply. Persuaders know this and use it to their advantage. For example, Howard (1990) points to the following excerpt from a lecture offered on fund-raising:

Before you ask anyone for a donation, you first ask them how they're feeling. After they tell you they're feeling good, and you tell them you're glad they're feeling good, they'll be more likely to contribute to helping someone who isn't. (p. 1185)

Research by Howard (1990) and Aune and Basil (1994) supports this conclusion. When asking for charitable donations, callers were more successful if they asked people how they were feeling, acknowledged the response, and then requested compliance than when they simply requested compliance. Howard (1990) argued that the tactic is especially useful given that, when acknowledging a greeting, people often mindlessly respond in a positive manner. Moreover, he noted:

What is diabolically clever about the technique is that, if properly used, it can be virtually undetectable "as a technique"; we feel the use of "common greetings" avoids the appearance of being part of a compliance ploy. (p. 1195)

optimistic. For example, Gorassini and Olson (1995) conducted a study that measured how helpful people perceived themselves to be after complying with a first, small request. They found that although people's self-ratings of helpfulness were affected by compliance with the small request, those changes did not always predict people's compliance with a second, larger request. Moreover, compliance with a second, larger request often occurred without people perceiving themselves as more helpful. Dillard (1990) argued that results of studies such as these show that more theorizing about the FITD tactic is necessary.

As an alternative to self-perception theory, Gorassini and Olson (1995) proposed a model that says the FITD strategy works if three changes can be brought about in the person from whom compliance is sought. By way of example, imagine that you want to get someone to donate money to the cancer society. Gorassini and Olson (1995) argued that your first task is to activate an attitude that would lead the person to behave in the way you want him or her to behave. In this case, for instance, you could make the person want to show compassion. Second, Gorassini and Olson noted that compliance also depends on how the person interprets the large request. That is, does the large request have anything to do with the attitude that has been activated? For example, donating money to the cancer fund is probably seen as a better opportunity to show compassion than donating money to a political candidate. Finally, the person being persuaded needs to learn something about norms regarding the attitude. For instance, the first, small request might ask a person to accept a pamphlet about children's cancer. This, in turn, might teach him or her that a person not making a donation is more callous than normal because such a behavior would be a rejection of sick children (Gorassini & Olson, 1995). If these three conditions are satisfied, the FITD tactic is more likely to be successful.

When Does a Foot in the Door Work?

Research tells us that some of the following conditions play an important role in determining the effectiveness of the FITD.

1. Size of the initial request. Is getting a person to comply with any request enough to get them to comply with later requests? Research shows that the initial request should be neither too large or too small. Seligman, Bush, and Kirsch (1976) argued that "the first request must be of sufficient size for the foot in the door technique to work" (p. 519). On the other hand, the initial request cannot be so large that it is rejected. Thus, the persuader must strike a balance between making a large enough initial request to trigger the FITD effect, but not so large that it is declined. For instance, asking for a penny so you might later get a larger donation probably would not work because the penny might be perceived as inconsequential. On the other hand, asking the average person for $1,000 to begin with might be a bit much. In short, the persuader wants to use the largest possible request that will be accepted.

2. Prosocialness of the request. In a review of several studies, Dillard and colleagues (1984) found that the FITD tactic is more effective when used for prosocial causes than it is when used for self-serving reasons. With this in mind, the FITD tactic would probably be more useful to social workers who are trying to raise money to help the homeless than it would be for commission salespeople.

3. External Incentives to Comply. Dillard and colleagues' (1984) study also indicated that people are less susceptible to the FITD tactic if they are offered external incentives for complying with the first request. Most researchers use self-perception theory to explain these effects. Specifically, if you are receiving a gift for agreeing to listen to a sales pitch, you do not form the impression of yourself as someone who is willing to comply readily with requests. You are only complying because you have a material reason for doing so. Thus, because the pregiving strategy (discussed earlier) uses external incentives, it may not be a good idea to use it and the FITD strategies together (see Bell, Cholerton, Fraczek, Rohlfs, & Smith, 1994; Weyant, 1996).

4. Who Makes the Requests. For the FITD strategy to work, the same person isn't required to make both the initial and the follow-up requests. Indeed, it is often the case that a person who complies with a request by one person will also comply with a second request, even when the second request is made by a different person.

THE DOOR IN THE FACE TACTIC: "ASK FOR THE STARS"

One of our students used to work selling jewelry in a large department store. She tells us that her approach to sales was very different from that of the other salespeople with whom she worked. Most of them, she tells us, started by showing their customers the "bottom of the line" merchandise. To increase their sales, they then moved to more expensive merchandise, demonstrating that "more money" meant "more quality." On the other hand, our student started by showing her customers the most expensive merchandise. Typically, they did not purchase what they were first shown but, even so, our student claims that while she worked at that store her sales were always higher than anyone else's.

Actually, we are not surprised by our student's success as a salesperson. Whether she knew it or not, she was using a tactic of persuasion that researchers have known to be effective for many years. Often called the *door in the face*, or DITF, this tactic is just the opposite of the FITD strategy. It works by first making a request so large that it is turned down, then following it up with a second, smaller request. Of course, just as with the FITD tactic, compliance with the second request is what the persuader has been aiming for all along.

Based on conversations with students, friends, and colleagues, it seems that the DITF tactic is quite common. For example, a person we know told us about his dealings with a particular fund-raising organization. Frequently, the organization sends him letters asking for donations of $400 to $1000—too high for his pocketbook. By now, he has received so many of these letters that he has figured out the organization's pattern: whenever he gets a letter, he is certain of what will come next—a follow-up call from the organization. Typically, the person making the call asks our friend if he received their letter. When our friend tells the caller that he can't afford the suggested donation, the caller tells him that anything he can afford would be appreciated. In other words, the letter is a DITF tactic that sets up the potential persuadee for a subsequent smaller request.

The first empirical study of the DITF tactic was conducted by Robert Cialdini and his colleagues at Arizona State University (Cialdini, Vincent, Lewis, Catalan, Wheeler, & Darby, 1975). Cialdini (1993) explains what happened:

> Posing as representatives of the "County Youth Counseling Program," we approached college students walking on campus and asked if they would be willing to chaperon a group of juvenile delinquents on a day trip to the zoo…As we expected, the great majority (83 percent) refused. Yet we obtained very different results from a similar sample of college students who were asked the very same question with one difference. Before we invited them to serve as unpaid chaperons on the zoo trip, we asked them for an even larger favor—to spend two hours per week as a counselor to a juvenile delinquent for a minimum of two years…By presenting the zoo trip as a retreat from our initial request, our success rate increased dramatically. Three times as many of the students approached in this manner volunteered to serve as zoo chaperons. (p. 37)

Since the 1975 study of Cialdini and colleagues, the effectiveness of the DITF tactic has been demonstrated again and again (e.g., Cann, Sherman, & Elkes, 1975; Pendleton & Batson, 1979; Schwarzwald, Raz, & Zvibel, 1979; Shanab & O'Neill, 1979). But rather than examining those studies, we turn now to a discussion of *why* the DITF tactic is thought to be so effective.

Why is a Door in the Face So Persuasive?

During our years of teaching public speaking courses, we've heard the expression "That's a tough act to follow" more than once. We imagine that this phrase is especially meaningful to students who have speeches of questionable quality. Indeed, no one wants to present a mediocre speech *after* a student who has dazzled the professor and the rest of the class with his or her eloquence. The speech would undoubtedly look worse than it really was. This is known as the *perceptual contrast effect.*

As an explanation for the effectiveness of the DITF tactic, the contrast effect says this: People are likely to comply with a second, smaller request because, compared to the initial, larger request, the second request seems much smaller than it normally would have (Cialdini, 1993). In other words, a $500 diamond ring seems inexpensive compared to the $3,000 rings. Compared to the $100 rings, however, it seems expensive.

A second explanation for the effectiveness of the DITF tactic is known as *reciprocal concessions* (Cialdini et al., 1975). This explanation is related to the norm of reciprocity we discussed earlier, that is, when someone does us a favor, we feel obligated to return that favor. A similar thing happens when someone makes a concession. When that happens, we are motivated to make a concession in return. If the other person gives up something, we should too.

So how does this relate to the DITF strategy? Quite simply, when a persuader follows up with a smaller request, it is often perceived as a concession. The persuader has made a more reasonable offer so we too should be reasonable. Thus, to "return the favor," people frequently comply with the second request. (The "that's not all" tactic is another approach to sequential persuasion that might be explained by the contrast effect and the norm of reciprocity—see Box 12.2.)

In the real world, negotiations often operate according to this process of reciprocal concessions. That is, negotiators often try to appear more reasonable by starting

---

BOX 12.2   The That's Not All Tactic: Seeking Compliance by Sweetening the Deal

Remember our friend who sold encyclopedias? We began this chapter by telling you how he used to weasel his way into houses with the foot in the door tactic. But that's not all he did to sell his books. According to him, he also used what he calls the "But wait, there's more" strategy. Here's how it worked: After presenting the books and before asking for the sale, he showed his customers several other items they could receive for free (an atlas, a dictionary, a thesaurus), *if* they agreed to buy the encyclopedias. Perhaps you've observed this strategy used in other contexts. For instance, haven't we all seen those commercials for food and vegetable slicers and dicers? Typically, after a demonstration, you're asked, "How much would you pay for this?" Then you're presented with an add-on knife. How much would you pay now? How about if a carrot cleaner was added? Well, you get the idea, so "call now!"

To see whether this tactic was effective, Jerry Burger (1986) conducted several studies. In one, the tactic was used on customers at a bake sale. When customers asked about the price of a cupcake, they were told one of two things. Some customers were told that a cupcake and two cookies sold for 75 cents. Other customers, however, were not told about the cookies right away—a few seconds after they'd been told that the cupcakes sold for 75 cents each, it was explained that that price included the cost of two cookies. Results of the study showed that the that's not all tactic sold more cupcakes. Specifically, although only 40 percent of the customers who had been presented cookies and cupcakes at the same time made a purchase, 73 percent of the that's not all customers made a purchase.

Why does this tactic work so well? According to Burger (1986), the that's not all tactic's effectiveness may be due to the norm of reciprocity and contrast effect (discussed earlier in this chapter). First, because the seller has sweetened the deal by adding on items, the customer may feel obligated to buy the product, thereby reciprocating the seller's action. Second, in contrast to the original deal, the revised deal may seem much better than it would have without the comparison.

Before concluding this discussion, we should note that the that's not all tactic can include more than adding on items to make a deal look better; it can also involve lowering the price of an item. For example, Burger (1986) found that more people bought cupcakes when the price was dropped form $1 to 75 cents than when the price was simply stated as 75 cents. You might have noticed that, in this form, the that's not all tactic is a lot like the door in the face approach. The difference is that, when using the door in the face approach, the persuader waits for the initial request to be rejected before following up with a lesser request. On the other hand, persuaders using the that's not all tactic do not wait for the initial request to be rejected before sweetening the deal. Some evidence indicates that of the two techniques, the that's not all tactic is the most persuasive (Burger, 1986).

with a large request so they can make concessions later. In his book *Negotiate to Win: Gaining the Psychological Edge,* Schoonmaker (1989) noted,

> *A conservative first offer also creates the bargaining room needed for the mutual concession ritual (you give a little; they give a little; you give a little; and so on). You may regard this ritual as silly, but many people insist on it. If you do not perform it, they may feel you are not negotiating in good faith...It is far better for them to feel that they have defeated you, that they have driven you right to the wall. Lay the foundation for their victory with an initial offer that creates lots of bargaining room. (p. 46)*

A third explanation for the effectiveness of the DITF tactic is the *self-presentation explanation* (Pendleton & Batson, 1979). According to this account, when people reject an initial request, they become concerned that they will be perceived negatively by the persuader. Thus, they are more likely to comply with a second request in order to make themselves look better. Of the three explanations, the self-presentation account has received the least attention and the least empirical support (Reeves, Baker, Boyd, & Cialdini, 1991). However, Abrahams and Bell (1994) argued that although self-presentation concerns may not be necessary for DITF effect, such concerns may enhance the tactic's effectiveness.

In a study examining the viability of these three explanations for the DITF tactic (i.e., perceptual contrast effect, reciprocal concessions, and self-presentation explanation), Abrahams and Bell (1994) noted that each of the explanations may be flawed. They argued that future research may need to consider all three explanations together and that new theoretical approaches should be explored.

When Does a Door in the Face Work?

According to Dillard (1991) over 26 articles have been published on the DITF. As with the FITD tactic, recent reviews of these studies suggest that, given the right conditions, the DITF strategy is quite powerful (Dillard et al., 1984; Fern et al., 1986). Research tells us that some of the following conditions play an important role in determining the effectiveness of the tactic:

1. **Size of the initial request.** Earlier we saw that for the FITD strategy to work, the initial request must not be inconsequential but also must not be too large to be rejected. Obviously, the opposite is true of the DITF tactic; the first request must be large enough to guarantee rejection by the persuadee, but not so large as to appear incredulous (Cialdini et al., 1975). But is there a right size for the initial request? A study by Even-Chen, Yinon, and Bizman (1978) addressed this question and concluded that the initial request must be large for the door in the face to work. On the other hand, they noted that the request must not be so large that it evokes anger, resentment, or incredulity in the persuadee (Even-Chen et al., 1978).

2. **Prosocialness of the request.** As we saw in the last section, the FITD tactic seems to be most effective when used for prosocial causes. The same seems to be true of the DITF tactic. For instance, a meta-analysis by Dillard and colleagues (1984) found that

the DITF tactic is not effective when used for self-serving reasons but can increase compliance as much as 17 percent when used for altruistic purposes.

3. Elapsed time between first and second requests. In their reviews of studies on the DITF, Dillard and colleagues (1984) and Fern and colleagues (1986) argued that the timing between the initial and follow-up requests influenced the successfulness of the tactic. Specifically, in order to increase compliance, the delay between the two requests must be brief, perhaps to capitalize on the perceptual contrast effect. If there is too much of a delay between the requests, compliance may actually decrease.[3]

4. Can a different person make the second request? Researchers who support the reciprocal concessions explanation (discussed earlier) like to point out that the DITF strategy does not work if the first and second requests are made by different people. Indeed, if a door-to-door salesperson offers you a vacuum cleaner for $500, and a different salesperson offers you the appliance for $300, you might perceive a contrast but not a concession. On the other hand, if the same salesperson made both offers, you might be more likely to reciprocate the concession and comply with the second offer.[4]

5. Who answers the door. Research by Bell, Abrahams, Clark, & Schlatter (1996) indicated that some people are more susceptible to the DITF tactic than others. Specifically, to ensure that equity is maintained, exchange oriented people tend to keep track of what they owe others and of what others owe them (Murstein, Wadlin, & Bond, cited in Bell et al., 1994). An exchange oriented person, for instance, would not tend to forget if he or she borrowed money or owed you a favor. For that reason, perhaps, the DITF tactic is more effective on exchange oriented people than it is on nonexchange oriented people (Bell et al., 1996). (For an examination of sequential tactics used in combination, see Box 12.3).

BOX 12.3   Faces, Doors, and Feet: An Extension and Combination of Tactics

Although the other sections in this chapter discuss compliance-gaining tactics that require two steps, it is clear that sequential persuasion can be far more complex. Research by Goldman and his colleagues (Goldman & Creason, 1981; Goldman, Creason, & McCall, 1981; Goldman, Gier, & Smith, 1981) indicated that two doors in the face or two feet in the door made people more compliant than a single door or foot. Further research by Goldman (1986) found that the door in the face and foot in the door techniques also can be combined. Here's how it works: First, people are presented with a very large request that they are almost sure to reject (e.g., "Would you call 150 people and ask them questions about the zoo?"). Second, people are presented with a moderate request that serves as a foot in the door. Because this request follows the very large request, however, it can be more difficult than the initial request that is typically used in the foot in the door approach (e.g., "Would you participate in a 25-minute survey about the zoo?" versus "Would you answer three or four questions about the zoo?"). Finally, people are asked to comply with the request that the persuaders wanted them to comply with all along (e.g., "Would you stuff and address 75 envelopes with information about the zoo?"). Results of Goldman's (1986) study found that this combination approach was more persuasive than either tactic was alone.

CHANGING THE DEAL: THE LOWBALL TACTIC

If you've ever bought a car from a dealership, there's a chance that you've seen the *lowball tactic* in action. Here's how it works. First, the salesperson makes you a deal that looks too good to refuse. Perhaps the car you want is offered for several hundred dollars less than anyplace else you've shopped. Excited, you accept the offer. But then, a number of things might happen. For instance, the salesperson might inform you that the quoted price did not include an expensive option (e.g., air conditioning) that you thought was included. Or, the salesperson might check with his or her manager for approval and later report that the deal was rejected. Why? The dealership would lose money if the car was sold so cheap. In short, the original offer is taken back, and you are asked to pay a much higher price for the car (for a discussion of a similar tactic, see Box 12.4).

Slimy? You bet. But also very effective. Indeed, in several studies conducted by Cialdini and his colleagues (Cialdini, Cacioppo, Bassett, & Miller, 1978), the lowball tactic was found to increase compliance significantly. In one of the studies, Cialdini and colleagues wanted to see if they could get undergraduate students to wake up early. Here's what happened: Some students were simply asked to participate in a "thinking" experiment at 7 in the morning. Others, however, were asked to participate but were not told when the experiment would take place. If they agreed to participate, they were told the time of the experiment and asked if they were still willing to participate. In other words, the second group of students was lowballed. Results of the study showed that although only 31 percent of the non-lowballed students agreed to participate, 56 percent of the lowballed students agreed. Results of two other studies produced similar results (Cialdini et al., 1978).

As unethical as the lowball tactic seems, it is used far more often than might be expected. Credit card issuers, for instance, are known for tempting customers with introductory deals that give very low interest rates. The problem is that these rates may double or even triple in a few months. Rates on adjustable mortgages do this too; a few years at a very reasonable rate, then—BAM!—a balloon payment is due. Even colleges and universities are not above suspicion. To be sure, most schools want to recruit new students, and who knows what they will resort to? A recent article in *Financial World* (Williams, 1995) sounds the following warning:

> *When it comes to spelling out the true cost of schooling, all colleges—even the haughtiest Ivy League schools—lie through their teeth. If you think that makes colleges sound like car dealers, you've got it right, says Raymond Loewe, a financial planner in Marlton, N. J., whose firm, called College Money, specializes in helping parents pay school bills. "The dealer pulls you in by telling you the car costs $20,000 when it really costs $23,000 or $24,000 with options," says Loewe. "That's what colleges do. They lowball you on their estimates of what you will be paying and you only find out what it's really going to cost after you sign up."* (p. 69)

BOX 12.4   **"Sorry, We Don't Have any More of Those in Your Size. But…": The Bait and Switch Tactic**

The next time you see a big sale advertised, be careful. If you aren't you may fall victim to a persuasion tactic that some authors (Joule, Gouilloux, & Weber, 1989) call "the lure:"

> This tactic…is frequently used when goods are put on sale. For example, a beautiful pair of shoes marked 40% off is displayed quite conspicuously in a store window. The enticed consumer enters the store with the intention of taking advantage of this exceptional offer, but the salesperson informs him that they are out of the shoe in his size. Just when the disappointed customer is ready to leave the store, he is shown a new pair that resembles the shoes on sale but that is being sold at the regular price. (p. 742)

The travel industry has been known to increase their profits using the same tactic. For instance, a company might advertise an inexpensive vacation package or airline seats as part of a promotion. However, as many prospective travelers discover, very few of these seats or packages are available and are often sold out by the time people have committed themselves to the idea of a vacation. The only solution is to go home and mope or buy a more expensive option.

Research by Joule and colleagues (1989) indicates that the lure is an effective strategy for gaining compliance. For instance, in one study, these researchers got several students to sign up to participate in a rather interesting and well-paid experiment. When the students showed up for the experiment, however, they were told that it had been canceled. Even so, these students, compared to those who were not lured, were more willing to participate in another experiment that was less interesting and unpaid.

According to Joule and colleagues (1989), the lure is similar to the lowball and foot in the door tactics but is also distinct. Like the lowball tactic, the lure requires that the persuadee make two decisions, one made before and one made after the real cost of compliance is known. However, while a decision in the lowball situation concerns the same behavior (e.g., buying red shoes for $30 or buying the same shoes for $40), a decision in the lure situation concerns different behaviors (e.g., buying one pair of red shoes for $30 or buying a different pair of red shoes for $40). Likewise, both the lure and the foot in the door tactics involve a less costly act followed by a more costly one. However, while the foot in the door requires a person to comply with a smaller request, in the lure, a person is unable to comply with the smaller request (Joule et al., 1989).

Why Lowballing Works

According to Cialdini and colleagues (1978), commitment may be the reason for the lowball tactic's effectiveness. Let's use the automobile customer as an example. Cialdini and his colleagues would argue that when the customer agrees to the initial offer, he or she becomes cognitively committed to the idea of owning the car. Thus, even when the reasons for buying the car change, the customer has a hard time altering his or her decision and commitment.

A second reason for the lowball tactic's effectiveness was proposed by Burger and Petty (1981). These researchers thought that people fall victim to the tactic because agreeing with the initial request creates an unfulfilled obligation. In other words, people agree to a second, more costly request because they feel obligated to make good on their promises. In support of this hypothesis, Burger and Petty (1981) found that the lowball tactic works only when the same person who made the first request also makes the less attractive request. It does not work when a different person makes the less attractive request.

SUMMARY

This chapter examined the effectiveness of several sequential tactics of persuasion. Pregiving involves making a persuadee feel indebted so that he or she will be more compliant. The foot in the door tactic involves making a small request and following up with a large one. The door in the face tactic involves just the opposite: a large request followed by a smaller one. Finally, when using the lowball tactic, persuadees are asked to agree with an attractive request but are expected to agree with a less attractive request later.

ENDNOTES

1. Although we don't think it's common, we don't rule out the possibility of women using this same approach on men.

2. Initially, the three meta-analyses on the foot in the door indicated that the effectiveness of the tactic was small (Beaman et al., 1983; Dillard et al., 1984; Fern et al., 1986). However, analysis of studies which showed that at least 80% of research subjects complied with the first request indicated that the strategy was much more effective. Thus, for the foot in the door tactic to work, the initial request needs to be small enough to achieve a sufficient level of compliance.

3. In contrast, a delay between the first and second request does not seem to hinder the effectiveness of the foot in the door strategy as long as the second request reminds the persuadee of his or her earlier compliance (see DeJong, 1979).

4. Some prior research suggests that the foot in the door strategy works even when the first and second requests are made by different people.

REFERENCES

Abrahams, M. F., & Bell, R. A. (1994). Encouraging charitable contributions: An examination of three models of door-in-the-face compliance. *Communication Research, 21,* 131–153.

Aune, R. K., & Basil, M. D. (1994). A relational obligations approach to the foot-in-the mouth technique. *Journal of Applied Social Psychology, 24,* 546–556.

Beaman, A. L., Cole, C. M., Steblay, N. M., Preston, M., & Klentz, B. (1983). Compliance as a function of elapsed time between first and second requests. *Journal of Social Psychology, 128,* 233–243.

Bell, R. A., Abrahams, M. F., Clark, C. L., & Schlatter, C. (1996). The door-in-the-face compliance strategy: An individual differences analysis of two models in an AIDS fundraising context. *Communication Quarterly, 44*(1), 107–124.

Bell, R. A., Cholerton, M., Fraczek, K. E., Rohlfs, G. S., & Smith, B. A. (1994). Encouraging donations to charity: A field study of competing and complementary factors in tactic sequencing. *Western Journal of Communication, 58,* 98–115.

Bem, D. J. (1972). Self-perception theory. In L. Berkowitz (Ed.), *Advances in experimental social psychology* (Vol. 6, pp. 2–62). New York: Academic Press.

Burger, J. M. (1986). Increasing compliance by improving the deal: The that's-not-all technique. *Journal of Personality and Social Psychology, 31,* 277–283.

Burger, J. M., & Petty, R. E. (1981). The low-ball compliance technique: Task or person commitment? *Journal of Personality and Social Psychology, 40,* 492–500.

Cann, A., Sherman, S. J., & Elkes, R. (1975). Effects of initial request size and timing of a second request on compliance: The foot in the door and the door in the face. *Journal of Personality and Social Psychology, 32,* 774–782.

Cialdini, R. B. (1993). *Influence: The psychology of persuasion* (Rev. ed.). New York: Quill William Morrow.

Cialdini, R. B., Cacioppo, J. T., Bassett, R., & Miller, J. A. (1978). Low-ball procedure for producing compliance: Commitment then cost. *Journal of Personality and Social Psychology, 36,* 463–476.

Cialdini, R. B., Vincent, J. E., Lewis, S. K., Catalan, J., Wheeler, D., & Darby, B. L. (1975). Reciprocal concessions procedure for inducing compliance: The door in-the-face technique. *Journal of Personality and Social Psychology, 31,* 206–215.

DeJong, W. (1979). An examination of self-perception mediation of the foot-in-the-door effect. *Journal of Personality and Social Psychology, 37,* 2221–2239.

Dillard, J. P. (1991). The current status of research on the sequential-request compliance techniques. *Personality and Social Psychology Bulletin, 17,* 283–288.

Dillard, J. P. (1990). Self-inference and the foot-in-the-door technique: Quantity of behavior and attitudinal mediation. *Human Communication Research, 16,* 422–447.

Dillard, J. P., Hunter, J. E., & Burgoon, M. (1984). Sequential-request persuasive strategies: Meta-analysis of foot-in-the-door and door-in-the-face. *Human Communication Research, 10,* 461–488.

Even-Chen, M., Yinon, Y., & Bizman, A. (1978). The door in the face technique: Effects of the size of the initial request. *European Journal of Social Psychology, 8,* 135–140.

Fern, E. F., Monroe, K. B., & Avila, R. A. (1986). Effectiveness of multiple request strategies: A synthesis of research results. *Journal of Marketing Research, 23,* 144–152.

Freedman, J. L., & Fraser, S. C. (1966). Compliance without pressure. *Journal of Personality and Social Psychology, 4,* 195–202.

George, W. H., Gournic, S. J., & McAfee, M. P. (1988). Perceptions of postdrinking female sexuality. *Journal of Applied Social Psychology, 18,* 1295–1317.

Goldman, M. (1986). Compliance employing a combined foot-in-the-door and door-in-the-face procedure. *Journal of Social Psychology, 126,* 111–116.

Goldman, M., & Creason, C. R. (1981). Inducing compliance by a two-door-in-the-face procedure and a self-determination request. *Journal of Social Psychology, 114,* 229–235.

Goldman, M., Creason, C. R., & McCall, C. G. (1981). Compliance employing a two feet-in-the-door procedure. *Journal of Social Psychology, 114,* 259–265.

Goldman, M., Gier, J. A., & Smith, D. E. (1981). Compliance as affected by task difficulty and order of tasks. *Journal of Social Psychology, 114,* 75–83.

Gorasini, D. R., & Olson, J. M. (1995). Does self-perception change explain the foot-in-the-door effect? *Journal of Personality and Social Psychology, 69,* 91–105.

Greenberg, M. S. (1980). A theory of indebtedness. In K. Gergen, M. Greenberg, & R. Willis (Eds.), *Social exchange: Advances in theory and research* (pp. 3–26). New York: Plenum.

Groves, R. M., Cialdini, R. B., & Couper, M. P. (1992). Understanding the decision to participate in a survey. *Public Opinion Quarterly, 56,* 475–495.

Howard, D. (1990). The influence of verbal responses to common greeting in compliance behavior: The foot-in-the-mouth effect. *Journal of Applied Social Psychology, 20,* 1185–1196.

Joule, R. V., Gouilloux, F., Weber, F. (1989). The lure: A new compliance procedure. *Journal of Social Psychology, 129,* 741–749.

Kellerman, K., & Cole, T. (1994). Classifying compliance gaining messages: Taxonomic disorder and strategic confusion. *Communication Theory, 4,* 3–60.

Lammers, H. B. (1991). The effect of free samples on immediate consumer purchase. *Journal of Consumer Marketing, 8,* 31–37.

Marwell, G., & Schmitt, D. R. (1967). Dimensions of compliance-gaining behavior: An empirical analysis. *Sociometry, 30,* 350–364.

Pendleton, M. G., & Batson, C. D. (1979). Self-presentation and the door-in-the face technique for inducing compliance. *Personality and Social Psychology Bulletin, 5,* 77–81.

Pliner, P., Hart, H., Kohl, J., & Saari, D. (1974). Compliance without pressure: Some further data on the foot-in-the-door technique. *Journal of Experimental Social Psychology, 10,* 17–22.

Regan, D. T. (1971). Effects of a favor and liking on compliance. *Journal of Experimental Social Psychology, 7,* 627–639.

Reeves, R. A., Baker, G. A., Boyd, J. G., & Cialdini, R. B. (1991). The door-in-the-face technique when established customs exist. *Journal of Applied Social Psychology, 9,* 576–586.

Schoonmaker, A. N. (1989). *Negotiate to win: Gaining the psychological edge.* Englewood Cliffs, NJ: Prentice-Hall.

Schwarzwald, J., Raz, M., & Zvibel, M. (1979). The applicability of the door-in-the-face technique where established behavioral customs exist. *Journal of Applied Social Psychology, 9,* 576–586.

Seligman, C., Bush, M., & Kirsch, K. (1976). Relationship between compliance in the foot-in-the-door paradigm and size of first request. *Journal of Personality and Social Psychology, 33,* 517–520.

Shanab, M. E., & O'Neill, P. (1979). The effects of contrast upon compliance with socially undesirable requests in the door-in-the-face paradigm. *Canadian Journal of Behavioral Science, 11,* 236–244.

Snyder, M., & Cunningham, M. R. (1975). To comply or not to comply: Testing the self-perception explanation of the "foot-in-the-door" phenomenon. *Journal of Personality and Social Psychology, 31,* 64–67.

Wagener, J. J., & Laird, J. D. The experimenter's foot-in-the-door: Self perception, body weight, and volunteering. *Personality and Social Psychology Bulletin, 6,* 441–446.

Weyant, J. M. (1996). Application of compliance techniques to direct-mail requests for charitable donations. *Psychology and Marketing, 13,* 157–170.

Williams, G. (1995, Sept. 26). Tuition financing 101. *Financial World, 164,* 69.

Wiseman, R. L., & Schenck-Hamlin. W. (1981). A multidimensional scaling validation of an inductively-derived set of compliance-gaining strategies. *Communication Monographs, 48,* 251–270.

13

DECEPTION

Do you think you can tell when someone is lying to you? If so, what kinds of things do you look for to detect deception? Think about it a minute. How do people behave when they are lying? What gives them away?

When we ask our students these questions, the most common response we get is this: eye contact. When people are lying, our students suggest, they can't look you in the eye. And, at least on the face of it, this hypothesis rings true. Indeed, our mothers used eye contact as their personal polygraphs all of the time. "Look me straight in the eye and tell me you didn't break the (fill in the blank)," they used to say.

If you've ever thought the same thing about lying and eye contact, you, our students, and our moms are not alone. Research indicates that eye contact is one of the most commonly used behavioral cues for detecting deception (DePaulo, Stone, & Lassiter, 1985; Riggio & Friedman, 1983). Here's the catch, though: Not only has research shown that *people do not look away* when they are lying (DePaulo et al., 1985), it shows that people may actually engage in *more* eye contact when lying than when telling the truth (Riggio & Friedman, 1983). In other words, when trying to detect deception, we may be using cues that are exactly the opposite of those we should be using. No wonder we're such lousy lie detectors!

That's right—humans, in general, tend to be fairly inaccurate when trying to detect deception. Research shows that the average person can detect a liar with about the same accuracy as someone flipping a coin. It makes sense that if others were better at detecting deception, people wouldn't lie so much. And lie they do. Whether one observes teenagers embellishing their accomplishments on a first date, card players bluffing in a poker game, negotiators stretching the truth in negotiations, politicians making promises they have no intentions of keeping, criminals lying in police interrogations, researchers serving up cover stories to their subjects, or parents claiming the existence of Santa Claus, it is clear that deception is a ubiquitous form of communication. Indeed, in one study, Turner,

Edgley, and Olmstead (1975) asked 130 subjects to record the veracity (e.g., truth) of their communication in natural situations and found that over 61 percent of their subjects' overall conversations involved deception! Similarly, Hample (1980) found that people reported lying an average of 13.03 times a week.

The fact that people are not very accurate at detecting deception is unfortunate when you consider the practical and professional contexts within which accurate detection would be desirable (e.g., jurists, consumers, law officers, negotiators, customs inspectors, job interviewers, secret service, and so forth). Clearly, there are practical advantages to improving detecting abilities, an observation that leads us to the following questions: Are there any reliable cues that can be used to detect deception? If so, what are they? Are some people better at deceiving us than others? Can some people detect deceit more accurately than others? Are there factors that can improve peoples' ability to detect a liar?

These are some of the questions that we will address in this chapter. Before we get started, however, some definitions are in order. Thus, the following section identifies some common conceptualizations of deception and includes a discussion of how deception is related to the study of persuasion. You may not automatically think of deception as a tool for influence. Yet, whenever deception is used in an attempt to gain compliance from another, or resist the compliance gaining attempts of another, it is being used to influence. The rest of the chapter examines research on the enactment and perception of deception.

WHAT IS DECEPTION? LIES AND DAMN LIES

Knowing that people lie a lot, although perhaps another justification for studying deception, does little to help us understand *what* deception entails conceptually. To answer the "conceptual question," scholars have attempted to outline several types of communication that might be considered deceptive. Most attempts to do so have focused on liars' motivations for telling lies. Goffman (1974), for example, discussed two forms of deception: *benign fabrications*, which are "engineered in the interest of the person contained by them, or, if not quite in his interest and for his benefit, then at least not done against his interest" (p. 87) and *exploitive fabrications*, which are motivated by the private interests of the deceiver.

Although some motivations for lying are self-evident, others are less obvious. For example, various researchers have posited all of the following reasons for lying (see Camden, Motley, & Wilson, 1984; Hample, 1980; Knapp & Comadena, 1979; Lindskold & Walters, 1983; Seiter, Bruschke, & Bai, 1998; Turner et al., 1975):[1]

- **Lie to benefit other:** Because she knows that her husband does not want to be disturbed, Babbs tells a door-to-door salesman that her husband is not home.
- **Lie to affiliate:** Buffy wants to spend some time with her father, so she tells him she needs help with her homework even though she is capable of doing it herself.

- **Lie to avoid invasion of privacy:** Muffy tells a co-worker that she is younger than she really is because she believes her age is no one's business but her own.
- **Lie to avoid conflict:** Biff tells his neighbor, who has called to complain about Biff's barking dog, that he cannot talk at the moment because dinner's on the table.
- **Lie to appear better:** To impress a date, Rex tells her that he was captain of his football team when, in reality, he was only vice president of the Latin Club.
- **Lie to protect self:** Trudy breaks her mother's vase but tells her the cat did it.
- **Lie to benefit self:** Favio tells his parents he needs extra money for textbooks so that he can go to a Hootie and the Blowfish concert with the money.
- **Lie to harm other:** Barney's in a bad mood so he points in the wrong direction when a motorist asks him directions.

In addition to looking at peoples' motivations for lying, another approach to conceptualizing deception is to view it as a strategy for manipulating information. In other words, this perspective argues that there are several strategies people can use to deceive others. For example, Metts (1989), Ekman (1985), and Burgoon, Buller, Ebesu, and Rockwell (1994) distinguished three deception strategies: *distortion* (or equivocation), *omissions* (or concealment), and *falsification.* Yet other researchers have come up with other categories of deception (e.g., see Hopper & Bell, 1984).

In addition to looking at different types of deception, a final way of conceptualizing deception was proposed in McCornack's (1992) *information manipulation theory.* This theory argues that when we are talking with others we typically assume that the information they give us is not only truthful, but also informative, relevant, and clear. We're not always right, however. Indeed, deception occurs when speakers alter the *amount* of information that should be provided (i.e., quantity), the *veracity* of the information presented (i.e, "quality"), the *relevance* of information provided, or the *clarity* of information provided. And if that seems complex, consider this: People can alter the amount, veracity, relevance, and clarity of information all at the same time or in different combinations. In other words, there is infinite variety in forms of deception (McCornack, Levine, Solowczuk, Torres, & Campbell, 1992). To give you an idea, examples of the ways in which people manipulate information along each of these dimensions are presented in Box 13.1.

What is clear from this discussion so far is that deceptive messages come in many forms and that people can be motivated to lie for any number of reasons. But, before concluding this section, we would like to make a final point. You might be asking yourself, "Why is a chapter on deception in a book on persuasion?" In response, we would argue that deception is a form of persuasion. Even from the standpoint of pure cases of persuasion, deception involves an intentional attempt to get someone to believe what the liar knows to be false. As Miller (as cited in Miller & Stiff, 1993) argued:

BOX 13.1   Information Manipulation Theory: Examples of Deceptive Dimensions of Messages

Deceptive Provoking Situation

You have been dating Terry for nearly 3 years. You feel very close and intimate toward this person. Because Terry goes to a different school upstate, the two of you have agreed to date other people. Nevertheless, Terry is very jealous and possessive. You see Terry only occasionally; however, you call each other every Sunday and talk for an hour. On Friday one of your friends invites you to a party on Saturday night, but the party is "couples only," so in order to go you need a date. There is no way that Terry can come down for the weekend so you decide to ask someone from your persuasion class to whom you've been attracted. The two of you go to the party and end up having a great time.

On Sunday your doorbell rings and it is Terry. Terry walks in and says, "I decided to come down and surprise you. I tried calling you all last night, but you weren't around. What were you doing?"

Example of responses that:

1. *Are clear, direct and truthful*—"Terry, I was out at a party. Since I figured you couldn't make it and we decided to date other people, I asked someone from my persuasion class who I kind of like if he or she'd go.

We had a good time. If there was a way that you could have made it to the party, I would have wanted to go with you. If you feel like we need to talk through dating other people again then let's do it."

2. *Violate assumptions about the quantity of information that should be provided*—"Terry, I went to a party one of my friends was having. It was a blast."

3. *Violate assumptions about the quality of information that should be provided*—"Oh, I was out running errands and my car broke down. I was out all night trying to get a tow truck back. It was a total drag!"

4. *Violate assumptions about the clarity of information that should be provided*—"Oh, I was just out goofing around."

5. *Violate assumption about the relevance of information that should be provided*—"Why didn't you tell me you were coming? I mean, I know you get paranoid some times, but driving all the way down here just to check on me is a bit ridiculous, don't you think? How would you like it if I paid a sneak visit to you and acted obnoxious by surprising you and asking you what you had been doing?"

Examples adapted from McCornack, S. A. (1992). Information manipulation theory. *Communication Monographs, 59* (1), 1–16, and McCornack, S. A., Levine, T. R., Solowczuk, K., Torres, H. I., & Campbell, D. H. (1992). When the alteration of information is viewed as deception: An empirical test of information manipulation theory. *Communication Monographs, 59*(1), 17–29. Used by permission of the National Communication Association.

> *Deceptive communication strives for persuasive ends; or, stated more precisely, deceptive communication is a general persuasive strategy that aims at influencing the beliefs, attitudes, and behaviors of others by means of deliberate message distortion. (p. 28)*

Having laid the groundwork for examining deception, we now discuss what happens during the process of deception. That is, what goes on while deception is being enacted and how is deception detected?

TELLING LIES: THE ENACTMENT OF DECEPTION

If all liars had noses like Pinocchio, deception detection would not be a problem. Unfortunately, detecting deceptive behavior is not as simple as looking for a growing nose or, as we have learned, the aversion of eye contact. In fact, even empirical research has been inconsistent when trying to identify the types of behaviors that we can expect out of liars. (Some of the behaviors that have been associated with deception are listed in Box 13.2.)

Theoretical Frameworks

Despite these inconsistencies, however, several theories of deception have been proposed that provide an understanding of the types of behaviors that are typical of liars. One such framework, known as the *four-factor model*, was proposed by Zuckerman and his colleagues (Zuckerman, DePaulo, & Rosenthal, 1981; Zuckerman & Driver, 1985). Another, known as *interpersonal deception theory*, was proposed by Burgoon and Buller (1994; Buller & Burgoon, 1994). The following sections discuss each of these perspectives.

The Four-Factor Model

Rather than simply list all of the things that people do when telling lies, the four-factor model tries to explain the underlying processes governing deceptive behavior. In other words, rather than tell us what people do when lying, the model tries to tell us why people behave differently when lying than when telling the truth. According to the model, four factors that influence behavior when lying are arousal, attempted control, felt emotions, and cognitive effort.

First, the model assumes that people are more aroused or anxious when telling lies than when telling the truth. This is also the principle on which the polygraph operates. Of course, we know that results from polygraphs can not be used as evidence in courts because they are not 100 percent accurate. Why? Because a sociopath, for instance, who feels no remorse for murder certainly won't get anxious when lying. Even so, not all people are sociopaths. We know that many people do feel anxious when they lie. Perhaps they fear getting caught. Perhaps telling the lie reminds them of information they want hidden. Perhaps they are simply motivated to succeed in the deceptive task. Whatever the case, we know that such arousal can lead to certain behaviors during deception. Poker players, for example, are said to wear sunglasses because their pupils dilate when they get a good hand. Similarly, pupil dilation can be a reliable indicator of deception (Zuckerman et al., 1981). What other cues to arousal accompany deception? A few that researchers have investigated include speech errors, speech hesitations, word–phrase repetitions, increased adaptors (e.g., finger fidgeting), eye blinks, vocal pitch, and leg movements.

Second, because people do not want to get caught telling lies, the four-factor model argues that they try to control their behaviors when lying. This claim is supported in research conducted by Ekman and Friesen (1969, 1974). According to

BOX 13.2   How Do Liars Behave?

A meta-analysis is a summary of several studies. Such an analysis attempts to resolve inconsistencies in research. Three such analyses (DePaulo et al., 1985; Kraut, 1980; and Zuckerman and Driver, 1985) have examined cues that were associated with deception in a large number of studies. Based on these reviews, the following cues were found to be associated with deception:

- **Blinks:** Liars blinked more often than did people telling the truth (DePaulo et al., 1985; Kraut, 1980; Zuckerman & Driver, 1985).

- **Adaptors:** Liars moved their hands more (fidgeted, scratched, rubbed themselves) when giving responses (DePaulo et al., 1985; Kraut, 1980; Zuckerman & Driver, 1985).

- **Speech Errors:** Liars made more errors when speaking than did truth tellers (DePaulo et al., 1985; Kraut, 1980; Zuckerman & Driver, 1985).

- **Message Duration:** Liars' messages were more brief than truth tellers' messages (DePaulo et al., 1985; Kraut, 1980; Zuckerman & Driver, 1985).

- **Pupil Dilation**—Liars' pupils are more dilated than truth tellers' pupils (DePaulo et al., 1985; Zuckerman & Driver, 1985).

- **Irrelevant Information**—Liars include less relevant material in their responses than truth tellers (DePaulo et al., 1985; Zuckerman & Driver, 1985).

- **Negative Statements**—Liars' responses contain more negative expressions than truth tellers' responses (DePaulo et al., 1985; Zuckerman & Driver, 1985).

- **Shrugs**—Liars shrug more than truth tellers (DePaulo et al., 1985).

- **Immediacy**—Liars communicate less involvement in their communication (DePaulo et al., 1985; Zuckerman & Driver, 1985).

- **Pitch**—Liars' vocal pitch is more anxious than truth tellers' vocal pitch (DePaulo et al., 1985; Zuckerman & Driver, 1985).

- **Hesitations**—Liars, compared to truth tellers, hesitate more when communicating (DePaulo et al., 1985; Zuckerman & Driver, 1985).

- **Leveling**—Liars use more leveling terms than truth tellers (i.e., make more overgeneralized statements) (DePaulo et al., 1985; Zuckerman & Driver, 1985).

- **Message Discrepancy**—Liars' messages contain more discrepancies than do truth tellers' messages (Zuckerman & Driver, 1985).

- **Facial Segmentation and Body Segmentation**—Measured by the number of units identified in the stream of behavior (Zuckerman & Driver, 1985). According to Miller and Stiff (1993), segmentation cues have little practical utility for deception detection, are vague, and lack clear conceptual meaning.

their "sending capacity hypothesis," when we are telling lies, we try to control our behaviors but, in the process, tend to pay more attention to some parts of our bodies than others. Because it is difficult to monitor all parts of our bodies, we try to control those parts that communicate the most information, like our faces. But, while busy monitoring our faces, we tend to forget about those parts that communicate little information such as our legs and feet. So, according to Ekman and

Friesen, those parts of our bodies that typically communicate little information reveal the most when we are being deceptive. In other words, because we are concentrating so much on our faces, deception "leaks" from other parts of our bodies. At least some research tends to support this notion. For example, one study found that people who watched liars' heads and faces (higher sending capacity) were less accurate at detecting deception than people who watched liars' bodies (lower sending capacity) (Ekman & Friesen, 1974). Moreover, in a summary of more than 30 studies in which judges tried to detect others' deception from either single channels (i.e., only the face, body, tone of voice, or words of the liar) or from particular channel combinations, DePaulo and colleagues (1985) found that in all conditions in which judges relied on facial cues, detection accuracy was lower. This study also concluded that when judges paid attention to what liars were saying, they were more accurate at deception detection than when verbal channels were unavailable.

In addition to arousal and attempted control, the four-factor model asserts that affective factors influence our behaviors when telling lies. And if you stop to think about it, you could probably figure out what types of emotions would be associated with telling a lie. Indeed, in our culture, deception is generally frowned upon. Children are taught that "the truth shall set them free," "honesty is the best policy," "what tangled webs are weaved," and often chide one another with rhymes such as "liar, liar, pants on fire." We grow up with stories about "Honest Abe" Lincoln and George "I cannot tell a lie" Washington. It's no surprise, then, that deceptive behavior would be associated with negative emotions such as guilt. It is because of these negative affects that researchers (e.g., Knapp, Hart, & Dennis, 1974; Mehrabian, 1971) hypothesized that when compared to truthful communicators, deceivers display fewer nods, smiles, and other interest statements and make more disparaging remarks. We should note, however, that not all deception is associated with negative emotions. Paul Ekman (1985), for instance, argued that liars may also experience "duping delight," as the result of facing or successfully meeting the challenge of deceiving another person (see Figure 13.1).

Finally, the four-factor model asserts that cognitive factors play a role in the way people behave when lying. Stated differently, lying requires you to think a lot harder than telling the truth does. Why? Because it's fairly easy to tell a story about something you've already heard or experienced. When you lie, however, you are oftentimes required to "make things up as you go along." Not only that, you have to be careful not to contradict something you've said before. (Remember the old saying?: Liars need a good memory.) Because lying requires extra cognitive effort, it's no wonder that researchers have hypothesized that liars, compared to people telling the truth, would take a longer time to respond, pause more when speaking, and deliver messages with few specifics (Zuckerman & Driver, 1985).

Interpersonal Deception Theory

Interpersonal deception theory (Buller & Burgoon, 1994, 1996; Buller, Strzyzewski, & Comstock, 1991; Burgoon & Buller, 1994) is by far the most comprehensive summary of deception research. Its goal is to view deception as an interactional phenomenon in which both senders and receivers are involved simultaneously

FIGURE 13.1   Duping delight in action.

encoding and decoding messages over time. Both the liar's and the detector's goals, expectations, and knowledge affect their thoughts and behaviors in an interaction. In turn, such thoughts and behaviors affect how accurately lies are detected and whether liars suspect that they are suspected. Later in this chapter, we'll examine other assumptions of the theory. At this point, however, the aspect of interpersonal deception theory that is most relevant is its distinction between strategic and nonstrategic behaviors during deception. Specifically, interpersonal deception theory argues that a liar's communication consists of both intentional (strategic) attempts to appear honest and unintentional (nonstrategic) behaviors that are beyond the liar's control.

First, interpersonal deception theory says that to avoid being detected liars strategically create messages with certain characteristics. For instance, liars might (1) *manipulate the information in their messages* in order to dissociate themselves from the message (e.g., liars might refer to themselves very little so they distance themselves from the responsibility of their statements), convey uncertainty or vagueness (because creating messages with a lot of specific details would increase the likelihood of detection), or withhold information (e.g., liars might create brief messages). Liars might also (2) *strategically control their behavior* to suppress deception cues (e.g., liars might withdraw by gazing or nodding less than people who tell the truth). And, finally, liars might try to strategically (3) *manage their image* by smiling or nodding to make themselves appear more credible (Buller, Burgoon, White, & Ebesu, 1994).

Second, although liars try to control their behaviors strategically, they also exhibit some *nonstrategic communication.* In other words, some behaviors "leak out" beyond the liar's awareness or control. As noted above (see the four-factor model), such communication might result from arousal (e.g., blinks, pupil dilation, vocal nervousness, speech errors, leg and body movements, and shorter responses) and/or negative emotions (e.g., less nodding, less smiling, more negative statements).

What Makes a Liar Persuasive?

Are some people better at "pulling the wool over our eyes" than others? Is it easier to get away with telling some lies than others? Do certain situations make deception more difficult to accomplish? In this section we discuss the ways in which characteristics of the liar, the lie, and the deceptive situation affect the process of deception.

The "Wool Pullers"

The boy who cried wolf should have quit while he was ahead. Or, before he got eaten, he should have at least taken a personality test. If he had, our guess is that he would have scored high on a test that measures a trait known as *Machiavellianism.* The Machiavellian personality is not interested in interpersonal relationships, manipulates others for selfish purposes, and has little sense of social morality (Christie & Geis, 1970; Geis & Moon, 1981). Machiavellian personalities are truly "wolves in sheeps' clothing"; when lying, they appear more innocent than their counterparts (i.e., low Machiavellians).[2] Indeed, a classic study by Braginsky (1970) backs up this claim. In the study, high and low Machiavellian children tasted bitter crackers and then were offered a nickel for each cracker they could get their little classmates to eat. The results of the study showed that the high Machiavellian children were not only the most successful in their persuasive attempts, they were also seen as more innocent and honest than the low Machiavellian children.

In addition to Machiavellianism, the social skills possessed by a person also influences how successful he or she is at deceiving others. For example, high self-monitors, people who use situational information to behave more appropriately, tend to be more skilled at deception than low self-monitors (Elliot, 1979; Miller, deTurck, & Kalbfleisch, 1983). Moreover, people skilled at communicating basic emotions are particularly good at convincing others to believe their deceptive messages (Riggio & Friedman, 1983), while those who are apprehensive in their communication tend to leak more deceptive cues (see O'Hair, Cody, & Behnke, 1985).

Similarly, people who are expressive and socially tactful (Riggio, Tucker, & Throckmorton, 1987), socially skilled (Riggio, Tucker, & Widaman, 1987), competent communicators (Feeley, 1996), and are attentive, friendly, and precise in their communication (O'Hair, Cody, Goss, & Krayer, 1988) are more successful at deceiving others than those who do not possess such skills.

Are Some Lies Easier to Tell Than Others?

Imagine, for a moment, Babbs, a 15 year old, high school sophomore with a curfew of 9 P.M. It's Thursday, a school night, but Babbs is on the dance floor, partying it up when she suddenly notices the time: 11 P.M! Knowing that her parents usually go to bed around 8, she hopes they'll be asleep but, on arriving home, she finds herself face to face with her parents, who have been waiting up for her. Both have frowns on their faces. "Where have you been?" they demand to know, at about the same time Babbs decides that she had better start lying her pants off if she doesn't want to spend the next 2 weeks in solitary confinement.

How successful do you think Babbs will be? According to research by Cody and his colleagues (Cody, Marston, Foster, 1984; Cody & O'Hair, 1983; O'Hair, Cody, & McLaughlin, 1981), behavior during deception depends, to a large extent, on whether the liar is telling a prepared lie or a spontaneous lie. To be sure, think about some of the components of the four-factor model we discussed earlier. When telling a prepared lie, compared to a spontaneous lie, Babbs should be less aroused, have more control, and should not find lying as cognitively difficult. Not surprisingly, research on deceptive cues supports this idea; in general, spontaneous lies are accompanied by more cues associated with deception than are prepared lies. And, because prepared liars make a more credible impression, they are more difficult to detect than spontaneous liars (Littlepage & Pineault, 1979; deTurck & Miller, 1985). The implication for detecting deception, then, is that if you suspect someone might be lying to you, try to get them to talk about things they might not be prepared to talk about. For instance, in the above example, if Babbs were prepared to tell her parents that she missed her curfew because she was studying in the library, her parents might be smart to ask follow-up questions such as, "What books were you reading?", "What did the books teach you?", "Where were you sitting in the library?", and so forth.

Spontaneity, though, is not the only dimension of a lie that seems to affect deceptive success. Indeed, research has also shown the length and the content of a lie influences how well a person can tell it. Longer lies, for instance, are more difficult to tell than short ones (Kraut, 1978). And concerning content, in a study by Thackray and Orne (1968), subjects played the role of an espionage agent who attempted to conceal both his or her identity and certain code words he or she had learned. The results of the study showed that subjects were more successful when telling lies about personally relevant information (i.e., their identity) than when telling lies about neutral information (i.e., code numbers). Similarly, it seems that people may be more accurate when detecting lies about factual information than when detecting lies about emotional information (see Hocking, Bauchner, Kaminski, & Miller, 1979).

Deceptive Situations and Deceptive Success

The context in which the lie is told can also influence how successful the liar is. Several situational features have been found to influence deception success. One is motivation. Certainly, there are some times when you are simply more motivated to lie successfully than others. A fisherman, for example, may not care so much when someone discovers that his "bass" was really a guppy. A playboy husband cheating on his wife, however, might have more at stake if his affair was discovered. So who then is the better liar: the fisherman or the cheat?

A study by DePaulo, Lanier, and Davis (1983) examined the effect of motivation on deception by telling some subjects that their messages would be carefully scrutinized and that deception was a skill associated with professional success. Other subjects were not motivated. Afterwards, judges tried to detect subjects' lies by either reading transcripts, listening to an audiotape, watching a videotape, or watching a videotape and hearing an audiotape of the subjects' messages. The results of the study showed that judges who read a transcript were more successful at detecting deception of low motivated subjects, although all the other judges were more successful at detecting the highly motivated subjects. Thus, high motivation may cause behavioral changes that lead to increased detectability. Presumably, highly motivated subjects are more aroused and try to control their behavior more.

The relationship between motivation and successful deception, however, may not be so simple. For instance, Buller and Aune (1987) hypothesized that people would be more motivated to lie successfully to intimates than to friends and more motivated to lie successfully to friends than to strangers. They found, however, that strangers leaked more nonverbal cues to deception than friends and intimates. Similarly, liars who were confronted with suspicious feedback (e.g., "Your story doesn't sound very plausible, can you tell me more?") leaked less deceptive cues and were judged as less deceptive than those that got more encouraging cues (Buller, Comstock, & Aune, 1989; Stiff & Miller, 1986). In other words, those liars that were presumably more motivated, were the most successful.

DETECTING DECEPTION: I CAN SEE RIGHT THROUGH YOU

Someone once told one of the authors that the word "gullible" is not in the dictionary. And he fell for it; he actually went to check the dictionary (for you gullible folks's information—he found the word). Perhaps that's why we're so interested in deception detection. After all, aren't we most interested in the things we're bad at?

Whatever the case, just as persuaders need someone to persuade, liars need someone to lie to. And just as some people are less resistant to persuasion, some people are just downright gullible. In the previous pages we discussed deception from the liar's perspective. In this section, we examine the opposite side of the coin: deception detection.

Factors That Influence Detection

"Look Me in the Eye": Stereotypes about Deception

When the actor Jon Lovitz used to be a regular on Saturday Night Live, he played a character with a compulsive lying problem. Upon meeting up with old friends, for example, he claimed that he was president of his own company and was married to the beautiful Morgan Fairchild ("Whom," he claimed, "I've slept with."). Of course, while he was telling these stories, he paused a lot, took a lot of time to think of his answers, and—after telling the stories—seemed so surprised that we were sure he had convinced himself of their truth ("Yeah, that's right! That's the ticket!"). So why was this character so funny? Perhaps it was because he was playing on some common stereotypes that people have about deception. We knew he was lying because he did everything that a liar does. Right?

Wrong! The fact is that many of the behaviors we perceive as deceptive simply aren't. Recall that we already talked about eye contact as one of these behaviors. For example, Riggio and Friedman (1983) found that although liars tend to gaze more, detectors *believe* that liars gazed less. Similar results were found in a meta-analysis of several studies on deception (DePaulo et al., 1985) that also found that people tend to perceive others as deceptive when they gaze less, smile less, shift their posture more, speak slowly, and take a long time to answer although none of these behaviors signaled actual deception. It's not surprising, then, that people tend to be fairly inaccurate when detecting deception. Take heart, however, for there are several factors that improve detection accuracy. Like the stereotypes we discussed in this section, though, other factors impede accuracy. We discuss these factors next.

Humans as Polygraphs

Just as some people are better at deceiving others, some people are more skillful at detecting deception. Earlier we talked about high self-monitors as being skillful deceivers and, at least when it comes to this personality trait, we can say that "it takes one to know one," because high self-monitors also tend to be better at detecting deception (Brandt, Miller, & Hocking, 1980b; Geizer, Rarick, & Soldow, 1977). Because they attend to more nonverbal cues out of a concern for social appropriateness, high self-monitors tend to pick up on deceptive behaviors that other people miss!

Results from studies examining the role of gender and deception detection are not so conclusive, however. For example, Rosenthal and DePaulo (1979) found that although females have been reported to be more adept at reading nonverbal cues than males, females were fooled more easily by deceptive messages than were males. DePaulo, Zuckerman, and Rosenthal (1980) reported that females were less successful at detection because they read the cues that deceivers want them to read rather than the cues that are true indicators of deception. This explanation seems plausible because other research has shown that when several of the cues that can fool females are not available, they do better than men in their deception detection. For instance, Fay and Middleton (1941) found that females were better than males at detecting deceptive messages that were projected over a public address system.

Another factor that may interact with gender to influence deception detection is the type of relationship between the liar and the detectee. For example, a study by Comadena (1982) found that females were more accurate at judging the deceptive communication of their spouses than were males. Males and females did not differ, however, when trying to judge the deception of a stranger. Thus, the degree to which you are familiar with the person you are trying to detect might influence how accurately you detect deception. We explore this issue next.

Familiarity, Biases, and Deception Detection

Does knowing a person help us detect his or her deception better? Several researchers have asked this question but, for quite some time, results of such studies seemed mixed. For instance, in five studies (Brandt, Miller, & Hocking 1980a, 1980b, 1982; Feeley & deTurck, 1997; Feeley, deTurck, & Young, 1995), people rated communicators' veracity after either watching or not watching videotapes of the communicators' normal, truthful behavior. The results of such studies showed that those people who were familiar with the communicators' previous, truthful behaviors were more accurate in their judgments than those who were unfamiliar.[3] Similarly, Comadena found that spouses could detect each others' deception better than friends could. On the other hand, Miller, Bauchner, Hocking, Fontes, and Kaminski (1981) found that when judging lies about emotional information, friends were more accurate than either strangers or spouses, and Seiter and Wiseman (1995) found that people who tried to detect the deception of people from their own ethnic group (e.g., those with whom they would presumably be the most familiar) were less accurate than people who tried to detect the deception of people from ethnic groups other than their own.

Although such results may seem inconclusive, interpersonal deception theory (Buller & Burgoon, 1996) suggests that they may not be when you consider the possible effects of familiarity on deception. The theory argues that familiarity is a double-edged sword: In some ways, it may help you be a better deception detector, in other ways, it might hinder your ability to detect deception. First, because of certain biases, the better you know someone, the less effective you are at detecting his or her lies. Specifically, McCornack and Parks (1986) found that familiarity increased a person's confidence about judging veracity which, in turn, leads to a *truth bias* (a perception that others are behaving honestly). The results of their study and others (Stiff, Kim, & Ramesh, 1992) support this idea by showing that truth bias was positively associated with familiarity and negatively associated with detection accuracy. In other words, people were less accurate when judging familiar others because they thought the others were always honest and trustworthy. In positive relationships based on trust, a truth bias is likely. However, in "negative" relationships, a *lie bias* (i.e., the perception that people are being dishonest) becomes more likely (McCornack & Levine, 1990). Whatever the case, both the truth and lie biases make you less accurate when judging veracity because they prevent you from distinguishing truths from lies.

Although truth and lie biases make you less accurate at detecting the deception of familiar others, the knowledge you've gained about familiar others can also make you more accurate at detecting them (Buller & Burgoon, 1996). Specifically, because you have more background information about a familiar other, you might be more likely to notice contradictions in what they say (e.g., your significant other has told you that he or she has never been to San Francisco but later says, "The view from the Golden Gate Bridge is fantastic."). Moreover, because you have more knowledge about the way a familiar other typically behaves, you may be more likely to detect his or her deception when the behavior suddenly changes (e.g., your significant other, who is normally calm, becomes very nervous whenever he or she talks about espionage agents). In short, then, familiarity can both help and hinder accurate deception detection. Familiarity is related to biases that decrease accuracy but is related to knowledge that increases accuracy.

Suspicion

According to interpersonal deception theory (Buller & Burgoon, 1996), "The receiver's counterpart to deception is perceived deceit or suspicion" (p. 205). Buller and Burgoon (1996) suggest that, as a deceptive interaction is unfolding, people may become suspicious of being lied to and, in turn, may behave in certain ways because of it. In some cases, they may hide their suspiciousness. For example, at least two studies show that when we suspect that someone is lying to us, we alter our behavior so that we don't look suspicious (Buller, Strzyzewski, & Comstock, 1991; Burgoon, Buller, Dillman, & Walther, 1995). Specifically, suspicious people tend to use shorter responses, take longer to answer, and manage their body movements more. In others situations, however, our behaviors may reveal our suspicion and, in turn, may affect our partner's behavior. Indeed, if someone lying to us thinks we are suspicious, the liar may try even harder to be convincing.

Although it is apparent that suspiciousness plays a role in both sender's and receiver's behavior, another issue concerns whether suspicion affects detection accuracy. Specifically, when people are more suspicious are they better at detecting deception? The evidence for this claim does not look too good. Even though we know that suspicious people have more negative perceptions of the people they are judging (DePaulo, Lassiter, & Stone, 1982), some scholars have found that suspicious subjects are no more accurate at detecting deception than naive subjects (see Mattson, 1994). Bond and Fahey (1987) argued that this could be because suspicious people are more likely to construe ambiguous information as lies rather than truths. McCornack and Levine (1990) argued that accuracy may depend on the level of suspiciousness. Specifically, they found that moderate levels of suspiciousness led to greater accuracy when judging deception.

Probing and Deception Detection

In the previous section we learned that when trying to detect deception, people sometimes try to alter their behavior so they don't look suspicious. But sometimes, probing a potential liar for more information may be necessary. To be sure, if a liar won't talk, it's difficult to find contradictions or inconsistencies in his or her story. Interestingly, however, most research indicates that probing suspects for more information (e.g., Tell me more about where you were when the bookbag was stolen?) does *not* increase the accuracy with which you can detect that suspect's deception (Buller, Comstock, Aune, & Strzyzewski, 1989; Buller et al., 1991). Perhaps even more interesting is the fact that probing a suspect for more information causes third parties to perceive the suspect as more honest (Buller et al., 1989, 1991). This phenomenon has been called the *probing effect* by those who study deception (e.g., Levine & McCornack, 1996a).

Although scholars agree that the probing effect occurs, there is some disagreement on what causes it (for a more detailed debate, see Buller, Stiff, & Burgoon, 1996; Levine & McCornack, 1996a, 1996b). For instance, several authors argue in favor of the *behavioral adaptation explanation*. In a nutshell, this explanation asserts that when probing occurs, liars realize they are suspected of lying and alter their behavior to be more believable. Levine and McCornack (1996a), however, assert that this explanation is flawed.

Before concluding this section, we should note that, in contrast to a probing effect, Ekman (1985) suggests that an opposite phenomenon may occur: When suspected of deceit, a *truthful* communicator may become anxious. This, in turn, may cause a detector to commit what Ekman calls the *Othello error*. That is, the detector wrongly assumes the anxious behavior is indicative of deception.

Cognitions and the Process of Deception Detection

Up to now, you've seen that a considerable amount of research has examined which factors influence how *accurately* people can detect deception. Such research, however, tells us very little about the process by which judgments of veracity are made. For example, when trying to detect deception, how do we make sense of all the information at our disposal (e.g., verbal and nonverbal cues, past knowledge, inferences, and so forth)? What do we do if the information we receive is contradictory (e.g., a person seems nervous but tells a plausible story)? How might our attributions change as we receive new information? For instance, as a juror, you might initially perceive a defendant as an honest person of high integrity. After hearing testimony from witnesses, however, you might change your mind. Ultimately, however, you might be convinced by the intensity of the defendant's testimony that he or she is not lying. In short, due to a number of different pieces of information, your conclusions about a person's veracity might change over time (Seiter, 1997).

A recent study by Seiter (1997) attempted to address these questions by applying a "connectionist" cognitive science approach to the study of deception. In essence, this approach suggests that when we are trying to detect deception, there are generally two "hypotheses" (or mental models) in competition with one another in our minds. One hypothesis suggests that the person we are observing is lying, the other suggests that the person is telling the truth. Eventually, one of these hypotheses "wins out over the other" and determines the attribution we make about the person we are judging. Whichever hypothesis "wins" depends on how we integrate the vast array of verbal and nonverbal information (e.g., Biff is twitching), past knowledge (e.g., Biff doesn't like turkey sandwiches), and inference (e.g., Biff is nervous). In other words, the way we integrate such information leads us to support one hypothesis or the other.[4]

Now, if deception detection can be thought of as a competition between hypotheses, you might be wondering how it is that one hypothesis wins out over another. The rules or principles by which one hypothesis "racks up points" were specified by Thagard (1989; also see Miller & Read, 1991). By way of example, one rule states that the best hypothesis is the one that can explain the most facts. Thus, if the hypothesis "he is lying" can be used to explain why "he is nervous" and why "his messages contradict one another," while the hypothesis "he is telling the truth" cannot explain either of these facts, the hypothesis "he is lying" wins.

Although Thagard (1989) discussed six additional rules, we do not have the space to cover them here. Even so, we should note that these rules or principles may be valid for describing the process by which deception detection operates (see Seiter, 1997). Moreover, the results of Seiter's study offer other important insights about deception detection. First, it suggests how people can change their minds once they decide that someone is being honest or deceptive. If, for example, their hypothesis for deception supports the most facts but, over time, they learn more facts that can be explained by their hypothesis for truthfulness, they should change their mind. Second, results of the study indicate that deception detection is highly idiosyncratic. For example, the data that one person uses to detect deception may be much different from the data that another person uses.

SUMMARY

Deception is a multifaceted and complex communication phenomenon that has been broadly conceptualized. In this chapter we explored some of these conceptualizations. We also learned that although people are not very good at detecting deception, some factors (e.g., personality) improve their accuracy. Other factors (e.g., the truth bias), however, can impede detection accuracy. We also examined some of the behaviors that distinguish truthful from deceptive individuals and some of the frameworks that explain such differences. Many of the distinguishing behaviors, we saw, were nonverbal in nature. Finally, we examined a cognitive framework that describes the process by which deception detection occurs and provides insights into the ways in which attributions on veracity can change over time.

ENDNOTES

1. Research shows that peoples' motivations for lying affect the frequency with which a lie is told and perceptions of the lie's acceptability. For instance, Camden and colleagues (1984) found that most lies are told for selfish reasons. Moreover, selfishly motivated lies and lies that cause people to lose some resource are seen as more reprehensible than lies that are altruistically motivated (Hopper & Bell, 1984; Lindskold & Walters, 1983; Maier & Lavrakas, 1976; Seiter et al., 1998).

2. Research by Exline, Thibaut, Hickey, and Gumpert (1970) showed that, when lying, high

Machiavellians maintained more eye contact than low Machiavellians.

3. Detection accuracy is increased even more if the questions being answered in the "normal," truthful video are relevant to the questions that are asked in the follow-up video. For example, imagine that you have to decide whether a person cheated on an exam. Imagine also that you've seen two video clips beforehand, one in which a person tells you the truth about his or her profession, the other in which he or she tells you the truth about not cheating on an exam. Previous research sug-

gests that seeing the latter video would help you more because it is more relevant to the topic about which the person is lying.

4. To make this material more understandable, we've used terms such as "hypotheses" and "support," even though cognitive scientists might prefer terms such as "mental models" and "activate." For example, rather than saying that one "hypothesis" received more "support" than another, cognitive scientists might say that one "mental model" received more "activation" than another.

REFERENCES

Bond, C. F., & Fahey, W. E. (1987). False suspicion and the misperception of deceit. *British Journal of Social Psychology, 26,* 41–46.

Braginsky, D. D. (1970). Machiavellianism and manipulative interpersonal behavior in children. *Journal of Experimental Social Psychology, 6,* 77–99.

Brandt, D. R., Miller, G. R., & Hocking, J. E. (1980a). The truth deception attribution: Effects of familiarity on the ability of observers to detect deception. *Human Communication Research, 6,* 99–108.

Brandt, D. R., Miller, G. R., & Hocking, J. E. (1980b). Effects of self-monitoring and familiarity on deception. *Communication Quarterly, 22,* 3–10.

Brandt, D. R., Miller, G. R., & Hocking, J. E. (1982). Familiarity and lie detection: A replication and extension. *The Western Journal of Speech Communication, 46,* 276–290.

Buller, D. B., & Aune, R. K. (1987). Nonverbal cues to deception among intimate, friends, and strangers. *Journal of Nonverbal Behavior, 11,* 269–290.

Buller, D. B., & Burgoon, J. K. (1994). Deception: Strategic and nonstrategic communication. In J. A. Daly & J. M. Wiemann (Eds.), *Strategic interpersonal communication* (pp. 191–223). Hillsdale, NJ: Lawrence Erlbaum.

Buller, D. B., & Burgoon, J. K. (1996). Interpersonal deception theory. *Communication Theory, 6*(3), 203–242.

Buller, D. B., & Burgoon, J. K., White, C., & Ebesu, A. S. (1994). Interpersonal deception: VII. Behavioral profiles of falsification, concealment and equivocation. *Journal of Language and Social Psychology, 13,* 366–395.

Buller, D. B., Comstock, J., Aune, R. K., & Strzyzewski, K. D. (1989, May). *The effect of probing on deceivers and truthtellers.* Paper presented at the annual meeting of the International Communication Association, San Francisco, CA.

Buller, D. B., Stiff, J. B., & Burgoon, J. K. (1996). Behavioral adaptation in deceptive transactions: Fact or fiction: Reply to Levine and McCornack. *Human Communication Research, 22*(4), 589–603.

Buller, D. B., Strzyzewski, K. D., & Comstock, J. (1991). Interpersonal deception: I. Deceivers' reactions to receivers' suspicions and probing. *Communication Monographs, 58,* 1–24.

Burgoon, J. K., & Buller, D. B. (1994). Interpersonal deception: IV. Effects of deceit on perceived communication and nonverbal behavior dynamics. *Journal of Nonverbal Behavior, 18* 155–184.

Burgoon, J. K., Buller, D. B., Dillman, L., & Walther, J. B. (1995). Interpersonal deception: IV. Effects of suspicion on perceived communication and nonverbal behavior dynamics. *Human Communication Research, 22*(2), 163–196.

Burgoon, J. K., Buller, D. B., Ebesu, A. S., & Rockwell, P. (1994). Interpersonal deception: V. Accuracy in deception detection. *Communication Monographs, 61,* 303–325.

Camden, C., Motley, M. M., & Wilson, A. (1984). White lies in interpersonal communication: A taxonomy and preliminary investigation of social motivations. *The Western Journal of Speech Communication, 48,* 309–325.

Christie, R., & Geis, G. (1970). *Studies in Machiavellianism.* New York: Academic Press.

Cody, M. J., Marston, P. J., & Foster, M. (1984, May). *Paralinguistic and verbal leakage of deception as a function of attempted control and timing of questions.* Paper presented at the annual meeting of the International Communication Association, San Francisco, CA.

Cody, M. J., & O'Hair, H. D. (1983). Nonverbal communication and deception cues to gender and communicator dominance. *Communication Monographs, 50,* 175–192.

Comadena, M. E. (1982). Accuracy in detecting deception: Intimate and friendship relationships. In M. Burgoon (Ed.), *Communication yearbook 6* (pp. 446–472). Beverly Hills, CA: Sage.

DePaulo, B. M., Lanier, P. S., & Davis, T. (1983). Detecting the deceit of the motivated liar. *Journal of Personality and Social Psychology, 45,* 1096–1103.

DePaulo, B. M., Lassiter, G. D., & Stone, J. I. (1982). Attitudinal determinants of success at detecting deception and truth. *Personality and Social Psychology Bulletin, 8,* 273–279.

DePaulo, B. M., Stone, J. I., & Lassiter, G. D. (1985). Deceiving and detecting deceit. In B. R. Schlenker (Ed.), *The self and social life* (pp. 323–370). New York: McGraw-Hill.

DePaulo, B. M., Zuckerman, M., & Rosenthal, R. (1980). Humans as lie detectors. *Journal of Communication, 30,* 129–139.

deTurck, M. A., & Miller, G. R. (1985). Deception and arousal: Isolating the behavioral correlates of deception. *Human Communication Research, 12,* 181–201.

Ekman, P. (1985). *Telling lies.* New York: W. W. Norton.

Ekman, P., & Friesen, W. V. (1969). Nonverbal leakage cues to deception. *Psychiatry, 32,* 88–106.

Ekman, P., & Friesen, W. V. (1974). Detecting deception from the body or face? *Journal of Personality and Social Psychology, 54,* 414–420.

Elliot, G. C. (1979). Some effects of deception and level of self-monitoring on planning and reacting to a self-presentation. *Journal of Personality and Social Psychology, 37,* 1282–1292.

Exline, R., Thibaut, J., Hickey, C., & Gumpert, P. (1970). Visual interaction in relation to Machiavellianism and as unethical act. In R. Christie & F. Geis (Eds.), *Studies in Machiavellianism* (pp. 53–75). New York: Academic Press.

Fay, P. J., & Middleton, W. C. (1941). The ability to judge truth-telling or lying from the voice as transmitted over a public address system. *Journal of General Psychology, 24,* 211–215.

Feeley, T. H. (1996, November). *Conversational competence and perceptions of honesty in interpersonal deception.* Paper presented at the annual meeting of the Speech Communication Association, San Diego, CA.

Feeley, T. H., & deTurck, M. A. (1997). Case-relevant vs. case-irrelevant questioning in experimental lie detection. *Communication Reports, 10*(1), 35–46.

Feeley, T. H., deTurck, M. A., & Young, M. J. (1995). Baseline familiarity in lie detection. *Communication Research Reports, 12*(2), 160–169.

Geis, G. L., & Moon, Y. Y. (1981). Machiavellianism and deception. *Journal of Personality and Social Psychology, 41,* 766–775.

Geizer, R. S., Rarick, D. L., & Soldow, G. F. (1977). Deception judgment accuracy: A study of person perception. *Personality and Psychology Bulletin, 3,* 446–449.

Goffman, E. (1974). *Frame analysis: An essay on the organization of experience.* New York: Harper and Row.

Hample, D. (1980). Purposes and effects of lying. *The Southern Speech Communication Journal, 46,* 33–47.

Hocking, J. E., Bauchner, J., Kaminski, E. P., & Miller, G. R. (1979). Detecting deceptive communication from verbal, visual, and paralinguistic cues. *Human Communication Research, 6,* 33–46.

Hopper, R., & Bell, R. A. (1994). Broadening the deception construct. *Quarterly Journal of Speech, 70,* 288–302.

Knapp, M. L., & Comadena, M. E. (1979). Telling it like it isn't: A review of theory and research on deceptive communications. *Human Communication Research, 5,* 270–285.

Knapp, M. L., Hart, P. R., & Dennis, H. S. (1974). An explanation of deception as a communication construct. *Human Communication Research, 1,* 15–29.

Kraut, R. E. (1978). Verbal and nonverbal cues in the perception of lying. *Journal of Personality and Social Psychology, 36,* 380–391.

Kraut, R. E. (1980). Humans as lie detectors: Some second thoughts. *Journal of Communication, 30,* 209–216.

Levine, T. R., & McCornack, S. A. (1996a). A critical analysis of the behavioral adaptation explanation of the probing effect. *Human Communication Research, 22* (4), 575–588.

Levine, T. R., & McCornack, S. A. (1996b). Can behavioral adaptation explain the probing effect? Rejoinder to Buller et al. *Human Communication Research, 22* (4), 604–613.

Lindskold, S., & Walters, P. S. (1983). Categories for the acceptability of lies. *Journal of Social Psychology, 120,* 129–136.

Littlepage, G. E., & Pineault, M. A. (1979). Detection of deceptive factual statements from the body and the face. *Personality and Psychology Bulletin, 5,* 325–328.

Maier, R. A., & Lavrakas, P. J. (1976). Lying behavior and the evaluation of lies. *Perception and Motor Skills, 42,* 575–581.

Mattson, M. (1994, November). *Reactive strategies to suspicious information in intimate relationships.* Paper presented to the annual meeting of the Speech Communication Association, New Orleans, LA.

McCornack, S. A. (1992). Information manipulation theory. *Communication Monographs, 59,* 1–16.

McCornack, S. A., & Levine, T. R. (1990). When lovers become leery: The relationship between suspicion and accuracy in detecting deception. *Communication Monographs, 57,* 219–230.

McCornack, S. A., & Parks, M. R. (1986). Deception detection and relational development: The other side of trust. In M. L. McLaughlin (Ed.), *Communication yearbook 9* (pp. 377–389). Beverly Hills, CA: Sage.

McCornack, S. A., Levine, T. R., Solowczuk, K., Torres, H. I., & Campbell, D. M. (1992). When the alteration of information is viewed as deception: An empirical test of information manipulation theory. *Communication Monographs, 59,* 17–29.

Mehrabian, A. (1971). Nonverbal betrayal of feeling. *Journal of Experimental Research in Personality, 5,* 64–73.

Metts, S. (1989). An exploratory investigation of deception in close relationships. *Journal of Social and Personal Relationships, 6,* 159–179.

Miller, G. R., Bauchner, J. E., Hocking, J. E., Fontes, N. E., Kaminski, E. P., & Brandt, D. R. (1981). "…and nothing but the truth:" How well can observers detect deceptive testimony? In B. D. Sales (Ed.), *Perspectives in law and psychology: Vol. II. The jury judicial, and trial process* (pp. 145–179). New York: Plenum.

Miller, G. R., deTurck, M. A., & Kalbfleisch, P. J. (1983). Self-monitoring, rehearsal, and deceptive communication. *Human Communication Research, 10,* 97–117.

Miller, G. R., & Stiff, J. B. (1993). *Deceptive Communication.* Newbury Park, CA: Sage.

Miller, L. C., & Read, S. J. (1991). On the coherence of mental models of persons and relationships: A knowledge structure approach. In G. J. O. Fletcher & F. Fincham (Eds.), *Cognition in close relationships* (pp. 69–99). Hillsdale, NJ: Lawrence Erlbaum.

O'Hair, D., Cody, M. J., & Behnke, R. R. (1985). Communication apprehension and vocal stress as indices of deception. *Western Journal of Speech Communication, 49,* 286–300.

O'Hair, D., Cody, M. J., Goss, B., & Krayer, K. J. (1988). The effect of gender, deceit orientation and communicator style on macro-assessments of honesty. *Communication Quarterly, 36,* 77–93.

O'Hair, D., Cody, M. J., & McLaughlin, M. L. (1981). Prepared lies, spontaneous lies, Machiavellianism, and nonverbal communication. *Human Communication Research, 7,* 325–339.

Riggio, R. E., & Friedman, H. S. (1983). Individual differences and cues to deception. *Journal of Personality and Social Psychology, 45,* 899–915.

Riggio, R. E., Tucker, J., & Throckmorton, B. (1987). Social skills and deception ability. *Personality and Social Psychology Bulletin, 13,* 568–577.

Riggio, R. E., Tucker, J., & Widaman, K. F. (1987). Verbal and nonverbal cues as mediators of deception ability. *Journal of Nonverbal Behavior, 11*, 126–143.

Rosenthal, R., & DePaulo, B. M. (1979). Sex differences in eavesdropping on nonverbal cues. *Journal of Personality and Social Psychology, 37*, 273–285.

✓ Seiter, J. S. (1997). Honest or deceitful?: A study of persons' mental models for judging veracity. *Human Communication Research, 24*(2), 216–259.

Seiter, J. S., Bruschke, J., & Bai, C. (1998, July). *Lies and damn lies: The acceptability of deception as a function of perceivers' culture and liars' intentions.* Paper presented at the annual meeting of the International Communication Association, Jerusalem, Israel.

Seiter, J. S., & Wiseman, R. (1995). Ethnicity and deception detection. *Journal of the Northwest Communication Association, 23*, 24–38.

Stiff, J. G., Kim, H. J., & Ramesh, C. (1992). Truth biases and aroused suspicion in relational deception. *Communication Research, 19*, 326–345.

Stiff, J. B., & Miller, G. R. (1986). "Come to think of it…": Interrogative probes, deceptive communication and deception detection. *Human Communication Research, 12*, 339–357.

Thackray, R. I., & Orne, M. T. (1968). Effects of stimulus employed and the level of subject awareness on the detection of deception. *Journal of Applied Psychology, 52*, 234–239.

Thagard, P. (1989). Explanatory coherence. *Behavioral and Brain Sciences, 12*, 435–467.

Turner, R. E., Edgley, C., & Olmstead, G. (1975). Information control in conversations: Honesty is not always the best policy. *Kansas Journal of Sociology, 11*, 69–89.

Zuckerman, M., DePaulo, B. M., & Rosenthal, R. (1981). Verbal and nonverbal communication of deception. In L. Berkowitz (Ed.), *Advances in experimental social psychology* (pp. 2–59). New York: Academic Press.

Zuckerman, M., & Driver, R. E. (1985). Telling lies: Verbal and nonverbal correlates of deception. In A. W. Siegman and S. Feldstein (Eds.), *Multichannel integrations of nonverbal behavior* (pp. 129–147). Hillsdale, NJ: Lawrence Erlbaum.

14

MOTIVATIONAL APPEALS

If real life was a cartoon, the salesman who showed up at the home of one of the authors could have been Elmer Fudd. The author needed to install a rain gutter on his house. On the advice of a neighbor, he contacted a company located a good 40 miles from where he lived to come out and provide an estimate. The salesman, a balding fellow in his mid-forties, arrived in a beat-up, 1970s vintage car. He looked tired and disheveled as he got out. He fumbled with his clipboard, calculator, and an armload of gutter samples as he made his way up the sidewalk.

"Find the place O. K.?" the author asked, greeting him at the door.

"The diwections wuh gweat," the salesman answered, "but the twaffic was tewwible, and I got a ticket on the way."

"That's too bad," the author replied.

"I didn't have my seatbelt on," the salesman lamented, "because it's bwoken, and it costs $300 to fix. I can't affawd it wight now."

Owing to the salesman's unkempt appearance, his speech impediment, and his sad tale about the traffic ticket, the author immediately felt sympathy for the poor man. Even though the salesman's estimate was slightly higher than that of several local businesses, the author signed a contract with him on the spot. How could he do otherwise? The salesman had come all that way—risked his life, in fact—to provide an estimate. He'd gotten a ticket for his trouble. The way the author saw it, the difference in the salesman's price from that of the local competitors was probably less than the cost of the ticket. And the guy obviously needed the sale.

Or did he? After the salesman drove away, the author began to wonder if it was all an act. What if the salesman told every potential customer he'd gotten a ticket en route? What if his seat belt worked just fine? What if he faked or exaggerated the speech problem to elicit sympathy and help make the sale? The author never did find out whether the salesman was being genuine or not, but the rain gutters have worked splendidly.

Whether the salesman's strategy was honest or not, it's clear that his success was based, to a large extent, on pity. His sad plight tugged at the author's heartstrings.

And in the end, the author was willing to pay more for the work because he felt sorry for the salesman. The salesman's appeal to pity, if it was designed as such, represents but one example of a *motivational appeal,* the topic of this chapter. Motivational appeals may be generally defined as external inducements, often of an emotional nature, which are designed to increase an individual's drive to undertake some course of action. By external inducements, we mean incentives that exist apart from the substance of a message itself. Such external inducements typically seek to alter people's moods, feelings, or emotions as a means of persuasion.

INTRINSIC VERSUS EXTRINSIC MOTIVATION

Motivational appeals can be thought of as attempts to jump start an individual's drive to do something. They provide an external incentive for performing some action. *Intrinsic motivation* is drive that comes from within (Deci, 1975; Deci & Ryan, 1978). If you are reading this chapter purely for knowledge and enlightenment, your motivation is internal. *Extrinsic motivation* is instilled by some outside factor (Petri, 1991). If you are reading this chapter because it was assigned, your motivation is external. All the motivational appeals we'll be discussing here can be thought of as extrinsic in nature. Motivational appeals are found everywhere. As Mortensen (1972) emphasizes:

> The daily bombardment of television commercials, political announcements, sermons, and editorials constantly enjoins us with appeals to our feelings and emotions: anxiety, guilt, sympathy, psychological well-being, physical comfort, security, pleasure, joy. A plethora of injunctions are aimed at attributes of loyalty, generosity, devotion, compassion, dedication, and patriotism. (p. 174)

Before discussing specific motivational appeals, however, we examine supposed differences between logical and emotional appeals.

LOGICAL AND EMOTIONAL APPEALS: A FUZZY DISTINCTION

People often think of "logical" and "emotional" appeals as opposites. This distinction dates back to Aristotle, who classified *logos* (logic, reasoning) and *pathos* (passion, emotion) as separate, distinct forms of influence (Aristotle, trans. 1932). This way of thinking, however, represents something of an artificial dichotomy.[1] Whether a message is perceived as logical or emotional has as much to do with the person *perceiving* the message as it does with the message itself (Becker, 1963). In fact, researchers (Lefford, 1946; Reuchelle, 1958) have learned that when people agree with a message, they tend to perceive it as being more logical or rational in nature. When they disagree with a message, they tend to think of it as being more emotional in nature. Hence, when a dispute arises, a person tends to think, "I'm being rational, why is he or she being so emotional?" In addition to our prior beliefs, our moods can also influence the way we process messages. We're more likely to be critical of messages when we're in a bad mood and accepting of messages when we're in a good mood. That's why so many commercials try to create a positive mood. Our emotional state thus affects our reasoning and vice versa (Bohner & Schwartz, 1993; Rosseli, Skelly, & Mackie, 1995).

A now classic study by Langer, Blank, and Chanowitz (1978) illustrates the sometimes fuzzy distinction between logical, psychological, and emotional appeals. The purpose of the study was to see how successful a person was at "taking cuts" in line, based on the quality of the reason he or she offered. In the study, a person (serving as a confederate) asked for permission to cut in line at a photocopy machine. In one condition, the person provided an actual reason for cutting in line: "Excuse me, I have 5 pages. May I use the Xerox machine, because I'm in a rush?" In a second condition, the person gave a semblance of a reason: "Excuse me, I have 5 pages. May I use the Xerox machine, because I have to make some copies"? In a third condition, the person offered neither a reason nor the pretext of a reason for cutting in line: "Excuse me, I have 5 pages. May I use the Xerox machine?" The confederate then repeated the process, with different strangers, but asked to make 20 copies, rather than 5.

Table 14.1 displays the compliance rates for each of the conditions. Notice that for the smaller request (five copies) a semblance of a reason was nearly as effective as a genuine reason. Thus, it was not so much the actual use of reasoning that mattered as the *appearance* of reasoning. In short, merely including rational sounding words and phrases in a message, such as "because," "therefore," and "it is only logical that…" can achieve much the same effect as providing genuine reasons (Bettinghaus, 1968). This was not the case with the larger request, however. When the confederate asked to make 20 copies, people were less likely to comply unless a genuine reason was offered.

FEAR APPEALS: IF YOU DON'T STOP DOING THAT, YOU'LL GO BLIND

"If you cross your eyes, they'll stay that way." "Don't run with scissors, you'll poke your eye out." "Don't touch that! It has germs." What child hasn't heard these or similar admonitions from a parent? Fear appeals are not only a frequent staple of

TABLE 14.1 Compliance rates in response to the size of the request and the type of reason offered.

Size of Request	Absence of a Reason	Semblance of a Reason	Genuine Reason
Smaller (5 copies)	60% compliance	93% compliance	94% compliance
Larger (20 copies)	25% compliance	25% compliance	42% compliance

Adapted from Langer, E., Blank, A., Chanowitz, B. (1978). The mindlessness of ostensibly thoughtful action: The role of "placebic" information in interpersonal interaction. *Journal of Personality and Social Psychology, 36*(6), 635–642.

child-rearing, they are also prevalent in the workplace, in public health messages, and in advertising. Advertisements for dandruff shampoos, deodorants, mouthwashes, and acne medications, for example, are often predicated on the fear of social ostracism.

But does scaring people or increasing their anxiety level really work? And if so, how? Research suggests that the effectiveness of fear appeals depends on several factors, which we examine next.

Fear Level or Intensity: The Goosebump Factor

Pioneering work on the study of fear appeals began with Janis and Feshbach in 1953. They presented three groups of high school freshman with persuasive messages on the subject of oral hygiene. One group was exposed to a strong fear appeal, which consisted of gory photographs of abscessed gums and rotting teeth. A second group was exposed to a moderate fear appeal, which consisted of information on the harms of dental neglect, such as cavities. Finally, a third group was exposed to a mild fear appeal, which consisted of a highly factual presentation on proper oral hygiene, with few references to the consequences of not brushing.

Surprisingly, the investigators discovered a negative or inverse relationship between the intensity of fear arousal and the messages' persuasiveness. That is, the students in the mild fear condition were more likely to modify their attitudes than the students in the other two groups. On the basis of these initial results, a number of authors "jumped the gun" and proclaimed that mild fear appeals were superior to moderate or strong fear appeals (see reviews by Higbee, 1969; Mongeau, 1994). This notion persists even today (see, for example, Bennett, 1996).

The answer was not so simple, however. Janis and Feshbach's study was criticized on a number of grounds. Katz (1960), for example, pointed out that the results could have been due to the lack of clear-cut recommendations in the high fear message. Participants weren't told what to do to avoid gangrenous gums and oral cancer. Higbee (1969) surmised that the relative unimportance of the topic to high school students also could account for the findings. Mortensen (1972) attributed the results to the sheer unbelievability of an exotic gum disease as portrayed in the high fear message. A variety of other explanations for Janis and Feshbach's results also have been advanced.

Whatever the limitations of Janis and Feshbach's study, subsequent investigations have tended to discount their results. In fact, researchers are now fairly confident that the relationship between fear intensity and persuasion is generally positive and linear. That is, greater fear tends to produce greater persuasion. This conclusion is borne out by both qualitative (Dillard, 1994; Gass, 1983; Higbee, 1969) and quantitative (Boster & Mongeau, 1984; Mongeau, 1994; Sutton, 1982; Witte & Allen, 1996) reviews of the fear literature. The more fear that is aroused, the more vulnerable receivers feel, and the more likely it is they will be persuaded (see Figure 14.1).

For this general rule to apply, however, a number of conditions must hold true. The most important of these involves the *perceived efficacy* of the recommendations.

FIGURE 14.1   A fear appeal in action.

To understand what perceived efficacy means and why it is so important, you'll
need to know more about how fear appeals work.

The Extended Parallel Process Model: There's Nothing to Fear but Fear Itself

There are a number of models of how fear appeals work, but we think Kim Witte's
(1992, 1994) *Extended Parallel Process Model* is among the best. Assuming that an
appeal arouses fear in a receiver, the receiver can be expected to do something
about it. Witte suggests two basic alternatives: The receiver can engage in danger

control or fear control. Let's say, for example, that Biff is exposed to an AIDS aware-ness message that says "Would you trade your life for a one night stand? Play it safe, use a condom!" If Biff concentrates on ways of reducing the danger, such as using condoms or refraining from sex, he would be resorting to *danger control*. If, on the other hand, Biff concentrates on ways of reducing his fear, such as telling himself to remain calm and not panic, he would be resorting to *fear control*. Danger control tends to be a more constructive means of coping with a fear appeal than fear control. Why? Because danger control focuses on the solution. Fear control, conversely, focuses on the problem and essentially involves "worrying about worry." Such an approach often results in denial, avoidance, or panic. A per-suader's goal in using fear appeals, therefore, should be to trigger danger control in receivers which, in turn, will cause them to take positive, constructive steps to avoid the harm and avoid triggering fear control.

This is where perceived efficacy enters into the picture. Perceived efficacy has to do with whether a receiver thinks a recommended action is both an effective and a feasible means of avoiding the harm portrayed by a fear appeal. For a fear appeal to trigger danger control, the person must perceive that (1) an effective response is available, termed *response efficacy*; and (2) that he or she is capable of undertaking that response, termed *self-efficacy*. If a person thinks no remedy is available, or that he or she cannot exercise the remedy, then fear control will take over.

Returning to our previous example, if the fear appeal convinces Biff that con-doms work and are easy to use, he'll be more likely to use them. The fear appeal would thus have high perceived efficacy. If, however, the appeal leaves Biff worry-ing that condoms are unreliable or impractical, he'll be less likely to use them. The fear appeal would have low perceived efficacy.

The trick, then, is to use fear appeals that include workable, practical remedies, thereby triggering danger control which, in turn, leads to constructive responses. The challenge is to avoid fear appeals that are nonefficacious, because they tend to trigger fear control, which leads to counterproductive responses. The bottom line, then, is that to maximize fear's effectiveness, receivers must be given some "out," which they perceive as being both effective and practical. If this is not done, the use of fear appeals may prove unsuccessful, or even backfire.

In addition to perceived efficacy, a number of other factors affect the success of fear appeals. Some of these other moderating variables, as researchers like to call them, are detailed in Box 14.1. When these additional factors are taken into account, and the message is adapted accordingly, fear appeals can be one of the most effective tools a persuader can use.

We would be remiss if we didn't acknowledge that there are serious ethical concerns surrounding the use of fear appeals. We address these in Chapter 16. For the time being, suffice to say that a persuader should exercise considerable caution in using fear appeals. Nevertheless, if the harmful consequences contained in a fear appeal are real or genuine, we would suggest it is not only acceptable for a per-suader to employ fear appeals, but that the persuader has an obligation to use them.

BOX 14.1   Additional Moderating Variables Affecting the Success of Fear Appeals

- **Perceived vulnerability:** Receivers must perceive themselves as vulnerable for a fear appeal to succeed (see Sigelman, Miller, & Derenowski, 1993). If receivers say, "That can't happen to me," the appeal will fail. To increase feelings of vulnerability a fear appeal should emphasize three things: the *noxiousness* or severity of the harm, the *probability* or likelihood of the harm's occurring, and the *imminence* or immediacy of the harm, as opposed to the harm being distant or remote. In short, the receiver should think, "It's bad, it's likely, and it could happen at any moment!"

- **Specificity of recommendations:** Specific recommendations have been shown to be more effective than general or vague guidelines (Leventhal, Jones, & Trembly, 1966; Leventhal & Niles, 1964; Leventhal, Singer, & Jones, 1965). Specific recommendations give receivers a clearer idea of what to do to avoid or lessen the dangers identified in a fear appeal.

- **Positioning of recommendations:** Studies show that the best place to put the recommendations about what to do is *immediately after* the fear appeal, a problem–solution format (Harris & Jellison, 1971; Leventhal & Singer, 1966; Skilbeck, Tulips, & Ley, 1977; Witte & Allen, 1996). Placing the recommendations before the fear appeal (a solution–problem format) is less effective, as is offering the recommendations at a later time.

- **Argument quality:** Several investigations have shown that fear appeals that contain high-quality arguments are more persuasive than fear appeals with low-quality arguments (Gleicher & Petty, 1992; Rodriguez, 1995; Smith, 1977). This is probably related to the issue of perceived vulnerability. A high-quality argument is more likely to convince receivers that the risk is genuine.

- **Self-Esteem:** The self-esteem of message recipients plays a role in the effectiveness of fear appeals. The relatively consistent finding has been that strong fear appeals are most successful on receivers with high self-esteem (Dabbs & Leventhal, 1966; Kornzweig, 1968; Leventhal & Trembly, 1968; Ramirez & Lasater, 1977). For receivers with low esteem, strong appeals tend to be less effective or even counterproductive (Leventhal, 1970; Leventhal & Trembly, 1968; Rosen, 1973; Rosen, Terry, & Leventhal, 1982). Receivers with high esteem appear better able to cope with fear arousal and respond in constructive ways.

- **Anxiety level:** Some people tend to be more worried, nervous, or anxious than others. This trait is known as *anxiety*. Janis and Feshbach (1953) attributed their results to the chronic anxiety levels of the participants. They hypothesized that increasing levels of fear invoked feelings of anxiety which, in turn, inhibited fear's effectiveness. Subsequent studies, however, have found little support for this conclusion. The majority of studies show that strong fear appeals are only marginally superior in individuals with low anxiety (Boster & Mongeau, 1984; Mongeau, 1994; Wheatley & Oshikawa, 1970; Witte, 1996). This may have to do with highly anxious individuals resorting to fear control (an undesirable response), as opposed to danger control (a desirable response) when confronted with a fear-arousing message.

APPEALS TO PITY AND GUILT: WOE IS ME, SHAME ON YOU

It happens every Labor Day weekend. Comedian Jerry Lewis hosts the Muscular Dystrophy telethon. Begun in 1966, the MD telethon relies heavily on pity as an instrument for fund-raising. The telethon is carried by more than 200 stations and attracts upwards of 100 million viewers. A "poster child," typically full of innocence and wearing leg braces and crutches, is chosen for each year's campaign. Throughout the telethon, children with MD are paraded before the cameras to tug at viewers' heartstrings and thereby elicit pledges.

The technique works. The telethon raised a record 126 million dollars in 1996. But Jerry Lewis has been criticized for relying on pity as a means of fund-raising. Organizations representing the disabled say the use of pity is demeaning, paternalistic, stigmatizing, and marginalizing (DeAngelis, 1993; Del Valle, 1992; Ervin, 1995). Opponents of Lewis' tactics say the good the telethon does is outweighed by the damage caused by portraying the disabled as "broken" and in need of "fixing" or as less than whole human beings.

But is it possible to engage in successful fund-raising without using pity or guilt? If the disabled are depicted by charities as independent and self-reliant will the dollars keep rolling in? One study suggests it may not be possible to have it both ways. Eayres and Ellis (1990) asked males and females to evaluate 10 posters

These cards were given to one of the authors at the food court of a mall. The author gave each deaf person $1.00 in return.

for charitable causes based on a number of criteria. Some posters portrayed people with mental or learning disabilities in a negative light (dependent, incapable), while others portrayed them in a positive light (valued, capable). The researchers found that the posters that evoked the strongest feelings of guilt and sympathy, the negative portrayals, were most likely to make the participants want to donate money. Participants were less likely to make a donation if the posters included positive portrayals. As the researchers noted, "this tends to validate the supposition that in order to produce a successful poster in charity terms it is necessary to play on people's feelings of guilt and pity" (p. 356). Interestingly, the participants were more willing to become actively involved in, and donate time to, charitable causes that were featured positively in the posters. This bodes well for charities seeking increased voluntarism, but not for ones seeking monetary contributions.

In a related vein, several investigations have examined people's emotional reactions to others who possess varying maladies or stigmas. Weiner, Perry, and Magnusson (1988) argue that how people react to others' stigmas (obesity, paraplegia, blindness, AIDS, etc.) depends on the causal inferences they make about those stigmas. For example, these researchers analyzed college students' emotional reactions

Which homeless person would you be most likely to give money to? Why?

Photos by Jennifer Nicholson.

to people with varying stigmas (obesity, drug addiction, etc.), based on how controllable the students thought the stigma was. Students expressed more feelings of guilt and sympathy if the stigma was uncontrollable (e.g., obesity ascribed to a glandular dysfunction) and more feelings of anger and reluctance to help if the stigma was controllable (e.g., obesity due to overeating). Thus, persuaders seeking to use emotional appeals such as pity or guilt for fund-raising or other purposes need to ensure that the beneficiaries are *not* perceived as having a physical or social malady that they brought upon themselves.

A research grant in which one of the authors was involved shows how this principal can be applied to real world settings (Emry et al., 1991). The problem facing the researchers was how to alert motorists in San Diego, California, near the Mexican border, that undocumented aliens might be crossing the freeway. At the time of the study, some 30 undocumented persons were being hit and killed per year and dozens more seriously injured (Morgan, 1989). The researchers tested 14 variations of signs alerting motorists to this hazard. The most effective sign was one that included the silhouette of a child with a family. The child's silhouette evoked the most sympathy and compassion from motorists. Why? Because the inclusion of a child's silhouette fostered the perception that, from the child's standpoint, the decision to dash across the freeway was not controllable—she had to go where the family went. The final version of the sign which was posted is displayed in Figure 14.2. Following the posting of the sign, along with a host of other measures,[2] pedestrian fatalities declined.

FIGURE 14.2   A silhouette of a child evoked the most sympathy from motorists.

Photograph courtesy of Robert A. Emry.

HUMOROUS APPEALS: STOP ME IF YOU'VE HEARD THIS ONE

The use of humor in persuasion is pervasive. Humorous advertisements account for 15 to 42 percent of all advertising (Madden & Weinberger, 1984). Almost one fourth of prime-time commercials include humor (Weinberger & Gulas, 1992). Humor is also common in the board room, the court room, the classroom, in interpersonal conversations, and even in the pulpit.

Using humor to influence is like skinning a cat; there's more than one way. A persuader can *do* something funny, *say* something funny, or both. A humorous appeal can consist of a pun, satire, an anecdote, innuendo, irony, a metaphor, or just a plain old joke, as in "an armadillo walks into a bar...." Humor can be directed at oneself, which is known as *self-disparaging humor,* or at others. Goldstein and McGhee (1972) have broadly classified all humor as falling into one of three categories; *aggressive* (insults, put-downs), *sexual,* and *nonsense* humor. Also with respect to the type of humor, Weinberger and Gulas (1992) suggest that humor may be related, that is, relevant or connected to the substance of the message, or unrelated, that is, not germane to the message's content. All in all, Berger (1976) identified 45 different techniques that can be used to create humor.

Humor as an Indirect Form of Influence

On occasion the content of a joke might alter another person's attitudes. Typically, however, jokes themselves don't persuade. As a means of persuasion, humor tends to operate in a more roundabout manner, akin to what Petty and Cacioppo (1986) call the peripheral route to persuasion (see Chapter 2). The first way in which humor assists persuasion is by *capturing attention.* Advertisers see humor as a way of breaking through media clutter. If a funny commercial appears on TV, such as the "Got Milk?" campaign, a viewer may keep watching rather than flip channels or head to the kitchen to fix a snack. Weinberger and Gulas (1992) note that nine of eleven advertising studies have found a positive relationship between humor and attention, while only two have found a mixed relationship. And if only those studies employing *related* humor (e.g., directly connected to message content) are considered, the results are even more convincing (Weinberger & Gulas, 1992). Humor's ability to capture attention has also been demonstrated in educational settings (Bryant & Zillman, 1989).

A second way in which humor may indirectly facilitate persuasion is through *distraction* (Cantor & Venus, 1980; Sternthal & Craig, 1973). Humor may divert attention away from the content of a message, thereby interfering with the ability of listeners to carefully scrutinize the message or engage in counterarguing (e.g., mentally rehearsing opposing arguments). In terms of Petty & Cacioppo's (1986) ELM model (see Chapter 2) humor can be thought of as a peripheral cue. In situations in which listeners would otherwise evaluate a message via the central route (e.g., thought, reflection), humor can be used to encourage peripheral processing instead. Simply stated, if listeners are laughing at the jokes, they may pay less attention to the content of a message. A persuader facing a hostile audience, for example, could incorporate humor to "soften up" or disarm listeners.

The third way in which humor indirectly facilitates persuasion is by increasing liking for the persuader, which indirectly increases the chances for persuasion. The use of humor tends to make a persuader seem more friendly and helps establish rapport with receivers. A sizable number of studies have shown this to be the case (see Weinberger & Gulas, 1992). Importantly, no studies suggest humor inhibits liking. This explains why some comedians make good celebrity endorsers. It isn't necessarily the hilarity of the commercials themselves that matters, but rather the likeability of the sources who, in turn, make consumers more receptive to the messages.

This doesn't mean, however, that a person who acts like a complete clown will be influential (Gruner, 1967). If a source doesn't seem to take his or her own message seriously, neither will others. Similarly, the use of inappropriate humor can decrease perceptions of credibility (Derks, Kalland, & Etgen, 1995; Munn & Gruner, 1981).

Relatedness of Humor

Humor that is integrated into a message is called *related*, while humor that is offered in a stand-alone fashion is called *unrelated*. Both types of humor have been shown to be effective. However, related humor enjoys an advantage over unrelated humor (Kaplan & Pascoe, 1977; Weinberger & Campbell, 1991; Weinberger & Gulas, 1992; Weinberger & Spotts, 1995). This makes perfect sense. When humor is integrated into the message content, the receiver doesn't have to make a mental detour to "get" the joke, then return to the message.

Humor and Credibility: Laugh Clown Laugh

Does humor enhance source credibility? The answer depends on the specific dimensions of credibility in which one is interested. Some studies have shown that humor enhances perceptions of trustworthiness (Gruner, 1967; Speck, 1987). This seems reasonable, given that we're more inclined to trust people we like. At the same time, some types of humor have been shown to diminish perceptions of competence or expertise (Chang & Gruner, 1981; Gruner, 1967, 1970; Gruner & Lampton, 1972; Speck, 1987; Tamborini & Zillmann, 1981; Taylor, 1974). Although not directly tied to dynamism, the use of humor has also been shown to increase a communicator's perceived social attractiveness (Murnstein & Burst, 1985; Wanzer, Booth-Butterfield, & Booth-Butterfield, 1996). And humor has been shown to enhance perceptions of "communication competence," or the ability to exhibit social "know how" in communicative situations (Wanzer, Booth-Butterfield, & Booth-Butterfield, 1996). Coupled with the finding that humor tends to increase likability, it seems the use of humor is beneficial for the communicator in all but the expertise dimension.

Self-Disparaging Humor: I Get No Respect:

At this point in the text, you've already read a number of humorous accounts (at least, we *hope* they were humorous) of the authors' own gullibility. Related to the issue of credibility, some studies have examined the effects of self-disparaging humor on persuasion (Graham, Papa, & Brooks, 1992). This involves making oneself the object or brunt of a humorous appeal. On the one hand, it might seem that putting oneself down, even light-heartedly, would lower one's credibility. On the other hand, it might seem that the ability to poke fun at oneself would increase one's credibility. Which is it? The answer is: it depends. It depends upon the specific credibility dimensions in which one is interested. A study by Hackman (1988) revealed that self-disparaging humor led to lower ratings of speaker competence. A study by Chang and Gruner (1981), however, demonstrated that self-disparaging humor enhanced liking for the source. In Chang and Gruner's study, the speaker's initial credibility was high and the speaker used indirect humor. The indirect humor consisted of a psychologist who was giving a presentation and defined a psychologist as "a guy who would father a set of twins, have one baptized, and keep the other as a control."

Our advice is to avoid using self-disparaging humor if you think you have low credibility to begin with or if you need to bolster your credibility in the "competence" dimension. If you have moderate to high credibility to begin with, then making light of some of your human frailties might make you appear more likable and less pretentious.

Humor and Gender

Several investigations have explored whether males and females respond differently to humor. In some ways their responses are the same. For instance, the fairly consistent finding is that both males *and* females enjoy female-disparaging humor (e.g., jokes at women's expense) more than male-disparaging humor (Cantor, 1976; McGhee & Duffy, 1983; Moore, Griffiths, & Payne, 1987). This tendency is more pronounced if receivers hold traditional views regarding sex roles and less pronounced if receivers hold nontraditional views regarding sex roles, but is evident either way (Moore, et al., 1987).

In other ways, the responses of males and females differ. Several studies have concluded that men find humor more amusing than do women (Hassett & Houlihan, 1979; Wilson & Molleston, 1981). The latter study has been criticized, however, for including *Playboy* cartoons as source material, which males would predictably enjoy more than females. A more recent investigation, using jokes about the Gulf War as source material, found that females found the jokes to be *funnier* and *less offensive* than males, a surprisingly counterintuitive finding (Sereno, Seiter, Robinson, & McDonald, 1996). Bryant, Comisky, Crane and Zillmann (1980) found that the use of humor enhanced the credibility of male, but not female, college teachers. In a related vein, Decker (1986) found that aggressive jokes, when told by male managers, were considered more appropriate than when told by female managers. The last two studies sound an important warning: female persuaders should be more cautious about employing humor than males.

Humor as Social Proof: Smile and the World Smiles with You

Humor has also been shown to function as an effective form of social proof. Social proof involves modeling our behavior after the actions or reactions of others (see

Chapter 7). The use of "laugh tracks" or live audience laughter on television sit-coms illustrates this principle. Researchers have found that the perceived funniness of low to medium-quality jokes is enhanced via the inclusion of canned laughter (Cupchick & Leventhal, 1974; Leventhal & Cupchick, 1975, 1976). Parents sometimes use laughter as a form of social proof with toddlers. If a toddler falls down, he or she may look to a parent to gauge the parent's reaction. If the parent looks concerned, the child may begin to cry, but if the parent laughs, the child may decide the fall was harmless. This suggests a persuader may use humor to temper receivers' responses to particular situations or circumstances.

Is Humor Itself Persuasive?

We've seen that humor can facilitate persuasion indirectly in a variety of ways. We've also seen that a variety of other factors affect the success of humorous appeals. The question remains, however, does humor itself persuade? Unfortunately, attempts to answer this question have yielded mixed results (see Table 14.2). In a review of the humor literature, Weinberger and Gulas (1992) reported that five studies found humor facilitated persuasion, but another fifteen were either inconclusive or found no such effects. Two studies found a negative relationship between the use of humor and persuasion.

At least one investigation not considered by Weinberger and Gulas *did* find that humor facilitated persuasion. O'Quin and Aronoff (1981) simulated a bargaining situation in which a buyer attempted to buy a painting from a seller. Sellers who made a final offer and added "and I'll throw in my pet frog!" were more successful in getting buyers to make a larger concession than sellers who did not include a humorous appeal. We don't find the joke too funny ourselves, but hey, it worked!

Based on the preceding, the best we can offer is that sometimes humor itself persuades, though usually it does not, yet rarely does it backfire. Attempts at generalizing about humor are complicated by the fact that there is considerable dispar-

TABLE 14.2   Number of studies reporting a positive, neutral, or negative relationship between humor and persuasion.

	Positive Relationship	Neutral or Mixed Relationship	Negative Relationship
Advertising Studies (TV, radio, print media)	5	8	1
Nonadvertising Studies (public speeches, direct mail, textbook cartoons, etc.)	0	7	1
Total	5	15	2

Adapted from Weinberger, M. G., & Gulas, C. S. (1992). The impact of humor in advertising: A review. *Journal of Advertising, 18*(2), 43–44.

ity in how studies were conducted. There are disparities as to the type of humor used, how funny receivers perceived the material to be, the relatedness of the humor to the rest of the message, as well as issues such as timing and delivery.

Bear in mind that laboratory studies of humor may not generalize well to the real world. The jokes are often read, rather than heard, and the presentation of humorous material may seem more artificial in a laboratory setting. Also noteworthy is the fact that most laboratory studies involve one-shot measurements of humor's effectiveness. If, in fact, humor operates as an indirect method of persuasion, then evaluating its effectiveness might require more long-term measures. One study that did include follow-up measures found that participants who were exposed to a humorous appeal generated more arguments in favor of the message advocated than those who were exposed to a nonhumorous appeal, *but only after a period of time had elapsed* (Lammers, Leibowitz, Seymour, & Hennesy, 1983).

So should you play a banjo and wear a fake arrow through your head the next time you want to persuade someone? The bottom line is that humor does appear to facilitate persuasion, but it does so indirectly, and is no more effective than alternative approaches such as reasoning and evidence. The use of humor rarely seems to inhibit persuasion (except for judgments of expertise). For some additional suggestions on how to maximize humor's effectiveness as a persuasive tool, see Box 14.2.

BOX 14.2   Advice and Tips on Using Humor as a Persuasive Tool

- If you can't tell a joke, *don't*. If you tend to forget key elements of jokes, mess up the punch lines, or have poor timing and delivery, find another way to get your message across.

- Be sure you have good material. The problem with some studies on humor and persuasion was that the stimulus material wasn't funny (Perloff, 1993). One investigation found that non-funny humor was not only ineffective, but irritating as well (Duncan & Nelson, 1985).

- Self-disparaging humor can actually enhance your likeability and social attractiveness. Don't put yourself down excessively or repeatedly, however.

- Integrate the humor into the substance of your message. Related humor has been consistently shown to be more effective than unrelated or irrelevant humor.

- Make sure the humor is appropriate for your audience. Humor that is perceived as offensive or tasteless will lower your credibility and undermine your message's effectiveness (Gruner, 1985).

- Female persuaders need to exercise more caution than male persuaders when using humor. The times they are a-changing, but some receivers still adhere to the notion that being "lady-like" doesn't include telling jokes or clowning around.

- As a peripheral cue, humor may help convince someone to make a minor decision or incidental purchase (Weinberger, Spotts, Campbell, & Parsons, 1995). However, the use of humor probably won't tip the scales in your favor if the decision or purchase is a major one.

FOR MATURE AUDIENCES: SEX APPEALS

There is a reason why *Baywatch* is televised in more countries throughout the world than any other TV show, and it *isn't* because of the solid acting. TV is replete with sexual appeals. TV talk shows sizzle with sexual themes. TV "magazines" abound with "T&A" stories presented under the guise of newsworthiness. And there is plenty of jiggle and bounce among the evening sitcoms and dramas too. Sex appeals aren't limited to TV, though. Magazine ads often include partial nudity and models in suggestive poses. The stories themselves often involve topics such as "How to Look and Feel More Sexy," or "Ten Steps to a More Sensual You." And then there's the Internet. There's more sex on the Web than flies on a cow-pie.

"Sex sells," goes the advertising adage. Sex appeals have been used to sell jeans, cosmetics, fragrances, undergarments, liquor, and automobiles, to mention only a few applications. The use of sexual appeals has been a fixture of advertising for decades. What has changed, however, is that the use of overt sexual appeals has increased considerably (La Tour, 1990). Whereas older ads tended to allude to sex, modern ads often contain more overt, visually based sex appeals (Miller, 1992a, 1992b; LaTour & Henthorne, 1993).

DARRIN BELL / For The Times

Cartoon by Darrin Bell. Copyright © 1998 Los Angeles Times Syndicate. Reprinted with permission.

Historically, females have been depicted as sex objects in advertisements (Eagle, 1979; Kerin, Lundstrom, & Sciglimpaglia, 1979; Venkatesan & Losco, 1975), a situation decried by feminists and other media critics. But rest assured ladies, the sexual objectification of males is now also well underway. For example, a recent Coke commercial showed female office workers rushing to the window to ogle a well-muscled construction worker as he removed his shirt. There is a growing acceptance of males as sex objects, especially hypermasculine males (Neimark, 1994). The idealized male of today is more muscular, more of a "hunk," if you will, than the male ideal of the past.

How do sex appeals work? Generally speaking, they function as peripheral cues to persuasion. The whole point of a sexual appeal, after all, is to stimulate an emotional reaction in the receiver, a vicarious experience of sexuality or sensuality (LaTour & Henthorne, 1993). For this reason, sex appeals are usually conveyed visually. Typically, the unspoken message in ads employing sexual appeals is either (1) if you use product "X" you will look, act, or feel more sexy or (2) if you use product "X" other sexy people will be attracted to you. This simple formula explains how most sex appeals operate. Of course, such ads rarely make explicit cause–effect claims about the benefits of the product. Rather, following the dictates of consistency theory (see Chapter 4), the product is paired with sexually laden imagery. Through this associative process the receiver comes to identify the product with sexiness or sensuality.

A simple example involves a Miller Genuine Draft beer commercial. In the commercial, three guys—who are average looking at best—are sitting in folding chairs at the beach. Three sexy women stroll by in bikinis. One of the guys taps his beer bottle on the chair, causing the women to "rewind" like a videotape, whereupon they stroll by all over again. The commercial represents a sexual fantasy. What red-blooded heterosexual male wouldn't like to see an instant replay of a gorgeous "babe" walking by? Notice that the beer is what makes it all possible. The beer brand is the key to the sexual fantasy because tapping the beer bottle is what produces the instant replay. This is how the association between the product and sex is made.

Caveats and Cautions

While it is true that sexual appeals can be effective, there are also cautions regarding their use. In some cases, nontargeted receivers may become angered over sexually charged advertisements. This happened several years ago when Calvin Klein ran a series of ads for its jeans depicting young teens in provocative positions. Critics charged the ads were tantamount to child pornography. In response, the manufacturer quickly pulled the ads ("Calvin's world," 1995).

In other cases, the targeted audience itself may resent the use of sexual appeals. For example, sexual stimuli are frequently included in ads aimed at women. Yet if women perceive the ads as sexist, the ads will inhibit purchases and may damage the advertiser's image (Ford & LaTour, 1993). A study by LaTour and Henthorne (1994), for example, found that both females and males perceived a jeans ad with a strong, overt sexual theme to be more offensive than one containing a mild sexual theme. Women's perceptions of the strong sexual theme, however, were significantly more negative than men's. Nowadays, an advertiser must walk a fine line between creating ads that are considered sexy and ads that are considered sexist (Lippman, 1991; Miller 1992b).

A second liability in using sex appeals is that they may function as a distraction, thereby inhibiting receiver recall. If a person is salivating over a sexy model in a magazine ad, he or she may be unable to pay attention to the product being advertised. Several studies have shown this to be the case (Steadman, 1969; Judd & Alexander, 1983). For example, Grazer and Keesling (1995) found that jeans ads containing moderate sexual stimuli elicited greater brand-name recall than ads containing strong sexual stimuli. Advertisers face something of a dilemma here: A sexual appeal that is too mild may not stand out in the crowd, yet a sexual appeal which is too strong may serve as a distraction.

A third downside to using sexual appeals is that they may produce undesirable social consequences. The idealized female body type depicted in the media is extremely thin, a body shape that is unattainable for most women. No wonder, then, that 56 percent of women, according to a recent survey, reported they were dissatisfied with their bodies (Garner, 1997). Some even develop eating disorders trying to emulate the gaunt look of movie idols and runway models. Media portrayals of the ideal male body are equally unrealistic, which makes many males feel inferior by comparison. According to one survey, some 43 percent of males were dissatisfied with their overall appearance (Garner, 1997). Some turn to steroids in an effort to acquire a more muscular physique. We don't fault the media entirely for the current obsession people have with their bodies. We do think, however, that advertisers, the movie industry, and the fashion industry must shoulder some of the blame for exploiting people's insecurities about their looks.

WARMTH APPEALS: STRAIGHT FROM THE HEART

"Nothing says lovin' like something from the oven, and Pillsbury says it best." Some advertisements convey a warm, cozy feeling. They emphasize family, friends, and a sense of belonging. They make us feel sentimental or nostalgic about life. Such ads are based on "warmth." Aaker and Bruzzone (1981) identify warmth as one of a half dozen basic dimensions people use to describe advertisements. The use of warmth in advertising is quite common. A little more than one in five prime-time commercials includes warmth as an advertising theme (Aaker & Stayman, 1990). State Farm's "Like a good neighbor...State Farm is there" campaign is based on this theme. So are ads for Saturn automobiles, Hallmark cards, Kodak film, "Poppin' Fresh," the Pillsbury doughboy, and Snuggle fabric softener, which features a cuddly teddy bear. Banks, insurance companies, airlines, health care providers, restaurants, and hotel chains all use warmth to convey an image of folksiness, hominess, friendliness, and familiarity (see Goldman & Papson, 1996).

So how do they work? Warmth appeals operate in much the same way as sex appeals. They work through association. A product or service is associated with the image of being warm, caring, or friendly. When we think of that product or service we get a warm, fuzzy feeling. Do you recall the Ford commercial featuring Lindsey Wagner playing with a litter of puppies in an Aerostar van? If you like dogs, you probably got a warm feeling while watching the commercial. Because the puppies were paired with the minivan, you might associate warm feelings with the minivan as well. These good vibes might carry over into a purchase decision if you were in the market for such a car.

Studies have shown that ads using warmth produce temporary mood changes in people. The feelings of warmth are induced fairly quickly, typically in a 7- to 15-second period (Aaker, Stayman, & Hagerty, 1986). This means that warm, fuzzy feelings can be created within a single commercial of fairly short duration (Aaker & Stayman, 1990). The feelings of warmth also tend to wear off after a while, so airing one warm commercial after another isn't as effective as interspersing warm ads with other kinds of ads (serious ads, humorous ads, etc.). In fact, some of the effectiveness of a warmth appeal is based on a contrast effect involving the material that immediately precedes and follows it (Aaker et al., 1986). Thus, what happens in the last scene of a television show, just before a commercial break, can affect how viewers respond to a warmth appeal during the first part of the break. A cat food commercial featuring a cute kitten, for example, would tend to be more effective if it followed a show like *America's Most Wanted* as opposed to *Touched by an Angel*.

Warmth appeals aren't limited to television advertising. Real estate listings often use words like "charming," "cozy," or "rustic" to describe houses that are for sale. Restaurants boast of "home style" cooking. Frozen foods claim to be based on "authentic family recipes" that are "made the old fashioned way." In interpersonal encounters warmth can be conveyed through actions that generate a sense of friendship, bonding, or camaraderie. The Wal-Mart "greeter" is a living embodiment of a warmth appeal. When a food server introduces himself or herself by name and smiles, the food server is also conveying warmth.

Warmth appeals can be quite effective, but their success depends upon their believability. The warm, fuzzy images being portrayed must come across as sincere for the appeal to work (Aaker and Stayman, 1989). As Aaker & Stayman note, the appeal "need[s] to avoid creating the perception of an ad's being phony, pointless, or contrived; such perceptions could interfere with the emotional response" (1990, p. 59). Warmth appeals, then, are a persuader's friend. They offer a positive approach to using motivational appeals by engendering warm, happy feelings in receivers.

INGRATIATION: "THAT'S A LOVELY DRESS YOU'RE WEARING, MRS. CLEAVER"

You may know it as "brown-nosing," "sucking up," or "boot-licking," but the term researchers use for flattery as a motivational inducement is *ingratiation*. Ingratiation has been thoroughly studied in organizational settings (see Liden & Mitchell, 1988). An overall assessment of the research to date suggests that ingratiation works, and works well (Gordon, 1996). For instance, a study by Watt (1993) found that ingratiators were perceived by their supervisors as being more competent, more motivated, and more qualified for leadership positions than their noningratiating counterparts. Another study (Wayne, Kacmar, & Ferris, 1995) found that the use of ingratiation tactics by subordinates resulted in higher satisfaction for the supervisor and co-workers. In fact, one study recently quantified the advantage enjoyed by ingratiators over non-ingratiators. In a study of 152 pairs of managers and employees, Deluga (cited in Kelleher, 1997) found that ingratiators enjoyed a 5 percent edge over noningratiators in getting favorable evaluations.

But, you might ask, wouldn't the other person *know,* or at least suspect, that the compliments were designed to curry favor? What if the target sees through the strategy? Not surprisingly, a transparent attempt at ingratiation has less chance of succeeding than an apparently genuine attempt. According to Burgoon (1994), ingratiation works best when the ingratiator's ulterior motives remain concealed. Surprisingly, however, ingratiation often works even when the other person is aware of the ingratiator's attempt. What's more, flattery produces almost as much liking for the ingratiator even when the compliments are false (Cialdini, 1993). Tempering these results somewhat, one study did find that when employees were perceived by their superiors as genuinely desiring to be good organizational citizens, they received greater rewards than employees whose behavior was perceived as purely ingratiating (Eastman, 1994). Hence, sincerity, or at least the appearance of sincerity, does count for something.

Researchers know that ingratiation works, but just how does it work? What is the secret behind its success? There are three interrelated explanations for ingratiation's effectiveness (Dubrin, cited in Kelleher, 1997). First, ingratiatory behavior tends to increase *liking* ("I love that outfit on you!"). Second, ingratiatory behavior can create perceptions of *similarity* ("You love polka music? Hey, I do too!"). Third, ingratiation can work through *social labeling.* The use of positive social labels ("You sure are in a good mood today," "You are so thoughtful.") can produce changes in the target's self-concept which, in turn, lead to changes in the target's behavior (Kraut, 1973). The person being ingratiated thus lives up to the positive label bestowed on her or him.

Reprinted with special permission of King Features Syndicate.

How may kinds of ingratiation are there? Edward Jones, who authored the first major work on ingratiation in 1963, identified three basic categories of ingratiation. The first is *other enhancement,* such as paying compliments, or engaging in flattery. A derivative of this technique is to have a third party deliver the compliment, so that it seems more genuine ("Biff speaks highly of you. He says you are the nicest boss he's ever had."). The second technique is *opinion conformity.* This involves agreeing with the target's statements, ideas, and views. A variation on this technique is to initially disagree, then subsequently yield, creating the impression the target has changed your mind ("OK, you've convinced me, there is life on Mars"). A third approach is *self-presentation.* This involves bragging or otherwise displaying one's attributes to increase the target's evaluation of oneself ("Gee, I'd love to play golf with you, but I'm helping at the homeless center this weekend"). So you see, there is more than one way to engage in brownnosing.

You might think of ingratiation as an unethical influence strategy. We tend to agree, but only if the flattery, compliments, or positive social labels used are believed to be untrue by the ingratiator. If the ingratiator *believes* in the praise he or she is offering, we see no ethical problem in focusing on the positive side of things. Indeed, if the praise is genuine, this strategy offers the prospect for a "win–win" communication encounter. We discuss the ethical implications of ingratiatory behavior in more detail in Chapter 16.

MIXED EMOTIONS: OTHER APPEALS AND COMBINATIONS OF APPEALS

There are many other types of motivational appeals that we do not have space to cover here. Some of these include appeals to pride, honor, patriotism, youth, beauty, shame, and freedom. Almost any human drive or emotion can serve as the basis for a motivational appeal.

Motivational appeals also can be used in combination. A threat of punishment can be coupled with a promise of reward, for example. A prosecutor might tell a defendant, "If you cooperate, I'll cut you a deal. If you don't, I'll throw the book at you." The "good cop/bad cop" technique used in police interrogations[3] also combines positive and negative appeals (Cialdini, 1993; Inbau, Reid, & Buckley, 1986; Kassim & McNall, 1991).

Guilt is commonly coupled with pity in charity fund-raisers ("If you don't help, who will?"). In a twist involving "strange bedfellows," the animal rights group known as PETA (People for the Ethical Treatment of Animals) has collaborated with *Penthouse* magazine for the last few years to produce an anti-fur advertisement. The ads feature sexy supermodels who proclaim they would rather go naked than wear fur, thus combining a sex appeal with a guilt appeal.

We see definite advantages in combining appeals. If one appeal proves ineffective, another may still work. And there is always the prospect that combinations of appeals will have an additive effect. That is, the combination of appeals may work better than they would individually. The danger in combining appeals is that they

BOX 14.3   Funeral Home Persuasion

"You can't take it with you...but you don't have to give it all to the mortuary!"

Funerals are expensive. The average price of a funeral nowadays is about $5,000 (Jaffe, 1996). Funerals rank beside weddings, automobiles purchases, home remodeling, and vacations in overall cost. Yet the process of negotiating the price of a funeral comes at the worst possible time: when our thinking is impaired by the loss of a loved one. We also may feel it is crass to engage in hard bargaining over prices (Gentry, Kennedy, Paul, & Paul, 1995). Unfortunately, this is exactly when some unscrupulous funeral home directors try to take advantage of us. They know that a person who is grieving is an easy mark.

Certainly, not all, or even most, mortuaries prey upon those who are grieving, but some clearly do (Wasik, 1995). As just one illustration, one undertaker tried to push silk coffin lining instead of rayon by arguing, "We find rayon is a lot more irritating to the skin" (Mitford, 1979, p. 82). Since when do dead people have sensitive skin? To increase your consumer awareness, and to arm you against the unscrupulous practices employed by some funeral homes, we offer the following list of "Do's" and "Don'ts" when making funeral arrangements. The suggestions apply to a traditional burial. If cremation, burial at sea, or some other option is chosen, not all the suggestions will apply.

1. **Do try to be as rational as possible.** Grieve for the deceased with all your heart, but negotiate the price of the funeral with your head. A funeral home is a for-profit enterprise. You need to be a savvy consumer when negotiating the arrangements and the price.

2. **Don't give in to guilt appeals,** such as "Don't you think _____ deserves genuine brass handles on his/her coffin?" The amount you love someone isn't measured by the amount you spend on that person's funeral. You can always spend more on that person later, when you are

thinking more clearly. For example, you could make a donation in the deceased's name to a worthwhile charity or social cause.

3. **Do conduct price comparisons,** just as you would when buying a car or making any other major purchase. Telephone mortuaries and ask for quotes over the phone. The FTC now requires funeral homes to provide prices by phone. Ask what a complete funeral would cost, including embalming, casket, burial, flowers, etc. If you don't feel up to making the calls, ask a trusted friend.

4. **Do ensure that everything you are promised is itemized** *in writing on a contract.* The FTC now requires mortuaries to provide itemized prices. Don't take the funeral director's word for it if he or she says "leave it to us, we'll take care of everything."

5. **Do shop around for prices on caskets.** Funeral homes mark up casket prices astronomically. You can save thousands of dollars by purchasing a casket factory-direct from a manufacturer and having it delivered to the funeral home (Cavanaugh, 1996; Interfaith Funeral Information Committee, 1996). Federal law prohibits funeral homes from turning away a casket purchased elsewhere or from charging "handling fees" for having a casket delivered to a mortuary.

6. **Don't pay for unnecessary frills.** Rather than paying more for brass handles, silk ruffles, carved wood panels, or other high-priced options, consider personalizing the casket with family photos, mementos, poetry, or artwork (Interfaith Funeral Information Committee, 1996). Decide what is within your budget and have the funeral director accommodate your needs. If the price isn't right, use outside vendors of your own choosing to provide additional services.

BOX 14.3 *Continued*

7. **Don't pay more than you have to for basic services.** Some mortuaries charge thousands of dollars for basic services like transporting the body to a mortuary, church, or cemetery. These services can be obtained for under $1,000 just by calling around ("R.I.P. Off." 1996).

8. **Don't get ripped off by "professional fees."** Some funeral homes charge frivolous fees for such things as "extra visitations" or "grief counseling." These pseudo-services can add to the price of a funeral. Pay only for what you need. If a mortuary lists professional fees as "non-declinable" on their contract, shop elsewhere (Interfaith Funeral Information Committee, 1996).

9. **Don't pay for a costly rubber or neoprene "protective sealer" for the casket.** These can actually do more harm than good. The seals serve as a catalyst for the growth of anaerobic bacteria, the kind that thrive in an airless environment inside the casket. The bacteria actually accelerate the decomposition of the body (Interfaith Funeral Information Committee, 1996).

10. **Don't pre-pay for a plot, casket, or other services without discussing the contract with an attorney or accountant.** Pre-paid plans might seem like a good idea, but most consumer groups advise against them. If you change your mind about where you want to be buried, or how you want to be disposed of, it may be impossible to alter the contract or obtain a refund. You also lose the potential interest your money could earn in a bank account (see below).

11. **Do consider opening a "Totten" trust,** a payable-on-demand account at a bank or savings institution for the cost of a funeral. The trust is revocable, so it can be moved, altered, or closed completely. Put the account in the name of several trusted family members. This way, you preserve liquidity (you may decide to be buried elsewhere, or be disposed of in some other way) and earn interest (Jaffe, 1996).

12. **Do make use of helpful information sources.** You can locate mortuaries in your area through the Funeral and Memorial Societies of America. The Interfaith Funeral Information Committee maintains an excellent website with consumer information on funerals at **www.xroads. com/%7Efunerals/.** The American Association of Retired Persons publishes an excellent report on planning and making funeral arrangements.

may appear contradictory or cancel one another out. Combining humor with pity, for instance, might create the appearance that a persuader was insensitive or disingenuous. In selecting motivational appeals, then, a persuader must be judicious.

Along this same vein, Stiff (1994) cautions against combining rational with emotional appeals. He warns that the heightened emotional arousal that accompanies motivational appeals may impair cognitive processing (e.g., thinking about the information). Box 14.3 on "Funeral Parlor Persuasion" highlights this very problem. People who are grieving are often too upset to negotiate rationally with funeral homes over prices.

SUMMARY

Motivational appeals are external inducements used to increase another's drive to do something. The use of motivational appeals is an omnipresent phenomenon. Attempts to cast logical and emotional appeals as opposites are suspect. Although motivational appeals aren't necessarily rational, neither are they irrational. Seven types of motivational appeals were discussed: fear, pity, guilt, humor, sex, warmth, and ingratiation. These represent only a fraction of the appeals available to persuaders. Experimental studies have shown some of these to be highly effective in facilitating persuasion, while others have been shown to be less effective. It also was suggested that motivational appeals can be successfully combined if certain precautions are followed.

ENDNOTES

1. The subject of what emotions actually are is a rather complicated one. For a discussion of whether emotions are best thought of as physiological responses, cognitive reactions, or some other form of neural activity, see Leventhal (1980).

2. Some of the other measures included the installation of a fence along the median barrier, flyers placed in utility bills, and public service announcements. Drawing a cause–effect inference between the signs and the decline in fatalities is complicated by the fact that U.S. Immigration and Naturalization Service policies also changed during the course of the grant.

3. Using this technique one interrogator plays the role of the "bad cop." The bad cop treats the suspect with disdain, threatens the suspect in various ways, and claims to have the goods on the suspect. A second interrogator, playing the role of the "good cop," comes to the suspect's rescue. The second interrogator befriends the suspect, for example, by offering coffee or a cigarette. The good cop tells the bad cop to back off. The good cop displays empathy for the suspect's situation. The technique can be quite effective. After being subjected to verbal abuse by the bad cop, the suspect is often more willing to talk to the sympathetic good cop.

REFERENCES

Aaker, D. A., & Bruzzone, D. E. (1981). Viewer perceptions of prime-time television advertising. *Journal of Advertising Research, 21*(5), 15–23.

Aaker, D. A., & Stayman, D. M. (1989). What mediates the emotional response to advertising? The case of warmth. In P. Cafferata & A. M. Tybout (Eds.), *Cognitive and affective responses to advertising* (pp. 287–303). Lexington, MA: Lexington Books.

Aaker, D. A., & Stayman, D. M. (1990). A micro approach to studying feeling responses to advertising: The case of warmth. In S. J. Agres,

J. A. Edell, & T. B. Dubitsky (Eds.), *Emotion in advertising: Theoretical and practical explorations* (pp. 53–68). New York: Quorum Books.

Aaker, D. A., Stayman, D. M., & Hagerty, M. R. (1986). Warmth in advertising: Measurement, impact, and sequence effects. *Journal of Consumer Research, 12*(4), 365–381.

Aristotle. (1932). *The Rhetoric*, (L. Cooper, Trans.). Englewood Cliffs, NJ: Prentice-Hall.

Becker, S. L. (1963). Research on emotional and logical proofs. *The Southern Speech Journal, 28*(3), 198–207.

Bennett, R. (1996). Effects of horrific fear appeals on public attitudes toward AIDS. *International Journal of Advertising, 15*, 183–202.

Berger, A. A. (1976). Anatomy of a joke. *Journal of Communication, 26*, 113–115.

Bettinghaus, E. P. (1968). *Persuasive communication.* New York: Holt, Rinehart, & Winston.

Bohner, G., & Schwartz, N. (1993). Mood states influence the production of persuasive arguments. *Communication Research, 20*(5), 696–722.

Boster, F. J., & Mongeau, P. A. (1984). Fear-arousing persuasive messages. In R. N. Bostrum & B. H. Wesley (Eds.), *Communication yearbook 8* (pp. 330–375). Beverly Hills, CA: Sage.

Bryant, J., Comisky, P. W., Crane, J. S., & Zillmann, D. (1980). Relationship between college teachers' use of humor in the classroom and students' evaluations of their teachers. *Journal of Educational Psychology, 72*(4), 511–519.

Bryant, J., & Zillmann, D. (1989). Using humor to promote learning in the classroom. *Journal of Children in Contemporary Society, 20*(1–2), 49–78.

Burgoon, J. K. (1994). Nonverbal signals. In M. Knapp & G. M. Miller (Eds.), *Handbook of interpersonal communication,* 2nd ed. (pp. 229–285). Thousand Oaks, CA: Sage.

Calvin's world (1995, September 11) *Newsweek, 126*(11) 60–66.

Cantor, J. R. (1976). What is funny to whom? *Journal of Communication, 26*, 164–172.

Cantor, J., & Venus, P. (1980). The effect of humor on recall of a radio advertisement. *Journal of Broadcasting, 24*(1), 13–22.

Cavanaugh, T. (1996, September). Bargain pine boxes. *American Demographics, 18*(9), 21–25.

Chang, M., & Gruner, C. R. (1981). Audience reaction to self-disparaging humor. *Southern Speech Communication Journal, 46*, 419–426.

Cialdini, R. (1993). *Influence: Science and practice* (3rd ed.). New York: HarperCollins.

Cupchik, G. C., & Leventhal, H. (1974). Consistency between expressive behavior and the evaluation of humorous stimuli: The role of sex and self-observation. *Journal of Personality and Social Psychology, 30*, 429–442.

Dabbs, J. M., Jr., & Leventhal, H. (1966). Effects of varying the recommendations in a fear-arousing communication. *Journal of Personality and Social Psychology, 4*, 525–531.

DeAngelis, T. (1993, August). Trivializing disabilities gives immunity to fears. *APA Monitor, 24* [Lexis-Nexis].

Deci, E. L. (1975). *Intrinsic motivation.* New York: Plenum.

Deci, E. L., & Ryan, R. (1978). *Intrinsic motivation and self-determination in human behavior.* New York: Plenum Press.

Decker, W. H. (1986). Sex conflict and impressions of managers' aggressive humor. *The Psychological Record, 36*, 483–490.

Deluga, R. J., & Perry, J. T. (1994). The role of subordinate performance and ingratiation in leader–member exchanges. *Group Organization Management, 19*(1), 67–86.

Del Valle, C. (1992, September 14). "Some of Jerry's kids are mad at the old man." *Business Week,* (3283), 36.

Derks, P., Kalland, S., & Etgen, M. (1995). The effect of joke type and audience response on the reaction to a joker: Replication and extension. *Humor, 8*(4), 327–337.

Dillard, J. P. (1994). Rethinking the study of fear appeals: An emotional perspective. *Communication Theory, 4*, 295–323.

Duncan, C. P., & Nelson, J. E. (1985). Effects of humor in a radio advertising experiment. *Journal of Advertising, 14*, 33–39.

Eagle, J. (1979). The bad, the bare, and the beautiful, *Media Scope, 13*, 39.

Eastman, K. K. (1994). In the eyes of the beholder: An attributional approach to ingratiation and organizational citizenship behavior. *Academy of Management Journal, 37*(5), 1379–1391.

Eayres, C. B., & Ellis, N. (1990). Charity advertising: For or against people with a mental handicap? *British Journal of Social Psychology, 29*, 349–360.

Emry, R. A., Gass, R. H., Page, N., Wiseman, R. L., Sachsman, D., Mayes, B. T., Mousouris, N., & Watson, G. (1991). *Study of pedestrian crossings by undocumented aliens of interstates 5 and 805 in San Diego County near the international border* (No. F90TE11). Washington, DC: Federal Highway Administration.

Ervin, M. (1995, June). The ragged edge [review of *The ragged edge*]. *The Progressive*, 39.

Ford, J. B., & LaTour, M. S. (1993). Differing reactions to female role portrayals in advertising. *Journal of Advertising Research, 33,* 43–52.

Garner, D. M. (1997, January/February). The *Psychology Today* 1977 body image survey results. *Psychology Today, 30*–44, 75–76, 78, 84.

Gass, R. H. (1983). *Threat of punishment versus promise of reward: A comparison of the relative effectiveness of two types of verbal appeals.* Unpublished doctoral dissertation, University of Kansas, Lawrence, Kansas.

Gentry, J. W., Kennedy, P. K., Paul, K., & Paul, K. (1995). The vulnerability of those grieving the death of a loved one: Implications for public policy. *Journal of Public Policy and Marketing, 14*(1), 128–142.

Gleicher, F., & Petty, R. E. (1992). Expectations of reassurance influence the nature of fear-stimulated attitude change. *Journal of Experimental Social Psychology, 28,* 86–100.

Goldman, R., & Papson, S. (1996). *Sign wars: The cluttered landscape of advertising.* New York: Guilford Press.

Goldstein, J., & McGhee, P. (Eds.). *The psychology of humor.* New York: Academic Press.

Gordon, R. A. (1996). Impact of ingratiation on judgments and evaluations: A meta-analytic investigation. *Journal of Personality and Social Psychology, 71*(1), 54–70.

Graham, E. E., Papa, M. J., & Brooks, G. P. (1992). Functions of humor in conversation: Conceptualization and measurement. *Western Journal of Communication, 56,* 161–183.

Grazer, W. F., & Keesling, G. (1995). The effect of print advertising's use of sexual themes on brand recall and purchase intention: A product specific investigation of male responses. *Journal of Applied Business Research, 11*(3), 47–57.

Gruner, C. R. (1967). Effect of humor on speaker ethos and audience information gain. *Journal of Communication, 17*(3), 228–233.

Gruner, C. R. (1970). The effect of humor in dull and interesting informative speeches. *Central States Speech Journal, 21*(3), 160–166.

Gruner, C. R. (1985). Advice to the beginning speaker on using humor—What the research tells us. *Communication Education, 34,* 142–147.

Gruner, C. R., & Lampton, W. E. (1972). Effects of including humorous material in a persuasive

sermon. *Southern Speech Communication Journal, 38,* 188–196.

Hackman, M. Z. (1988). Reactions to the use of self-disparaging humor by informative public speakers. *The Southern Speech Communication Journal, 53,* 175–183.

Harris, V. A., & Jellison, J. M. (1971). Fear-arousing communications, false physiological feedback, and the acceptance of recommendations. *Journal of Experimental Social Psychology, 7,* 269–279.

Hassett, J., & Houlihan, J. (1979, January). Different jokes for different folks. *Psychology Today, 12*(8), 64–71.

Higbee, K. L. (1969). Fifteen years of fear-arousal: Research on threat appeals. *Psychological Bulletin, 72,* 426–444.

Inbau, F. E., Reid, J. E., & Buckley, J. P. (1986). *Criminal interrogations and confessions,* 3rd ed. Baltimore: Williams & Wilkins.

Interfaith Funeral Information Committee (1998). *Funerals and ripoffs.* Available: www.xroads.com/~funerals

Jaffe, C. A. (1996, October 16). "Shopping for your funeral makes financial sense." *Los Angeles Times,* pp. D3, D9.

Janis, I. L., & Feshbach, S. (1953). Effects of fear-arousing communications. *Journal of Abnormal and Social Psychology, 48,* 78–92.

Jones, E. (1963). *Ingratiation.* New York: Appleton-Century-Crofts.

Judd, B. B., & Alexander, M. W. (1983). On the reduced effectiveness of some sexually suggestive ads. *Journal of the Academy of Marketing Science, 11,* 156–168.

Kaplan, R. M., & Pascoe, G. C. (1977). Humorous lectures and humorous examples: Some effects upon comprehension and retention. *Journal of Educational Psychology, 69*(1), 61–65.

Katz, D. (1960). The functional approach to the study of attitudes. *Public Opinion Quarterly, 24,* 163–204.

Kassim, S. M., & McNall, K. (1991). Police interrogations and confessions. *Law and Human Behavior, 15,* 233–251.

Kelleher, K. (1997, February 24). "Flattery will get you…everywhere." *Los Angeles Times,* pp. E1-E2.

Kerin, R., Lundstrom, W. J., & Sciglimpaglia, D. (1979). Women in advertisements: retrospect and prospect. *Journal of Advertising, 8,* 37–42.

Kornzweig, N. D. (1968). *Behavior change as a function of fear-arousal and personality.* Unpublished doctoral dissertation, Yale University.

Kraut, R. E. (1973). The effects of social labeling on giving to charity, *Journal of Experimental Social Psychology, 9,* 551–562.

Lammers, H. B., Leibowitz, L., Seymour, G. E., & Hennesy, J. E. (1983). Humor and cognitive responses to advertising stimuli: A trace consolidation approach. *Journal of Business Research, 11,* 173–185.

Langer, E., Blank, A., Chanowitz, B. (1978). The mindlessness of ostensibly thoughtful action: The role of "placebic" information in interpersonal interaction. *Journal of Personality and Social Psychology, 36*(6), 635–642.

LaTour, M. S. (1990). Female nudity in print advertising: An analysis of gender differences in arousal and ad response. *Psychology and Marketing, 7,* 65–81.

LaTour, M. S., & Henthorne, T. L. (1993). Female nudity: Attitudes toward the ad and the brand and implications for advertising strategy. *Journal of Consumer Marketing, 10*(3), 25–32.

LaTour, M. S., & Henthorne, T. L. (1994). Ethical judgments of sexual appeals in print advertising. *Journal of Advertising, 23*(3), 81–90.

Lefford, A. (1946). The influence of emotional subject matter on logical reasoning. *Journal of General Psychology, 34,* 127–151.

Leventhal, H. (1970). Findings and theory in the study of fear communications. In L. Berkowitz (Ed.), *Advances in experimental psychology,* (Vol. 5, pp. 119–186). New York: Academic Press.

Leventhal, H. (1980). Toward a comprehensive theory of emotion. In L. Berkowitz (Ed.), *Advances in experimental social psychology* (Vol. 13, pp. 140–207). New York: Academic Press.

Leventhal, H., & Cupchik, G. C. (1975). The informational and facilitative effects of an audience upon expression and evaluation of humorous stimuli. *Journal of Experimental Social Psychology, 11,* 363–380.

Leventhal, H., & Cupchik, G. C. (1976). A process model of humor judgment. *Journal of Communication, 26,* 190–204.

Leventhal, H., Jones, S., & Trembly, G. (1966). Sex differences in attitude and behavior change under conditions of fear and specific instruc-

tions. *Journal of Experimental Social Psychology, 2,* 387–389.

Leventhal, H., & Niles, P. (1964). A field experiment on fear arousal with data on the validity of questionnaire measures. *Journal of Personality, 32,* 459–479.

Leventhal, H., & Singer, R. P. (1966). Affect arousal and positioning of recommendations in persuasive communications. *Journal of Personality and Social Psychology, 4,* 137–146.

Leventhal, H., Singer, R. P., & Jones, S. (1965). Effects of fear and specificity of recommendations upon attitudes and behavior. *Journal of Personality and Social Psychology, 2,* 20–29.

Leventhal, H., & Trembly, G. (1968). Negative emotions and persuasion. *Journal of Personality, 36,* 154–168.

Liden, R., & Mitchell, T. (1988). Ingratiatory behaviors in organizational settings. *Academy of Management Review, 13,* 572–587.

Lippman, J. (1991, September 30). Sexy or sexist? Recent ads spark debate. *The Wall Street Journal, 218,* pp. B1.

Madden, T. J., & Weinberger, M. G. (1984). Humor in advertising: A practitioner view. *Journal of Advertising Research, 24*(4), 23–29.

McGhee, P. E., & Duffy, N. (1983). The role of identity of the victim in the development of disparagement humor. *Journal of General Psychology, 108,* 257–270.

Miller, C. (1992a, March 16). No sex please, we're censors. *Marketing News, 26,* 1, 17.

Miller, C. (1992b, November 23). Publisher says sexy ads are O. K., but sexist ones will sink sales. *Marketing News, 26,* 8–9.

Mitford, J. (1980). Americans don't want fancy funerals. In J. Mitford (Ed.), *Poison Penmanship: The gentle art of muckraking* (pp. 79–88). New York: Vintage Books.

Mongeau, P. (1994). Another look at fear-arousing appeals. In M. Allen & R. Preiss (Eds.), *Prospects and precautions in the use of meta-analysis* (pp. 75–100). Dubuque, IA: William C. Brown.

Moore, T. E., Griffiths, K., & Payne, B. (1987). Gender, attitudes towards women, and the appreciation of sexist humor. *Sex Roles, 16*(9–10), 521–531.

Morgan, N. (1989, August). San Diego: Where two California's meet. *National Geographic, 176*(2), 176–205.

Mortensen, C. D. (1972). *Communication: The study of human interaction.* New York: McGraw-Hill.

Munn, W. C., & Gruner, C. R. (1981). "Sick" jokes, speaker sex, and informative speech. *Southern Speech Communication Journal, 46,* 411–418.

Murnstein, B. L. & Burst, R. G. (1985). Humor and interpersonal attraction. *Journal of Personality Assessment, 49,* 637–640.

Neimark, J. (1994, November). The beefcaking of America: Sexual objectification of men by women. *Psychology Today, 27*(6), 32–39, 70–72.

O'Quin, K., & Aranoff, J. (1981). Humor as a technique of social influence. *Social Psychology Quarterly, 44*(4), 349–357.

Perloff, R. M. (1993). *The dynamics of persuasion.* Hillsdale, NJ: Lawrence Erlbaum.

Petri, H. (1991). *Motivation: Theory, research, and application* (3rd ed.). Belmont, CA: Wadsworth.

Petty, R. E., & Cacioppo, J. T. (1986). *Communication and persuasion: Central and peripheral routes to attitude change.* New York: Springer-Verlag.

Ramirez, A., & Lasater, T. L. (1977). Ethnicity of communicator, self-esteem, and reactions to fear-arousing communications. *The Journal of Social Psychology, 102,* 79–91.

Reuchelle, R. C. (1958). An experimental study of audience recognition of logical and intellectual appeals in persuasion. *Speech Monographs, 25*(1), 49–58.

"R. I. P. Off." Television feature that aired on ABC's "20/20" program, August 30, 1996.

Rodriguez, J. I. (1995). *Confounds in fear arousing persuasive messages: Do the paths less traveled make all the difference?* Unpublished doctoral dissertation, Michigan State University, East Lansing, MI.

Roselli, F., Skelly, J. J., & Mackie, D. M. (1995). Processing of rational and emotional messages: The cognitive and affective mediation of persuasion. *Journal of Experimental and Social Psychology, 31,* 163–190.

Rosen, T. J. (1973). *The role of fear and danger in persuasion following a fear communication.* Unpublished doctoral dissertation, Northwestern University.

Rosen, T. J., Terry, N. S., & Leventhal, H. (1982). The role of esteem and coping in response to a threat communication. *Journal of Research in Personality, 16,* 90–107.

Sereno, K., Seiter, J. S., Robinson, J., & McDonald, V. (1996, November). When you hate yourself for laughing: An examination of receivers' gender and perceptions of offensive humor. Paper presented at the annual meeting of the Speech Communication Association, San Antonio, TX.

Sigelman, C. K., Miller, A. B., & Derenowski, E. B. (1993). Do you believe in Magic? The impact of Magic Johnson on adolescents' AIDS knowledge and attitudes. *AIDS Education and Prevention, 5*(2), 153–161.

Skilbeck, C., Tulips, J., & Ley, J. (1977). The effects of fear arousal, fear position, fear exposure, and sidedness on compliance with dietary instructions. *European Journal of Social Psychology, 7,* 221–239.

Smith, M. J. (1977). The effects of threat to attitudinal freedom as a function of message quality and initial receiver attitude. *Communication Monographs, 44,* 196–206.

Speck, P. S. (1987). On humor and humor in advertising. Unpublished doctoral dissertation, Texas Tech University, Lubbock, TX.

Steadman, M. (1969). How sexy illustrations affect brand recall. *Journal of Advertising Research, 9,* 15–19.

Sternthal, B., & Craig, S. (1973). Humor in advertising. *Journal of Marketing, 37*(4), 12–18.

Sutton, S. R. (1982). Fear-arousing communication: A critical examination of theory and research. In J. R. Eisner (Ed.), *Social psychology and behavioral medicine* (pp. 303–337). London, England: John Wiley & Sons.

Stiff, J. B. (1994). *Persuasive communication.* New York: Guilford Press.

Tamborini, R., & Zillmann, D. (1981). College students' perceptions of lectures using humor. *Perceptual and Motor Skills, 52,* 427–432.

Taylor, P. M. (1974). An experimental study of humor and ethos. *Southern Speech Communication Journal, 39,* 359–366.

Venkatesan, M., & Losco, J. (1975). Women in magazine advertisements. *Journal of Advertising Research, 15,* 49–54.

Wanzer, M. B., Booth-Butterfield, M., & Booth-Butterfield, S. (1996). Humor and social attraction: Are funny people popular? An examination of humor orientation, loneliness, and social attraction. *Communication Quarterly, 44*(1), 42–52.

Wasik, J. F. (1995, September/October). "Fraud in the funeral industry." *Consumer's Digest, 34,* pp. 53–59.

Watt, J. D. (1993). The impact of frequency of ingratiation on the performance evaluation of bank personnel. *Journal of Psychology, 127*(2), 171–177.

Wayne, S. J., Kacmar, K., & Ferris, G. R. (1995). Co-workers response to others' ingratiation attempts. *Journal of Managerial Issues, 7*(3), 277–289.

Weiner, B., Perry, R. P., & Magnusson, J. (1988). An attributional analysis of reactions to stigmas. *Journal of Personality and Social Psychology, 55,* 738–748.

Weinberger, M. G., & Campbell, L. (1991). The use and impact of humor in radio advertising. *Journal of Advertising Research, 31,* 44–52.

Weinberger, M. G., & Gulas, C. S. (1992). The impact of humor in advertising: A review. *Journal of Advertising, 21*(4), 35–59.

Weinberger, M. G., & Spotts, H. E. (1989). Humor in U.S. versus U. K. TV and advertising. *Journal of Advertising, 18*(2), 39–44.

Weinberger, M. G., Spotts, H., Campbell, L., & Parsons, A. L. (1995). The use and effect of humor in different advertising media. *Journal of Advertising Research, 35*(3), 44–56.

Wheatley, J., & Oshikawa, S. (1970). The relationship between anxiety and positive and negative advertising. *Journal of Marketing Research, 7,* 85–89.

Wilson, D. W., & Molleston, J. L. (1981). Effects of sex and type of humor on humor appreciation. *Journal of Personality Assessment, 45,* 90–96.

Witte, K. (1992). Putting the fear back into fear appeals: The extended parallel process model. *Communication Monographs, 59,* 329–349.

Witte, K. (1994). Fear control and danger control: A test of the extended parallel process model. *Communication Monographs, 61*(2), 113–134.

Witte, K. (1995). Using scare tactics to promote safe sex among juvenile detention and high school youth. *Journal of Applied Communication Research, 23*(2), 128–142.

Witte, K., & Allen, M. (1996, November). When do scare tactics work? A meta-analysis of fear appeals. Paper presented at the annual meeting of the Speech Communication Association, San Diego, CA.

15

ESOTERIC FORMS OF PERSUASION

Previous chapters have dealt with fairly "mainstream" types of persuasion, the kinds of topics and variables covered in most persuasion texts. In this chapter we examine some of the more esoteric forms of persuasion. The topics we discuss in this section often receive short-shrift or are neglected entirely by other texts. Yet we find these are among the most interesting topics to students and laypersons. We include them here partly because they are so intriguing, partly because there are important research findings on these topics, and partly to debunk some of the myths and superstitions surrounding these topics. The topics we'll examine are subliminal persuasion, music as persuasion, and the role of smell in persuasion.

SUBLIMINAL PERSUASION: HIDDEN MESSAGES OR HOKUM?

A good deal of misinformation surrounds the topic of subliminal persuasion. Most Americans, 75 to 80 percent, according to some accounts, believe subliminal messages are not only omnipresent in advertising, but that they work (Rogers & Seiler, 1994; Zanot, Pincus, & Lamp, 1983). The advertising industry has repeatedly disavowed using subliminal stimuli (Rogers & Seiler, 1994), yet people continue to believe that the practice is widespread.

Public belief in subliminal persuasion dates back to a report by James Vicary, the "grandaddy" of subliminal advertising, in 1957. Vicary claimed to have used subliminal stimuli to increase popcorn and Coca Cola sales at a movie theater in Ft. Lee, New Jersey. He maintained that by flashing the words "Eat Popcorn" and "Drink Coca-Cola" for $1/2000$th of a second, every 5 seconds during a movie, he was able to boost popcorn sales by 57.5 percent and Coke sales by 18.1 percent (Rogers, 1992–93).

Vicary's study was subsequently faulted for failing to control for a variety of confounding variables (McConnell, Cutler, & McNeil, 1957; Moore, 1982). Most

You are very smart! You love this book! You are very smart! You love this book! You are very smart! You love this book! You are very smart! You love this book! You are very smart! You love this book!

notably, there was no control group (a group that wasn't exposed to the subliminal message), and the movie shown, *Picnic,* was about food. Attempts to replicate his findings proved unsuccessful (Beatty & Hawkins, 1989; Hawkins, 1970). Nevertheless, public belief in the technique was born.

In the 1970s and 1980s Wilson Brian Key renewed public interest in subliminal persuasion with his popular but unscientific books on subliminal advertising (Key, 1972, 1976, 1980, 1989). Key claims to have found phallic symbols in ads for Tanqueray (gin) and Chivas Regal (scotch), vulgar words in Ritz crackers, and female genitalia in, of all things, an ad for Betty Crocker cake mix. We've scrutinized the ads ourselves and while, in some cases, we can discern the symbols and shapes Key alludes to, we find his approach somewhat akin to staring at clouds. If one looks long enough and hard enough, one is bound to see something.

More recently, the Walt Disney Company has come under fire for using subliminals in some of its movies. Rumors circulated that the movies *Aladdin, Little Mermaid,* and the *Lion King* contained subliminal images and phrases, but most of these accounts were dismissed as urban myths (Emery, 1996). The Disney Company did acknowledge that the movie *Who Framed Roger Rabbit* contained some X-rated images embedded in-between frames. This was not by corporate design, however, but the result of a prank by a few employees (Harmon, 1995). We've also verified the rumor that the original cover of *The Little Mermaid* video contained a hidden phallic symbol. Next time you're at the video store, look carefully at the spires on the castle in the background and see for yourself. Again, we're convinced this is the work of a mischievous artist, not a corporate conspiracy. Such incidents, while rare, tend to reinforce the public's perception that subliminal messages abound in advertising.

What Makes a Message Subliminal?

There is more than a little confusion about what constitutes a subliminal message. The word "subliminal" literally means below (sub) the threshold (limen) of human consciousness. Thus, a subliminal message is one that is processed without conscious awareness. This is in contrast to "supraliminal" messages that are consciously recognized and processed. A sound that is reproduced so faintly or quickly that the human ear can't consciously detect it is subliminal. A sound that is played quietly, but which is nevertheless audible, is supraliminal. Advertisers frequently "plant" products in movies and television shows (Junior Mints on the *Seinfeld* show, Ford Explorers in *Jurassic Park*). Although the popular press sometimes refers to this practice as "subliminal persuasion," it is not. Product planting involves supraliminal processing because the advertisers *want* viewers to notice their products.

A problem with interpreting subliminal studies is that different researchers have employed different definitions of subliminal processing. Some researchers have set the threshold for subliminality as the point at which observers can no

Kit & Caboodle

The difference between "subliminal" and "supraliminal" messages.

longer detect the presence of a stimulus. Others have set the threshold as the point at which observers correctly guess what they hear or see half of the time (Cheesman & Merikle, 1985; Weiner & Shiller, 1960). These differences frustrate efforts to compare the results of subliminal studies.

Do you think of yourself as being smart? Do you like this book? We hope so. In fact, we included a subliminal message on the previous page to make you think so. Did you see it? Did you suddenly feel smarter or like the book more? (We doubt it.) The subliminal message consists of tiny type at the top of the last page.

Types of Subliminals

Researchers have studied a variety of forms of subliminal processing. Three of the major types include embedded images, sub-audible messages, and electronically altered signals. *Embedded images* consist of pictures or words that are shown fleetingly for only a few hundredths or thousandths of a second. The images may be displayed only once, or repeated at regular intervals. *Sub-audible messages* are those that are so faint that they can't be heard or, in some cases, are played at such high frequencies that the human ear cannot detect them. *Electronically altered signals* include backward-masked messages (messages played in reverse) and voice alteration. We examine each of these three types in turn.

Embedded Images: Now You See 'Em, Now You Don't

Vicary's "popcorn" study supposedly used embedded images to increase purchases. However, the consensus of the literature is that embedding has no effect on consumer behavior. In one of the earliest controlled studies, Champion and Turner (1959) exposed participants to a film containing a subliminal message for Wonder Rice. But the group that "saw" the subliminal image fared no better than a control group that was not exposed to the image when asked to identify a bowl of rice by its brand name. At roughly the same time, Byrne (1959) exposed participants to a subliminal message to eat beef. When the participants were later given an opportunity to choose a sandwich from among several types, those exposed to the subliminal message were no more likely to select beef than those in the control group. Other food studies using subliminal stimuli have obtained essentially the same results (for example, Theus, 1994).

Turning from food to sex, Vokay and Read (1985) found that ads with the word "sex" embedded in them were no more effective than ads containing nonsense syllables or ads with no embedding whatsoever. Follow-up tests conducted 2 days later showed the same negative results. Likewise, Gable, Wilkens, and Harris (1987) studied the effects of sexual stimuli embedded in advertisements. Identical pairs of photographs were shown to observers, except that one of each pair contained an embedded sexual image. No differences in preferences for the products featured in the photos were found. Contrary to what many consumers believe, then, embedded images appear to be ineffective at influencing brand preferences or sexual appetites. As one advertising executive put it, "How can showing someone a penis get him or her to switch from, say, Kent (cigarettes) to Marlboro?" (Kanner, cited in Rogers & Seiler, 1994, p. 37).

Smith and Rogers (1994) found supraliminal messages to be far more effective than subliminal messages when the words "choose this" were embedded in a television commercial. They did find a small, almost negligible effect for subliminals, but they found a much stronger effect for supraliminal messages. As they stated in their conclusions, "The largest possible effect of subliminal messages is much smaller than the effect of supraliminal messages" (p. 872). This makes practical sense, we believe. If subliminal messages were highly effective, why would advertisers bother to spend hundreds of thousands of dollars for 1-minute spots on prime-time TV? The trick in advertising is to gain receivers' attention. Advertisers go to great lengths to get their products noticed. If hiding products were a more effective strategy, advertisers would save themselves the trouble and expense of designing catchy ads.

Sub-Audible Messages: The Power of Suggestion

How would you like to lower your blood pressure, improve your memory, lose weight, reduce your stress level, prevent migraine headaches, release your body's natural healing forces, gain confidence, stop procrastinating, and win the lottery? These are just *some* of the claims that have been made on behalf of subliminal self-help audiotapes. There is a booming market in subliminal self-help tapes. More than 400 titles are currently available (Spangenberg, Obermiller, & Greenwald, 1992). Though precise figures are unavailable, it has been estimated that some 5 million subliminal audiotapes are sold annually (Oldenburg, 1990) representing

$50 million to $1 billion in sales (Spangenberg et al., 1992). When that many people pay that much money one would expect the tapes to work.

The fact is, however, they do not. Every controlled study to date has reached the same conclusion: There is no evidence that subliminal self-improvement tapes work any magic, apart from the *belief* that they work. Believing can, in and of itself, produce changes in people, but these changes are the result of a *placebo effect* and have nothing to do with the content of the tapes themselves. A placebo effect follows the age-old notion that "thinking makes it so." When a person believes something will work, he or she convinces him or herself that it has worked. The placebo effect is well-documented in the medical literature (see, for example, White, Tursky, & Schwartz, 1985).

By way of illustration, in one well-known study (Greenwald, Spangenberg, Pratkanis, and Eskenazi, 1991) volunteers were given one of two types of self-help tapes; one that claimed to improve memory or one that claimed to improve self-esteem. Unbeknownst to the volunteers, however, the researchers switched the labels on half of the tapes. Thus, half the volunteers who thought they had received a tape with an "improve your esteem" label actually got a tape designed to improve their memory, and vice versa. The volunteers took the tapes home and listened to them for a period of time. Some time later, the volunteers completed a survey asking them about their experiences. A strong placebo effect was found for whichever type of tape the volunteers thought they'd been given. Those with the tapes labeled for improving memory reported memory improvements, even those who received the mislabeled tapes. Those with the tapes labeled for improving self-esteem reported that they felt better about themselves, even those with the mislabeled tapes. Other tests of subliminal tapes have produced essentially the same results (Benoit & Thomas, 1992; Greenwald et al., 1991; Mitchell, 1995; Spangenberg et al., 1992; Staum & Brotons, 1992).

These results point strongly to the conclusion that subliminal audiotapes fail to confer any of the benefits claimed by their manufacturers. Rather, the results demonstrate the powerful effects of psychological expectancies. If they work at all, it is through "slight of mind."

Is it worth paying $19.95 to fool yourself? Don't answer yet. It gets worse. One study found there weren't even any subliminal messages on some tapes! That's right. A sophisticated acoustic analysis of a sampling of subliminal audiotapes by Merikle (1988) found no evidence of speech insertions in any of the tapes studied. Acoustic engineers found various nature sounds (crickets, birds, surf, etc.) but no actual self-improvement messages. This, of course, only strengthens the argument that any observed changes are due to a placebo effect.

The FDA has begun clamping down on some of the more extravagant claims, especially medical claims, made by subliminal cassette manufacturers (Oldenburg, 1990). The tape manufacturers are crafty, though. Rather than claiming, "You'll lose weight," they say, "See yourself at your ideal weight." They also rely heavily on testimonials from satisfied customers, rather than scientific studies to support their claims. Of course, such testimonials only verify the operation of the placebo effect.

Backward Masking and Electronic Alterations:
The Devil Made Me Do It

Sparks, Nevada, played host to an unprecedented product liability suit in 1990. The plaintiffs, the parents of two teenage boys, contended that subliminal lyrics contained in the song "Beyond the Realms of Death" by Judas Priest prompted their sons to commit suicide. The two teens, Raymond Belknap and James Vance, had spent the afternoon in Raymond's bedroom, drinking, getting high, and listening to Judas Priest's album "Stained Class." Later that afternoon they took a sawed-off, 12-gauge shot gun, headed for a nearby playground, and blew their brains out. Raymond died instantly. James died 3 years later from his self-inflicted wounds.

After hearing the case, the court decided for the defendants. The judge's final summary acknowledged that there were backward-masked lyrics in the album (the words "do it" had been inserted in reverse). However, the judge cited alternative causes as more likely explanations for the teens' suicide pact (Goleman, 1990; Phillips, 1990). Ozzie Ozbourne was involved in a similar suit in which the judge also ruled the evidence of subliminal suggestion was insufficient (Harmon, 1995).

The authors have listened to both albums in question and have experienced no suicidal tendencies. The repeated playing of Barry Manilow music, however, is another story! All kidding aside, many parents have serious concerns about backward-masked messages in rock and rap music and wonder if their kids are at risk.

The results of laboratory studies suggest parents have little to fear. Vokay and Read (1985), for instance, asked undergraduates to listen to backward-masked recordings while performing a variety of tasks. They found that the student's couldn't make out any of the words. They also observed no effects on the students' behavior. In fact, the only thing they did find was that the students could guess the sex of a voice played backwards. These results, which are consistent with other studies on backward-masking (Swart & Morgan, 1992), suggest that parents would be better off worrying about the influence of audible lyrics in music as opposed to backward-masked lyrics.

Flaws in Subliminal Research

We believe much of the information published in the popular press about subliminal persuasion can be dismissed as "junk science." Popular reports of subliminal effects typically haven't used control groups, thereby leaving open the possibility of placebo effects. None to our knowledge have employed a *double-blind procedure*, in which neither the experimenter nor the participants know which tape is which. Nor have they been published in reputable scholarly journals, where they would have been subjected to rigorous review. The few studies that have reported positive results haven't been successfully replicated. These sorts of limitations led Moore (cited in Gentry, 1990) to conclude, "any study that purports to have shown an influence on motivation or attitudes has got methodological flaws you could drive a truck through" (p. 1A).

Implicit Perception: Knowing Without Knowing It

Thus far, we've argued that subliminal messages are generally ineffective as a means of persuading people. From a marketing standpoint, they have little or no value. We would be remiss, however, if we failed to acknowledge the existence of a significant body of research showing that people can and do process information without realizing it. This area of research is called *implicit perception* or *perception without awareness* (Bornstein & Pittman, 1992). Researchers working in this area have found that messages that may or may not be subliminal are often processed outside the individual's awareness.[2] Insofar as persuasion is concerned, however, such implicit perception doesn't necessarily lead to changes in beliefs, attitudes, intentions, motivation, or behavior—the kinds of results persuaders are after. Thus far, the most noteworthy effects involving implicit perception center around affective or emotional responses to message stimuli.

In one of the earliest studies, Silverman (1976) presented the message "destroy mother" to a group of depressed individuals using a tachistoscope.[3] He found the message heightened their feelings of depression. Following this line, Schurtman, Palmatier, and Martin (1982) exposed an experimental group of alcoholics to the subliminal message "Mommy and I are one" and a control group to the message "People are walking." In comparison to the control group, the experimental group reported lower anxiety and depression, enhanced self-concept, and lower alcohol consumption after a 3-month follow-up. Not bad for a four-word sentence! Using normal subjects, Talbot, Duberstein, and Scott (1991) studied the effects of the message "Mommy is leaving me" compared to a neutral message, "Mona is loaning it." The group exposed to the first message reported less confidence in their interpersonal attractiveness.

These studies, and others like them, suggest that the emotional content of some messages can be processed without the individual's awareness. The messages can provoke feelings of anxiety or a sense of relief in message recipients without them realizing it. Weinberger and Hardaway (1990) conducted a meta-analysis of 72 studies using phrases like "Mommy and I are one" and found there were, indeed, significant effects. Some studies have even measured behavioral outcomes produced by the messages. For instance, Patton (1992) exposed normal college females and college females prone to bulimia to one of three subliminal messages; "Mama is leaving me," "Mona is loaning it," and "Mama is loaning it." Afterward, the participants were taken to another room where they were invited to participate in a taste-test involving crackers. The bulimia-prone females who were exposed to the maternal separation message ate twice as many crackers as the females in the other two groups. The anxiety-arousing nature of the message thus influenced their eating behavior. Other studies have produced similar results using images, rather than text (Niedenthal, 1990; Robles, Smith, Carver, & Wellens; 1987).

Thus receivers can process both words and images without realizing they are doing so. Implicit perception or perception without awareness is thus a very real phenomenon. Perhaps one day advertisers or other persuaders will figure out how to make use of this phenomenon in order to turn a profit. That day seems a long way off, however. The effects are difficult enough to create in a laboratory setting and require careful planning and execution (Masling, 1992). Many of the studies conducted have produced negative results, mixed results, or have found that supraliminal messages elicit greater affective responses than subliminal messages. The results also are temporary or transitory. Suffice to say that, at present, consumers have little to fear in the way of their emotions being manipulated via implicit perceptual processes.

I Want to Believe

Despite the disappointing research findings, ordinary people remain fascinated by the prospect of subliminal persuasion. Why the persistent belief, given that the preponderance of the scientific evidence is to the contrary? Perhaps it is because people find conspiracy theories attractive. There may be a certain appeal to the idea that Madison Avenue is secretly manipulating consumers. We don't mean to imply that all conspiracy theories are untrue. In the case of subliminals, however, the mere fact that some people believe they work, no more proves they do work, than a belief that Elvis Presley is alive proves he is alive.

In addition, convincing people that subliminals don't work is confounded by the impossibility of proving a "negative." How can one prove there aren't a lot of subliminals out there? A good subliminal, after all, can't be spotted. It only takes a few reported incidents of subliminals, like the Disney examples mentioned earlier, to reinforce the public's belief that subliminal persuasion is rampant. The best we can offer is that surveys of advertisers (Rogers & Seiler, 1994) indicate they do not use subliminals, even when asked about the practice in roundabout ways (e.g., "Do you know of *other* advertisers who use subliminal messages?"). At present there is no evidence to suggest that subliminal messages are being used on a grand scale and, given that the research to date demonstrates their general ineffectiveness, we don't see why advertisers would want to rely on them.

What Advertisers Really Do

Advertisers are not really interested in subliminals. As we noted in Chapter 4, what advertisers seek to do is to associate their products with positive images and idealized lifestyles. The pairing of products with positive images and lifestyles (equating beer with good times, associating cars with power and prestige) occurs at a low level of awareness, but is in no sense subliminal. Advertisers operate in the supraliminal world. They want you to see and hear their messages. The associations may be subtle at times because advertisers often want their messages to be processed in a peripheral manner (e.g., indirectly, as opposed to directly). Why? Because when receivers directly process messages (think about them or reflect upon them) they tend to ask more questions and scrutinize the messages more carefully. In sum, we believe consumers have little to fear from subliminal advertising.

BOX 15.1   Is There a Subliminal in Your Future?

Some department stores use subliminal messages (e.g., "stealing is wrong") to deter shoplifters (Harmon, 1995). We've seen no proof, however, that these techniques work. If there is a subliminal in your future, it just might be on your computer. In 1995 Time Warner released the first computer game to include subliminals. The game, Endorfin, contains 100 sub-audible messages in the background music. The *positive affirmations*, as they are termed, include phrases like "I am at peace," and "I am in harmony." All the messages are clearly identified in the packaging, so no attempt is being made to dupe unwary consumers.

Screen-savers also may become a haven for subliminal messages. Subliminal screen-savers are already being marketed (Harmon, 1995; Hoye, 1996). Subliminal messages also could be transmitted over the Internet, since they could be easily hidden in computer code. Subliminal messages could be inadvertently downloaded in the same way as computer viruses.

Before you panic, however, remember that there is no proof subliminal messages work. The fact that companies sell subliminal screen-savers only proves there is a profit to be made from those who *think* they work. Should computerized subliminals become a problem we are confident that the profit motive will spur software manufacturers to develop programs to detect and delete them.

MUSIC AS A FORM OF PERSUASION

Have you ever heard an advertising jingle and then been unable to get the tune out of your head the rest of the day? If you like the tune, all is well and good, but if you hate the tune it can be maddening. This illustrates the power of music as a means of facilitating product recall. Music is an important ingredient in persuasion. Almost half of radio and television commercials and more than two-thirds of prime-time commercials include music (Yalch, 1991). Music facilitates persuasion in a variety of ways: the music or lyrics can impart product information, conjure up favorable images and associations, reinforce advertising themes, help put listeners in a positive frame of mind, and regulate the pace of consumer shopping. Music can also serve as a mnemonic device, or memory aid. We now look at these and other ways in which music can assist persuasion.

Music as a Central and Peripheral Cue

Song lyrics persuade. The lyrics to the Virginia Slims song, "You've come a long way baby..." provide a case in point, as do the lyrics to the famous McDonald's song "You deserve a break today...." When song lyrics persuade, they do so through what Petty and Cacioppo (1986a, 1986b) call the central route to persuasion. That is, the song lyrics are cognitively processed (thought about, reflected upon) by listeners. This tends to be the case when the music is in the foreground, as opposed to the background, of a commercial. However, the processing of song lyrics may involve substantially less cognitive activity than the processing of words without music. This is because the music may make listeners feel more relaxed and, therefore, more likely to lower their guard to the possibility of being persuaded.

Music can also persuade via the peripheral route to persuasion. Peripheral ✓ processing occurs when listeners hear, but don't actively attend to, the music. Such is the case with background music. You may, for example, prefer to study with the radio on or a CD playing. Background music functions as an affective component that influences a person's mood or emotions, absent the person's cognitive involvement.

Music in Advertising and Sales

Reinforcing Products' Images: Not Your Father's Oldsmobile

Music figures heavily in commercial advertising both on radio and television. Music is often used to help foster a product's image. The type of music used in an ad says things about both the product and its user. For example, an ad for a luxury automobile might employ classical music to show that the car is classy and refined. An ad for a sports car might use rock music to convey a youthful, sexy image. Stores also use music to entertain shoppers and put them in a positive frame of mind for making purchases. Some stores, like Nature Company, Starbucks coffee, and Victoria's Secret even sell CDs and cassettes of their store music.

The Mere Exposure Hypothesis: Hearing Is Believing

Another way music helps to sell products is based on the *mere exposure hypothesis* (Zajonc, 1968), which we discussed in Chapter 10. The idea is simply that repeated exposure to a stimulus increases liking for the stimulus. If an ad for a given product includes a popular song or a likable jingle, repeat airings of the ad will facilitate liking for that product (Hargreaves, 1984; Obermiller, 1985). This is only true up to a point, however. Excessive repetition of a song or jingle can decrease liking for the product (Brentar, Neuendorf, & Armstrong, 1994). Remember how annoyed people became with Barney the Dinosaur's theme song after awhile ("I love you, you love me…")?

Music as a Mnemonic Device

Music also functions as a *mnemonic device* in advertising. A mnemonic device is simply a memory aid that facilitates recall. The saying, "spring forward, fall back" for remembering daylight saving time is an example of a mnemonic device. Some jingles help the consumer to spell out the product's name and thus remember it. The Oscar Meyer bologna and Jello brand gelatin songs do this. Other jingles surround the product's name with positive associations. Try supplying the following product's name while singing along: "Nothing says lovin' like something from the oven and _____ says it best." Here's another one, "The heartbeat of America, today's _____." And yet another one, "Like a good neighbor _____ _____ is there." If you are familiar with these commercials, as any red-blooded American consumer should be, you should have been able to supply the correct names: Pillsbury, Chevrolet, and State Farm.

Music is a very effective means of stimulating brand recall. Richard Yalch (1991) demonstrated this in a study involving undergraduate students. They were presented with 20 advertising slogans and asked to identify the brand name associated with each slogan. Half the slogans were taken from advertisements that included jingles, while the other half were not. The results demonstrated consistently better recall for the brands accompanied by jingles. When standing in the aisle at the store or supermarket, therefore, an effective jingle can make all the difference between choosing brand "A" or brand "B." Yalch's study also suggests that advertising jingles are most effective when the content of the ad is difficult to remember. If there are other clues for remembering a product's name or features, a jingle is less beneficial. To be effective the jingles also have to be simple. This is because the words in a jingle tend to be processed phonetically (e.g., as mere sounds) rather than semantically (as meanings).

You have undoubtedly heard a number of hit songs adapted for use in commercials. But an investigation by Tom (1990) revealed that original music, written specifically for a product, was more effective at facilitating brand recall than either borrowed hits or parodies of well-known songs. Song parodies were the second most effective at promoting recall, with borrowed hits finishing third. This finding makes sense, because some borrowed hits are poor matches for the products with which they are paired. In addition, hit songs may be remembered apart from the ads in which they are used.

Background Music: The Malls Are Alive with the Sound of Muzak

Background music also has come to play an important role in the persuasion process. Retailers rely heavily on background music, also dubbed environmental music, programmed music, or functional music. The most well-known supplier of background music is, of course, Muzak Corporation. Worldwide, Muzak's soothing but banal sound is heard by more than 80 million people everyday in stores, elevators, and while "on hold" on phones (Jones & Schumaker, 1992). In the United States roughly one in three people hears Muzak on a daily basis (Husch, 1984). Muzak has been roundly criticized as the scourge of popular music (Jones & Schumaker, 1992), yet the company maintains their music can yield as much as a 38 percent increase in sales. Background music, whether by Muzak or another supplier, can enhance a store's atmosphere, help regulate the pace of consumer shopping, and influence customers' moods.

Background Music and Shopping Pace.   Can music affect the speed at which you do things? Milliman carried out two well-known studies on the effects of music tempo on consumer behavior. In the first study, Milliman (1982) demonstrated that the pace of shopping in a store was significantly slower when slow tempo music (72 beats per minute) was played compared to fast tempo music (94 beats per minute). The sales volume was 38 percent higher with the slow tempo music. Presumably, the longer shoppers lingered, the more they bought. In the second study, Milliman (1986) demonstrated much the same thing for restaurant patrons. Customers in a restaurant who were exposed to slow tempo background music took longer to eat than those exposed to fast tempo music. Although the customers didn't order more food while lingering, they did order more drinks, increasing the bar tabs in the slow tempo condition. Of course there are limits to what tempo can accomplish. As with everything, the tempo of background music affects the pace of shopping but only up to a point (Bruner, 1990).

Are shoppers and diners aware that their behavior is being regulated by background music? Probably not. Because background music is processed via the peripheral route, people aren't actively thinking about the music. Furthermore, people's subjective estimates about the passage of time aren't necessarily accurate. One investigation (Kelleris & Kent, 1992) revealed that people's perceptions of the amount of time that had passed varied in relation to the type of music being played. Now that you know what to listen for, the next time you are in a department store, see if you can tell what the background music is trying to induce you to do.

Background Music and Mood. Because one of the authors has anxiety attacks whenever he visits the dentist, his dentist provides a blindfold and earphones that play relaxing music. Music can be an extremely effective tool for inducing relaxation and/or fostering a favorable mood. Alpert and Alpert (1988), for example, found that the type of background music played influenced participants' moods and their evaluations of the sentiments expressed in greeting cards. Of course, one needn't rely on experimental studies to reach the conclusion that music can arouse people's emotions. Any moviegoer can vouch for the fact that a good film score significantly heightens the emotional impact of a film. Gordon Bruner (1990) thus emphasizes "that music is an especially powerful stimulus for affecting moods is no revelation; it is attested to throughout history by poets, playwrights, composers, and, in the last two centuries, researchers" (p. 94).

From an advertising or sales perspective, the goal is to use background music to place consumers in a positive frame of mind, one that is conducive to making purchases. Music that arouses positive feelings, whether in a commercial or in a store, helps foster favorable attitudes toward the product which, in turn, may bring about a preference for the product. Studies reveal that most people exhibit a preference for melodic, consonant sounds, as opposed to atonal, dissonant sounds.

Bruner offers a useful rule of thumb for predicting when background music will have the greatest impact on consumer behavior. Music, he states, is most likely to promote purchases when consumers have *high affective involvement* and *low cognitive involvement* with the products. That is, music works best when consumers feel good about the products, but don't think about them too much. Examples of such products include perfume, jewelry, beer, trendy clothing, and impulse purchases. Music is least likely to be effective, Bruner says, when consumers have *high cognitive involvement* with the products, for example, they are likely to think about and reflect upon their purchases. Examples of such products include computers, cameras, major appliances, and insurance. Bruner's advice is borne out in a study by Park and Young (1986) who found music facilitated intentions to purchase, but only under conditions of low involvement. For highly involved consumers, music tended to function as a distraction. One would expect music to enhance impulse purchases or purchases involving disposable income, because little thought goes into such decisions. One would expect music to be less effective for purchases of expensive, durable goods, where considerably more thought is invested before making such decisions.

Background Music and Task Performance: Sweatin' to the Oldies.   Apart from studies of consumers, investigators also have examined the effects of background music on task performance and group productivity. Boutcher and Trenske (1990), for example, found that background music lowered the perceived exertion levels of women engaged in exercise on stationary bicycles. This study supports the widely held view that exercise is more fun and enjoyable when it is accompanied by music. Richard Simmon's gimmick of "Sweating to the Oldies," apparently has merit.

Turning from physical to mental exertion, Miller and Schyb (1989) studied whether different kinds of background music could enhance student performance on both verbal and nonverbal tasks. College students were exposed to one of four conditions; no music, classical music, pop music, and disco music. The researchers found that background music facilitated task performance, but surprisingly, only for females. Pop music especially, and to some extent disco, proved to be the most effective. Pearsall (1989) also examined type of music in relation to listening comprehension, also with surprising results. The somewhat counter intuitive finding was that listener comprehension was higher with dissonant (nonmelodic, atonal) background music than with consonant (melodic, tonal) music. Why would this be the case, given that people tend to prefer consonant sounds? A possible explanation is that because consonant music is more enjoyable, it may be more distracting. The more mentally taxing the task, the more distracting enjoyable music may be. Hence, the occasional utterance of "Keep it down! I can't hear myself think!" Research has shown that vocal selections can be more distracting that instrumental works (Dye, 1996). Thus you may want to study to either dissonant and/or instrumental music if you really need to concentrate.

Rather than the type of music, Mayfield and Moss (1989) examined the tempo of background music on task performance. In a simulated stock market setting, they found that workers in an up-tempo environment (rock music played at 120 beats per minute) were more productive than those exposed to a slow tempo (a heartbeat of 60 beats per minute). Lastly, Daoussis and McKelvie (1986) studied the effects of background music (selections from the Rolling Stones) and personality type on a reading comprehension task. They found that introverts scored significantly lower than extroverts when background music was playing. Interestingly, introverts reported studying to background music only 25 percent of the time, whereas extroverts reported studying to background music 50 percent of the time.

Music Videos and Persuasion: I Want My MTV

A great deal has been written about the influence of MTV and music videos on the attitudes and behaviors of young people. There is little doubt that music videos influence fashions, trends, slang, sexual mores, and model social behavior. The question is how much they do so and whether the modeling provided is beneficial or detrimental. On the negative side, music videos have been criticized for glorifying materialism and wealth (Kalis & Neuendorf, 1989) and for reinforcing sexism (Barongan & Hall Nagayama, 1995; Baxter, De Riemer, Landini, Leslie, & Singletary, 1985; Hansen & Hansen, 1990; Peterson & Pfost, 1989; Sherman & Dominick, 1986; Vincent, 1989). Let's face it, some music videos feature more limousines than the academy awards show and display more lingerie than a Victoria's Secret store! Rap or hip-hop music and, in particular, "gangsta rap," has been singled out for criticism for its reliance on profanity, sexism and misogyny, and violence. Who can deny that terms like "bitch" and "ho" (for whore) are endemic to rap?

In response to these charges, defenders argue that some music videos make important social statements and that others simply mirror the crass materialism and rampant sexism of the larger society. Rap and hip-hop artists respond that they are sending important sociopolitical messages, that the mainstream media paints a distorted picture of rap, and that the language and images used reflect the harsh realities of inner-city life (Brown & Campbell, 1986; Chambers & Morgan, 1992; Tiddle, 1996; Wideman, cited in "Tough Talk on Entertainment," 1995). Dyson (1993), for example, classifies rap music as a form of resistance that empowers African Americans. He stresses that rap combines social protest, musical creation, and cultural expression all at the same time.

Whether one perceives the messages in music videos as positive or negative, it is difficult to deny that such music does serve to shape attitudes, beliefs, intentions, motivations, and behaviors. This is particularly true for juveniles (those who don't yet date or drive) who readily admit they watch MTV to find out what is "cool." One must be cautious about making direct causal inferences, however, between what juveniles see or hear on MTV and their subsequent behavior. There are plenty of alternative sources for modeling behavior. Like them or not, music videos are now a routine feature of popular culture. Music videos will continue to influence into the foreseeable future how teens construct and interpret what is hip, cool, and trendy.

Cautions about Using Music to Persuade: Don't Try This At Home

Some of the persuasive uses to which persuasive music has been put have us scratching our heads. For instance, it was reported that the U.S. military played blaring music through loudspeakers in an effort to force former Panamanian general Manuel Noriega to surrender (Morrison, 1996). The songs that were played: "I Fought the Law and the Law Won," and "You're No Good," among others. We doubt that this was the pivotal factor in his eventual surrender. To the extent that the strategy was successful, we think the aforementioned Barney the Dinosaur theme song would have produced quicker results. It also has been reported that classical music has been used to drive away the homeless, panhandlers, and gang members from fast-food restaurants and convenience stores. Commented one officer, "If you're a tough guy and you like rock or rap, you're not going to sit there and listen to Tchaikovsky" (Holt, 1996, p. 2).

Before you get a hankering to use music to persuade others, bear in mind the following caveats. First, the type of music used must match the receivers' musical tastes. Adapt the music to suit your audience. Classical music, for instance, might not sell beer, while heavy metal music might not sell wine. Second, the music has to match the particular purpose for which it is used. Third, music shouldn't over-power the verbal content of a message. Otherwise, receivers may remember the music but forget the point of the message. In radio and TV commercials, for example, the music is turned down during the voice-overs so that receivers can attend to product names and features. Fourth, in a sales setting, quieter music allows for more interaction between the salesperson and the customer. In a retail setting in which such interaction is important, playing blaring music would be ill-advised. Fifth, music will probably have little effect on highly involved receivers who will concentrate on the substance of the message anyway. Music is best used on low-involved receivers who will tend to process the message indirectly (Park & Young, 1986). In most cases music functions as a useful supplement to verbal persuasion. Rarely can music be used as a substitute for verbal persuasion.

AROMA AND PERSUASION

Though few texts discuss the subject, smell plays an important role in the process of persuasion. Selling smells is a big business. Sales of fragrances and scented products total more than $20 billion in the United States annually (Foderaro, cited in Baron & Bronfen, 1994). Aromatherapy, the new-age upstart of the fragrance industry, is already generating annual sales of more than $200 million (Stolberg, 1994). Think of all the fragrances you can buy to make you feel better; you can douse yourself in perfume, scent your car's interior, and place air fresheners throughout your home. You can use scented deodorants, scented soaps, scented laundry detergent, scented dishwashing liquid, and scented toilet paper. There used to be a women's shampoo called, "Gee your hair smells terrific!" In addition to personal uses of fragrances, the use of "ambient" (background) fragrances in the workplace and in retail settings is beginning to play an increasingly prominent role. In this section we examine persuasion in the fragrance industry, with a view toward finding out whether perfumes, colognes, and aftershaves do what their ads imply they do; namely, increase one's sexual attractiveness. We also take a look at the field of "aroma-chology,"[4] the scientific study of ambient smells as a means of influencing people's moods, task performance, consumer behavior, and a variety of other functions.

Perfume: Romance in a Bottle

The fragrance industry is one in which a product often "wins by a nose." The marketing of perfumes, including colognes and aftershaves, is a $4.4 billion dollar industry (Ortega & McCartney, 1994). It seems as if every celebrity now has his or her own designer fragrance, and every magazine contains an aromatic insert of one sort or another. More perfume is bought and sold in the United States than in any other country, including France (Kalich, 1987). More fragrances are now being manufactured in the United States as well. This is due, in part, to the popularity of American celebrity fragrances and also, in part, to decisions by U.S. courts that fragrances are not patentable (Kalich, 1987). The latter factor explains the popularity of knockoff brands that imitate more expensive lines such as Georgio, Obsession, and Passion.

Of course, scent alone isn't what sells perfume. The promise of romance sells perfume. Hence, the marketing themes associated with fragrances revolve around images of romance, intrigue, sensuality, and, of course, sex. "Between madness and infatuation," a Calvin Klein ad proclaims, "lies obsession" (for Obsession perfume). Celebrity endorsers and supermodels often are used to hawk fragrances, especially their own. Packaging also plays a role. Unusual bottle shapes and sizes are a common means of distinguishing products in the fragrance industry. After all, at $100 per quarter ounce, the bottle should look like a work of art! A perfume's name also counts for a lot. Remember, the name attached to a smell influences how it is perceived. French-sounding names remain quite popular. "L' Eau d' Issey" note two commentators on the fragrance scene, "has a more romantic ring to it than Issey's water" (Ortega & McCartney, 1994, p. E1).

Did you know that the clerks behind the fragrance counter often receive hefty commissions from fragrance manufacturers? They do. In fact, at some department stores, the clerks work directly for the fragrance manufacturers (Ortega & McCartney, 1994). Hence, when you ask a clerk to recommend a fragrance for you or your amour, the clerk's suggestion may have more to do with the size of his or her commission than the person you describe. "It's you!" the clerk may fawn, but "I get a big rebate" may be what the clerk is really thinking.

Love Stinks

Through images and innuendo, fragrance ads create the impression that using their products will increase your sexual attractiveness. But do they make any actual difference? Do they help attract dates, win over lovers, or make one feel better about oneself? We've uncovered very few studies on the effects of fragrances and attraction. Those we've found present a mixed bag of results.

A study by Baron (1983) suggests fragrances do facilitate attraction. Female undergraduates wearing perfume were perceived as more attractive by male undergraduates than female undergraduates not wearing perfume. The results of two other studies, however, don't bode well for the fragrance industry. Cann and Ross (1989) asked males to rate the attractiveness of slides of females. While doing

A fragrance designer plies his trade.

Reprinted with permission by Joseph M. Tabacca.

so, the males were exposed to a pleasant smell (spray cologne), an unpleasant smell (ammonium sulfide), or no smell. The researchers found no significant differences in perceived attractiveness based on the different smells. In fairness, though, these results may be attributable to the fact that the slides featured only attractive or unattractive females (not "average" looking females). It may be that females whose looks tend toward one extreme or the other don't benefit from the use of fragrances, but females whose looks are closer to average do.

Another study that casts doubt on the allure of perfumes was conducted by Hirsch (cited in Stolberg, 1994). Male medical students were recruited as subjects for the study. Blood pressure monitors were attached to the volunteers' genitals while they smelled a variety of fragrances, including Chanel No. 5 and Obsession. The results? The only smell that consistently increased blood pressure, the measure of sexual arousal used in the study, was that of cinnamon buns! The results seem to reinforce the old adage that the way to a man's heart is, after all, through his stomach. As with the preceding study, these results may also be questioned. Let's face it, having an apparatus attached to one's genitals doesn't approximate a real-world setting for arousal (not for most folks, anyway). In such a clinical environment, the participants may not have responded as they otherwise would.

Lastly, an investigation by DeBono (1992) suggests that fragrances can side-track one's thought processes, predisposing one to respond more emotionally, and less rationally, in a given situation. In the study, college students were asked to observe a perfume advertisement featuring either an attractive or unattractive spokeswoman. The spokeswoman provided either strong arguments or weak arguments on behalf of the perfume. Before seeing the ad, however, some participants smelled a sample of the perfume. Those who smelled the sample beforehand were influenced more by the spokeswoman's looks than by her arguments. For those who didn't smell the sample beforehand, the results were just the opposite: the quality of the arguments mattered more than looks. The results suggest that the fragrance promoted peripheral processing, à la Petty and Cacioppo's Elaboration Likelihood Model of Persuasion (1986a, 1986b), at the expense of central processing. If the goal of a perfume wearer is to prompt another to feel more and think less, this study suggests perfume achieves that goal.

Overall, two studies suggest perfume increases attraction, while two studies suggest it does not. All four studies have limitations. Thus, the best answer to the question, "Do perfumes really increase attraction?" is an equivocal "It depends." In questioning whether perfumes and other fragrances work any magic, bear in mind that there are huge individual differences in preferences for smells. Bear in mind, too, that scent is only *one* factor in the overall attractiveness equation. Other factors include such things as physical appearances, personalities, and common interests, to name but a few. One would be foolish, indeed, to believe that fragrance alone could serve as the basis for a meaningful, lasting relationship.

Ambient Aromas and Social Influence: Something Special In the Air

Although there is little research on the relationship between fragrance and attraction, there is a sizable body of research on the ways in which ambient aromas affect people generally. Smells have been shown to influence a variety of physiological processes, including brain waves (Lorig & Schwartz, 1988; Sugano, 1989, 1992), blood pressure (Jellenik, 1994), heart rate (Kikuchi, Tanida, Uenoyama, Abe, & Yamaguchi, 1991; Oguri, Iwaki, Ogata, Okazaki, & Torii, 1992), and pupil dilation (Steiner, 1986). Physiological changes like these are only indirectly related to persuasion, but they may signal changes in arousal or cognitive activity that are conducive to persuasion.

Aromas and Moods: Am I Blue?

Smells have been shown to affect people's moods, feelings, and emotions in significant ways. Do you get nervous when you enter a doctor's office or visit a hospital? For patients undergoing cancer screening tests, the experience produces considerable anxiety. At the Memorial Sloan-Kettering Cancer Center physicians have used vanilla fragrance to relax patients who are about to undergo a magnetic resonance image (MRI) exam (Stolberg, 1994). Similarly, Redd and Manne (1991) exposed patients undergoing MRI's for cancer to the scent of heliotropin (similar to baby powder). The results revealed that patients in general felt more relaxed by the heliotropin, particularly those who rated the smell as pleasant. Not just any smell will do, however. In a follow-up study, the same researchers found that the scent of wintergreen (a menthol fragrance) had no calming effect because it was perceived as invigorating rather than relaxing by the patients (Manne & Redd, 1993).

Researchers have found that scents can influence people's moods in nonmedical settings as well. One of our favorite studies (Hanisch, 1982), because of its unusual method, examined whether pleasant fragrances could reduce arachnophobia (fear of spiders) among females. The researcher dangled a spider at varying distances from the participants' faces. Part of the time the participants were exposed to a pleasant, unfamiliar scent. Part of the time they were not. The researcher found that the pleasant fragrance reduced fear and anxiety and allowed the spider to be placed closer to the participants' faces than the no-fragrance condition. The researcher didn't mention whether the spider liked the fragrance or not.

Other studies also support the conclusion that ambient smells can alter moods and emotions. Nagai and colleagues (1992) found that the smell of sweet fennel oil reduced the psychological stress and fatigue associated with doing math problems on a computer. And Knasko (1992) found that the smell of chocolate and baby powder (separately, not in combination) elicited more positive moods than no smell. A variety of other studies have achieved similar results (Nakano et al., 1992; Schiffman, 1993a, 1993b; Schiffman, Suggs, & Sattely-Miller, 1995; Warren & Warrenburg, 1993). The fairly consistent conclusion is that ambient fragrances can alter people's moods, providing the right fragrances are used. Fragrances that have proven successful in one setting or another include vanilla, chocolate, heliotropin, sweet fennel oil, baby powder, and floral scents.

Aromas and Task Performance: Whistle While You Work

Another area in which scents have been shown to have an effect is on task performance. Several studies have shown that mild fragrances can improve the speed, accuracy, and efficiency with which people complete tasks (Hirsch, cited in Stolberg, 1994; Rotten, 1983; Sugano & Sato, 1991; Warm, Parasuraman, & Dember, 1990). For example, Baron and Bronfen (1994) asked students to solve word problems under both high and low stress conditions. Some students were placed in a room with a pleasant fragrance (either Glade "Powder Fresh" or Glade "Spiced Apple") while they solved the problems, and others were not. The students who were exposed to the powder fragrance completed significantly more word problems than those who were not. This was true for both the low and high stress conditions. The students who were exposed to the spiced apple scent also fared better than the no-scent group, but the results fell short of being statistically significant. Thus, it appears the right fragrance can improve task performance. A follow-up study by the same researchers (Baron & Bronfen, 1994) found that the degree of improvement in task performance from exposure to a pleasant fragrance (in this case lemon) was on par with the improvement brought about by giving someone a small gift (candy).

Other studies have shown ambient fragrances, such as lavender, can facilitate learning and recall (Frank & Ludvigh, 1931; Smith, Standing, & de-Man, 1992; Steiner, 1986). For best results, however, the fragrance concentrations should be mild rather than strong. An investigation that used stronger levels found no beneficial effects on memory (Ludvigson & Rottmann, 1989). A fragrance that is too powerful can be distracting and may even trigger an allergic reaction.

Findings in the area of task performance highlight the differences in the way individuals respond to smells. By way of illustration, Warm, Dember, and Parasuraman (1992) found that both the smell of muguet (Lily of the Valley) and peppermint improved participants' performance on a difficult visual attention task. But a follow-up study using peppermint (Nelson, Grubb, Warm, & Dember, 1992) found that the beneficial effects applied only to those participants who said they became bored with the task, not for those who reported remaining alert and attentive. Perhaps you should consider eating a peppermint just before a class with a particularly boring professor!

Ambient Aromas and Consumer Behavior

A number of retail stores use ambient odors in an effort to regulate shopping behavior (Miller, 1991). Does pumping fragrances into the air make customers buy more? Researchers seem to agree that purchasing decisions are too complex to be influenced solely by smell. However, fragrances can lend assistance by putting shoppers in a more pleasant mood, or by regulating the amount of time spent shopping. In one investigation (Hirsch, cited in Stolberg, 1994), shoppers visited both a scented (mixed floral) and an unscented (purified, odor-free) room. The rooms were otherwise identical. The shoppers were asked to examine Nike tennis shoes, estimate their worth, and indicate their willingness to buy them. When in the scented room, the shoppers evaluated the worth of the Nike shoes more highly, by an average of more than $10. They also expressed more interest in purchasing the shoes. Surprisingly, even those shoppers who said they *disliked* the floral scent expressed more interest in buying the shoes in the scented as opposed to the unscented room! Eau my! Before attaching too much importance to the above study, however, you should know other researchers using a similar approach came up empty-handed (Steiner, cited in Jellenik, 1994).

Although it may not qualify as "shopping," the same researcher (Hirsch, 1993) also found that gamblers in a pleasantly scented casino room put significantly more money into slot machines than gamblers in an unscented room. Gamblers fed 53 percent more money into the slot machines when the scent concentration was higher and 33 percent more when the scent concentration was lower. This study, along with others by Hirsch, has been criticized for lacking scientific rigor (Stolberg, 1994).[5] It does seem reasonable, though, that if a pleasant fragrance can put people in a good mood, they might feel more optimistic or lucky, and hence bet more.

Several studies have also shown that pleasant fragrances can make consumers linger longer in stores. Teerling, Nixdorf, and Koster (1992), for instance, found that two ambient fragrances increased the time spent shopping in a fabric store. Likewise, Knasco (1989) found either a floral or a spicy scent made customers stay longer in a jewelry store. Much the same was found using a museum as the setting (Knasco, 1993). You may recall that similar effects were produced by background music in both store and restaurant settings.

Caveats and Qualifications

Before you rush out to buy a case of room air fresheners to make you feel better, study harder, and work more efficiently, keep the following in mind: First, there are large variations in individual preferences for smells. A scent that works on one person may not work on another. One of the authors, for example, actually likes the smell of a skunk from afar. Second, as was the case with subliminal research, some of the effects reported in these studies may be due to a placebo effect. That is, the participants' expectations that smells can alter human behavior might account for the changes observed. For instance, Schiffman (1993a, 1993b) found that participants who were told they were exposed to a fragrance reported favorable mood shifts even though, in reality, they were given an odorless substance. Third, the repetitive use of scents could lead to counterconditioning such that an initially pleasant scent comes to be perceived as unpleasant. The smell of vanilla, for example, has been shown to be relaxing. But if it is introduced every time a child receives a vaccination, the smell may become aversive. Fourth, easy does it where ambient scents are concerned. An overpowering odor that draws attention may not produce the results you're after. Lastly, there may be ethical as well as health-related concerns involved in using fragrances to influence people. Remember, people can close their eyes or look away from an image that offends them. They can't stop breathing or turn off their noses, however. We address some of the ethical questions arising from the use of fragrances in Chapter 16.

What Will the Future Smell Like?

More than a dozen years ago, one of the authors went to see a film being shown in "odor-rama."[6] Audience members were given a "scratch n' sniff" card as they entered the theater. At the appropriate points in the movie a number would appear on the screen, at which point viewers would scratch and sniff the corresponding card number. The experience was fun, but gimmicky. Obviously, "odor-rama" and "smell-a-vision" never caught on. What about the future of smell as a form of influence? Will there come a day when you wake up, not only to your alarm clock's buzzer, but to a fragrance that will make you feel perky and chipper as well? Will your gym or aerobics class pipe in a fragrance that makes you want to exercise

DILBERT reprinted by permission of United Feature Syndicate, Inc.

harder and longer? Or perhaps your employer will use similar ambient odors to make you work harder and be more productive on the job. Perhaps you'll be able to buy a scented "blue book" or "Scantron" form that will improve your concentration and recall while taking a test. Granted, such hypothetical scenarios seem far-fetched. Pleasant smells can only do so much. A clever attorney isn't going to get his or her client off by wearing the right fragrance. Even so, keep in mind that fragrances are already being put to use in some hospitals, retail stores, and office buildings (Baron & Bronfen, 1994). To the extent that fragrances can alter moods, they may become increasingly important tools for persuaders.

SUMMARY

In this chapter we examined three esoteric forms of persuasion: subliminal messages, music as persuasion, and smell as persuasion. Despite the public's belief in subliminal persuasion, controlled laboratory studies show the technique produces few if any results. Embedded images, self-help tapes, and backward-masking do little if anything. Implicit perception, on the other hand, is a very real phenomenon and can be used to influence moods. Music was shown to be an important component of persuasion. Music facilitates persuasion in a variety of ways, such as reinforcing advertising images, serving as a mnemonic device, and influencing receivers' moods. Though overlooked by most persuasion researchers, smell also was shown to be a useful tool for persuasion if the right conditions are met. Ambient fragrances can enhance moods, improve task performance, and influence consumer behavior.

ENDNOTES

1. Aside from the Disney films mentioned, we know of only two other movies that have used subliminals, *The Exorcist,* and *Jade* (Emery, 1996; Goodkin & Phillips, 1983).

2. Researchers in this area prefer the term *awareness* over that of *consciousness,* because the latter implies Freudian notions about the unconscious. Awareness or non-awareness, these researchers say, probably involves much more rudimentary brain processes.

3. A tachistoscope is an old-fashioned device that looks something like a Viewmaster. It was originally designed to simulate three-dimensionality when viewing travel postcards. Researchers have used it to show two different images to the left and right eyes. When confronted with two different images, the brain tends to makes sense of the two by merging them into one.

4. Aroma-chology involves the scientific study of human olfactory processes (Jellinek, 1994). Unlike aromatherapy, which tends to be nonscientific and anecdotal in nature (Baron & Bronfen, 1994), aroma-chology involves the systematic study of the effects of aromas on human behavior through verifiable laboratory experiments.

5. The fragrances used weren't identified by the researcher, complicating any effort aimed at replication. Factors that could have confounded the results include the number of gamblers in the casino, the amount of money they had with them, and variations in gambling habits as a function of the time of day and day of week.

6. The film was *Polyester,* by cult film director John Waters.

REFERENCES—SUBLIMINALS

Beatty, S. E., & Hawkins, D. (1989). Subliminal stimulation: Some new data and interpretation. *Journal of Advertising, 18*(3), 48.

Benoit, S. C., & Thomas, R. L. (1992). The influence of expectancy in subliminal perception experiments. *Journal of General Psychology, 119*(4), 335–341.

Bornstein, R. F., & Pittman, T. S. (Eds.) (1992). *Perception without awareness.* New York: Guilford Press.

Byrne, D. (1959). The effect of a subliminal food stimulus on verbal responses. *Journal of Applied Psychology, 43*(4), 245–252.

Champion, J., & Turner, W. W. (1959). An experimental investigation of subliminal perception. *Journal of Applied Psychology, 43*, 382–384.

Cheesman, J., & Merikle, P. M. (1985). Word recognition and consciousness. In D. Besner, T. G. Waller, & G. E. Mackinnon (Eds.), *Reading research: Advances in theory and practice* (Vol. 5, pp. 311–352). New York: Academic Press.

✓ Emery, C. E., Jr. (1996, March/April). When the media miss the real messages in subliminal stories. *Skeptical Inquirer, 20*(2), 16–17+.

Gable, M., Wilkins, H., & Harris, L. (1987). An evaluation of subliminally embedded sexual stimuli. *Journal of Advertising, 16*(1), 26–30.

Gentry, C. (1990, August 13). "Subliminal messages in mind of beholder." *St. Petersburg Times,* p. 1A.

✓ Goleman, D. (1990, August 14). "Research probes what the mind senses unaware." *New York Times,* pp. B7–B8.

Goodkin, O., & Phillips, M. (1983). The subconscious taken captive. *Southern California Law Review, 54,* 1077–1140.

Greenwald, A. G., Spangenberg, E. R., Pratkanis, A. R., & Eskenazi, J. (1991). Double-blind tests of subliminal self-help audiotapes. *Psychological Science, 2,* 119–122.

✓ Harmon, A. (1995, October 1). "High-tech hidden persuaders." *Los Angeles Times,* pp. A1, A28–29.

Hawkins, D. (1970). The effects of subliminal stimulation on drive level and brand preference. *Journal of Marketing Research, 8,* 322–326.

Hoye, D. (1996, May 4). "You will buy this software: Computer program inspires subliminally." *The Arizona Republic,* p. A1.

Key, W. B. (1972). *Subliminal seduction: Ad media's manipulation of a not so innocent America.* Englewood Cliffs, NJ: Prentice-Hall.

Key, W. B. (1976). *Media sexploitation.* Englewood Cliffs, NJ: Prentice-Hall.

Key, W. B. (1980). *Clam-plate orgy: And other subliminal techniques for manipulating your behavior.* Englewood Cliffs, NJ: Prentice-Hall.

Key, W. B. (1989). *The age of manipulation: The con in confidence, the sin in sincere.* New York: Henry Holt.

Masling, J. M. (1992). What does it all mean? In R. F. Bornstein & T. S. Pittman (Eds.), *Perception without awareness,* (pp. 259–276). New York: Guilford Press.

McConnell, J. V., Cutler, R. L., & McNeil, E. B. (1957). Subliminal stimulation: An overview. *American Psychologist, 13,* 229–242.

Merikle, P. M. (1988). Subliminal auditory messages: An evaluation. *Psychology and Marketing, 5*(4), 297–316.

Mitchell, C. W. (1995). Effects of subliminally presented auditory suggestions of itching on scratching behavior. *Perceptual and Motor Skills, 80*(1), 87–96.

Moore, T. E. (1982). Subliminal advertising: What you see is what you get. *Journal of Marketing, 5*(4), 355–372.

Niedenthal, P. M. (1990). Implicit perception and affective information. *Journal of Experimental Social Psychology, 26*(6), 505–527.

Oldenburg, D. (1990, April 3). "Hidden messages; Subliminal self-help: too good to be true?" *The Washington Post,* p. C5.

Patton, C. J. (1992). Fear of abandonment and binge eating: A subliminal psychodynamic activation investigation. *Journal of Nervous and Mental Disorders, 180,* 484–490.

Phillips, C. (1990, July 16). "Trial to focus on issue of subliminal messages in rock." *Los Angeles Times,* pp. F10-F11.

Robles, R., Smith, R., Carver, C. S., & Wellens, A. R. (1987). The influence of subliminal visual images on the experience of anxiety. *Personality and Social Psychology Bulletin, 13*(3), 399–410.

Rogers, M., & Seiler C. A. (1994). The answer is no: A national survey of advertising industry practitioners and their clients about whether they use subliminal advertising. *Journal of Advertising Research, 34*(2), 36–45.

Rogers, S. (1992–93). How a publicity blitz created the myth of subliminal advertising. *Public Relations Quarterly, 37*(4), 12–17.

Schurtman, R., Palmatier, J., & Martin, E. (1982). On the activation of symbiotic gratification fantasies as an aid in the treatment of alcoholics. *International Journal of Addictions, 17*(7), 1157–1174.

Silverman, L. H. (1976). Psychoanalytic theory: The reports of my death are greatly exaggerated. *American Psychologist, 31*(9), 621–637.

Smith, K. H., & Rogers, M. (1994). Effectiveness of subliminal messages and television commercials: Two experiments. *Journal of Applied Psychology, 79*(6), 866–874.

Spangenberg, E. R., Obermiller, C., & Greenwald, A. G. (1992). A field test of subliminal self-help audiotapes: The power of expectancies. *Journal of Public Policy and Marketing, 11*(2), 26–36.

Staum, M. J., & Brotons, M. (1992). The influence of auditory subliminals on behavior: A series of investigations. *Journal of Music Therapy, 29*(3), 130–185.

Swart, L. C., & Morgan, C. L. (1992). Effects of subliminal backward-recorded messages on attitudes. *Perceptual and Motor Skills. 75*(3, Pt. 2), 1107–1113.

Talbot, N., Duberstein, P., & Scott, P. (1991). Subliminal psychodynamic activation, food consumption, and self-confidence. *Journal of Clinical Psychology. 47,* 813–823.

Theus, K. T. (1994). Subliminal advertising and the psychology of processing unconscious stimuli: A review of research. *Psychology and Marketing, 11*(3), 271–290.

Vokay, J. R., & Read, J. D. (1985). Subliminal messages: Between the devil and the media. *American Psychologist, 40*(11), 1231–1239.

Weinberger, J., & Hardaway, R. (1990). Separating science from myth in subliminal psychodynamic activation. *Clinical Psychology Review, 10,* 727–756.

Weiner, M., & Shiller, P. H. (1960). Subliminal perception or perception of partial cues. *Journal of Abnormal and Social Psychology, 61*(1), 124–137.

White, L., Tursky, B., & Schwartz, G. E. (1985). *Placebo: Theory, research, and mechanisms.* New York: Guilford Press.

Zanot, E. J., Pincus, D. J., & Lamp, E. J. (1983). Public perceptions of subliminal advertising. *Journal of Advertising, 12,* 39–45.

REFERENCES—MUSIC

Alpert, J. I., & Alpert, M. I. (1988). Background music as an influence on consumer mood and advertising responses. In T. K. Scrull (Ed.), *Advances in consumer research* (Vol. 16, pp. 485–491). Honolulu, HI: Association for Consumer Research.

Barongan, C., & Hall Nagayama, G. C. (1995). The influence of mysogynous rap music on sexual aggression against women. *Psychology of Women Quarterly, 19*(2), 195–207.

Baxter, R. L., De Riemer, C., Landini, A., Leslie, L., & Singletary, M. W. (1985). A content analysis of music videos. *Journal of Broadcasting and Electronic Media, 29,* 333–340.

Boutcher, S. H., & Trenske, M. (1990). The effects of sensory deprivation and music on perceived exertion and affect during exercise. *Journal of Sport and Exercise Psychology, 12*(2), 167–176.

Brentar, J. E., Neuendorf, K. A., & Armstrong, G. B. (1994). Exposure affects and affective response to music. *Communication Monographs, 61*(2), 161–181.

Brown, J. D., & Campbell, K. (1986). Race and gender in music videos: The same beat but a different drummer. *Journal of Communication, 36,* 94–106.

Bruner, G. C., II. (1990). Music, mood, and marketing. *Journal of Marketing, 54,* 94–104.

Chambers, G., & Morgan, J. (1992, September 12). "Droppin' knowledge: A rap roundtable." *Essence,* pp. 83–120.

Daoussis, L., & McKelvie, S. J. (1986). Musical preferences and effects of music on a reading comprehension test for introverts and extroverts. *Perceptual and Motor Skills, 62*(1), 283–289.

Dye, L. (1996, December 2). "Studying emotional chords of music." *Los Angeles Times,* p. D-5.

Dyson, M. E. (1993). *Reflecting Black: African-American cultural criticism.* St. Paul, MN: University of Minnesota Press.

Hansen, C. H., & Hansen, R. D. (1990). The influence of sex and violence on the appeal of rock music videos. *Communication Research, 17,* 212–234.

Hargreaves, D. J. (1984). The effects of repetition on liking for music. *Journal of Research in Music Education, 32,* 35–47.

Holt, D. (1996, April 24). "Fighting crime with violins." *Dallas Morning News,* p. 31-A.

Husch, J. (1984). Music of the workplace: A study of Muzak culture. Unpublished doctoral dissertation, University of Massachusetts, Amherst, Massachusetts.

Jones, S. C., & Schumaker, T. G. (1992). Muzak: On functional music and power. *Critical Studies in Mass Communication, 9*(2), 156–169.

Kallis, P., & Neuendorf, K. A. (1989). Aggressive cue prominence and gender participation in MTV. *Journalism Quarterly, 66*(1), 148–154, 229.

Kelleris, J. J., & Kent, R. J. (1992). The influence of music on consumers' temporal perceptions: Does time fly when you're having fun? *Journal of Consumer Psychology, 1*(4), 365–376.

Mayfield, C., & Moss, S. (1989). Effects of music tempo on task performance. *Psychological Reports, 65*(3, Pt. 2), 1283–1290.

Miller, L. K., & Schyb, M. (1989). Facilitation and interference by background music. *Journal of Music Therapy, 26*(1), 42–54.

Milliman, R. E. (1982). Using background music to affect the behavior of supermarket shoppers. *Journal of Marketing, 46*(3), 86–91.

Milliman, R. E. (1986). The influence of background music on the behavior of restaurant patrons. *Journal of Consumer Research, 13,* 286–289.

Morrison, P. (1996, April 26). "City brass hopes piped-in classics drive out loiterers." *Los Angeles Times,* p. A3.

Obermiller, C. (1985). Varieties of mere exposure: The effects of processing style and repetition on affective response. *Journal of Consumer Research, 12,* 17–30.

Park, C. W., & Young, S. M. (1986). Consumer response to television commercials: The impact of involvement and background music on brand attitude formation. *Journal of Marketing Research, 23,* 11–24.

Pearsall, E. R. (1989). Differences in listening comprehension with tonal and atonal background music. *Journal of Music Therapy, 26*(4), 188–197.

Peterson, D. L., & Pfost, K. S. (1989). Influence of rock videos on attitudes of violence against women. *Psychological Reports, 64,* 319–322.

Petty, R. E., & Cacioppo, J. T. (1986a). *Communication and persuasion: Central and peripheral routes to attitude change.* New York: Springer-Verlag.

Petty, R. E., & Cacioppo, J. T. (1986b). The elaboration likelihood model of persuasion. In L. Berkowitz (Ed.), *Advances in experimental social psychology* (Vol. 19, pp. 123–205). New York: Academic Press.

Sherman, B. L., & Dominick, J. R. (1986). Violence and sex in music video: TV and rock n' roll. *Journal of Communication, 36,* 79–93.

Tiddle, C. (1996, December 2). Tales from 'hood need to be told. *Los Angeles Times,* p. F-3.

Tom, G. (1990). Marketing with music. *Journal of Consumer Marketing, 7*(2), 49–53.

Tough talk on entertainment. (1995, June 12). *Time,* pp. 32–33.

Vincent, R. C. (1989). Clio's consciousness raised? Portrayal of women in rock videos, re-examined. *Journalism Quarterly, 66,* 155–160.

Yalch, R. F. (1991). Memory in a jingle jungle: Music as a mnemonic device in communicating advertising slogans. *Journal of Applied Psychology, 76,* 268–275.

Zajonc, R. B. (1968). Attitudinal effects of mere exposure. *Journal of Personality and Social Psychology Monograph Supplement, 9*(2, Pt. 2), 1–28.

REFERENCES—SMELL

Baron, R. A. (1983). "The sweet smell of success?" The impact of pleasant artificial scents (perfume and cologne) on evaluations of job applicants. *Journal of Applied Psychology, 68,* 709–713.

Baron, R. A., & Bronfen, M. I. (1994). A whiff of reality: Empirical evidence concerning the effects of pleasant fragrances on work-related behavior. *Journal of Applied Social Psychology, 24*(13), 1179–1203.

Cann, A., & Ross, D. A. (1989). Olfactory stimuli as context cues in human memory. *American Journal of Psychology, 102,* 91–102.

DeBono, K. G. (1992). Pleasant scents and persuasion: An information processing approach. *Journal of Applied Social Psychology, 22,* 910–919.

Frank, J. B., & Ludvigh, E. J. (1931). The retro-active effect of pleasant and unpleasant odors on learning. *American Journal of Psychology, 43,* 102–108.

Hanisch, E. (1982). The calming effect of fragrances and associated remembrances. *drom Report* "The nose: Part 2," pp. 18–19.

Hirsch, A. R. (1993). Effect of ambient odor on slot-machine usage in a Las Vegas casino. *Chemical Senses, 18,* 578.

Jellinek, S. J. (1994). Aromachology: A status review. *Cosmetics and Toiletries, 109*(10), 83–101.

Kalich, T. (1987, October). "What's in a smell?" *Atlantic Monthly, 260*(4), 34–38.

Kikuchi, A., Tanida, M., Uenoyama, S., Abe, T., & Yamaguchi, H. (1991). Effect of odours on cardiac response patterns in a reaction time task. *Chemical Senses, 16,* 183.

Knasco, S. C., (1989). Ambient odor and shopping behavior. *Chemical Senses, 14,* 718.

Knasko, S. C. (1992). Viewing time and liking of slides in the presence of congruent and incongruent odors. *Chemical Senses, 17,* 652.

Knasco, S. C. (1993). Lingering time in a museum in the presence of congruent and incongruent odors. *Chemical Senses, 14,* 718.

Laird, D. (1935). What can you do with your nose? *Scientific Monthly, 41,* 126–130.

Lorig, T. S., & Schwartz, G. E. (1988). Brain and odor: I. Alteration of human EEG by odor administration. *Psychobiology, 16,* 281–289.

Ludvigson, H. W., & Rottmann, T. R. (1989). Effects of ambient odours of lavender and cloves on cognition, memory, affect, and mood. *Chemical Senses, 14,* 525–536.

Miller, C. (1991). Research reveals how marketers can win by a nose. *Marketing News, 25* [Lexis-Nexis].

Manne, S. L., & Redd, W. H. (1993). Fragrance administration to reduce patient anxiety during magnetic resonance imaging in cancer diagnostic work-up. Final Report to the Olfactory Research Fund.

Nagai, H., Nakamura, M., Fujii, W., Inui, T., & Asakura, Y. (1992). Effects of odors on humans: II. Reducing effects of mental stress and fatigue. *Chemical Senses, 16,* 198.

Nakano, Y., Kikuchi, A., Matsui, H., Hatayama, T., et al. (1992). A study of fragrance impressions, evaluation, and categorization. *Tohoku Psychologica Folia, 51,* 83–90.

Nelson, W. T., Grubb, P. L., Warm, J. S., & Dember, W. N. (1992). The effects of fragrance administration and attentiveness on vigilance performance. Paper presented at the annual meeting of the Southern Society for Philosophy and Psychology, Memphis, TN.

Oguri, M., Iwaki, T., Ogata, S., Okazaki, Y., & Torii, S. (1992). Coincidental variations between heart rate and contingency negative variation during odor condition. *Chemical Senses, 16,* 197–198.

Ortega, B., & McCartney, S. (1994, December 21). "Perfume clerks try to make sense of those scents." *The Orlando Sentinel Tribune,* p. E1.

Petty, R. E., & Cacioppo, J. T. (1986a). The Elaboration Likelihood Model of persuasion. In L. Berkowitz (Ed.), *Advances in experimental social psychology* (Vol. 19, pp. 123–205). New York: Academic Press.

Petty, R. E., & Cacioppo, J. T. (1986b). *Communication and persuasion: Central and peripheral routes to attitude change.* New York: Springer-Verlag.

Redd, W. H., & Manne, S. L. (1991). Fragrance administration to reduce patient anxiety during magnetic resonance imaging in cancer diagnostic work-up. Report to the Fragrance Research Fund. (Now called the Olfactory Research Fund.)

Rotten, J. (1983). Affective and cognitive consequences of malodorous pollution. *Basic and Applied Social Psychology, 38,* 213–228.

Schiffman, S. S. (1993a). The effect of fragrance on the mood of women at mid-life. *The Aroma-Chology Review, 2*(1), 1–5.

Schiffman, S. S. (1993b). The effect of pleasant odor: On mood of males at mid-life. Final Report to the Olfactory Research Fund.

Schiffman, S. S., Suggs, M. S., & Sattely-Miller, E. A. (1995). Effect of pleasant odors on mood of males at midlife: Comparison of African-American and European-American men. *Brain Research Bulletin, 36*(1), 31–37.

Smith, D. G., Standing, L., & de-Man, L. (1992). Verbal memory elicited by ambient odor. *Perceptual and Motor Skills, 74*(2), 339–343.

Steiner, W. (1986). The effect of the fragrances on human experience and behaviour. *drom Report*, "The nose: Part 3," pp. 6–21.

Stolberg, S. (1994, June 29). "Trying to make sense of smell." *Los Angeles Times*, pp. A1, A20, A21.

Sugano, H. (1989). Effects of odors on mental function. *Chemical Senses, 14*, 303.

Sugano, H. (1992). Psychophysiological studies of fragrances. In S. Van Toller & G. H. Dodd (Eds.), *Fragrance: The psychology and biology of perfume* (pp. 221–228). London: Elsevier.

Sugano, H., & Sato, H. (1991). Psychophysiological studies of fragrance. *Chemical Senses, 16*, 183–184.

Teerling, A., Nixdorf, R. R., & Koster, E. P. (1992). The effect of ambient odours on shopping behavior. *Chemical Senses, 17*, 886.

Warm, J. S., Dember, W. N., & Parasuraman, R. (1992). Effects of olfactory stimulation on performance and stress in a visual sustained attention task. *Journal of the Society of Cosmetic Chemists, 42*, 199–210.

Warm, J. S., Parasuraman, R., & Dember, W. N. (1990). Effects of periodic olfactory stimulation on visual sustained attention in young and older adults. Progress Report No. 4 to the Fragrance Research Fund.

Warren, C., & Warrenburg, S. (1993). Mood benefits of fragrance, *Perfumes & Flavors, 18*(2), 9–16.

16

THE ETHICS OF PERSUASION

"The most dangerous animal in the world," it has been said, "is a freshman with one semester of psychology." If that is true, then the second most dangerous animal must surely be a freshman with one persuasion class under his or her belt. If you give a child a toy hammer, the child will invariably find that every object he or she encounters is in need of pounding (Kaplan, 1964). In much the same vein, it is not uncommon for a student who has completed a course in persuasion to think that every communication encounter requires a test of her or his newfound persuasive skills. At best, this can be tedious for the recipients of the influence attempts. At worst, it can damage or destroy relationships if the persuader is perceived as being obnoxious and/or unethical. Like a hammer, persuasion is a useful tool. But one shouldn't use it to pound on others.

For this reason and others, we consider in this chapter the ethics of influence attempts. Although this is the last chapter of the text, it is by no means the least important. We decided to place this chapter at the end of the book so that we could discuss the ethical concerns that were raised throughout the preceding chapters. In this chapter we attempt to ask and answer a number of ethical questions and to provide guidelines, albeit tentative ones, to determine if and when persuasion is ethically defensible.

We make no bones about the fact that we've tried to teach you how to become a more effective persuader, as well as a more discriminating consumer of persuasive messages. Hence we feel morally obliged to offer some prescriptions and proscriptions on the ethical uses of persuasion. Before you go out and attempt to wield your persuasive skills on unsuspecting roommates, absent-minded professors, unwitting family members, unfortunate co-workers, or hapless strangers, we want to make sure you understand the importance of respecting others' dignity, of showing concern for others' welfare and, as they say in comic books, "of using your powers for good instead of evil." Quite seriously, we believe that the power to persuade carries with it a corresponding duty to persuade ethically. We don't claim to have a "corner" on the ethics market. Feel free to disagree with any of our guidelines. Your time will be well spent thinking through the bases for your own ethical standards and in coming to terms with what you consider to be moral and immoral influence attempts.

IS PERSUASION IN GENERAL UNETHICAL?

A frequent charge leveled against persuasion is that it is unethical. Some people equate persuasion with manipulation and see it as a one-sided approach to communication. Communication, they argue, should emphasize cooperation, trust, and shared agreement. We see this view of communication and human relationships as overly idealistic. What happens when people don't agree? What happens when their goals contradict? Enter the need for persuasion. Persuasion is what people rely on when things aren't "hunky dory," "peachy keen," or "super duper." Persuasion is what people turn to when their needs haven't been met or their relationships are less than ideal.

We argued in the first chapter that persuasion is not a dirty word. But persuasion *is* used to do the "dirty work" of convincing others when disagreements develop. Attempts at convincing others, however, are not necessarily one-sided. Persuasion can be, and often is, two-sided. Persuasion can, and often does, result in mutually satisfactory solutions. Persuasion is not the antithesis of cooperation. Persuasion can be based on trust and mutual respect. In a relationship based on equality, for example, each party is free to influence the other.

As we noted in Chapter 1, persuasion performs a number of positive, prosocial functions. For example, persuasion is used to increase public awareness about a variety of social problems such as spousal abuse, homelessness, and HIV transmission. And like it or not, persuasion is here to stay. To the extent that some persuaders are unethical, it makes even more sense to learn how unethical influence attempts work and why they succeed.

We don't deny that persuasion can be used in manipulative ways. Persuasion is a tool. Tools can be misused. In such cases, however, one should blame the tool's user, not the tool. By way of analogy, when someone uses the English language to belittle or demean another person, no one suggests we should do away with language. Why then, when persuasion is used unethically, do people blame persuasion rather than the persuader? Granted, some persuasive tools, such as fear appeals, hold greater potential for abuse, in the same way that a saw is more dangerous than a pair of pliers. Stronger safeguards need to be taken when using such persuasive tools, even when their use is for the receiver's own good.

THE MOTIVES COLOR THE MEANS

Consistent with our tool analogy, James McCroskey has commented that "the means of persuasion themselves are ethically neutral" (McCroskey, 1972, p. 269). Contrasting this view, Jacksa and Pritchard (1994) adopt the position that "virtually any act of communication can be seen from a moral point of view" (p. 12). We concede that ethics and persuasion are closely intertwined. We maintain, however, that the moral quality of an influence attempt is derived primarily from the motives or ends of the persuader, and only secondarily from the means of persuasion which are employed. In our view, the means of persuasion take on the moral character of the persuader's ends.

To illustrate our view, imagine that three persuaders each employ one of three strategies of influence: deception, fear appeals, or ingratiation. Is it possible to determine which persuader is the most ethical, or least ethical, merely by knowing the strategy each employs? We think not. We don't see how an ethical evaluation of the strategies could be made absent any knowledge of the purposes for which the strategies would be used. In Table 16.1, we list these three strategies (in column one), along with two contrasting sets of motives (in columns two and three). Notice that when paired with the first set of "good" motives, the use of the strategies appears justified. However, when paired with the second set of "evil" motives, the strategies appear highly unjustified.

Thus, in our view, the ethical quality of a persuader's motives tends to "rub off" on the persuasive strategy employed. The strategy itself is essentially neutral or amoral, until such time as it is paired with a particular motive or end. At that point, the entire influence attempt (motive and strategy) takes on a moral/immoral dimension.

To take our point one step further, even coercion can be defended as a justifiable means of achieving certain ends (remember that, according to our model, coercion represents a "borderline" case of persuasion). A child, for example, might be forced to get a vaccination by her or his parents. Psychotic or delusional persons might be forcibly restrained to prevent them from harming themselves or others. Or consider the "ticking bomb" scenario: A terrorist group announces it will set off a nuclear bomb in a major city within 24 hours. The detonation and ensuing radi-

TABLE 16.1 **The motives color the means. In our view, a persuader's motives color the means of persuasion that are used, as these examples illustrate.**

Strategy or Means	"Good" Motive or End	"Evil" Motive or End
Use of Deception	Trying to conceal a surprise birthday party from the person in whose honor the party is being given	Trying to swindle an elderly person out of his or her life savings
Use of Fear Appeals	Trying to convince a child never to accept a ride from a stranger	Threatening to demote an employee for refusing a superior's sexual advances
Use of Ingratiation	Trying to cheer up a friend who is depressed about a poor grade on a test	Lavishing attention on a dying relative, in order to inherit the relative's money

ation will likely kill thousands of people. The police have caught one of the terrorists, who refuses to talk. If the police torture the terrorist, however, they are 90 percent certain they can learn the bomb's location and disarm it. Is it morally permissible for the police to extract the information they need through torture in order to save thousands of lives?

The so-called ticking bomb scenario has left a number of moral ethicists scratching their heads. Sure it is wrong to torture someone, even a terrorist. But is it not *more wrong* to condemn millions of innocent people to die? Now consider this: the ticking bomb situation isn't purely hypothetical. In a recent Israeli court case, a ruling was made that limited physical abuse was permissible if it would save lives (Trounson, 1996; "U. N. Panel," 1997). Whether one agrees with the Israeli court's decision or not, the ruling underscores the point that even a conscientious persuader may reach the conclusion that the use of coercion is occasionally justified. We're not saying persuaders should relish the use of coercion. We're just saying that in some cases it may be the only way to prevent a greater harm.

ETHICS, CULTURE, AND THE ISSUE OF CENTRAL VERSUS PERIPHERAL PROCESSING

We readily admit that some persuasive strategies may seem more ethically desirable than others. For example, the use of reasoned argument might seem more ethically justifiable than the use of flattery or charm. The use of facts and statistics might appear more defensible than the use of emotional appeals. This highlights a general preference among Western societies for logical, rational thought, consistent with what Petty and Cacioppo (1986) call central processing. You may recall from our earlier discussion of the Elaboration Likelihood Model of Persuasion model in Chapter 2, that the central route to persuasion involves actively thinking about issues, reflecting upon information, and scrutinizing the content of messages. The peripheral route, on the other hand, is based on factors such as source credibility, imagery, or social cues. In American culture, the central route is generally the preferred route for persuasion. Not all cultures place the same emphasis, however, on rational, linear thought processes. Other cultures value different ways of knowing, favor other means of gaining adherence to ideas, and prefer other methods of securing behavioral compliance. As just one example, some Asian cultures emphasize the importance of fitting in, of conforming to group norms, and of not "rocking the boat." In such cultures, greater emphasis tends to be placed on *indirect* strategies of influence (such as hinting or stressing the importance of following group norms) than on *direct* strategies (arguing, open disagreement). The preference for indirect strategies reflects the importance of such cultural values as avoiding confrontation and preventing the loss of face (Wiseman, Sanders, Congalton, Gass, Sueda, & Ruiqing 1995).

Within Western culture there are also exceptions to the general preference for "rational" persuasion. A person who comes across as being overly logical or emotionless, like the character Mr. Spock, of *Star Trek* fame, may be viewed as "cold," "calculating," or "heartless." The ability to display compassion, convey empathy, and respond to the entreaties of others based on these same emotions are considered desirable qualities. Recent trends toward the use of "victim impact statements" in criminal trials illustrate the value placed on emotional appeals. A growing number of states now permit victims and/or victims' family members to testify during the sentencing phase of a criminal trial (Reske, 1996; Schulhofer, 1995; "Victim Justice," 1995). The survivors tell of the pain and grief they've experienced. They explain in vivid terms the losses they've suffered. The purpose is to focus attention on the emotional consequences of crime, a side that often gets overlooked amidst the legal and procedural wrangling that occurs during a trial. Thus, even though it may seem that some forms of influence are more ethically defensible than others, this depends to some extent on cultural and situational factors.

ETHICAL QUESTIONS THAT CAN'T BE ANSWERED THROUGH THE STUDY OF PERSUASION

We've argued that the moral character of a persuasive act is derived primarily from the persuader's motives. Persuasion research, however, tends to focus almost exclusively on the means of persuasion (strategies and tactics) rather than on the motives of persuaders. For this reason, persuasion research is ill-equipped to answer questions about what are good or evil ends. Take any current social controversy, for example; abortion, assisted suicide, drug legalization, and so forth. The study of persuasion cannot tell a persuader what side of the controversy to be on. The study of persuasion can't enlighten persuasion researchers as to what causes are good or bad or what values are right or wrong. Persuasion researchers tend to defer to moral philosophers, religious leaders, the judicial system, and other ethical arbiters to make such determinations.

Perhaps persuasion researchers should give greater consideration to the possible uses of the strategies and tactics they are busy investigating. Bear in mind, though, that it is difficult for a researcher to know how a particular tool of influence will be used. If a persuasive tool can be used for good *or* evil ends, what is a persuasion researcher to do? In Box 16.1, we identify some well-known approaches to ethics that you might study in a course on ethics. In practice, individuals tend to follow a combination of the approaches identified in Box 16.1, making most of us ethical relativists. A complete discussion of the field of ethics and moral philosophy is beyond the scope of this text. Fortunately, several excellent works are available if you wish to learn more about ethics and communication (Christians, Rotzoll, & Fackler, 1991; Jacksa & Pritchard, 1994; Johannesen, 1983; Johannesen, Thayer, & Hardt, 1979; Nilsen, 1966; Rivers, Christians, & Schramm, 1980).

The inability of persuasion researchers to distinguish good from bad applications of persuasion is similar to the situation facing other researchers in other fields. Recall the recent furor over cloning, for example, when a Scottish researcher, Ian Wilmut, announced he had successfully cloned "Dolly," a sheep, from DNA. The media was quick to pick up on the story. Could the technique be applied to

BOX 16.1   Approaches to Ethics

Ends versus means: An ethical controversy centering on whether the means or method of influence is justified by the desirability of the outcome. Can a persuasive outcome be so good or desirable that the use of force or coercion is justified to achieve it?

Consequentialism: An ethical approach emphasizing that which is pragmatic or functional. A persuader should weigh the benefits and drawbacks of his or her actions. Those actions that produce the greatest balance of good over bad are ethical.

Deontological systems: An ethical approach that is idealistic in nature. Such an ethical system focuses on the inherent rightness or wrongness of intentions. It isn't the persuasive outcome, but the morality of the persuader's intent that counts.

Amoralism (or Machiavellianism): This ethical approach authorizes whatever a persuader can get away with and is constrained only by laws or fear of social ostracism. The self-interest of the persuader is all that matters; others better watch out for themselves. Suckers deserve what they get. They should learn from their mistakes

Situational ethics/relativism: This ethical approach maintains that there are no moral absolutes. There are no ethical maxims. It isn't possible to write a moral code that applies to all cultures, persons, times, and places. There are always exceptions to every rule. There can be good or bad forms of persuasion, but whether they are good or bad depends upon the situation, the parties involved, the nature of the issue, and other related factors.

Universalism: This ethical approach maintains that there are universal, immutable "do's" and "don'ts." Morals and values can be ordered into enduring codes of conduct. Some actions are right or wrong for all people, places, and times. For example, torture is always wrong. Certain universal human rights must be honored. There are "hard" and "soft" versions of universalism, meaning that some perspectives are more absolute than others.

Egalitarianism (also known as the "Golden Rule"): This approach to ethics involves doing unto others as you would have them do unto you. Treat other people as you would have them treat you. A more modern derivative of this principle is "What goes around comes around."

Free market ethics: This ethical approach is based on the metaphor of the free market or capitalism: *Caveat emptor,* let the buyer beware. There should be little or no prior restraint on persuasive messages. This approach places greater responsibility on the receivers to critically evaluate persuasive messages.

Utilitarianism (John Stuart Mill): This is a teleological approach, based on the greatest good for the greatest number of people. The *Star Trek* version of this principle involves balancing "The needs of the many with the needs of the one."

humans? What if Albert Einstein or Ludwig van Beethoven could be cloned? What if Adolf Hitler were replicated? The prospect that the technique might be used to clone human beings whipped public sentiment into a frenzy. Legislation was quickly drafted to ban research on the cloning of human beings ("Scientists Argue Against Ban," 1997; Stolberg, 1997).

The scientist who developed the technique never dreamed his discovery would prompt such an outcry. He was simply going about his research. The same may be said for persuasion researchers. They are aware their findings have ethical implications. For the most part, however, they are simply interested in learning more about how persuasion works. Their focus is not on whether a particular strategy or tactic should be used. Nor is their focus on what causes should or should not be furthered through the use of persuasion. We don't deny that persuasion researchers should take heed of the ethical implications of the strategies and tactics they are investigating. We merely wish to point out that persuasion researchers are more interested in pursuing knowledge for its own sake and less on discovering techniques for mind control. We readily admit, however, that like Dr. Frankenstein in Mary Shelley's novel, persuasion researchers—and all researchers for that matter—are ethically responsible for the knowledge they uncover and pass along.

OUR APPROACH: CHARACTERISTICS OF ETHICAL INFLUENCE

The authors claim no special expertise in the field of ethics. We certainly don't possess the moral credentials of a Mother Teresa or the Dalai Lama. We feel obliged, nonetheless, to offer our own set of guidelines and recommendations for ethical persuasion. Just as we believe the power to persuade entails a responsibility to persuade ethically, we also believe that teaching others how to persuade entails an obligation to teach them how to do so ethically. Our views don't emanate from a single ethical perspective, so we can probably best be described as situationistic or relativistic in our approach (see Box 16.1). We don't expect you to accept our advice as gospel. But we do hope you'll think about our guidelines and recommendations carefully. We believe that the more you think about the ethical dimensions involved in persuasion, the more conscientious you will tend to be as a persuader.

Ethics and Our Model of Persuasion

You will recall that in our model of persuasion (see Chapter 2) we distinguished between pure and borderline cases of persuasion. You also will recall from our model that there are five criteria that distinguish pure cases of persuasion from borderline cases. Pure cases of persuasion are those that are intentional, which occur with the receiver's conscious awareness, which involve free choice on the part of the receiver, which take place through language or symbolic action, and which involve two or more persons. We believe the first four of these criteria hold important ethical implications for persuaders.

Intentionality

A number of scholars subscribe to the view that only intentional influence attempts count as persuasion. From an ethical standpoint, however, this view is problematic. We maintain that such a view lets persuaders "off the hook" for the unintended consequences of their persuasion. A persuader whose influence attempts result in harmful, unforeseen consequences can avoid responsibility by saying, "That's not what I intended." A persuader whose influence attempts reach the wrong audience can say, "That's not where I was aiming." Studies have shown that unintended messages, such as an overheard ethnic slur, can damage a person's reputation in the eyes of other persons (Greenberg & Pyszczynski, 1985; Kirkland, Greenberg, & Pyszczynski, 1987). Thus, we think persuaders should be held accountable for the unintended consequences of their persuasion. Our definition and model of persuasion, which acknowledges the existence of unintentional persuasion, is better suited to holding persuaders accountable for the unintended effects of their persuasion.

Conscious Awareness

Pure cases of persuasion, according to our model, occur with the conscious awareness of the participants. Borderline cases of persuasion, on the other hand, require no such realization on the part of the participants. We maintain that persuasion that takes place with the conscious awareness of all the parties involved is far more ethical than persuasion that does not. If a person knows he or she is the target of an influence attempt he or she can take active steps to resist the attempt or counter with an attempt of his or her own. All else being equal, an above-board attempt at persuasion is ethically superior to a hidden, disguised, or surreptitious attempt to persuade.

Free Choice/Free Will

Pure cases of persuasion, according to our model, are those that allow participants to make free, informed decisions as to whether they wish to comply with persuasive messages. Borderline cases of persuasion, on the other hand, involve coercion in varying degrees. We believe, quite obviously, that persuasive attempts that allow persons to make free choices are ethically superior to those that do not. Free choice includes the ability to question others' influence attempts, to counter with influence attempts of one's own, and to resist complying with others' attempts. As a general rule, we believe the more freedom one has to say "No," the more ethical a given influence attempt is. The more coercive pressure that is brought to bear on a person, we maintain, the less ethical is the influence attempt. This also explains why conscious awareness, discussed previously, is an important ingredient in ethical persuasion. A person cannot *choose* to comply with an influence attempt if the person is unaware he or she is the target of an influence attempt.

An interesting side issue with respect to free choice and persuasion is whether a person should have the right to avoid influence attempts altogether. Do people in public places have the right not to be asked for donations by panhandlers and, in a related vein, how aggressive or assertive can panhandlers be when asking for donations? Does a woman seeking an abortion have the right to avoid a persuasive attempt by a pro-choice advocate on the steps of an abortion clinic? The courts have recently wrestled at length with these very kinds of issues (Cain, 1996; Ellickson, 1996). In general the courts have decided that the right to free speech outweighs the right to be left alone. The courts have, however, imposed a number of "time and place" restrictions on solicitors, panhandlers, and anti-abortion protesters. Telephone solicitors, for example, can't call at unreasonable hours of the day (Cain, 1996) (see Box 16.2). Pro-choice advocates must stand a certain distance

BOX 16.2   Telephone Solicitations: Don't Fall for a Phony Line

It happens all the time. You've just sat down to dinner, or you're in the shower, and the telephone rings. "Hello," the voice at the other end says, "How are you this evening? I'm calling to tell you about a wonderful opportunity..." You guessed it—another telephone solicitation. Telemarketing is a big business. More than 18 million Americans are called by telemarketers each day (Cain, 1994). Although most telemarketing calls are merely a nuisance, some are downright fraudulent. No one knows for sure, but one estimate is that telemarketing fraud amounts to $40 billion a year and that roughly 10 percent of all telemarketing sales are fraudulent (Kristoff, 1997).

Some measures have been enacted to protect consumers. For instance, in 1995, Congress passed the Telemarketing and Consumer Fraud and Abuse Prevention Act. The act specifically forbids (1) automatically dialed calls to emergency service providers, cellular phones, pagers, and patients' rooms in hospitals; (2) prerecorded calls to residences; and (3) unsolicited fax advertisements (Cain, 1996).*

At the same time, however, more and more telemarketing scams are being launched from outside the United States, making it difficult for law enforcement agencies to prosecute perpetrators or for victims to seek restitution. Of course, there are many legitimate charities and worthwhile causes out there. But because you have no way of knowing whether a given telemarketer is on the up and up, we suggest you *exercise considerable caution* before buying anything or donating money via a telephone solicitation. With this in mind, we've provided a number of suggestions for dealing with telephone solicitors. The friendly, kind-hearted voice at the other end of the phone could be a con artist. Some of the strategies are, admit-

tedly, rude. Keep in mind, however, that the telephone solicitor is counting on your being too polite to hang-up.

- **The polite but swift rebuff:** As soon as you've established the call is a telephone solicitation, say "No thanks, I'm not interested, good-bye" and hang up before the other party can utter another word. Remember, the solicitor wants to engage you in conversation, get you to answer questions, and listen to his or her pitch. You don't have to.

- **My home is my castle:** If a telemarketer calls at a particularly inopportune time, say "I consider this an unwarranted intrusion on my privacy in my own home. Never call here again."

- **The "do not call" list:** Did you know you can simply ask a telemarketer to exclude you from any future calls? You can. As part of the Telephone Consumer Protection Act of 1991, the FCC adopted a requirement that any consumer can ask to be placed on a "do not call" list, which must be honored thereafter. Companies are required by law to maintain a "do not call" list.

- **Mail it to me:** One of the author's always uses this approach. Whatever the telemarketer is selling, the author says, "Mail me all the information. That way I can read it over carefully, and make a rational, informed decision." If the telemarketer persists, hang up. Any offer that can't be communicated in writing is probably a scam.

- **I need to think it over:** Tell the telemarketer, "I want to think it over. I want to consult my accountant or attorney first." If the telemarketer persists, say, "You seem to be trying to push me into an impulse decision, so my impulse is to hang up. Bye."

*The legislation excludes calls to persons with whom the caller has an established business relationship, calls from tax-exempt nonprofit organizations, and calls made with the person's prior express permission (Cain, 1994).

(Continued)

BOX 16.2 *Continued*

- **The walk away method:** A friend of ours gets rid of telephone solicitors in the following way: When they ask, "Is Mr. or Mrs. Boswell home?" He says, "Yeah, I'll go get em'." He then walks away leaving them to languish for 5 to 10 minutes. When he returns, they've invariably hung up. "They're wasting my time," he says, in defense of this strategy, "so I'm wasting theirs."

- **The Seinfeld method:** This technique for getting rid of a telephone solicitor was featured on an episode of the *Seinfeld* show. In response to a telemarketing call, Jerry Seinfeld said, "I'm busy right now. Why don't you give me *your* home phone number and I'll call you back later?" Following an apparent pause at the other end, Seinfeld says, "What's the matter, you don't like people calling you at home?"

Whatever technique you use, here are two important pieces of advice to avoid being conned. First, never give out a credit card number or bank account number to anyone who has called you. You have no way of knowing if the person is really who he or she claims to be. Only give out credit card information if you initiated the call. Second, if a telephone offer sounds promising ask for the name of the business, their business license number, the city in which the business is incorporated, and then a name and phone number so you can make a return call. Any telemarketer who is reluctant to provide this information is waving a red flag. This gives you a chance to verify the legitimacy of the business. If it is a charity, you can verify their tax-exempt status. If you have concerns or suspicions, call your local Chamber of Commerce or police department.

away from the entrance to an abortion clinic. Thus, even though we enjoy a constitutionally recognized right to privacy, we don't have a constitutional right to be free from all types of persuasive messages.

Language and Symbolic Action

According to our model, pure cases of persuasion center around the use of language (the spoken or printed word) and symbolic actions (protests marches, sit-ins, etc.). Borderline cases of persuasion include persuasion via nonverbal and/or behavioral means. Using physical attractiveness or behavioral modification to alter another's behavior would both constitute instances of borderline persuasion. We believe that persuasion that takes place through language and/or symbol usage is generally more ethical than persuasion via nonverbal and/or behavioral means. Our preference for the former is based on the fact that language-based influence attempts are generally more easily recognized and more readily understood. Nonverbal appeals, on the other hand, are less recognizable as persuasive attempts. This hearkens back to our previously stated preference for influence attempts that occur with the conscious awareness of the participants. In general, it is easier to know one is being persuaded when the persuasion occurs through language.

Of course, it is possible for persuaders to let receivers know that they will be the targets of nonverbal influence attempts and/or behavioral modification techniques. Sit-ins and protest marches, for example, are fairly obvious instances of nonverbal persuasion. Or, in behavioral modification, a person who checked into a smoking cessation clinic would be told that negative stimuli (nausea, electrical shock) might be used to help her or him kick the smoking habit. Where the recipient is made aware that nonverbal and/or behavioral strategies will be employed, we see little ethical difference between language-based and non-language-based persuasion.

Persuaders as Lovers

In a widely acclaimed essay Wayne Brockriede (1974) posited three metaphors describing the ways people go about arguing. "Seducers," he argued, used trickery, deceit, charm, flattery, and beguilement to achieve their ends. Seducers do not view others as equals, but as unwitting victims. "Rapists," the second category identified by Brockriede, use threats, force, and coercion in an effort to win their arguments. They resort to brow-beating, personal attacks, threats, and ultimatums to get their way. Like seducers, rapists view others as inferior. Others are treated as objects to satisfy the rapist's needs. "Lovers," the third of Brockriede's categories, respect one another's dignity and base their relationships on equality. They don't treat each other as victims or objects, but rather as partners. They are open and receptive to one another's arguments and look for mutually satisfactory solutions to their differences.

We believe Brockriede's characterization of these three styles of argument applies equally well to persuasive encounters. We extend his approach here by ascribing what we believe to be three essential attributes or qualities of "persuaders as lovers." The first quality is *respect*. Ethical influence attempts tend to reaffirm the other person's sense of self-worth. Persuaders who use ethical strategies and tactics tend to demonstrate respect for one another's dignity. In contrast, unethical influence attempts tend to express disdain for others. The target of an unethical influence attempt is viewed as a "mark," a "sucker," or a "patsy."

The second quality is *equality*. Influence attempts are most ethical when the parties enjoy equal status in a relationship. This is because in unequal relationships status or power differences are more likely—whether intentionally or unintentionally—to impinge upon the choice-making ability of the lower status person. The person enjoying more status or power may find it difficult to resist using "carrots" or "sticks" to gain compliance. The person occupying the lower status position may find it difficult to believe that the person with higher status will not resort to rewards or punishments.

Does this mean a manager or supervisor cannot engage in ethical influence attempts with subordinates or employees? Does this mean parents are necessarily unethical when they try to persuade children? Certainly the *potential* for unethical influence, or the *perception* of unethical influence, exists in any hierarchical relationship. Nevertheless, we believe ethical influence attempts are possible even when there are power disparities, but only if the more powerful party allows communication to take place on an equal footing. In organizational communication, for example, the very concepts of "downward" and "upward" communication suggest inequality. To minimize such inequality, the possibility for reciprocal influence would have to be established. This would require a superior to make it clear that he or she was suggesting, not ordering. The superior also would need to promise that there would be no reprisals for disagreement and make good on that pledge. Finally, the superior would have to be open to having her or his mind changed as well. These same requirements—suggesting, not ordering, avoiding reprisals, and remaining open to influence—would apply to parental influence as well.

The third quality is *tolerance*. Each party to a persuasive encounter must be patient with the other, giving the other a chance to make his or her case. Each party also should be open to the other's point of view, making persuasion a two-way street. If a person wishes to influence another, we maintain, then he or she also must be willing to be influenced. Turn-taking plays an important role in this process. Persuaders need to be willing to hear one another out. A person who enters a persuasive encounter with the mind-set, "I will persuade, but I will not be persuaded," is not displaying tolerance for the other person or the other person's point of view. Taken together, we believe that these three qualities have the potential to make persuasive encounters more ethical and more pleasant.

ETHICAL ISSUES ARISING FROM PREVIOUS CHAPTERS

Having offered some of our own guidelines for ethical persuasion, we now turn our attention to some of the ethical issues introduced elsewhere in this text. A number of ethical questions regarding persuasive strategies and tactics emanate from the preceding chapters. Here, we examine some of those key questions and explore possible answers.

Ethics and Credibility

A number of ethical questions center around the use of source credibility as a tool for persuasion (see Chapter 5). Among the key questions on the ethical uses of credibility are the following:

1. Is it unethical for a celebrity endorser to promote a product or service he or she does not actually use or about which he or she lacks expertise?
2. Does the use of authority become an abuse of authority if receivers place too much faith or reliance in a particular source? For example, can a TV evangelist hold too much sway over his or her followers, thereby clouding their judgment and independent thinking?

Although we don't have specific answers to the above questions, we can offer some general advice. Because credibility tends to function as a peripheral cue, a reliance on credibility as the principle means of persuasion tends to short-circuit thoughtful deliberation. We believe that persuasive appeals that emphasize central processing are generally superior to those that emphasize peripheral processing.

The former are ethically preferable, we believe, because they enable receivers to analyze messages, scrutinize evidence, and generally think for themselves.

We believe that a reliance on source credibility, at the expense of thoughtful reflection, is ethically suspect. In cases where credibility is used to enhance the persuasiveness of a message, we believe a qualified source should be used. By "qualified," we mean a source who possesses expertise in the area in which she or he is offering advice or making recommendations. Tiger Woods, for example, knows a great deal about the game of golf, so his endorsement of a brand of golf clubs would be meaningful. He's not an expert on vacuums, however, so his recommendation of a brand of vacuum cleaner would possess no more validity than that of the average person.

Ethics and Communicator Characteristics

We noted in Chapter 6 that some receivers are particularly vulnerable to influence attempts. Young children, for example, have difficulty distinguishing what toys featured in television commercials can and cannot do. Patients with terminal illnesses are highly vulnerable to hucksters peddling "miracle" cures. Elderly citizens, some of whose mental faculties are diminished, are highly susceptible to scams perpetrated by con artists. And some new immigrants are uniquely vulnerable, owing to their naivete, to language barriers, or both. Concerns such as these invite several ethical questions on persuasion aimed at specialized audiences:

1. What ethical safeguards should be followed when attempting to persuade children?
2. What ethical responsibilities does a persuader have when attempting to persuade highly vulnerable audiences?

With respect to the first question, we strongly believe that special care must be taken when targeting children. Children are highly impressionable and, unfortunately, highly gullible. They often fail to grasp the full meaning of messages or disclaimers attached to messages. Although a variety of private and public agencies already regulate mass media messages aimed at children, advertisers have been criticized for a number of unfair practices. As Treise, Weigold, Conna, and Garrison (1994) have commented:

> *Most notable of these criticisms include the arguments that advertising to children promotes the use of products, such as sweets, that are harmful to children (Gore, 1989); manipulates and disappoints children with exaggerated claims; creates conflicts with parents over purchases; has the potential to influence children to experiment with alcoholic beverages and/or drugs (Atkin, 1987); and creates confusion over product and commercial distinctions (Kunkel, 1988; Englehardt, 1987). (Lexis–Nexis)*

In addition to following those strictures that are already in place, we would advise those seeking to influence youngsters to follow three basic guidelines. First, they should ensure that they have a parent or legal guardian's permission before attempting any persuasion. Persuading without such permission not only usurp's parental autonomy, but invites lawsuits as well. Second, they should communicate using words and concepts that children can understand. Persuasive messages should be geared to the developmental level of the age group being targeted. Third, they should make sure they have the children's best interests at heart. Whose interest was R. J. Reynolds promoting through the use of the now discontinued "Joe Camel" campaign? Critics charged that the use of the cartoon-like character was a transparent attempt to attract underage smokers (Bromberg, 1990). In our view, public awareness messages that target kids for their sake (e.g., anti-drug spots or stranger-danger messages) are less ethically suspect than for-profit advertisements that target kids in order to make money.

With respect to the second question, there clearly are cases in which vulnerable groups are targeted by persuaders. As just one example, people who live in inner city areas are subjected to more billboards promoting cigarettes and alcohol than people who live in more affluent, suburban areas. The Detroit Planning Commission found that in low-income, inner-city neighborhoods 55 to 58 percent of the billboards advertised cigarettes and alcohol, whereas only 34 percent of the billboards in higher income neighborhoods did so (Koeppel, 1990).

We believe that many of the concerns involving highly vulnerable groups or individuals can be allayed by adhering to the aforementioned values of mutual respect, relational equality, and mutual tolerance. Part of the task of persuading vulnerable receivers involves displaying interpersonal and/or intercultural sensitivity. This includes the ability to empathize with others' feelings and points of view. Part of the task also involves avoiding the temptation to prey upon others' fears, weaknesses, or vulnerabilities. The motto *caveat emptor* (let the buyer beware) may make sense when one is dealing with fully functioning, informed consumers. When applied to vulnerable groups, however, the motto simply becomes an excuse for taking advantage.

Ethics and Deception

The study of deception and deception detection constitutes one of the most ethically sensitive areas of persuasion research. A number of ethical issues were addressed in the chapter on deception (see Chapter 13). Of these, one overriding question will be reexamined here:

> *Is deception ever justified? Or, stated somewhat differently, is honesty always the best policy?*

While some may feel that lying is always wrong, we believe that there are numerous situations in which telling "white lies" is beneficial for relationships. Such social rituals as complimenting another's clothing, praising a dinner host's cooking, or telling the host of a party you had a good time seem like fairly harmless, innocuous uses of deception to us. Even where candor is called for, we believe there is an important difference between being honest and being *brutally* honest.

Our view is that although deception is sometimes socially justified, one should examine the motives of the persuader by asking, "In whose interest is the lie being perpetrated?" Self-serving lies, we believe, are the least ethical. Lies told for the benefit of another, we maintain, are the most ethical. In assessing the ethical merits of deception, one should also keep in mind that outright falsehoods and misrepresentations constitute only one type of deception. Deception also can include withholding information or purposeful ambiguity. The latter types of deception, we suggest, are more ethically defensible than "bald-faced" lies. A person might be "diplomatic," for example, to spare another the pain or loss of face that being blunt or frank might cause. Both the withholding of information and purposeful ambiguity thus can be used to benefit another.

A final note on the "honesty is the best policy" approach is that it only works if some of the preceding conditions for ethical persuasion exist, for example, there is mutual respect, a relationship is based on equality, and tolerance for one another's views exists. If these conditions do not exist, then being honest may simply result in the honest person being fired, punished, or ridiculed.

Ethics of Using Threats as a Compliance-Gaining Strategy

In Chapter 11 we discussed a number of strategies and tactics related to compliance gaining. Among the strategies identified was the threat of punishment (Marwell & Schmidt, 1967). As a general rule, studies have shown that using threats achieves greater compliance than not using them (Gass & Canary, 1988; Heisler, 1974; Nevin & Ford, 1976; Tittle & Rowe, 1973). Their effectiveness notwithstanding, however, there are serious ethical questions regarding the use of threats. Hence, we focus here on the ethics of using threats as a means of persuasion.

> *Is the use of threats of punishment ever ethically justifiable and, if so, under what circumstances?*

Every attempt to persuade involves ethical questions. To a greater extent than with other influence strategies, however, we believe the use of threats should raise red flags in the persuader's mind. There are numerous reasons why. First, we believe threats are unethical inasmuch as their effectiveness hinges upon creating a state of psychological distress in receivers. Second, threats tend to be exploitative of power and/or status differences in relationships. As we noted previously, persuasion is more ethically defensible when it is based on a relationship of equality. Third, both issuing and carrying out threats tends to diminish the morale and self-esteem of the recipient. Fourth, a reliance on threats is damaging and destructive to relationships. In the long-run threats do more harm than good. Fifth, the use of threats can foster resentment or trigger aggression toward the threatener. If you rely on threats, you'd better watch your back! Sixth, threats must be carried out from time to time, an unpleasant prospect for both the threatener and the recipient. Seventh, the threatener is modeling a negative form of behavior for others to follow, thereby teaching others to rely on threats as well. Can you tell we're not too fond of threats?

When, if ever, then, should a persuader use threats? Our advice is that threats, although sometimes unavoidable, should never be the strategy of first resort. They should be used only when prosocial alternatives are unavailable, or have failed, and only when they are clearly in the best interests of the receiver and/or society. As an illustration, imagine that a spouse or intimate is destroying himself or herself through alcohol abuse. The partner has pleaded with him or her to join Alcoholics Anonymous or to seek some other form of help, all to no avail. We believe that the partner would be well-justified in threatening, "I'm leaving you if you don't get help." Making such a threat, and following through on it if necessary, might well be in the long-term interests of both people.

Other examples of what we consider justifiable uses of threats can be summoned: We believe parents are within their rights in threatening their children with punishment to deter them from running into the street. An office worker who is the object of repeated, unwelcome sexual advances by a co-worker is justified in threatening legal action to stop the untoward behavior. Highway safety agencies have legitimate grounds for threatening motorists with fines for exceeding the posted speed limit.

The above examples notwithstanding, a reliance on threats produces so many undesirable social consequences that we think their use is rarely justified. A persuader who is contemplating the use of threats should therefore ask himself or herself if that is the only way to achieve an objective and if the objective is even worth achieving if threats must be used. Too often, we suspect the use of threats represents reflex behavior on the part of the threatener. A reliance on threats can become habitual. If persuaders would reflect upon their strategy selection more, they would recognize that pro-social alternatives are usually available and are more conducive to promoting and preserving relationships.

Ethics and Fear Appeals

Some persuaders live by the motto, "If you've got em' by the balls, their hearts and minds will follow." Although the research we reviewed in Chapter 14 shows that fear appeals are generally effective, considerable caution should be used when using these types of appeals as tools of influence.

Is the use of fear appeals ever ethically justifiable and, if so, under what conditions or circumstances?

If the dangers alluded to in a fear appeal are real or genuine, then we believe it is not only acceptable to use them, but desirable to do so as well. People should be informed about dangers and hazards to which they are exposed. One of the risks posed by the use of strong fear appeals, however, is that they may induce panic in some receivers. Receivers with high chronic anxiety and/or low self-esteem are more likely to overreact to fear appeals. Hence, persuaders should avoid using intense fear appeals on such groups or take extra care when doing so. Two other guidelines should be observed when using fear appeals. The first is that specific recommendations for avoiding the harmful consequences must be included in the appeal. The specific recommendations must tell receivers how to cope with the dangers identified. The second is that the persuader should include reassuring recommendations telling receivers that everything will be O.K. if they follow the prescribed course of action. In our judgment, fear appeals should never be used if the alleged harms are exaggerated or, worse yet, fabricated. Nor should fear appeals be used if receivers are given no recourse for avoiding the harms. What is the point in scaring people if there is nothing they can do about it?

By way of comparison, we believe the use of threats is a much more serious matter than the use of fear appeals. As we noted previously, threats should be a strategy of last resort, to be used only after pro-social forms of influence, like encouragement, praise, or other positive inducements have been exhausted.

Ethics and Emotional Appeals

Some people take the view that emotional appeals, which tug at receivers heart-strings, are unjustified precisely because they appeal to emotion rather than to reason. Persuasion, they say, should aim higher, at the mind, not the heart, and certainly not below the belt. In response to this concern, we raise the following ethical questions:

1. Is playing on others' emotions ethically justifiable?
2. Are some types of emotional appeals better, or more ethically defensible, than others?

Our answer to the first question is a qualified "Yes." You'll recall from Chapter 14, however, that the distinction between logical and emotional appeals represents something of an artificial dichotomy anyway. People tend to perceive messages they agree with as "logical" or "rational" and messages they disagree with as "emotional." To the extent that logical and emotional appeals can be differentiated, we believe they work perfectly well side by side. We see nothing wrong with using emotional appeals, so long as their use compliments, rather than contradicts or substitutes, for other more cognitively oriented approaches to persuasion. We do not think emotional appeals should constitute the sole means of persuasion, nor do we believe emotional appeals should be used if they contradict sound reasoning and evidence. As we mentioned earlier, our preference is for central processing of persuasive messages. To the extent that emotional appeals are used to promote peripheral processing, at the expense of central processing, we believe their use is undesirable.

In answer to the second question, we tend to believe that negative, divisive appeals are less ethically defensible than positive, prosocial appeals. When one thinks of emotional appeals one may envision "negative" sorts of appeals such as appeals to pity, shame, or guilt. Bear in mind, however, that emotional appeals have a positive side as well. Emotional appeals can be inspiring or uplifting. They can motivate one to try harder, to excel, to give one's all. We hardly think that coaches, teachers, politicians, and clergy who provide emotional encouragement are behaving unethically. Quite the contrary. We believe positive emotional appeals have a legitimate role to play in the persuasion process and that they function as useful compliments to the use of reasoning and evidence.

Ethics and Ingratiation

Everyone claims to hate brownnosers, unless the brownnosing is directed at them, that is. In his seminal work on the subject Jones (1963) defined ingratiation, the polite term for brownnosing, as an "illicit" form of strategic behavior (see Chapter 14). Thus it would seem that ingratiation operates through unethical means. We thus explore the question:

> Is ingratiation an unethical practice or just an honest acknowledgment of the way things work?

We typically tend to think of ingratiation as a form of deception. That is, we envision the ingratiator as being non-genuine in his or her use of flattery. But what if the ingratiator *believes* in the praise he or she bestows upon another? We see no problem with the use of praise or compliments if the persuader genuinely believes in what she or he is saying. In fact, this is one of the ethical questions that allows us to draw a "bright line" between what we consider to be ethical and unethical persuasion. Sincere compliments, we maintain, are ethical, and insincere compliments unethical. Genuine praise offers the prospect of a win–win communication encounter. Both parties benefit. When a persuader pays a compliment and means it, he or she is demonstrating respect for the other person, and respect, we contend, is one of the essential ingredients of ethical influence attempts.

Ethics and Subliminal Persuasion

Unlike many people, we aren't troubled by the use of subliminal messages. Why? Because, frankly, we don't believe they work. Virtually all the credible research that has been conducted to date supports our strong sense of skepticism. Thus, it is more as a matter of principle than out of genuine concern that we raise the ethical question:

> Should subliminal messages be allowed, and if so, should they be regulated by the government or some other institution?

We feel much the same about the first part of this question as we do about the use of voodoo dolls. We'd prefer that people *not* stick pins in dolls that resemble us, but we aren't much bothered by it if they do. As we noted in Chapter 15, there is no credible scientific evidence that subliminals work. The practice of embedding or hiding images in advertisements has proven fruitless as has the practice of planting sub-audible oral messages. Other than disliking subliminals as a matter of principle, then, we believe that there is little to fear from their actual use. If unscrupulous persuaders want to bombard us with subliminal messages, so much the better! The time and energy they waste on their fruitless endeavor may distract them from using other, more effective techniques of persuasion on us.

SUMMARY

We've argued in this chapter that persuasion is not an inherently unethical activity. To the contrary, we believe that persuasion can be used to advance all manner of positive, prosocial interests. Persuasion is a powerful tool that can be used for the noblest and basest of motives. Humankind's ability to persuade is thus both a blessing and a curse. Our view is that the moral quality of a given persuasive act is based primarily on the motives of the persuader and only secondarily on the strategies and tactics used by the persuader.

Based on our model of persuasion, we've argued that pure persuasion is more ethically defensible than borderline persuasion. That is, persuasion that is intentional, that occurs with the receiver's conscious awareness, that involves free choice, and that takes place through language or symbolic action is more ethically defensible than persuasion that takes place via other means. Furthermore, we offered three qualities that we consider to be characteristic of ethical persuasion—respect, equality, and tolerance.

Last, we examined a number of ethical questions associated with particular topics and issues related to persuasion. We attempted to answer these questions as best we could—without pussyfooting or dancing around the issues on the one hand and without claiming to have a corner on truth and ethics on the other hand. Above all, we urge you to contemplate the bases for your own ethical beliefs and not to let anyone else, including us, tell you what is right or wrong. The cause of ethics will be better served if you figure out for yourself what you ought, and ought not do, as a persuader.

We've told you about a number of tools of influence in these pages. Many of them have proven to be highly effective. Unfortunately, we can't give you a conscience to go with them (the publisher said it would be too expensive). We have to trust that you will let your conscience be your guide. When pondering which persuasive strategies you should employ, think not only about the persuasive ends you are seeking, but the kinds of relationships you want to have with other people. Long-term relationships, we're convinced, should never be sacrificed for short-term compliance. Mutual influence requires give and take, not just take, take, take. If you put people first, and persuasion second, we think you'll be more successful in the long run than if you put persuasion first and people second.

REFERENCES

Brockriede, W. (1974). Arguers as lovers. *Philosophy and Rhetoric, 5,* 1–11.

Bromberg, M. S. (1990). Critics fume at cigarette marketing. *Business and Society Review, 73,* 27–28.

Cain, R. M. (1994). Call up someone and just say 'buy'—Telemarketing and the regulatory environment. *American Business Law Journal, 31*(4), 641–698.

Cain, R. M. (1996). Recent developments in telemarketing regulation. *Journal of Public Policy and Marketing 15*(1), 135–145.

✓ Christians, C. G., Rotzoll, K. B., & Fackler, M. (1991). *Media ethics: Cases and moral reasoning* (3rd ed.). New York: Longman.

Ellickson, R. C. (1996) Controlling chronic misconduct in city spaces: Of panhandlers, skid rows, and public-space zoning. *Yale Law Journal, 105*(5), 1165–1248.

Gass, R. H., & Canary, D. J. (1988, May). *An experimental examination of threat of punishment and promise of reward on motivation.* Paper presented at the annual meeting of the International Communication Association, New Orleans, LA.

Greenberg, J., & Pyszczynski, T. (1985). The effect of an overheard ethnic slur on evaluations of the target: How to spread a social disease. *Journal of Experimental Social Psychology, 21,* 61–72.

Heisler, G. (1974). Ways to deter law violators: Effects of levels of threat and vicarious punishment on cheating. *Journal of Consulting and Clinical Psychology, 42*(4), 577–582.

✓ Jacksa, J. A., & Pritchard, M. S. (1994). *Communication ethics: Methods of analysis* (2nd ed.). Belmont, CA: Wadsworth.

✓ Johannesen, R. L. (1983). *Ethics and human communication* (2nd ed.). Prospect Heights, IL: Waveland Press.

✓ Johannesen, R. L., Thayer, L. O., & Hardt, H. (1979). *Ethics, morality, and the media: Reflections on American culture.* New York: Hastings House.

Jones, E. (1963). *Ingratiation.* New York: Appleton-Century-Crofts.

Kaplan, A. (1964). *The conduct of inquiry.* New York: Thomas Crowell.

Kirkland, S. L., Greenberg, J., & Pyszczynski, T. (1987). Further evidence of the deleterious effects of overheard derogatory ethnic labels: Derogation beyond the target. *Personality and Social Psychology Bulletin, 13*(2), 216–227.

Koeppel, D. (1990, January 29). "In Philadelphia, R. J. Reynolds made all the wrong moves." *Adweek's Marketing Week, 40* pp. 20–30.

Kristoff, K. M. (1997, January 19). "Groups band together to crack down on telemarketing fraud." *Los Angeles Times,* p. D-2.

Marwell, G., & Schmitt, D. R. (1967). Dimensions of compliance-gaining behavior: An empirical analysis. *Sociometry, 30,* 350–364.

McCroskey, J. C. (1972). *An introduction to rhetorical communication* (2nd ed.). Englewood Cliffs, NJ: Prentice-Hall.

Nevin, J. R., & Ford, N. M. (1976). Effects of a deadline date and a veiled threat on mail survey responses. *Journal of Applied Psychology, 61,* 116–118.

Nilsen, T. R. (1966). *Ethics of speech communication.* Indianapolis, IN: Bobbs-Merrill.

Petty, R. E., & Cacioppo, J. T. (1986). *Communication and persuasion: Central and peripheral routes to attitude change.* New York: Springer-Verlag.

Reske, H. J. (1996, October). Constitutional cooperation: Bipartisan support creates momentum for victims' rights amendment. *ABA Journal, 82,* 26.

Rivers, W. L., Christians, C. G., & Schramm, W. (1980). *Responsibility in mass communication* (3rd ed.). New York: Harper and Row.

Schulhofer, S. J. (1995). The trouble with trials: The trouble with us. *Yale Law Journal, 105*(3), 825–855.

"Scientists argue against ban on human cloning" (1997, April 14). *Milwaukee Journal Sentinel,* p. 4.

Stolberg, S. (1997, April 29). "Reproductive research far outpaces public policy." *Los Angeles Times,* A1, A20–21.

Telemarketing and Consumer Fraud and Abuse Prevention Act, 15 U. S. C. § 6101-6108 (1994).

Tittle, C. R., & Rowe, A. R. (1973). Moral appeal, sanction, threat, and deviance: An experimental test. *Social Problems, 20*(4), 488–498.

Treise, D., Weigold, M. F., Conna, J., & Garrison, H. (1994). Ethics in advertising: Ideological correlates of consumer perceptions: Special issue on ethics in advertising. *Journal of Advertising, 23*(3), 59–69.

Trounson, R. (1996, November 16). "Activists decry Israel's OK of force by interrogators." *Los Angeles Times*, p. A9.

"U. N. panel attacks Israel over 'torture' of detainees" (1997, May 8). *Orange County Register*, p. 26.

"Victim Justice" (1995, April 17). *The New Republic, 212,* 9.

Wiseman, R. L., Sanders, J. A., Congalton, K. J., Gass, R. H., Sueda, K., & Ruiqing, D. (1995). A cross cultural analysis of compliance gaining: China, Japan, and the United States. *Intercultural Communication Studies, 5*(1), 1–17.

NAME INDEX

Bostrom, R. N., 151
Boutcher, S. H., 304
Bower, G. H., 154
Bowers, J. W., 150, 154
Boyd, J. G., 236
Bradac, J., 154, 155, 157
Bradley, P. H., 156
Braginsky, D. D., 251
Brandt, D. R., 254, 255
Brashers, D. E., 156
Brauer, M., 137, 138
Brehm, J. W., 172, 199
Brehm, S. S., 172, 199
Brentar, J. E., 301
Brock, T., 162
Brock, T. C., 199
Brockner, J., 169
Brockriede, W., 329
Bromberg, S., 332
Bronfen, M. I., 306, 310, 313, 313n
Brooks, G. P., 275
Brotons, M., 296
Brown, J. D., 305
Brown, P., 215–216
Brownlow, S., 176
Bruner, G. C., 303
Bruschke, J., 244
Bruzzone, D. A., 280
Bryant, J., 273, 275
Buckley, J. P., 283
Buller, D. B., 163, 166, 177, 199,
    245, 247, 249, 251, 253, 255,
    256, 257
Bullis, C. A., 127
Burant, P. A., 211
Burger, J. M., 129, 235, 239, 240
Burgoon, J. K., 162, 163, 164, 169,
    171, 172, 178n, 197, 216, 245,
    247, 249, 251, 255, 256, 257
Burgoon, M., 80, 99, 155, 197, 213,
    216, 217, 230, 282
Burke, K., 127, 144
Burleson, B. R., 94, 218, 222
Burnkrant, R. E., 189
Burst, R. G., 274
Bush, M., 232
Buss, A. H., 134
Byers, E. S., 210
Byers, P. Y., 143
Byrne, J., 48

Cabitt, J., 169
Cacioppo, J. T., 18, 35, 50, 51, 74,
    83, 86, 110, 136, 162, 167, 175,
    184, 185, 186, 187, 198, 238, 273,
    300, 309, 322
Cain, R. M., 326, 327
Camden, C., 244, 258n
Cameron, P., 150
Campbell, D. M., 245
Campbell, D. T., 50, 189, 190, 201n
Campbell, J. D., 124
Campbell, K., 305
Campbell, L., 274, 277
Canary, D. J., 31, 217, 220, 333
Cann, A., 234, 307
Cantor, J., 273, 275
Cantrill, J. G., 205
Carli, L. L., 98, 157
Carter, L. F., 98
Carver, C. S., 298
Cassirer, E., 7
Cassotta, L. L., 129–130
Catalan, J., 234
Cavanaugh, T., 284
Chaiken, S., 28, 37n, 50, 98, 154
Chambers, G., 305
Champion, J., 295
Chandler, T. A., 111
Chandran, R., 191
Chang, M., 274, 275
Chanowitz, B., 265
Chave, E. J., 43
Cheesman, J., 294
Cheney, G. E., 127
Childers, T. L., 154
Cholerton, M., 233
Christians, C. G., 323
Christie, R., 108, 251
Christopher, F. S., 210
Chua-Eoan, H., 119
Cialdini, R. B., 70, 131, 172,
    175, 228, 229, 234, 236, 238,
    239, 282, 283
Clark, C. L., 237
Clark, R. A., 109, 223n
Clevinger, T., 113
Cochrane, S., 127
Cody, M. J., 21, 29, 31, 98, 99, 131,
    132, 175, 209, 210, 217, 218, 220,
    251, 252

Coker, D. A., 178n
Coker, R. A., 178n, 216
Cole, T., 218, 223n, 228, 230
Comadena, M. E., 173, 244, 255
Comisky, P. W., 275
Comstock, J., 249, 253, 256, 257
Condra, J., 95
Congalton, K. J., 99, 322
Conklin, F., 177
Conna, J., 331
Conrad, E., 75
Cooper, J., 60
Cooper, J. B., 50
Cooper, M., 22, 27
Copeland, L., 112
Corbett, E. P. J., 148, 182
Costanzo, P. R., 128
Couper, M. P., 229
Courtright, J., 154
Craig, R. T., 214
Craig, S., 273
Crane, J. S., 275
Creason, C. R., 237
Crockett, W. H., 109
Cronkhite, G., 77
Cruz, M. G., 211
Cunningham, M. R., 230
Cupach, W. R., 88, 90, 210
Cupchik, G. C., 276
Cutler, B. L., 107
Cutler, R. L., 292

Dabbs, J. M., 171, 269
Dallinger, J. M., 217
Daoussis, L., 304
Darby, B. L., 234
Darley, J. M., 134
Davis, O., 148
Davis, T., 253
Dawson, E., 100, 177
DeAngelis, T., 270
DeBono, K. G., 103, 108, 109, 309
Deci, E. L., 264
Decker, W. H., 275
DeJong, W., 231, 240n
Delia, J. G., 94, 109
Deluga, R. J., 282
Del Valle, C., 270
de-Man, L., 310
Dember, W. N., 310, 311

SUBJECT INDEX

Accommodation theory, 155–156.
    See also Mirroring
Acquiescence bias, 45
Adaptors, 167–168
Age and persuasion, 94–97.
    See also Children
Aggressiveness. *See* Verbal
    aggressiveness
Amoralism, 324
Anticlimax order in persuasive
    messages, 188–189
Anxiety-arousing appeals.
    See Fear appeals
Anxiety level
    and deception, 247
    and fear appeals, 102–103, 269
    and persuadability, 102–103
Appearance. *See* Physical
    appearance
Appearances
    fallibility of, 47
    as indicators of attitudes, 47
Argumentativeness, 110–112
Aristotle, 12, 77, 182, 264
Aroma, and persuasion, 306–313
Aroma-chology, 306, 313n
Artifacts, 173–174
Artists as persuaders, 5–6
Assertiveness, 110
Assimilation effect, 107
Associations, 47–49
Associative networks, attitudes
    as, 56–57
Asynchronous communication,
    31

Attentiveness, 162
Attitude. *See* Ch. 3 generally
    associative networks,
      attitudes in, 56
    attitude–behavior connection,
      40, 41, 42, 49
    definition of, 41
    functions of, 40
    scales for measuring, 43–47
Attractiveness, 125–127. *See also*
    Physical appearance
    and conformity to group,
      125–127
Audiences, analyzing and
    adapting to, 112–114
Authoritarianism, 107–109
Autokinetic effect, 121
Automobile purchases, 10–12

Backward-masked recordings,
    297
Bait and switch tactic, 239
    See also Old Switcheroo
Behavioral adaptation
    explanation, 257
Biases and detecting deception,
    255–256
Bidirectional indicators of
    attitudes, 50–51
Body language, 166–168.
    See also Mirroring
Body shape. *See* Physical
    appearance
Bolstering, and psychological
    consistency, 62

Borderline persuasion, 20
Brand loyalty, 63–64
Buyer's remorse, 67

Celebrity endorsers, 74–75,
    79, 307
Centrality of attitudes, 42, 61
Central processing, 35, 52, 53,
    185–186, 300–301
Charisma, 74, 90n. *See also*
    Credibility
Charismatic terms, 145–147
Children
    peer pressure, 128, 197
    persuadability, 94–97
    preventing molestation, 50,
      96–97
    seeking compliance, 94
    smoking, 197
Chronemics, 172–173
Cicero, 182
Climax order in persuasive
    messages, 188–189
Clothes. *See* Clothing
Clothing, 173–174
Coercion versus persuasion,
    25–26
Cognitive complexity, 109–110
Cognitive consistency. *See*
    Consistency, psychological
Cognitive dissonance, 66–72
Collectivism–individualism.
    See
    Individualism–collectivism
Commitment, 69–72, 239

53 more effective to make TAs think about your message & internalize it
129–30: evaluation of Hofstede's 4 dimensions
305: music to induce Noriega to surrender – effectiveness discounted